Revelation of the Devil

Revelation of the Devil

Laurence Gardner

dash house
Brockenhurst UK

First published in 2012 by dash house

dash house
PO Box 394
Brockenhurst
Hants SO41 1BP

The website address is www.dashhousepublishing.co.uk

ISBN 978 0 9567357 4 4

A catalogue record of this book is
available from the British Library

Printed and bound in Great Britain by
Lightning Source UK Ltd

Acknowledgements

Grateful thanks are once again due to Dash House for their invaluable assistance in bringing this work to fruition.

My very special thanks to Edmund Marriage of The Golden Age Project for his friendship and support over the years.

CONTENTS

INTRODUCTION

In the Gospel of Matthew, the opening book of the Christian New Testament, a figure known as the Devil is introduced as the tempter of Jesus. At a series of locations (the wilderness, a temple and a mountain), the Devil is said to have provoked Jesus with taunts about miracles, ultimately promising the kingdoms of the world in return for Jesus' allegiance. The offer was of course declined, and that is the end of the story — a mere 246 words in just eleven verses.[1] No description of the Devil is given, nor any hint as to his origin or identity. Apart from a repeat of the exact same story in the Gospel of Luke,[2] it is the one and only personal appearance of the Devil in the whole Bible. He receives no reference in the Old Testament, has a few passing mentions in the New Testament, and the final book of The Revelation claims that, during an envisioned war of the angels, the Devil was chained in a bottomless pit for a thousand years. The pit is described as being of 'everlasting fire'.[3] But, even though confined to the blazing abyss, the Devil is still referred to as the 'prince of the world'.[4]

That is the extent of the Devil's portrayal in the Bible — an undefined character, whose name derives from the Anglo-Saxon word *deofol*, relating to a 'nuisance'. Beyond this particularly English definition, other languages use variants of the original Greek *diabolos*: an 'accuser'. In this regard, he has long been associated by Christians with an argumentative Old Testament 'son of God' called Satan,[5] although with no scriptural basis for the association. The Hebrew term *satan* denotes an 'adversary'. In consideration of these nominal descriptions and limited Bible citations, the Devil's scriptural role is not especially malevolent. He is a nuisance, an accuser, an adversary and a tempter, but he is not presented as being particularly dangerous or evil. Yet, for what little was written about him, the Devil has spawned a 2,000-year culture of fear and trepidation on which the whole *Doctrine of Salvation* was founded.

Perceived for centuries in Church dogma as the Antichrist, and somehow direct opponent of God with incredible powers, the Devil's abominable tradition (again without any biblical foundation) is still an aspect of superstitious belief today. In their reporting of the terrorist destruction of the New York World Trade Center on 11 September 2001, some mischievous newspaper and television reporters fuelled a public frenzy with headlines such as 'The Face of Evil', when the supposed image of Satan was perceived in the smoke billowing from the Twin Towers. Subsequently, Lieutenant-General William Boykin, the US Undersecretary of Defense for Intelligence, announced that 'The war on terrorism is a Christian struggle against Satan'.

On 16 April 2007, South Korean student Seung-Hui Cho shot and killed thirty-two students and staff, and wounded many others at the Virginia Tech research university in Blacksburg, before committing suicide. Just as happened after the 9/11 attack in 2001, the Asian Tsunami and Madrid train bombings in 2004, the London Transport bombings and hurricane *Katrina* in 2005, the people, press and media posed the question: 'Why did God allow this to happen?' In response, Franklin Graham, president of the Billy Graham Evangelistic Association, told NBC News, 'I tag this on the Devil. He's responsible … He's the one who wants to destroy'.[6]

Based on the religious premise that God created all creatures in Heaven and on Earth, many people (struggling with comments such as those of Franklin Graham) have asked, 'Why would God have created the Devil to oppose him?' This same question was confronted as far back as 1215, when the Fourth Lateran Council in Rome concluded: '*Diabolus enim et alii dæmones a Deo quidem naturâ creati sunt boni, sed ipsi per se facti sunt mali*':

> The Devil and the other demons were created by
> God good in their nature, but they by themselves
> have made themselves evil.

This Lateran Palace decree was reckoned to exonerate God from the Devil's actions, but it also had the effect of rendering God ineffectual against such an all-powerful enemy. Thus it was that, although much had been made of the Devil and his wiles to that point in time, his cult soared to previously unparalleled heights from the 13th century. What hope was there for everyday people when even God was powerless against him? Even to this day, the Church of Rome clings tenuously to a Middle Ages belief in the Devil. In 1993, the *Catechism of the Catholic Church* was pronounced by Pope John Paul II, and later translated as a compendium in English as recently as 2005. The penultimate and consolidating item of the *Compendium of the Catechism* states:

> Evil indicates the person of Satan who opposes God and is the deceiver of the whole world. Victory over the Devil has already been won by Christ. We pray, however, that the human family be freed from Satan and his works. We also ask for the precious gift of peace and the grace of perseverance as we wait for the coming of Christ, who will free us definitively from the Evil One.[7]

Given the dearth of related information in the Bible, it is clear that the Devil of common perception is by no means a scriptural interpretation. Almost everything written and taught about the Devil, in the way he has come to be understood, is a product of Church doctrine and has absolutely no biblical authenticity. His character was developed onwards from the 4th century in an attempt to provide a base for the *Doctrine of Salvation* — a figure of threat and evil from whom those obedient to the Church could be saved. A foremost requirement in this regard was the ritual of baptism, which bound its candidates to the faith.

To make baptism effective, the 4th-century notion of *Original Sin* was introduced — a doctrine which prevails to this day. In this respect, the unnamed Old Testament serpent of Genesis, who seduced Eve in the G arden of Eden, was said by the Church of Rome to have been Satan. Thus it was determined that, owing to the transgression of Eve, all people are born in sin by virtue of having mothers! Consequently, a child at the font was, and still is, presumed sinful by the very nature of its birth. Baptism therefore supposes the infant to be under the influence of evil, requiring an abjuration of Satan by the sponsor in the name of the child.[8] By this means, the baptismal sponsor and child are united in a promise to 'renounce the Devil and all his works, the pomps and vanity of this wicked world, and all the sinful lusts of the flesh'.

From this strategic beginning, the Devil was associated thereafter with all forms of sin in the eyes of the Church. Then in the late 6th century, Pope Gregory the Great announced: 'The Devil has powers to control the weather'. Henceforth, storms and tempests were believed to be inflicted by Satan. At that time, in AD 590, Gregory also gave the first satanic description, proclaiming that 'Satan has horns and hooves, and a terrible stench'.

Gradually, as the centuries passed, an ever-growing list of evils was piled upon the Devil's head. He became responsible for every tragedy, whether natural or deliberate, from earthquakes to mortal crime. God appeared to have no direct control over the Evil One. Only the Church had the power to intervene, and the price for protection was absolute subservience. Those who did not comply with the rule of the bishops were declared sorcerers, witches and otherwise Devil worshippers. From the Middle Ages, hundreds of thousands were mercilessly tortured, hanged or burned at the stake, through a period of more than 500 years.

Even after such persecutions and executions were ruled illegal by the European secular courts from the latter 1600s, it was still maintained that the Devil and his demons were the greatest of all threats to social order. Both the Catholic and Protestant movements continued their war against satanic influence by the lucrative performance of exorcisms — a practice which remains extant today. Father Gabriele Amorth, the senior exorcist for Vatican City, reported recently that he had performed over 50,000 exorcisms. Additionally, he made headlines across the globe with his satanic opinion of JK Rowling's *Harry Potter* children's book series. The *Catholic News* reported on 4 January 2002 that Amorth stated in interview, 'Behind Harry Potter hides the signature of the king of darkness, the Devil'.[9]

Just as in medieval times, the Devil-based superstition remains an aspect of Christian religious belief. Although not so widespread as in past centuries, this belief is still used to great effect by the 'fire and brimstone' preachers, who seek to manipulate their congregations by means of threat and fear of the diabolical unknown. At the other end of the scale, the Devil has become a tactical marketing ploy for advertisers, who use him to convey images of pleasure and abandon to a more adventurous, though no less gullible, public. Thus, his temptations are promoted as the route to excesses of personal gratification in a modern environment that is completely divorced from any religious context.

Of all the mythological characters ever imagined, there is no doubt that the Devil has had a greater influence on social behaviour than any other for the past two millennia. Indeed, he has had a greater influence than most real figures of history. As related by Fyodor Dostoevsky's character, Ivan, in *The Brothers Karamazov*, 'The Devil does not exist, but man has created him in his own image and likeness'. The story of this creation and its strategized evolution through the centuries is, nevertheless, as fascinating as any true-life biography. Notwithstanding the Devil's erroneously presumed involvement in modern-day calamitous events of nature and terrorism, millions of innocent people have been tortured and executed specifically because they were reckoned to be the apostles of Satan. The absurdity of this charge was that it was levelled by the very Church establishment that invented the Devil in the first place.

Laurence Gardner
Exeter, 2010

'Baphomet' (*see* chapter 18)
A popular representation of the Devil from the late 19th century

1

THE EVIL ONE

King of the Demons

For nearly 2,000 years, Christian religious culture has presented a supernatural character called the Devil as the epitome of evil in opposition to the Judaeo-Christian God. Although noticeably absent from the Hebrew Bible, the Devil is very much a part of the Christian tradition in his role as the Antichrist figure. In this regard, he is associated with a provocative Old Testament son of God called Satan.[1] In the New Testament scriptures, the great dragon 'called the Devil and Satan'[2] is also referred to as Beelzebub, 'prince of the devils'.[3]

The questions that arise in this initial context are, Who or what were the devils? Were they a product of Israelite scribal lore, or was their origin in the demonology of earlier times?

The Old Testament of the Christian Bible relates on just four occasions to 'devils'.[4] But in the Hebrew Bible,[5] the terms used in these same verses are 'satyrs' and 'demons', not devils. From these entries we might presume that, in the oldest biblical sense, the definition of a devil refers to a satyr or demonic entity to which the various texts recount that sacrifices were made. The English translations into 'devils' stem from the Hebrew se'irim, meaning 'hairy ones', a type of shaggy demon that was reckoned to inhabit the wastelands.[6] There is, however, nothing in any of this to denote a particular being who might have been considered a prince of the devils as emerged in the Christian tradition.

In terms of Israelite biblical understanding, the idea that evil had any other source than God himself was out of the question. God was reckoned to instigate everything. It was therefore not possible that any other deity had the power to compete on the playing-field of creation. Thus, in the book of Isaiah 45:7, God is quoted as saying, 'I make peace and create evil'. In Amos 3:6, it is asked, 'Shall there be evil in a city, and the Lord hath not done it?' The early Christians, nevertheless, thought differently. God, they maintained, must have an evil competitor from whom people can be saved, and they called this adversary the Devil. Given that Jesus was considered to be the earthly son of God, then the Devil (as the Antichrist) was doubtless a supernatural son of God — a fallen angel, most probably the argumentative son referred to in the Old Testament book of Job 1:6 as Satan. Later, in the 10th-century culture of Bulgaria, the priest Bogomil defined the godhead *Trinity* as being God the Father and his two sons, Satanael (Satan) and Jesus Christ.[7]

According to the *Oxford English Dictionary*, the word 'devil' derives from the Old English *deofol* (a nuisance), relative to the Greek *diabolos* (an accuser or slanderer). Hence, someone whose actions are maligning or obstructive might be termed 'devilish' or 'diabolical'. As we have seen, the root of the term is in the Hebrew lore of the *se'irim* who, in Greek mythology, were wild, lustful satyrs depicted with goat-like ears and legs, a tail and sometimes horns. This early description is not dissimilar to the familiar portrayal of the Devil as he emerged in the later Christian tradition. In essence, the satyrs were pagan nature spirits as personified by Pan, the Arcadian god of the shepherds. When discussing Babylon, the city of Israelite captivity, the book of Isaiah 13:21 foretells that 'wild beasts of the desert shall lie there; and their houses shall be full of doleful creatures; and owls shall dwell there, and satyrs shall dance there'.

Along with the *se'irim*, another style of creatures in biblical lore are the *shedim*. They feature in Deuteronomy 32:17, when Moses explained the unholy practices of old to the Israelites: 'They sacrificed unto *shedim*, not to God; to gods whom they knew not ... whom your fathers feared not'. The theme is progressed in Psalm 106:37, which relates that, when the Israelites later ignored Moses and forsook the Lord, 'they sacrificed their sons and their daughters unto *shedim*'. In both instances, the Christian Bible translates *shedim* as 'devils', whereas the translation from the Hebrew text of the more authentic Jewish Bible renders 'demons'. According to the *Jewish Encyclopedia*, the *shedim* were storm demons represented in an ox-like form.[8]

2

In the ancient Mesopotamian regions of Babylonia and Assyria, *shedim* was a generic term, much like the word 'spirit'. It derives from the Mesopotamian *shedu* — winged animal-like spirit creatures, perhaps akin to the cherubim of biblical tradition. In referencing these enigmatic creatures, the Hebrew chronicler Flavius Josephus maintained in his 1st-century *Antiquities of the Jews*, 'Nobody can tell, or even conjecture, what was the shape of these cherubims'.[9] These days, the term *shedu* is generally applied to the mighty winged bull statues that guarded the gateways of the Assyrian royal palaces. In this regard it is perhaps significant that, when referring to the 'four living creatures' envisioned by Ezekiel near the Babylonian river of Chebar, Ezekiel 1:10 relates to their faces of a man, a lion, an ox and an eagle, whereas Ezekiel 10:14 later identifies the face of the ox as being that of a cherub.

There is no common agreement between the texts of various distant cultures as to the particular natures of the mythological spirit creatures. They differed in appearance, and were either good or bad in accordance with the time, place and purpose of their representation. They were, however, all demonized as pagan entities by the eventual Christian establishment. It is therefore with the notion of demons that our investigation of the satanic Devil, as an ultimate power-lord, should begin.

The oldest known documented references to demons come from the tablets of ancient Mesopotamia. These date back to the 3rd millennium BC, long before the original books of the Bible were written. From those early times it was understood that the world of existence was a realm of opposites, with the two cardinal spirits of conflict being those of light and darkness, good and evil. In this competitive environment, not all the gods were good, and there is much literature concerned with the battles between the combative factions. The ambassadorial hosts of the gods had many definitions in the early years — genies, daevas, demi-gods and such — but in time they became commonly known as angels. There were good angels and bad angels, the latter of which, by way of particular designation, were sometimes identified as demons.

In general terms, demons were primarily reckoned to be mischievous or malignant beings of gruesome appearance, and with unnatural abilities. Though not always wicked in the extreme, they were of high nuisance value, causing pain, anguish and disruption.[10] They were not initially portrayed in any religious context, but made their appearances in mythology and folklore as malevolent spirits. Eventually, they took literary form as invasive creatures that would possess living people. In this respect, demons were held responsible for physical illness, mental instability and antisocial behaviour. They were said to be responsible for splits in personality, in which context the word 'demon' evolved from the Greek *daimon*, emanating from the verb 'to divide'. In the ancient world, demons were usually perceived as upright hybrid creatures, as against monsters, which were mostly animal combinations with four legs.[11]

From distant recorded times come the formative examples of supernatural beings with wings. An original demon from the Mesopotamian kingdoms of Akkad (the region of Baghdad in modern Iraq) was Pazuzu, the 'demon of the southwest wind'.[12] Depicted with canine features, bulging eyes, and feet with talons, he was said to bring disease, plague and corruption, and was reckoned to be the king of the demons. If the satanic Devil of eventual Christendom had an archetype for his envisioned personality, then an early model for the concept might well have been Pazuzu.

According to the mythology of Sumer (southern Mesopotamia above the Persian Gulf), Pazuzu was not all bad. He was said to have challenged Lamastu, the lion-headed queen of the she-demons, and forced her back into the underworld. Lamastu was reckoned to attack nursing mothers, and was the supposed cause of many infant deaths. In Babylonia, during the 1st millennium BC, pregnant women used to wear amulets of Pazuzu to ward off the intervention of Lamastu. In nearby Assyria (northern Mesopotamia), she was treated as a goddess, albeit an evil one.

There are any number of demons, male and female, mentioned in the Bible-land tablets of old Mesopotamia. But, unlike the gods and certain transcendent figures, the demons were not recorded historically. They were deemed essentially part of the spirit world, and appeared mostly in magical incantations. By virtue of this, a great many amulets, pendants, inscribed bowls and small figurines were produced in order to ward off such malevolent spirits by confronting them with wild images of themselves. Alternatively, an inferior demon might be deterred if faced by the representation of a more powerful spirit being.

Apart from the fact that Pazuzu was perhaps a forerunner of the devilish concept in terms of his demonic presence, there is nothing yet to compare with the ultimate Devil who emerged in later times. There is no way that Pazuzu, or any other ancient demon, was ever a match for the legitimate gods of the old tradition. By contrast, the Devil of Christian demonology was conceived almost as a god figure in his own right, all-powerful as the Evil One in opposition to the God of the Bible.

Hostile Seduction

The books of the Christian Old Testament (The Hebrew Bible) were originally written between the 6th and 2nd centuries BC. They were commenced during the Babylonian captivity of the Israelites, and were concluded by subsequent generations back in Judaea — a series of separate accounts from Babylonian, Canaanite and Jewish sources. From about 586 BC, many thousands of Israelites were taken into bonded service by Prince Nebuchadnezzar of Babylon.[13] His ambition was to restore and rebuild that once magnificent city, but he needed architects, builders and engineers, together with an ongoing supply of labourers. He chose to supplement his requirement for these craftsmen and workers from Jerusalem, and this afforded the captive Israelites access to the old libraries of that Mesopotamian capital. Here they found tablets containing the early records of their ancestral heritage — the stories of Adam and Eve, the Great Flood and the Tower of Babel. From these ancient records the book of Genesis was born.

Not all the books which might have made it into the Jewish Bible were ultimately included in the final canon. One of the excluded works was the *Book of Jubilees*, a Pharisee chronicle from around 120 BC.[14] Between 1947 and 1956, some fifteen *Jubilees* manuscripts in Hebrew were discovered in five caves among the

Dead Sea Scrolls at Qumrân in Judaea.[15] In this work is found a close Jewish representation of a character who might be deemed another evolutionary archetype for the Christian Devil. His name is given as Mastema.

The name Mastema relates to 'hatred' or 'hostility', and he was considered to be the chief of the evil spirits. Mastema was said to have negotiated with God that one-tenth of the angels should be apportioned to his bidding: 'And the prince Mastema sent out his hand to do all wickedness and sin and transgression, and to destroy, and to murder, and to shed blood over the earth'.[16]

The significance of Mastema is that he is described as being subservient to God. He performed his evil with the aid of angels that were allocated to him for the express purpose of tempting mankind and leading the people into sin. This literary device provided a means by which to confront the persistent question of how evil could possibly exist if God was good and in charge of everything. It had the effect of keeping God in control, whilst the people's allegiance to him was put to the test. It was meant somehow to explain the fact that wickedness existed not because God could not prevent it, but because he allowed and encouraged it. By this means, the process of earned righteousness was determined by way of those who resisted Mastema's seduction.

Satan's Wager

The situation is much the same in the Old Testament, which presents Satan as an obedient, though mischievous, son of God. His aggressive behaviour is not beyond God's reproach or control, but is actioned by agreement and with God's approval. It was always the case in original biblical lore that nothing, not even diabolical evil, could exist without God's permission. Only by upholding this principle could the scribes explain the constant anomaly that humans, who were designed and created by God, had an inherent tendency towards wickedness. Clearly, God could not be seen as the immediate instigator, but he could commission others, like Mastema and Satan, to front what appeared to be schemes in opposition to his own objectives.

The biblical story in the book of Job provides a good example in this regard. It begins with God calling his sons before him. One of them, Satan, then questions the sincerity of Job's righteousness before the heavenly council. In this context, the name (or more precisely, the judicial term) *satan* is evident in its original Hebrew rendition, meaning 'accuser'.[17]

Job enters the scene as a wealthy and successful man who regularly offered sacrifices to the Lord. With a large family, much livestock and a splendid household, he was said to be 'the greatest of all the men of the east'. His adversity begins when Satan suggests that Job's loyalty should be put to the test, and he enters into a bet with God as to whether or not Job's faith can be destroyed. Job is then subjected to a series of unjust trials and persecutions in order to measure his virtue. The story appears to have no other purpose than to convey the message that true righteousness can only exist by way of intimidation and blind obedience.

Satan has only two other named mentions in the Old Testament. In 1 Chronicles 21:1 it is given that 'Satan stood up against Israel, and provoked King David to number Israel'. The relevance of the ensuing Davidic census was that, in about 1000 BC, it related to the introduction of Israelite taxation. For whatever reason, the concept of raising public money to manage the new kingdom was deemed sinful, and 'God was displeased with this thing'. King David then apologised saying, 'I have sinned greatly'. But although he was seen to be the transgressor, it was a transgression brought about by the provocation of Satan. Nevertheless, 'the Lord sent pestilence upon Israel, and there fell of Israel seventy thousand men'.[18]

In Zechariah 3:1-10, Satan is depicted standing at the right hand of God, arguing with him over a social matter. The scene relates to the Israelites' return from five decades of exile in Babylon. On re-entering their homeland in about 536 BC, they were attempting to regain their family stations in Jerusalem, but arrived to find a high priest and a governing establishment that ignored their ancestral claims. Satan accused Joshua, the high priest, of being a poor representative for the disaffected Jews, but God sided with Joshua and the residential Israelites.

In this example, Satan is not acting as a provocative agent of God, but as a confrontational adversary with a measure of right on his side. Nonetheless, despite the political stand-off, there is still no indication of anything remotely dark or sinister in his character. It is, however, his last appearance in the Old Testament.

Final Judgement

By way of chronological reference to characters and Israelite history, the Old Testament story concludes in about 400 BC. The writing began with the book of Genesis in about 550 BC during the Babylonian Captivity, and ended with the retrospective book of Daniel around 164 BC.[19] To that point, there is nothing in any literature that even remotely connects the original image of Satan with his portrayal in later Christian doctrine. He is never once claimed to be in any way demonic, nor associated with devils — only with the heavenly court, wherein his role was that of a judicial prosecutor. Prior to New Testament times, the notion of the Devil as an independent evil power ruling a demonic kingdom, and headed for judgement, is completely absent from any documented source.

As given in the *Anchor Bible Dictionary*, 'Satan's move from the position of a subordinate accuser to that of an independent tempter was a development of the intertestamental period'.[20] This might be attributed to a number of factors. A proposal of current theological scholarship is that the Christian notion of Satan was heavily influenced by Persian 'dualism' — the concept of two opposing and equally powerful gods.[21] In this ancient tradition of the Persian archpriest Zoroaster,[22] the leaders of the two cardinal spirits were said to be Ahura Mazda, the god of life and light,[23] and his opposer Ahriman, the lord of death and darkness.[24] These deities were destined to wage a continual war until Light prevailed in the Final Judgement — at which time Ahura Mazda would create the enchanted realm of Paradise (*Pairi Daize*) on Earth.

The significant difference between Satan and Ahriman was that the latter was perceived as having a godly status, whereas

Satan did not. But that does not rule out a strategic change of emphasis in order to heighten Satan's fearsome mastery.

The Persian influence on elements of the Judaeo-Christian culture is evident in the apocryphal references to Aeshma the 'demon of wrath', transposed into Hebrew lore with the name Asmodai.[25] A noted prince of darkness and lust, he was an angel of the god Ahriman, and appears in both the non-canonical *Book of Tobit* and the Hebrew *Talmud* (a traditional codification of Jewish law).[26] Asmodai is best known for his mythological help in building King Solomon's Temple,[27] as related in the 2nd-century *Testament of Solomon*. And, like Pazuzu in the Akkadian tradition, he was reckoned in Jewish lore to be king of the demons.[28]

It is apparent in the Qumrân *War Scroll*, from the 1st century BC, that the cult of the Persian Magi had a substantial impact on the community of Judaea in the period between the Testaments. The notion of an impending war between the Children of Light and the Sons of Darkness (as detailed in that work) subsequently found its way into the New Testament book of The Revelation. In the *War Scroll* account, the conflict of the Zoroastrian Day of Judgement is foretold as occurring at Har-Megiddo (the Heights of Megiddo), an historically important battlefield where a military fortress guarded the plains of Jezreel south of the Galilean hills. In transcript, the place-name was corrupted to Armageddon,[29] and many Christians believe that this final encounter is yet to come.

Along with Asmodai, King Solomon was said to have had dealings with a number of other demons, including Belial. He is identified in the *War Scroll* as the leader of the Sons of Darkness: 'His rule is in darkness, and his ambition is to bring about wickedness and iniquity'.[30]

The name Belial (from the Hebrew *beli ya'al*) relates to a worthless and wicked destroyer,[31] and the followers of Belial are referenced numerous times in the Hebrew Bible. Belial is cited as being distinct from Mastema in the *Book of Jubilees* and, although both names are often substituted for Satan in Christian literature, this was not the case during the Old Testament BC years. There are some similarities to be found between Mastema and Satan in that they both operated within God's allowable parameters, but the more formidable spirit of Belial was perceived as an evil force beyond any sanction.[32]

When discussing matters of righteousness in the New Testament, St Paul's epistle to the Corinthians specifically names Belial in opposition to Jesus Christ.[33] An early Judaeo-Christian manuscript entitled *Testaments of the Twelve Patriarchs*, from around AD 150, explains that Belial is the prince of darkness who will come as the Antichrist.[34]

From the 2nd to 5th centuries of the early Christian era comes a work entitled *The Sibylline Oracles* — a collection of twelve books, written in Alexandrian Greek and detailing a series of prophecies ascribed to different *Sibyls* (prophetesses).[35] In this compilation, Belial is named as the Antichrist figure who will appear at the time of ultimate contest between good and evil.[36] In this context, it is pertinent to note that, in the 5th-century Latin *Vulgate* Bible,[37] the same original Hebrew word as given in 1 Kings 21:10, 13 is rendered once as *belial* (worthless), and twice as *diaboli* (devil).[38]

Described in the *War Scroll* as 'lord of the inferno' and 'prince of the kingdom of wickedness', Belial features again in fragments of another Qumrân scroll manuscript known as the *Damascus Document*.[39] Written in about 100 BC, it discusses the Covenant of the Lord as made with the patriarchs of old, and tells of an impending period of temptation, explaining that 'During all those years Belial shall be unleashed against Israel'.[40]

When comparing the various Jewish documents of the culminating BC era with those of the Gospel period and beyond, Belial is undoubtedly the intertestamental model for the Devil as he emerged in the Christian doctrine about a century after the relevant *Dead Sea Scrolls* were written.

2

GATES OF HELL

A Fallen Angel

Before embarking on the Devil's own trail of evolution, we should perhaps consider the wider notion of 'fallen angels' in which category he is generally perceived. The concept that some angels fell from grace is not of biblical origin. A mention in Job 4:18 that God charged his angels with folly is the only direct accusatory remark in the Hebrew Bible. In the New Testament, Jesus is quoted as saying to his followers, 'I beheld Satan as lightning fall from heaven'.[1] But this is just a figurative response to the disciples after they reported their healing success in casting out demons.

A commonly held theological view is that certain angels attracted God's displeasure in the days before the Flood. The brief story in this regard is one of the most enigmatic in the Old Testament, and actually refers to the 'sons of God' rather than to angels.[2] Genesis 6:1–2 states:

> And it came to pass, when men began to multiply on
> the face of the earth, and daughters were born unto
> them, that the sons of God saw the daughters of men
> that they were fair; and they took them for wives all of
> which they chose'.

There is no mention in this item of the Devil, Satan or any other individual. Neither does it state thereafter that God admonished the said 'sons' — only that he punished mankind by way of a great deluge. But there is a particular Hebrew word used in the textual passage which relates, 'There were *nephilim* in the earth in those days'. In Christian Bibles, *nephilim* is mistranslated as

11

'giants', but the term correctly relates to 'those who descended' or 'those who came down'.[3] The original consonantal stem, NFL, meant 'cast down',[4] and during the intertestamental period the theory was developed that 'cast down' equated with 'fallen from grace'.

An early example of this comes from the ancient *Book of Enoch* which, like the Hebrew *Book of Jubilees*, was excluded from the Old Testament canon. Produced by a sect of traditional ascetics who occupied the first settlement at Qumrân from about 130 BC, parts of this work in Aramaic were discovered in the Dead Sea collection in 1947.[5]

Given that those termed the 'sons of God' were reputed to have caused their own dishonour by consorting with earthly women, they were said in the *Book of Enoch*,[6] to have fallen from the divine grace. Previously, the 'sons of God' had been identified as angels (*oi aggeloi tou theou*) in the Greek *Septuagint* Bible. This oldest known collection of biblical texts was translated from Hebrew between the 3rd and 1st centuries BC, and began as a commission from the pharaoh Ptolemy II Philadelphus in about 250 BC. The work was conducted in Alexandria, and it is believed that seventy-two scholars were employed overall for the ongoing translations. This led to the compilation becoming known as the *Septuagint* (relating to 'seventy').[7]

Owing to the general ambiguity of the Genesis entry, it is not clear whether the *nephilim* and the 'sons of God' were one and the same. Neither is it clear whether the sons of God were synonymous with angels as described in the *Septuagint*. In the 2nd century AD, Rabbi Simeon ben Jochai was adamant that they were not,[8] and the Jews traditionally said they were not. But, by whatever method of reasoning, a wholly new breed of phenomenal beings emerged in scriptural literature during the Qumrân era. They were the 'fallen angels', and the *Book of Enoch* explains that there were about 200 of them.

Having established the notion of fallen angels, *Enoch* then identifies them with a celestial group called 'watchers', who are also mentioned in the Old Testament book of Daniel.[9] *Enoch* further explains that the watchers were those same deiform beings who had mated with the earthly women,[10] while in Daniel we learn that the watchers were akin to the *nephilim* (those who came down):

> Behold, a watcher and an holy one came
> down from heaven.[11]
> The king saw a watcher and an holy one
> coming down from heaven.[12]

The *Book of Jubilees* states that Enoch 'was the first one from among the children of men that are born on the earth to learn writing and the knowledge of wisdom, and he wrote the signs of heaven'.[13] These signs are described as being the 'science of the watchers', which had been carved on a rock in distant times,[14] and the *Book of Enoch* relates that the watchers were the 'holy angels who watch'.[15]

A little while after *Enoch* and *Jubilees*, the Qumrân text of the *Damascus Document* was written. In this manuscript the 'fallen angel' and 'watcher' classifications were again brought together:

> I will uncover your eyes ... that you may not
> be drawn by thoughts of the guilty inclination
> and by lustful eyes. For many went astray
> because of this ... The watchers of heaven fell
> because of this.[16]

From the early Christian era comes another work known as the *Secrets of Enoch* (as distinct from the previously cited *Book of Enoch*).[17] It exists now only in Slavonic with an evident Christian influence, and is a good example of how Satan was identified with the Devil in those times:

> The Devil is an evil spirit of the lower places, a
> fugitive. His name was Satanael. Thus he
> became different from the angels, but his nature
> did not change his intelligence as far as his
> understanding of righteous and sinful things.[18]

The same text describes that Satanael endeavoured to place his throne higher than the clouds in order to have equality with God. As a result, God 'threw him out from the height, and he was flying in the air continuously above the abyss'.[19] This concept appears to emanate from an entry in the Old Testament book of Isaiah 14:13–15:

> I will exalt my throne above the stars of God ... I
> will ascend above the heights of the clouds; I will be
> like the Most High. Yet thou shalt be brought down
> to hell, to the sides of the pit.

Although sometimes presumed to relate to the Devil, these Isaiah verses were actually written about King Nabonidus of Babylon.[20] His reign had come to an end in 539 BC, when his empire was overrun by Shah Cyrus II of Persia. In respect of this humiliating defeat, Isaiah the prophet exclaimed, 'How art thou fallen from heaven, O day star, son of the dawn! How art thou cut down to the ground, that didst cast lots over the nations!'[21] In contrast to this poor translation, the original Hebrew phrase used in respect of the 'day star, son of the dawn' was *heilel ben-shachar*, which actually meant 'boastful one, son of Shachar'.[22] In those times, the words 'boastful' and 'bright' were interchangeable, and Shachar was the Babylonian god of the dawn.

Close to a millennium after this passage was written, Saint Jerome produced the Latin *Vulgate* Bible for the 5th-century Catholic Church. In this translation, the item concerning Nabonidus as the *'heilel ben-shachar'* was spuriously reapplied to the planet Venus which appears in the sky at dawn. The Greek *Septuagint* had referred to Shachar as the *heosphoros* ('dawn bringer'), and the transcription into Latin rendered this word as *lucifer*, meaning 'light bearer'. The resultant passage reads: *'Quomodo cecidisti de caelo lucifer qui mane oriebaris corruisti in terram qui vulnerabas gentes'*.

With a proper-noun connotation given to the 'light bearer', this morning star passage was later rendered in the King James Authorized Bible of 1611 as: 'How art thou fallen from heaven,

O Lucifer, who didst rise in the morning! How art thou fallen to the earth, that didst wound the nations!' Then in 1667, a related satanic interpretation was placed on the entry by the Protestant writer, John Milton, in his epic poem *Paradise Lost*.[23]

> Of Lucifer, so by allusion called,
> Of that bright star to Satan paragon'd.[24]

The perception of Satan (a fallen angel according to the *Secrets of Enoch*) was now firmly cemented to the earlier Isaiah verse, with the result that, from the 17th century, Lucifer became another attributed name of the Devil. Prior to that, the Latin term *lucifer* (*lux-fer*) had never been associated with a male entity — and certainly not with an evil demon. Even after Milton's death, the correct reference was still given in 18th-century dictionaries. The 1721 *Bailey's Etymological Dictionary* states: 'Lucifer: The morning or day star; the planet Venus, when it rises before the sun'.[25]

The ambiguity of the *Vulgate* translation can be seen from the word *heosphoros* ('dawn bringer') that was misrepresented as Lucifer. The direct Greek equivalent to Lucifer (Latin: *lux-fer* — 'light bearer') was *phos phoros*, from which the English word 'phosphorus' derives. Where this was used in the original New Testament (2 Peter 1:19), it was correctly translated as relating to Venus the 'day star'. *Lux-fer* and *phos phoros* are identical in referring to the light bearer, and the word 'phosphorus' is rightly given in today's *Oxford English Dictionary* as relating to the morning star. Neither *lux-fer* nor *phos phorus* were ever used as derogatory terms, and were even applied in respect of the Messiah in Revelation 22:16: 'I am the root and the offspring of David, and the bright and morning star'. The *Jewish Encyclopedia* states: 'It is obvious that the prophet Isaiah, in attributing to the Babylonian king a boastful pride followed by a fall, borrowed the idea from a popular legend connected with the morning star'.[26]

Not only was Milton's use of *lux-fer* thoroughly ill-conceived, it was (as derived from the *Vulgate* mistranslation) the wrong word in any event. That apart, Lucifer, along with Satan, Mastema

15

and Belial, has since become one of the commonly regarded names of the Devil.

Into the Underworld

In the New Testament gospels, Jesus is accused by the Pharisee priests of using the power of Beelzebub to cast out demonic possessions. In this context, Beelzebub is described as 'prince of the devils'[27] and 'chief of the devils'.[28] Jesus responds to the accusation by asking, 'How can Satan cast out Satan?'[29] Thus, another satanic name, that of Beelzebub, is added to those given above.

Since *beel* derives from the Phoenician *baal*, meaning 'lord', and *zebûb* was a Semitic collective noun relating to 'things in flight', it is generally accepted that Beelzebub (or Baalzebub) relates to one who is the 'lord of flying things'. The name first appears in the Old Testament book of 2 Kings 1:2-3, when King Ahaziah of Israel was sick: 'He sent messengers, and said unto them, Go, inquire of Baalzebub, the god of Ekron, whether I shall recover of this disease'.

Beelzebub also appears by name in the 3rd-century gospel of Nicodemus (*Evangelium Nicodemi*), which again records him as 'prince of the devils' and 'king of glory'. In this apocryphal context, Satan is addressed by Hades (the guardian of Hell) as 'Beelzebub, the heir of fire and torment'.[30] This raises the question: If Satan was supposedly the lord of Hell, then who was Hades?

In Greek mythology, Hades was described in Homer's *Odyssey* as the god of the underworld, and he retained this position in some early Christian literature from Alexandria and the Greek-speaking world. His realm was the universal destination of the dead, and was also denoted by the term Hades. Its Hebrew equivalent was 'Sheol', the abode of death. This designation became a persistent problem for the Christian Church since the bishops had defined two places appropriate to death: Heaven was the abode of righteous souls where God reigned, whereas the damned were condemned to an eternity of fire and torment in Hell. The cultural difference is seen in the interpretations of *Sheol* from Psalm 16:10. The Masoretic Hebrew translates as:

> For thou wilt not abandon my soul to the netherworld [*sheol*]; neither wilt thou suffer thy godly one to see the pit.

In the English King James Bible, it reads:

> For thou wilt not leave my soul in hell [*sheol*]; neither wilt thou suffer thine Holy One to see corruption.[31]

For a while it was early Christian practice to associate the Greek underworld of Hades with Hell — its master also being named Hades, as in the gospel of Nicodemus. But there were many who could not equate the two places, since Hades was reckoned to accommodate both the righteous and unrighteous dead alike. Among those who suffered bewilderment was the Church Father, Tertullian of Carthage (AD 155–230), who addressed the dilemma in his *Treatise on the Soul*. After some consideration, he determined that, whereas Hell was a phenomenal realm of the ungodly, Hades was an underground domain: 'It is a vast deep space in the interior of the earth … You must suppose Hades to be a subterranean region'.[32]

In the Jewish belief, Sheol was similarly an underground domain of souls protected by gates and bolts.[33] By the latter 5th century, however, there was further confusion as to which of the custodians was the ultimate Devil: Was he Hades or Satan? In settling the matter, the personal name of Hades was dropped, as were references to the infernal region of Hades, and Satan took his place in Christian literature as the guardian of Hell.

In strict etymological terms, Hell (in the same manner as Hades) also defines some kind of underground abode, rather than an inexplicable realm as commonly envisaged. The word 'hell' relates to a pit or hole, and is a derivative of the Anglo-Saxon verb *helan* (to hide). In contrasting doctrinal interpretation, Hell is an infernal domain (the *infernus*) of the damned.[34]

The Bible seems to indicate that Hell is underground, for it describes it as an abyss into which the wicked descend. We even read of 'things under the earth'.[35] But it is impossible to know whether the word 'under' refers to a place 'within' the earth or a dimension 'beneath' it. At the time when written, there was poor geological knowledge of the Earth's structure. All such writings emerged from the northern hemisphere, and it was widely assumed that the world was flat. St Augustine of Hippo in North Africa (AD 354–430)[36] wrote, 'It is my opinion that the nature of Hell-fire and the location of Hell are known to no man unless the Holy Ghost made it known to him by a special revelation'. The Catholic Church has no emphatic view on the matter, and states that the importance of understanding Hell is not a question of its location, but of how one might avoid being sent there![37]

In treating the Devil as custodian of the infernal region, Matthew 10:28 states: 'Fear not them which kill the body, but are not able to kill the soul; but rather fear him which is able to destroy both soul and body in hell'. Subsequently, when Jesus proclaimed the eternity of his mission, he decreed, 'The gates of hell shall not prevail against it'.[38]

The Watchers

Having established that the watchers and fallen angels were reckoned to be synonymous, and that Satan was defined as a fallen angel, it might well be inferred that he was by definition a watcher. To establish this more firmly if possible, we should consult the *Book of Enoch*. Apart from the lost *Book of Noah*, of which only a fragment remains, *Enoch* (which refers to the *Noah* manuscript) is the only fully extant work to list the individual names of the watchers. Section I of the compilation (36 of its 98 chapters) is classified as the *Book of the Watchers*.

In naming the eighteen chiefs of the watchers, who lusted after the daughters of men, *Enoch* identifies their senior chief as an angel named Semjaza.[39] Rather more is written, however, about his unruly comrade Azazel. He was said to have 'taught all

18

unrighteousness on earth and revealed the eternal secrets which were preserved in heaven'.[40] For this he was admonished by God, who instructed his archangel: 'Bind Azazel hand and foot, and cast him into the darkness ... and let him abide there for ever, and cover his face that he may not see the light. And on the day of the great judgement he shall be cast into the fire ... The whole earth has been corrupted through the works that were taught by Azazel. To him ascribe all sin'.[41]

Subsequently, in view of the watchers' said fornication with earthly women, God was angered with them all. Whereas in Genesis only mankind was punished, *Enoch* describes that so too were the angelic perpetrators. 'He instructed his archangel: Go bind Semjaza and his associates who have united themselves with women so as to have defiled themselves with them in all their uncleanliness'. Bind them 'in the valleys of the earth, till the day of their judgement ... In those days they shall be led off to the abyss of fire, and to the torment and the prison in which they shall be confined for ever'.[42] This confinement is recounted in the New Testament epistle of Jude 1:6, which states, 'And the angels which kept not their first estate, but left their own habitation, he hath reserved in everlasting chains under darkness unto the judgment of the great day'.

The name of Satan does not appear in the Enochian list of the chiefs of the watchers, neither do any of the other devilish names we have encountered. Foremost in the reckoning for particular blame by God are Semjaza and Azazel, but they are not directly aligned with the Devil in any Judaeo-Christian tradition. Nevertheless, Azazel does make nominal appearances in the Bible. The first is in Leviticus 16:8, when God orders the high priest Aaron to 'place lots upon two goats, one lot for the Lord and the other lot for Azazel'. The goat designated by lot for the Lord on this Day of Atonement (*Yom Kippur*) is to be used as a 'sin offering', whilst the goat designated for Azazel 'shall be set alive before the Lord, to make atonement over him, to send him away for Azazel into the wilderness'.[43] Aaron was to 'lay both his hands upon the head of the live goat, and confess over him all the iniquities of the children of Israel, and all their transgressions, even all their sins. And he shall put them upon the head of the goat, and shall send him away by the hand of an appointed man into the wilderness. And the goat shall bear upon him all their iniquities unto a land which is cut off'.[44]

In a 1530 English translation of the Bible, the Protestant reformer William Tyndale split the name Azazel into the component parts, *ez ozel* ('goat that escapes'). Consequently, Azazel's name was excluded from the subsequent King James Bible, and he was recorded therein as the 'scapegoat'.[45]

What emerges from all this is a direct association between sin and a wandering goat — a concept that did indeed enter the satanic tradition. It was well suited to the devilish image of the horned satyr with the legs and feet of a goat. Since the biblical Satan carries no physical description, he was traditionally considered to look like any other angel, albeit a fallen one with bat's wings, alluding to his association with darkness. But in AD 590 Pope Gregory I made a doctrinal announcement concerning the Devil's characteristics, thereby establishing a satyr-like personality which has been perpetuated from that time. 'Satan has horns and hooves', said Gregory, along with 'powers to control the weather, and a terrible stench'.[46]

The Devil's Children

Although not listed as being a chief of the watchers, Satan does feature prominently in the *Book of Enoch* as a senior figure in their midst. It describes that in a 'deep valley with burning fire', an angel makes 'iron chains of immeasurable weight' to bind the host of Azazel ... in the abyss of complete condemnation'. When explaining the reason for this confinement, the angel states that the captives are to be cast 'into the burning furnace ... for their unrighteousness in becoming subject to Satan'.[47] In this regard, Satan is portrayed as the ultimate master of the chiefs, and the formidable opponent of God, the Lord of Spirits.

Two women were deemed ultimately responsible for the fall from grace of the watchers. The first (in the early descent from

Cain) was Naamah, a biblical daughter of Lamech and sister of Tubalcain in Genesis.[48] It was said that 'her great beauty tempted the angels to sin'. For Azazel and Samjaza, it was a young woman named Istahar who proved fatal to their virtue. In their earthly surroundings the watchers succumbed to the wiles of these and other women, and were resultantly cast into the abyss, unable to return to Heaven. From that place Azazel was said to continue in his evil ways, 'dealing in rich adornments and fine garments for women, thereby seducing men into wickedness with his fanciful wares'. It was for this reason that the goat bearing the lot of these transgressions was sent especially to Azazel on the Day of Atonement.[49]

This story of the Fall of the Angels is very much in parallel with the said Fall of Man in that, as was most often the case in early Judaeo-Christian lore, women were seen to be the primary instigators of sin. In the Catholic tradition, this relates especially to that which is termed *Original Sin* — the sin committed by Eve, which we are all reckoned by the Church to inherit by way of our descent from her. This was the sin which resulted in Adam being deprived of immortality, leading to the final sin of death. Thus, it is presumed that we are not only born in sin, but prove our abiding sinfulness by the act of dying: 'Wherefore as by one man sin entered into the world, and death by sin; and so death passed upon all men, for that all have sinned'.[50]

In explanation of this peculiar assumption, St Augustine of Hippo first pronounced the 4th-century Catholic doctrine of *Original Sin* which prevails to this day. It maintains that, owing to the transgression of Eve, all people are born in sin by virtue of having mothers! A child at the font is therefore presumed sinful by the very nature of its birth. In accordance with Ephesians 2:1–3, all are spiritually dead in their trespasses and sins from the lusts of the flesh in past times. This is attributed to 'the prince of the power of the air, the spirit that now worketh in the children of disobedience'. As related in the gospel of John, the prince of power, the 'prince of this world' is reckoned to be Satan.[51] Christian baptism therefore supposes the infant to be under the power of evil, requiring an abjuration of Satan by the sponsor in

21

the name of the child.[52] Thus, the baptismal sponsor and candidate are united in a promise to 'renounce the Devil and all his works, the pomps and vanity of this wicked world, and all the sinful lusts of the flesh'.

At the root of all this is a common belief that the Christian term *Original Sin* and the resultant fall of Adam, had something to do with Eve's sexual misbehaviour in the garden of Eden, but this is an absurdity. To the point where Adam is banished from the garden, after eating from the Tree of Knowledge of Good and Evil, there is no mention whatever of any physical contact between him and Eve. Their offspring were conceived in their new environment some time after Genesis explains they had left the garden. Notwithstanding this, it is made clear from the outset in Genesis 2:24 that Eve was the 'wife' of Adam, a fact which is repeated numerous times along with the instruction that the man 'shall cleave unto his wife, and they shall be one flesh'.

What has any of this to do with Satan or the Devil? Absolutely nothing; he is not mentioned at any stage of the proceedings. The only other character in the Eden plot is an unnamed serpent. The story relates that God warned Adam away from the Tree of Knowledge, claiming that he would die if he ate its fruit. The serpent then asserted to Eve that this was untrue, and that they should partake of the knowledge: 'Ye shall not surely die, for God doth know that in the day ye eat thereof, then your eyes shall be opened, and ye shall be as gods'.[53] In the event, the serpent was right — the man and woman did eat of the tree, and they did not die. They gained the knowledge of good and evil, whereupon God sent Adam to till the ground as a punishment of servitude for his disobedience.[54]

In consideration of the Hebrew text, it is evident that there was not actually a serpent in the garden. The biblical term that became mistranslated to 'serpent' was *nahash*. Before the vowels were added, the original consonantal stem was *NHSH*, which meant 'to decipher' or 'to find out'.[55] Hence, there was no serpent in the common snake-like understanding of the word, and a better interpretation of *NHSH* would relate to a 'wise one'. This becomes especially evident from the early Hebraic expression of angels being *ha'neshim*, as against the quite separate definition *ha'neshek*, which referred to serpents.[56]

If Eve was perceived to have sinned, the notion could only relate to her eating from the forbidden tree along with Adam. In this regard, she accepted the wise one's advice that they would not die from the fruit, instead of heeding God's contrary warning that they would die.[57] The fact is, however, that God did not warn Eve against the tree; he only warned Adam at a time before Eve was even created.[58] It was for this reason that Adam alone was expelled from Eden, because he had 'hearkened to the voice of thy wife'.[59] Not until chapter 4 of Genesis do we discover that Eve followed Adam's footsteps out of the garden.

Having eaten the fruit from the Tree of Knowledge, another of the garden's trees then posed a secondary problem for Adam: the Tree of Life. God is said to have banished Adam from the garden 'lest he put forth his hand and take also of the Tree of Life, and eat, and live forever'. Not content with this, a revolving sword of fire was installed to prevent Adam's future access to the tree.[60] To complete the punishment, God then said to Eve, 'I will greatly multiply thy sorrow and thy conception; in sorrow thou shalt bring forth children'. Then, even though Adam had not touched the Tree of Life, he was expelled and deprived of its benefit in any event.[61]

What the Genesis narrative, concerning Adam and Eve, achieves by virtue of the strangely conveyed expulsion story is that it sets up women in general as being temptresses. Eve's said transgression (just like that of Naamah and Istahar) was to have seduced Adam into her wicked ways. Thus, the reasoning is used to establish a male supremacy that pervades the rest of the patriarchal scripture. For her said misbehaviour with the fruit, and for daring to influence Adam against God's will, Eve was told that, henceforth, 'thy husband ... shall rule over thee'.[62] Adam's offence was that he had listened to Eve instead of obeying God. As a punishment for this sin, Eve was to suffer the pain and sorrow of bearing children.

In complete contrast to the story as portrayed in Genesis, the Christian doctrinal view is that, since the serpent (the *nahash*) was powerful enough to oppose God in the garden, then the serpent must have been Satan. Given that all children thereafter have been born in sin as a result of Eve's transgression, their first step towards salvation is a commitment to God and the Church by way of baptism and a publicly announced renunciation of the Devil. The first explicit testimony in this regard comes from Tertullian's *De Corona* (The Chaplet). Written in the late 2nd century by this prominent leader of the early North African Church, it states,

> When we are going to enter the water, but a little before, in the presence of the congregation and under the hand of the president, we solemnly profess that we disown the devil, and his pomp, and his angels.[63]

3

CONFLICT WITH SATAN

Diabolic Perception

In the formative years of the Christian Church, it was deemed necessary to rewrite some of the Old Testament stories in order to set a more conducive scene for the Devil. The account of Adam and Eve was foremost for amendment in this regard since, to suit the new ideal, the Devil had to be acknowledged as being present from the very beginning. The serpent in the garden of Eden was vague and undefined in Genesis. This rendered him a suitably devilish candidate, and the revisionist scribes of Christendom began their work. Henceforth, from the 5th century, it was to be presumed that the unnamed serpent (the *nahash*: 'wise one') was Satan the Devil.

This change of physical image caused a certain amount of difficulty in subsequent portrayals and literary descriptions. Satan was, on the one hand, represented as a dark bat-winged angel, while on the other hand he was described as a goat-like satyr with horns and hooves. Now there was to be a new aspect to his appearance: dragon-like and scaly, with claws. As the centuries progressed, any one of these portrayals, or in some cases a combination of two or three of them, were used to identify the satanic presence of the Devil.

Initially, when dealing with the revised concept of portraying both God and the Devil in Eden, there was an anomaly to be considered in that, since God was reckoned to have created everything, then he must have created the Devil. Thus, the question arose: Why would God have given himself such a problem? This only presented itself as a difficult area of debate because of the way in which the Latin Bible had been translated. There are no fewer than 2,570 occasions in the Hebrew Old Testament where the term 'gods' (*elohim*) is used in the plural.[1]

But in the Christian Bible the vast majority of these were changed to the singular, 'God'. Of the few entries that remain as originally written, we have already encountered one, when the serpent said to Adam and Eve, 'Ye shall not surely die, for God doth know that in the day ye eat thereof, then your eyes shall be opened, and ye shall be as *gods*'.[2] Similarly, the Old Testament Psalm 82 opens in the King James Bible with: 'God standeth in the congregation of the mighty; he judgeth among the *gods*'. It is also of particular note that, when Adam had eaten the fruit of knowledge, God said to the serpent (the *nahash*), 'Behold the man is become as *one of us*',[3] thereby denoting the wise one as another god.

Clearly, since the book of Genesis emanated from the much older Mesopotamian archive, there were indeed many gods on record. The Jewish God (El-Yahweh) could not therefore be portrayed as the 'one and only' God because all other traditions contradicted this. At best he could be portrayed by the Old Testament scribes as the only God that mattered to the Hebrews and later Israelites. The Christian Church had, nonetheless, disclaimed the existence of other ancient deities and, with regard to the Devil, this posed a real dilemma. There was an advantage, however, in the fact that, for a good many centuries, people at large did not own their own Bibles, so the priests and bishops could preach whatever they wanted. It was also the case that few dared to question the authority of the Church and, on account of this, the satanic anomaly was pretty much ignored.

It was not until 1215 that the official teaching of the Church on this particular topic was established and set down by the Fourth Lateran Council. The decree maintained that 'In the beginning God created two types of creature, the spiritual and the corporeal [the angelic and the earthly]'. The decree continued: 'The Devil and the other demons were created by God good in their nature, but they by themselves have made themselves evil' (*Diabolus enim et alii dæmones a Deo quidem naturâ creati sunt boni, sed ipsi per se facti sunt mali*).[4] It was then added that 'Man sinned by the suggestion of the Devil, and in the next world the wicked shall suffer perpetual punishment with the Devil'. By virtue of this decree, it was further determined:

26

> The Devil and the other demons are but a part
> of the angelic creation, and their natural powers
> do not differ from those of the angels who
> remained faithful. Like the other angels, they
> are pure spiritual beings without any body, and
> in their original state they are endowed with
> supernatural grace and placed in a condition of
> probation. It was only by their fall that they
> became devils.

To support this fabricated notion, along with the theory that death was itself said to be the result of sin, there was placed into the Latin *Vulgate* Bible a work entitled the *Book of Wisdom*. It remains in some Catholic Bibles today,[5] and states: 'By the envy of the Devil, death came into the world'.[6]

The Lateran doctrine was all very well to a point, but there was a drawback in that the angels were described as 'pure spiritual beings without any body'. This plainly did not equate with the angels of the Old Testament, who were materially alive, on-the-ground figures. Among these were the angel who met Abraham's consort Hagar by the water fountain;[7] the angels who visited Lot's house and supped with him;[8] the angel who stopped Balaam's ass in its tracks;[9] the angel who spoke to Manoah and his wife,[10] and the angel who sat beneath the oak with Gideon.[11]

Furthermore, it was stated of certain angels that 'It was only by their fall that they became devils'. Among these was reckoned to be the fallen angel Satan, in which event another problem arose: How could he be spiritual, without a body, if he appeared to Adam and Eve in the garden? How could he be purely spiritual if he met with Jesus in the wilderness as related in Matthew 4:1–11? In fact, how could Pope Gregory have described the Devil's appearance with horns and hooves if he had no body to display? All of these questions remained unanswered within a confusing set of inconsistent dogmatic assertions. But they arose only because of a strategy to define the angels as being different from their Old Testament originals in an attempt to create a new doctrinal perception of Satan for Christendom.

The 'serpent-to-devil' transition was facilitated in the first instance by a tale known as the *Moses Apocalypse*. Written in the late 1st century BC, it was a short manuscript about Adam and Eve after their expulsion from the garden. In this work, the Devil and the serpent appear separately. The latter (based on the *nahash* connotation) is portrayed in this text as a wise counsellor:

> And the devil spake to the serpent saying, Rise up, come to me and I will tell thee a word whereby thou mayst have profit. And he arose and came to him. And the devil saith to him, I hear that thou art wiser than all the beasts, and I have come to counsel thee.[12]

Some years later, in the 1st century AD, a reworked version of the story appeared. It became known in Latin as the *Vita Adae et Evae* (Life of Adam and Eve).[13] In this adaptation, the Devil and the serpent were combined as one character, to the extent that the serpent does not appear by individual definition. The account focuses on Adam and Eve's search for food, and of how Satan approached Eve as she wept:

> Satan was wroth and transformed himself into the brightness of angels, and went away to the River Tigris to Eve, and found her weeping. And the devil himself pretended to grieve with her, and he began to weep and said to her, Come out of the river and lament no more.[14]

After some discussion between Adam, Eve and the Devil, which conveniently aligns Satan with the biblical serpent, Adam asks him why he was banished by God. 'And with a heavy sigh, the devil spake: O Adam! all my hostility, envy and sorrow is for thee, since it is for thee that I have been expelled from my glory, which I possessed in the heavens in the midst of the angels, and for thee was I cast out in the earth'.[15] Thus, the desired connections were made: The serpent was synonymous with the Devil, and he had fallen from grace because he had advised Eve to eat the fruit against God's command.

The scene was now conveniently set, and the time had come to rewrite the story of Adam and Eve in full. Whereas the biblical account of Eden and the expulsion amounts to just 1,900 words, the new Christianized version emerged as a lengthy 33,000-word exposition in 79 chapters. The work emanated from North Africa, a foremost department of early Christianity. The region spawned prominent Church Fathers such as Tertullian of Carthage and Origen of Alexandria, where the Episcopal See became second only to that of the Vatican in Rome. Produced in the 5th century AD, the revised Eden story was entitled *The Conflict of Adam and Eve with Satan*.[16]

This tactically designed work, also known as *The First Book of Adam and Eve*, cleverly amalgamates Satan and the serpent. This is not done by claiming that they were one and the same (as in the *Vita Adae et Evae*), but by explaining how the serpent was strategically possessed by the Devil. In a conversation with Adam, Satan confides to him,

> It is I who hid myself within the serpent, and who talked to Eve, and beguiled her until she hearkened to my command. I am he who sent her, through the wiles of my speech, to deceive thee, until thou and she ate of the fruit of the tree, and ye came away from under the command of God.[17]

In terms of the Devil's appearance and name, it is stated: 'Now his figure is hideous; he is become abominable among angels; and he has come to be called Satan'.[18] The anomaly concerning how it was that God allowed Satan to exist is also confronted in this text, with God saying, 'Were it not for my mercy, I would have destroyed thee and thy hosts from off the earth. But I have had patience with thee unto the end of the world'.[19]

With Satan described as being 'great in wickedness' and a constant embarrassment to the heavenly angels, most of the story focuses on a series of events in which he endeavours to taunt and torment Adam and Eve in their cave of residence:

He had gathered trees and dry grasses,
and had carried and brought them to
the cave, and had set fire to them, in
order to consume the cave and what
was in it.[20] He then said unto his host,
Ye know that this Adam, whom God
created out of the dust, is he who has
taken our kingdom. Come, let us all
gather together and kill him, or hurl a
rock at him and at Eve, and crush them
under it.[21]

A similarly constructed work, entitled *The Book of the Cave of Treasures*, was then produced in the 6th century.[22] This was a Syriac compendium of earthly history from the creation of the world to the crucifixion of Jesus. Once again, Satan appears as the constant protagonist of persecution. He arrives fourteen times to torment Adam and Eve in their cave, but each time an angel of God puts him to flight. A principal objective of this work was to show that the Christian tradition was foreshadowed in early times. It even maintains that a rod cut from the Tree of Life by Adam was eventually the staff used by Jesus Christ, which was then stolen by the apostle Judas Iscariot.

In many ways, *The Book of Adam and Eve* and *The Cave of Treasures* had the jointly desired effect of establishing a platform of operation for Satan, from which he could wage his violent campaign. But for all that, the earlier celestial enchantment of the watchers and the lustful *nephilim* was completely lost. There was nothing ethereal or otherworldly about this newly fashioned character, who acted more like a brutish neighbour than a fallen angel. He was neither dark nor sinister, and was in no way terrifying on any grand scale. He assaulted Adam and Eve with bonfires, sticks and stones, and drove wild animals to their door, but he achieved nothing and was constantly outwitted. It was all a far cry from the fearsome guardian of Hell or the mighty beast of the *Apocalypse*, who led the Sons of Darkness in the great War of Heaven.

The Temptation

Moving to the more original references to the Devil and Satan, his first and only actual appearance in the New Testament gospels is with Jesus in the wilderness. The story appears in Matthew 4:1–11, and is repeated in Luke 4:1–13. It begins, 'Then was Jesus led up of the Spirit into the wilderness to be tempted of the devil'. The continuing narrative relates that the tempter questioned Jesus' legitimacy as the son of God, and asked him to prove it by turning stones into bread. He then took Jesus to the pinnacle of a temple, suggesting that he cast himself down to prove that the angels would save him. After that, 'The devil taketh him up into an exceeding high mountain, and showeth him all the kingdoms of the world, and the glory of them; and saith unto him, All these things will I give thee, if thou wilt fall down and worship me'. With Jesus conceding to none of these requests, it is resultantly stated, 'Then the devil leaveth him, and, behold, angels came and ministered unto him'.

The devilish tempter of this passage is not presented as being in any way persuasive or influential, and he gives up remarkably easily. He bears absolutely no similarity to the terrible demon that later emerged in the satanic mythology of the 'fire and brimstone' preachers. In fact, just as with the Old Testament, there is nothing remotely fearsome about any of the satanic mentions in the New Testament gospels and epistles, and there is not even the vaguest reference to a physical description.

Apart from the story of the Devil and Jesus, other satanic entries of the New Testament are all symbolic. At the Last Supper it is stated, 'Then entered Satan into Judas surnamed Iscariot'.[23] Elsewhere, when the scribes admonished Jesus for performing exorcisms when he was not himself a priest, 'He called them unto him, and said unto them in parables, How can Satan cast out Satan?'[24] A few other references in The Acts and Epistles are of a similarly obscure nature.[25] The Revelation of St John then refers to blasphemers as being of the 'synagogue of Satan',[26] whilst claiming that, having been dismissed from heaven, Satan would remain imprisoned for a thousand years.[27]

31

In the midst of these entries, the most telling reference in terms of the obstructive nature of a *satan* ('accuser') arises in Matthew 16:23, when Jesus charges the apostle Peter with being satanic. It occurs when Peter rebukes Jesus for being too complacent, whereupon Jesus 'turned and said unto Peter, Get thee behind me satan; thou art an offence to me, for thou savourest not the things that be of God, but those that be of men'.[28]

The strategically designed evolution of Satan's role in the early Catholic faith was based entirely on the need to subject the masses to the dominion of the bishops. To facilitate this, an Antichrist figure was necessary as a perceived enemy from whose wrath the believers could be saved. This enemy was said to be Satan, the 'evil one', who would claim the souls of any who did not offer absolute obedience to the Church. Authority was then established on the back of a statement made by St Paul in his epistle to the Romans:

> Let every soul be subject unto the higher powers. For there is no power but of God; the powers that be are ordained of God. Whosoever therefore resisteth the power, resisteth the ordinance of God; and they that resist shall receive to themselves damnation.[29]

It then remained for the Church to become the self-appointed bridge between God and the people. This was done by granting an inviolable vicarious office to the Pope, who became the designated Vicar of the Son of God (*Vicarius Filii Dei*).

As for the Antichrist, so often preached to strike terror and subjugation, there is no such character in the New Testament. The word 'antichrist' appears only in the epistles of John, but not in respect of a specific figure. It is used simply as a term to define those opposed to the teachings of Jesus. 1 John 2:18 states, 'Even now are there many antichrists'. 1 John 2:22 continues with 'He that denieth that Jesus is the Christ; he is antichrist'.[30] There is nothing here that relates to any satanic being, and the author of the John epistles plainly recognized that Jesus had many opposers.

In much the same way, the word 'satanist' was used for hundreds of years, right up until Protestant times. Like the terms antichrist, atheist and infidel, it was a commonly used description of unbelievers in general, and its complexion did not begin to change until the 15th-century onset of the witch-hunts.[31] Even as late as 1559, the pamphlet *An Harbour for Faithful and True Subjects*, issued by John Aylmer, Bishop of London, refers to all those other than Christians as 'satanists'.[32]

The Apocalypse

There are any number of references in the New Testament to sick people thought to be possessed by demons and devils. But, apart from the above mentioned incident of the temptation of Christ, entries concerning the satanic Devil in particular are few. One is in a parable about crops and weeds (tares) in which Jesus says, 'The field is the world; the good seed are the children of the kingdom; but the tares are the children of the wicked one; the enemy that sowed them is the devil'.[33] On another occasion, when preaching to his disciples on the Mount of Olives near Bethany, Jesus refers to an 'everlasting fire prepared for the devil and his angels'.[34]

The work that is most often thought to be concerned with the Devil is the book of The Revelation. It is worth considering the relevant passages of this New Testament section in some detail, since they are at the root of the dark satanic lore and devilish superstitions that grew over the years from its 1st-century origin.

It was during the reign of the Roman Emperor Domitian (AD 81–96) that John the Evangelist was sentenced to confinement on the Greek island of Patmos,[35] where he was said to have compiled The Revelation.[36] Also known as *The Apocalypse of St John*, this alternative title derives simply from the Greek word *apocalypse*, meaning nothing more nor less than 'revelation'. Few distinctive words have come to be so inappropriately misused in the modern English language, with 'apocalypse' and 'apocalyptic' now so frequently misapplied to denote terrible or disastrous events.

The Revelation is presented as a series of visionary experiences, described in the manner of a fragmented stage-play with the various acts explained by John. As he watches the scenes, his task is to record what he is witnessing, and to send the details to the leaders of seven principal churches in Ephesus, Smyrna, Pergamos, Thyatira, Sardis, Philadelphia and Laodicea.

By its very nature, The Revelation is an allegorical work, wherein the strictly esoteric passages are heralded by the often used expression, 'He that hath an ear, let him hear'. This was a device used many times by Jesus when conveying his parables. It was very much a part of the *Dead Sea Scrolls* tradition to phrase things in such a manner that would be incomprehensible to the Roman overlords during a period of harsh occupation. It was an effective way of communicating politically sensitive information to those who understood the Qumrân community jargon. As Jesus said to the disciples in Mark 4:11–12:

> Unto you it is given to know the mystery of the kingdom of God; but unto them that are without, all these things are done in parables: that seeing they may see, and not perceive; and hearing they may hear, and not understand.

Only since the discovery and translation of the *Dead Sea Scrolls* from 1947 has it been possible to decipher some of the coded elements of this cryptic technique, which pervades a good deal of the New Testament.[37] Study of the scrolls (particularly the *Manual of Discipline*, the *Community Rule*, the *War Rule* and the *Angelic Liturgy*) reveals a number of such biblically coded words and pseudonyms that were previously misunderstood or considered to be of no particular importance. For instance, the 'poor' were not poverty-stricken, underprivileged citizens; they were those initiated into the higher echelons of the community, and had given up their property and worldly possessions. The 'many' was a title for the head of the celibate community, whereas the 'crowd' was a designation of the regional Tetrarch (Governor), and a 'multitude' was a governing council. Novices and students within the establishment were called 'children'. The doctrinal theme of the Nazarene community was known as The Way, and those who followed the principles of The Way were known as the Children of Light. The term 'lepers' was often used to denote those who had not been initiated into the community, or who had been denounced by it. The 'blind' were those who were not party to The Way, and could therefore not see the Light.

In this regard, we now have a better understanding of the terminology used in The Revelation. The great battle between the Children of Light and the Sons of Darkness, previously mentioned in connection with the *War Scroll*, and prophesied to take place on the Palestinian battlefield of Har-Megiddo (Armageddon) in Jezreel, was a contest between the community of The Way and the might of Imperial Rome. This is emphasized, for example, in Revelation 12:3, which states:

> And there appeared another wonder in
> heaven; and behold a great red dragon,
> having seven heads and ten horns, and
> seven crowns upon his heads.

The natural inference here is that we are dealing with some form of supernatural beast, but it is in fact a specific reference to the Roman occupational force. Not only did the Romans display a red dragon on their standard, but Rome was itself known as the City of the Seven Kings — the number of 'crowned heads' before the Republic was formed in 509 BC.[38]

There are many such instances in St John's *Apocalypse* where terms such as 'accuser of our brethren'[39] and the like are given a symbolic devilish significance. But as far as John, the brethren and all Israelites were concerned at that time, there was no greater devil than the Roman machine that had demolished Jerusalem before John and others were expelled by imperial dictate. What John foresaw, and predicted in his work, was a day of retribution when the seven-headed dragon would be defeated, when the satanic regime would be crushed, and peace might prevail in Judaea:

> And the great dragon was cast out, that old serpent, called the Devil and Satan, which deceiveth the whole world: he was cast out into the earth, and his angels were cast out with him.[40]

The coded symbolism for Rome does not mean that the demonic Satan's name is absent from The Revelation. It is certainly evident, as in the above quoted passage. But, in this context and others, his name is used to personify evil, rather than to depict a horned satyr creature or a fallen angelic watcher. In one instance, John uses Satan's name to criticize the Hebrew priests, who were happy to benefit from lucrative Roman employment at the expense of their Jewish neighbours, saying, 'Behold, I will make them of the synagogue of Satan, which say they are Jews, and are not, but do lie'.[41]

Interestingly, although John foresaw the fall of Rome and the casting out of the beast, he also reckoned that a devilish power would return at a future time:

> And I saw an angel come down from heaven, having the key of the bottomless pit and a great chain in his hand. And he laid hold on the dragon, that old serpent, which is the Devil and Satan, and bound him a thousand years. And cast him into the bottomless pit, and shut him up, and set a seal upon him, that he should deceive the nations no more, till the thousand years should be fulfilled … And when the thousand years are expired, Satan shall be loosed out of his prison. And shall go out to deceive the nations which are in the four quarters of the earth.[42]

In discussing the angel with the great chain and the key to the bottomless pit, John appears to have been referencing that similar scene in the *Book of Enoch*, when the angel with the chain bound Azazel and his fallen angels in the chasm of burning fire. They were confined 'for their unrighteousness in becoming subject to Satan'.[43] Such entries in the *Apocalypse* are clearly designed to draw parallels between mythological tradition and historical reality.[44] Thus, it can be said that, although The Revelation is allegorically compiled 'for those with ears to hear', it is without doubt a prophetic book about a war that must constantly be waged against an evil that will always exist even if confined to the abyss for periods of time. In this particular instance, however, John does not name Satan as the guardian of the abyss. Referring to its inhabitants, he states,

> And they had a king over them, which is the angel
> of the bottomless pit, whose name in the Hebrew
> tongue is Abaddon, but in the Greek tongue hath
> his name Apollyon.[45]

Abaddon (or Apollyon) means 'destroyer' and, by virtue of this passage, has become yet another of the names popularly ascribed to the Devil. In practice, John would more likely have been consistent in using the name Satan (as elsewhere in the text) if he were indeed the figure in question. It is fair to assume, therefore, that Abaddon was an independently conceived character. But the descriptions of Abaddon's swarming army, with iron breastplates, lions' teeth, wings and scorpions' tails, were sufficiently fearsome to be added to the list of scary attributes in subsequent portrayals of the Devil.

There are a number of differently described beasts in The Revelation, each with its own hideous identifications. None of them is the Devil as such, but it has been common practice for Church teaching to extract invividual passages of explanation from each description, and to assign them from the pulpit as if they all relate to a single satanic presence. There is however one beast in Revelation 13, which rose out of the sea and was said to receive its power from a great dragon who became worshipped. Although John actually ascribes the name of Satan to the seven-headed dragon of Rome, this other dragon bears the closest resemblance to the malevolent image of Satan as he emerged in the fiery invective of the later wrath-driven preachers. It is said of this particular creature:

> And there was given unto him a mouth speaking great things and blasphemies ... And he opened his mouth in blasphemy against God, to blaspheme his name, and his tabernacle, and them that dwell in heaven. And it was given unto him to make war with the saints, and to overcome them; and power was given him over all kindreds, and tongues, and nations. And all that dwell upon the earth shall worship him, whose names are not written in the book of life of the Lamb, slain from the foundation of the world.[46]

When summing up the book of The Revelation from a perplexed Christian perspective, as against its keenly esoteric Nazarene construction, it is apparent from the writings of early Church Fathers that the allegories of the book's terminology were beyond their understanding. In this respect, we can do no better than cite Dionysius, the Bishop of Alexandria AD 247–265. About 160 years after *The Apocalypse* was compiled, he wrote:

> I myself would never dare to reject the book, of which many good Christians have a very high opinion. But realizing that my mental powers are inadequate to judge it properly, I take the view that the interpretation of the various sections is largely a mystery, something too wonderful for our comprehension. I do not understand it, but I suspect that some deeper meaning is concealed within the words.[47]

In times to follow, it was this very incomprehensible aspect of *The Apocalypse* that rendered it so useful to the subjugative priests and preachers of Christendom. If the bishops did not understand it, then neither would people at large. It could therefore be interpreted for congregations at will. Thus, with certain individual passages strategically presented out of context,

The Revelation became a scary proclamation of foreboding and doom — the ultimate textual weapon of threat, intimidation and control.

In order that the rule of the bishops should prevail, it was decreed that the prophesied war of the angels and the Day of Judgement were still to come. Those who obeyed the dictates of the Church were promised the right of entry to the Kingdom of Heaven, as sanctified by the Vatican. The rest were condemned to eternal damnation in Hell. In the course of this, the one-time Palestinian hill-fort of Har-Megiddo was invested with a dark supernatural overtone, so that the very word *Armageddon* took on a hideous ring of terror. It implied the fearsome ending of all things at the hands of the Devil, from whom the only sure route to salvation was absolute compliance with the Rule of Rome. It proved to be one of the most ingeniously devised political manoeuvres of all time, and the malicious doctrine is still taught to this day.

4

A REIGN OF TERROR

The Adversary

In 1945, two years before the discovery of the *Dead Sea Scrolls*, a unique collection of documents was unearthed in the town of Nag Hammadi, near Luxor in Egypt. They were not scrolls, but codices — leather-bound books with parchment leaves from the 2nd and 3rd centuries, written in the ancient Coptic language of Upper Egypt.[1] Emanating from a tradition known as *Gnostic*, which relates to esoteric insight, their language is imbued with allegory, symbolism and metaphor. They are the scriptures and teachings of a philosophical Christian sect that flourished before the 4th-century establishment of the Church of Rome.

Throughout these works, the concept of opposing spirits — light and dark, good and evil — is manifestly evident. But among the sixty individual tractates there are surprisingly few mentions of the Devil or Satan — just a dozen or so overall. It is of note, however, that the Devil was regarded as real enough by the Gnostic Christians. He was called 'the adversary' and 'the deceitful one'. He was a fallen angel and, in line with the *Vita Adae et Evae*, was likened to the serpent of Eden because of his opposition to the spirit of God:

> In the *Apocryphon of James*, the disciples ask Jesus, 'Grant us not to be tempted by the Devil'.[2]

> In the *Gospel of Truth*, Jesus addresses his disciples: 'Do not become a dwelling place for the Devil'.[3]

> In the *Teaching of Sylvanus*, it is preached: 'Cast the deceitfulness of the Devil from you ... The schemes of the Adversary are not few, and his tricks are varied'.[4]

In the *Testimony of Truth*, Eve relates: 'The serpent is the one who instructed me. And He [God] cursed the serpent and called him the Devil'.[5]

Just as in the New Testament, these various comments do not amount to very much. The Devil's name is used in order to personify temptations of the darker side, but he makes no physical appearance and is in no way bodily described.

* * *

Following the confirmation of selected books for the New Testament at the Synod of Carthage in AD 397, the next official work of religious doctrine to appear was the 7th-century Islāmic Koran (*Al-Qur'an*).[6] In this holy book of the Muslims, God is called Allāh (the 'Only God'), and the Devil is referred to as Shaitān.

The Koran relates that Adam was created by Allāh to be his deputy on Earth, and that the angels were instructed to bow before Adam. They all complied willingly except for Shaitān, who lured Adam and his wife to eat from the forbidden Tree of Transgression.[7] This is not dissimilar to an item in the earlier *Vita Adae et Evae*, when God commanded the angels to bow before Adam. All obeyed except for Satan, who exclaimed, 'I will not worship one who is younger than I am, and inferior. He ought to worship me'.[8]

Once again, in accordance with the biblical Devil and devils, the Koran also has its Shaitān and its shaitāns. In strict terms, the Devil is referred to as *al-Shaitān* (the Satan), with 87 mentions in all. Sometimes he is called Iblis, a *jinn* creature (a genie) made of smokeless fire by Allāh, but expelled from his grace. He is portrayed as chief of the evil spirits, roaming the Earth in an attempt to deceive and misguide.

The character of Shaitān does not appear as an active player as such in the Koran. Aside from his part in the story of Adam and Eve, the other mentions are more in the nature of warnings against his malevolent influence. For example:

41

O you who believe;! enter into submission one and all,
and do not follow the footsteps of Shaitān; surely he is
your open enemy.[9]

Shaitān threatens you with poverty and enjoins you to
be niggardly, and Allāh promises you forgiveness from
Himself and abundance.[10]

The Shaitān only desires to cause enmity and hatred to
spring in your midst by means of intoxicants and games
of chance.[11]

So when you recite *Al-Qur'an*, seek refuge with Allāh
from the accursed Shaitān.[12]

The Millennium

We have now met with Satan as he appears in the Hebrew Bible,
the Christian New Testament and the Islāmic Koran. We have also
referenced his mentions in Jewish and Christian apocryphal
works, as well as in the Gnostic tradition. From all this, it is
evident that, although Satan features in the books of the three
primary monotheistic religions, he is still far removed from any
likeness to the awesome power-lord who later rose to induce fear
and trepidation on a monumental scale. To the point we have
reached, he would not begin to compete in the evil realm of
Gothic horror, and there has been no sign of any group that might
venerate him to the extent that would incite the hunts and
burnings of presumed satanists that occurred in later times.
Having now reached the 7th century, it is evident that the Devil is
still far from being in his prime.

Through the 8th and 9th centuries the Devil moved into
heightened prominence when Christian baptism, the accepted
doorway to a spiritual and godly life, also became a ritual of
exorcism. In 743, at the Synod of Liptina, an abjuration of the
Devil was added to the *Confession of the Catholic Faith*, and it was

taught that the unbaptised would be tormented for ever in Hell. But it was not until the approaching year 1000 that fear of the Devil truly began to break out in Christendom.

Before that time, thoughts of the Devil had remained largely in the back of people's minds, if indeed he was considered at all. Religious people in general had felt secure in the knowledge that, in accordance with The Revelation of St John (written in about AD 90), Satan had been consigned to the abyss for a thousand years. He had been bound and incarcerated in the bottomless pit with a seal upon him. But the time had now come for his release from the chains, destined to begin a new reign of terror from the turn of the first millennium, or thereabouts.

Rodulfus Glaber, a monk of St Bénigne at Dijon through the change of millennium, wrote of the events that took place during that period:

> A multitude began to flock from all parts of the world to the sepulchre of our Saviour at Jerusalem … The lower orders of people led the way, after whom came those of middle rank, and then all the greatest kings and counts and bishops. Lastly, many noble ladies and poorer women journeyed thither. For many purposed and desired to die before they should see their homes again … Moreover, some of those most concerned in these matters, answered with some caution that it portended no other than the advent of that reprobate Antichrist, whose coming at the end of this world is prophesied in holy scripture.[13]

The prophecy of Revelation 20:3 had claimed that the loosing of the Devil would prevail for 'a little season', but this was an indefinite period of time — a long or short period; nobody knew. Whatever the case, it was reckoned to be followed by the return of Christ himself, leading to the war of Armageddon, the great Day of Judgement and the end of the world. This presented an enormous threat in the minds of many who supposed they might be judged, or even misjudged, as sinners, and committed to eternal damnation in Hell. The disorder and misery which resulted from the acts committed in anticipation of the approaching wrath of the millennium were considerable. Some squandered their property in order to enjoy the last days of their lives; some sold all they had and gave to the poor; others invested all their possessions in Masses and Church donations, and a great many fell into wretched poverty and distress.[14]

The fiery and torturous concept of Hell, although not defined in the Bible, had become well enough understood through the subjugative pulpit teachings of ages. Its vivid descriptions came from a pseudoepigraphical 2nd-century document called the *Apocalypse of Peter*. Its author remains unknown, but the now fragmented manuscript details how the damned would be required to present themselves at the gates of Hell for judgement. Read in Catholic churches onwards from the 5th century, it was written in the supposed revelatory words of St Peter, and people believed the work was truly penned by him. The drama of this work is savage, and as fearsome as needs be to hold people in thrall, with no room in the judgemental process for any reason or mediation. Having witnessed the environment of that dreadful place, the pseudo Peter explains:

> Behold now what they shall experience in the last days … Women are hung up by their neck and by their hair, and cast into the pit. These are they who plaited their hair, not to create beauty, but to turn to fornication … The men who lay with them are hung up by their thighs in that burning place … And other men and women stood in flames up to the middle of their bodies, and were cast into a dark place, and were scourged by evil spirits and had their entrails consumed by worms … Other men and women, who cast themselves down from a high slope, came to the bottom and were driven by their torturers to go up to the precipice, and were then thrown down again, and they had no rest from this torture … And still other men and women were burned and turned in the fire and baked.[15]

Unleashing the Antichrist

One of the problems that confronted people of the era was that they were unsure of how they might differentiate between Christ and the Antichrist when they appeared. After all, it was written in Matthew 24:23–24 that 'If any man shall say unto you, Lo, here is Christ, or there; believe it not. For there shall arise false Christs, and false prophets, and shall show great signs and wonders'. Some also remembered Jesus' words in Matthew 7:15, 'Beware of false prophets, which come to you in sheep's clothing, but inwardly they are ravening wolves'. On that basis, Satan was just as likely to come in the guise of a Christian bishop, or a nun, or even as Christ himself. In fact, it became a matter of wide speculation as to whether the Antichrist would actually be Satan, or maybe an emissary sent to prepare the way.

The millennium fever appears to have begun in the year 950, when the Benedictine monk Adso of Montièr-en-Der wrote his treatise, *Libellus de Antichristo*, on the coming of the Evil One. Adso seems to have preferred the idea that the Antichrist would be the contrived son of the Devil, rather than Satan himself:

> He will be born from the union of a mother and father, like other men, not as some say from a virgin alone. Still, he will be conceived wholly in sin, will be generated in sin, and will be born in sin. At the very beginning of his conception the Devil will enter his mother's womb at the same moment. The Devil's power will foster and protect him in his mother's womb, and it will always be with him.
>
> Just as the Holy Spirit came into the mother of Our Lord Jesus Christ, and overshadowed her with his power and filled her with divinity so that she conceived of the Holy Spirit, and what was born of her was divine and holy, so too the Devil will descend into the Antichrist's mother, will completely fill her, completely encompass her, completely master her, completely possess her within and without, so that with the Devil's

cooperation she will conceive through a man and what will be born from her will be totally wicked, totally evil, totally lost. For this reason that man is called the Son of Perdition, because he will destroy the human race as far as he can, and will himself be destroyed at the last day.[16]

The Antichrist concept of the Son of Perdition (the 'man of sin') was interpreted by Adso from St Paul's second epistle to the Thessalonians 2:3–10, which explains,

Let no man deceive you by any means: for that day shall not come, except there come a falling away first, and that 'man of sin' be revealed, the Son of Perdition, who opposeth and exalteth himself above all that is called God, or that is worshipped; so that he as God sitteth in the temple of God, shewing himself that he is God. Remember ye not that, when I was yet with you, I told you these things? And now ye know what withholdeth that he might be revealed in his time. For the mystery of iniquity doth already work: only he who now letteth will let, until he be taken out of the way. And shall that wicked one be revealed, whom the Lord shall consume with the spirit of his mouth, and shall destroy with the brightness of his coming: Even him, whose coming is after the working of Satan with all power and signs and lying wonders, and with all deceivableness of unright-eousness in them that perish; because they received not the love of the truth, that they might be saved.

A good deal of what transpired in the following centuries, through the Inquisition, the witch hunts and the so-called Burning Times, resulted from the predictions of Adso's treatise. Even in modern times it has fueled the material for cinema films such as *Rosemary's Baby*, *The Omen* and *The Calling*. It is therefore worth extracting a further sequence from the text, since it is from this particular literary beginning that the Devil, as we have come to know him, was truly born:

He will first convert kings and princes to his cause, and then through them the rest of the peoples. He will attack the places where the Lord Christ walked and will destroy what the Lord made famous. Then he will send messengers and his preachers through the whole world. His preaching and power will extend from sea to sea, from east to west, from north to south. He will also work many signs, great and unheard-of prodigies. He will make fire come down from heaven in a terrifying way, trees suddenly blossom and wither, the sea become stormy and unexpectedly calm.

He will make the elements change into differing forms, divert the order and flow of bodies of water, disturb the air with winds and all sorts of commotions, and perform countless other wondrous acts. He will raise the dead in the sight of men in order to lead into error, if possible, even the elect. For when they shall have seen great signs of such a nature even those who are perfect and God's chosen ones will doubt whether or not he is the Christ who according to the scriptures will come at the end of the world.

He will arouse universal persecution against the Christians and all the elect. He will lift himself up against the faithful in three ways: that is by terror, by gifts, and by prodigies. To those who believe in him he will give much gold and silver. Those he is not able to corrupt with gifts, he will overcome with terror; those he cannot overcome with terror, he will try to seduce with signs and prodigies. Those he cannot seduce with prodigies, he will cruelly torture and miserably put to death in the sight of all. Then there will be tribulation such as has not been on earth from when the nations began to exist up to that time.

Then those who are out in the field will flee to the mountains, and he who is on the roof will not go down into his house to take anything from it. Then every faithful Christian who will be discovered will either deny God, or if he will remain faithful, will perish, whether through sword, or fiery furnace, or serpents, or beasts, or through some other kind of torture. This terrible and fearful tribulation will last for three and a half years in the whole world. Then the days will be shortened for the sake of the elect, for unless the Lord had shortened those days, mankind would not have been saved.[17]

Five years later, another Benedictine monk, Abbo of Fleury, heard a preacher in Paris announce that the Antichrist would be unleashed in the year 1000, and that the Last Judgment would soon follow. At about the same time, panic occurred in the German army of Emperor Otto I, because of a solar eclipse that the soldiers took for a sign of the end of the world. And when the Carolingian dynasty fell in France with the death of King Louis V in 987, many saw this as a precursor to the arrival of the Antichrist. In 989 a comet (later known as Halley's Comet) was seen, followed by a supernova event in 1006, both of which were interpreted as signalling the end. Then in 1066, the comet was seen again when the Saxon King Harold fell at the Battle of Hastings in England, and this was regarded as a final omen.[18]

This century or so of millennium frenzy was very convenient for the Church establishment. It performed wonders for the coffers of penance and baptism, bringing hoards to confession and to the font in order to 'renounce the Devil and all his works' in the hope of deliverance. In the event, however, absolutely nothing happened; there was no earth-shattering revelation of the Antichrist. But there were those who said that this is just the way it would appear, for the Devil had many tricks and would make himself known when he was good and ready. As suggested by the 19th-century French poet, Charles Pierre Baudelaire, 'The greatest trick the Devil ever pulled was convincing the world he did not exist'.[19]

By the same token, it could be said conversely that the greatest trick the Church ever pulled was convincing so many that the Devil did exist. The most despicable of all ecclesiastical legacies is that the establishment has thrived by making people fearful of death and its consequences. Presumably, people have always had concerns regarding the particular nature of their dying. But death itself, as an inevitable consequence of life, is not recorded as being feared for its own sake before the onset of strategically motivated religious propaganda. Warriors even perceived death in battle as a noble estate. Christian dogma, however, introduced fear based on the possibilities of two distinct realms of afterlife, with one — the notion of Hell — being so awful that subservience in life to the bishops was the only perceived route to reprieve by way of the *Doctrine of Salvation*.

The Devil's Magic

Given that the Devil was reckoned to be a master trickster, it was perhaps natural enough for the Church to proclaim magic as being the work of the Devil. But quite apart from the familiar miracles of Jesus Christ, there are many occasions cited in the Gospels when Jesus and the apostles performed exorcisms and feats of healing by the laying on of hands, or by other expressions of faith. Mark 3:14–15 explains that Jesus 'ordained the twelve, that they should be with him, and that he might send them forth to preach, and to have power to heal sicknesses, and to cast out devils'.

Such things from a Christian perspective are presented as holy miracles, but when performed by those of another religion or none, they are classified as unacceptable magic or witchcraft. The tables were turned on Jesus in this regard when the Jerusalem Temple scribes accused him of healing by the appropriation of a devilish spirit.[20] The perceived difference in attitude lies simply in the recognized legitimacy of the act in accordance with various standpoints of religious belief. If a Christian saint or priest performs a healing, it is reckoned to be done with the aid of God. But if a heretic achieves the same result, it is said to be magic, the work of the Devil. The former is boasted as a glory of the Church; the latter is denounced as an abomination.

The very fact that a religion proposes to accomplish success and salvation, by way of sacraments, pilgrimages, Mass readings, exorcisms, or the sprinkling of holy water, presupposes the expectation of a contra-natural result. This automatically renders it a 'religion of magic', altered only in the minds of believers by substituting the premise of divine action. Once that religion (as in the case of Christianity) becomes an established institution, it discriminates between its own miracles and those of other belief systems, condemning the others as diabolical.[21]

It was determined that God and the angels could not in any way be compelled; they could only be supplicated. Evil spirits and demons, on the other hand, necessarily had to be compelled, as was demonstrated in authorized exorcism. But the Devil could only be compelled by God, or by his appointed representatives. Satan's power was said to be so awesome, so overwhelming, that anyone attempting to command him or his demonic emissaries would end up instead being controlled by them.[22] Thus it was that those who practised magic, without licence from God or the Church, were identified as sorcerers who attracted the spirits of evil by their rituals of invocation. They would therefore become servants of the demons and, as such, would be subject to enslavement by Satan himself.

The right of the godly to punish such misguided sorcerers was presumed to be sanctioned by the event in the New Testament book of The Acts, when St Paul confronted the magician Elmyas:

> Then Saul, who also is Paul, filled with the Holy Ghost, set his eyes on him and said, O full of all subtlety and all mischief, thou child of the Devil, thou enemy of all righteousness, wilt thou not cease to pervert the right ways of the Lord? And now, behold, the hand of the Lord is upon thee, and thou shalt be blind, not seeing the sun for a season. And immediately there fell on him a mist and a darkness; and he went about seeking some to lead him by the hand.[23]

50

The concept of prayer (from the Old French *preie*, and Latin *precarius*: 'to obtain by entreaty')[24] is a form of mysticism which supplicates aid or support from a supernatural or phenomenal source. Associated with prayer throughout the Old Testament was the Israelite custom of slaying and burning animals as sacrifices to God. This Jewish tradition was also common in many other ancient religious cultures, but if performed today would be deemed wicked and unnecessarily cruel. In contrast, the Christian practice of seizing innocent women who were thought to be witches, and burning them alive, was reckoned to be a divinely approved manner of exorcism!

As an accompaniment to the ancient mantra of the Asian mystics, circular beads on strings were handled in a ritual process. The beads reflected various colours and substances that had symbolic religious meaning. For the Christians, St Basil, the 4th-century Bishop of Caesarea, introduced a similar device — a woollen cord of 100 knots called a *chokti*,[25] divided every 25 knots with a larger knot or a bead. But it was said, at around the same time, that when the Eastern monk St Pachomius prayed with a knotted cord, the Devil was able to undo the knots. So Pachomius devised a secret method of sewing the knots in position. His contemporary, St Paul the Hermit, made use of pebbles to accompany his prayers. Pebbles were still being used in 12th-century Christian worship, along with beans, nuts, berries and assorted bits of bone. Then eventually, St Dominic, the 13th-century founder of the Friars Preachers, reintroduced the knotted cord. From this evolved the Catholic Church's now familiar string of 'Hail Mary' *Rosary* beads. This took the concept right back to where it all began with the original Asian mystics, whose own use of the beads had been condemned by the Church as a form of sorcery.

Stemming from the Greek *telesma*, relating to 'consecrated or sacred objects', all such items (beads, nuts, pebbles, knots, beans, berries or bones) are ritualistic talismans. Whether used for counting, divination, or as aids to meditation, they are deemed to represent the logical extension of a spiritual process. The same is the case with holy water, crucifixes, saintly relics and other

Christian devices. They are all 'charms', designed to influence people and environmental situations by way of a particular religious motivation. Once again, as with sacraments and exorcisms, all such charms render Christianity an undoubted 'religion of magic' in terms of employing 'an inexplicable or remarkable influence to produce surprising results'.[26] And yet the Church denounces the performance of magic by any other group or religion as being unholy. Catholic theology even goes so far as to maintain that the magic of other cultures is 'an attempt to perform miracles not by the grace of God'. It is thereby determined that when either Jesus or his mother are invoked by a believer, such an action constitutes a 'legitimate rite'. But the doctrine further states:

> Magic is the art of performing actions beyond the power of man with the aid of powers other than the divine. The Church condemns magic ... because all magical performances, if undertaken seriously, are based on the expectation of interference by demons or lost souls.[27]

Those who undertook such illegitimate magic were classified as heretics, sorcerers, wizards and witches. They were the performers of miracles without the licence of a Christian establishment that presumes its own monopoly over the supernatural. The Church thereby retains its position as the self-appointed institution of sacred sorcery.

Inasmuch as the Church encountered so many problems that supposedly emanated from the forces of the Devil, it also had to acknowledge that most of those problems were of its own making. The monks and bishops had, for the most part, invented the Devil as he became envisaged in the prime of his cultism. Laws were introduced against meddling with the occult, but those laws were like riverside signs that warn 'No Fishing', from which the natural assumption is that there are good fish to be had for those who dare. Even in early times, the churchmen managed to frighten themselves with their own superstitions. On one occasion in the late 6th century, Pope Gregory was consecrating a one-time Arian church for Catholic worship, in the course of which, with the aid of sacred relics, he performed an exorcism of the Devil. The proceedings were disrupted, however, when Satan appeared in the shape of a large pig, causing an immediate evacuation of the premises.[28]

The Possessed

Exorcism is described as a means of driving out demons from the possessed. To perform an exorcism against the supposed molestations of evil spirits naturally requires a belief in their existence. Even those churchmen who were convinced were also aware that most of the cases they encountered had more to do with hallucinations and hysteria than with demons. In this context, the 18th-century Benedictine theologian, Dominic Schram, wrote, 'Very often what are supposed to be demoniacal obsessions are nothing else than natural ailments, or morbid imaginings, or even distractions of actual lunacy'.[29] Given the obscure nature of the condition, it was not uncommon for criminals to claim demonic possession in their attempts to avoid punishment.

The opposing rationalist view asserted that there were no demons. But the Church countered this argument by way of the numerous citations in the Gospels, and that Jesus himself referred many times to devils and evil spirits.[30] Indeed, Matthew 4:24 identifies that even lunacy is the result of demonic possession, and Luke 13:32 has Jesus saying, 'Behold, I cast out devils and do cures'. On other occasions, it is said of Jesus that 'He healed many that were sick of divers diseases, and cast out many devils; and suffered not the devils to speak, because they knew him'.[31] The Church maintained that for anyone to claim that Jesus and his apostles deliberately told untruths was a punishable heresy, and so the dissenters kept their views pretty much to themselves.

Early writers on the subject claimed that not only the clergy, but lay Christians as well, were able to deliver demoniacs from their possessions by invoking the power of Christ. Some, like the

2nd-century Christian apologist Justin Martyr, admitted that they were themselves former practitioners of the magical arts,[32] and their apparent success was used as a strong argument for the divinity of the Christian religion. The exorcists were said to have employed a simple and authoritative address to the demon in the name of God, or more precisely in the name of Jesus Christ. Seemingly, this was sufficient to fulfil the task, and the said demons were not especially obstinate.

Sometimes, when the devils were more difficult, various symbolic actions were employed, such as breathing deeply and exhaling three times before spitting the demon onto the floor![33] The laying of hands on the subject was also popular. Justin Martyr wrote of demons that flew helplessly from the touch and breathing of dutiful Christians.[34] The crucifix was also extolled by many Church Fathers for its efficacy against all kinds of demoniac molestation. It was said to banish the evil power of the Devil, who was repeatedly denounced for fostering paganism and sorcery in his fight against the Kingdom of God and the divine plan of salvation.[35] The latter-day and modern rite of exorcism, as given in the 17th-century *Rituale Romanum*, fully agrees with this early teaching, and supports a continuity of Catholic tradition in the matter.[36]

Although exorcism became an aspect of the baptismal sacrament, this did not assume that the candidate was actually possessed — only that he or she was a victim by birth as a consequence of *Original Sin*. Thus, they were subject to the power of the Devil, whose pomps and evil works the candidate, or sponsor, was required to renounce. In the 4th century, St Cyril of Jerusalem gave a detailed description of baptismal exorcism, from which it appears that anointing with exorcised oil was sometimes employed. Alternatively, the 'breathing out' of the Devil by the candidate was accompanied by a 'breathing in' of the Holy Ghost by others present.

According to Catholic tradition, demons and fallen angels retain their natural powers as intelligent beings, and can use material objects to direct powerful forces for their own wicked ends. Although these forces are deemed limited by the control of divine providence, they are believed to have gained a wider scope for activity by virtue of the *Original Sin*.[37] Thus, it is somehow determined that places and objects are equally subject to the possibility of diabolical infestation as are people themselves.

Among those things considered most susceptible to such assault, and therefore most commonly exorcised, are water, salt and oil. Once blessed and free from possession, these things are used in turn as part of the exorcism process. Hence, they are employed to bless and consecrate churches, altars, sacred vessels, church bells and the like, as well as for personal exorcisms. Sacramental holy water is a mixture of exorcised water and exorcised salt, and God is besought to endow these material elements with supernatural powers, to protect those who use them against all attacks by the Devil.

The rite of ordination for exorcists was established in AD 398 at the Fourth Council of Carthage in North Africa. In this ritual, the bishop presented the exorcist with a book containing the formulae of exorcism, saying, 'Receive, and commit to memory, and possess the power of imposing hands on the *energumens* [demoniacs], whether baptized or *catechumens* [novices]'. These days, instead of the *Book of Exorcisms*, the *Pontifical* or *Missal* is used.[38] It is assumed at all times, however, that possessed demoniacs worthy of exorcism must be members of the Catholic faith. The ministry of the Church in this regard is not intended for pagans or those of other belief systems.

The *Apostolic Constitutions* of the early Christian era state expressly that, over and above ordination for the purposes of exorcism, anyone who possesses the charismatic power for that office should be recognized and ordained, as needs be, to the position of deacon or subdeacon.[39] These days, it is only priests who are authorized to use the exorcising power conferred by ordination.

A great many stories and weird accounts emerged concerning exorcisms. They were often used in congregational sermons in order to convey the power of the Church, or sometimes merely as simple anecdotes. One such tale in the early 1200s came from the German monastic prior, Caesar of Heisterbach, who wrote:

At a Mass near Aachen, a possessed woman was brought to the abbot. When he placed his hand upon her head, the Devil gave such a terrible roar that we were all terrified. 'Adjured depart', he cried, 'The Most High does not wish it'. When asked in what manner he entered the woman, the Devil did not reply. But the woman confessed that, in anger, her husband had told her, 'Go to the Devil', and she felt the Evil One enter through her ear.[40]

Although it is reckoned by the Church that demonic possession must be rife in pagan environments, it is reluctantly admitted that cases of possession do sometimes occur in Christian countries. Therefore, every priest, especially a parish priest, is liable to be called upon to perform his duty as an exorcist. In so doing, he is instructed to follow the prescriptions of the *Rituale Romanum* and the laws of provincial or diocesan synods. These require that the bishop should first be consulted, and his authorization obtained, before any exorcism is attempted.

5

PRINCE OF THE WORLD

Sorcery and Sin

From the earliest Christian times, magic was construed as a device of the Devil, and a belief in satanic interference with the forces of nature led easily to fears of malevolent sorcery. When confronting this prospect, and to distinguish iniquitous magic from its own divine miracles, the medieval Church was aided by an assortment of writings and ecclesiastical decrees.

There had been emphatic warnings against magical practice in a 2nd-century treatise called the *Didache* (Teaching). In describing sinful actions such as murder, rape and adultery, which are 'evil and accursed', it cites magic arts and witchcraft among the devilish crimes 'from which sincere Christians should seek deliverance'.[1] From the same era comes the *Epistle of Barnabus*, which also lists magic and witchcraft among those transgressions which are of the 'crooked and cursed way of the Black One'.[2]

Churchmen in the Middle Ages were very aware of entries in the Old Testament concerning the abomination of magic. Deuteronomy 18:11 warns against charmers, wizards and necromancers, whereas Exodus 22:18 states, 'Thou shalt not suffer a witch to live'. Additionally, Leviticus 20:27 proclaims that 'a man also or woman that hath a familiar spirit, or that is a wizard, shall surely be put to death'. In the New Testament, Galatians 5:20 inveighs against witchcraft and heresies, and Revelation 21:8 advises the righteous to fear sorcerers. Clearly, this belief in magic and sorcery was not just an idle superstition. Nowhere is it suggested that the perceived evil of these practices was assumed to be a mere pretence of powers that were thought not really to exist.[3]

The Council of Elvira in AD 306 refused the right of a *Viaticum* sacrament (as in the Last Rites) to anyone who had killed a man by way of a spell, since such a crime could not be committed without the aid of the Devil. The Council of Ancyra in AD 314 imposed a five-year penance upon those who consulted magicians. And the Council of Paderborn in 785 enacted that sorcerers must be reduced to serfdom and made over to the service of the Church. A very strange decree was also passed to the effect that 'Whosoever, blinded by the Devil and infected with pagan errors, holds another person for a witch that eats human flesh, and therefore burns her and eats her flesh, shall be punished with death'.

In the early centuries of the Christian era, a few individual prosecutions for witchcraft and sorcery took place, with torturous interrogation as permitted by Roman civil law. The first recorded torture and execution of a heretic, by way of civil charges for sorcery and the practice of magic, as determined by the Church, was in AD 385. The victim was the Gnostic preacher Priscillian of Avila in Spain.[4] A deeply ascetic and spiritual Christian, Priscillian was inclined towards apocryphal texts that were not short-listed at the time for the New Testament canon. Based on the Nazarene philosophies of old Judaea, these documents were deemed occult and sinful because they discussed beliefs that had been superseded by new Church doctrines. Moreover, of all diabolical things, one of Priscillian's leading disciples was a woman! Her name was Egeria, and it was she who had obtained certain of the proscribed manuscripts whilst travelling in the East. They were said to be concerned with devilish matters of conjuring and enchantment, in consequence of which Priscillian and six of his companions were condemned, tortured and burned to death at Trier in Germany.[5]

In 866 Pope Nicholas I prohibited the use of torture, but conceded that suspected witches, with hands and feet tied together, could be subjected to the ordeal of immersion in deep water. Given that the sinking or drowning of the victim was regarded as a proof of innocence, it seems that a majority of results were posthumous verdicts of acquittal.

In later medieval times the concept of malevolent witches grew ever wilder in people's minds, so that even some clerics endeavoured to dissuade the public from believing all they were told. In 906 the Benedictine abbot, Regino of Prüm, wrote in his book of Church procedures, entitled *De Ecclesiasticis Disciplinis*:

> It is not to be passed over that certain abandoned women, turning aside to follow Satan, being seduced by the illusions and phantasms of demons, believe and openly profess that, in the dead of night, they ride upon certain beasts along with the pagan goddess Diana and a countless horde of women. And that in these silent hours they fly over vast tracts of country and obey her as their mistress, while on other nights they are summoned to pay her homage.

Regino then remarked:

> If it were only the women themselves who were deluded, it would be a matter of little consequence, but unfortunately an immense number of people believe these things to be true. It is the duty of priests earnestly to instruct the people that these things are absolutely untrue, and that such imaginings are planted in the minds of misbelieving folk not by a divine spirit, but by the spirit of evil.[6]

This did not of course amount to a clerical disbelief in witchcraft, only that there were limits to what might be presumed possible. But in suggesting a cause for the wild imaginings, there was a clear admission that evil spirits were actually thought to exist.

From around 1020, came the extensive *Decretum* of Burchard, Bishop of Worms. One of its sections, known as *The Corrector*, was circulated widely as an individual text, and was revered as a practical confessor's guide.[7] Burchard plainly believed in witchcraft — in magical potions for instance, which might sinfully be employed to bring about impairment and infirmity. But, like Regino, he rejected the possibility of the many marvellous powers that were popularly credited to witches: nocturnally riding through the sky, shapeshifting and control of the weather. Burchard suggested that belief in such things constituted a sin in itself, deserving of a seriously assigned penance. As a result of writers such as Regino and Burchard, in 1080 Pope Gregory VII forbade witches to be put to death for having caused storms, crop failure or pestilence. But this was a comparatively short-lived period of reprieve, and things changed dramatically with the institution of the 13th-century Catholic Inquisition.

The Face of Transgression

In the lead-up to an horrendous period of tortures and executions that went on for centuries, the age-old question of the Devil's status prevailed just as it had in the Dark Ages. Witches and sorcerers were deemed to be instruments of the Devil. But why was there a Devil in the first place? If God is all good and all powerful, then why does evil exist? How can it exist? It was therefore argued: Maybe God is not all good, or maybe he is all good but not all powerful. Ancient documents were scoured to find a solution, especially since there was a general consensus that the Devil was created by God, who must have had a justifiable reason. Maybe the Devil was good to begin, but fell into wicked ways beyond God's control. This of course implied that either God was not all powerful, or that he had some ulterior motive for allowing evil to exist.

In the first instance, the writings of the 2nd-century Church Father, Clement of Alexandria, proved helpful in this regard. He had indeed asserted that the Devil must have been created good because it was impossible that God would hate anything he creates. Hence, it was clear that the Devil turned to evil of his own free will. Then, following his fall from grace, he did everything in his power to alienate people from God. But, stated Clement, since people also have free will, the Devil's licence to tempt is not an ability to compel anyone into sin.[8]

The Devil's presumed seniority in the ranks of the fallen angels was ascertained from Clement's contemporary, Origen of

Alexandria. In detailing a schedule of non-biblical Christian beliefs, Origen maintained that the Devil, 'who in the Hebrew language is named Satan ... was the first among those that were living a peaceful and happy life to lose his wings, and to fall from blessedness'.[9]

Another early writer whose work aided the inquiry was the 3rd-century Christian apologist Lactantius, a professor of rhetoric in Nicomedia, Asia Minor. His theory was that because God exists, the Devil must also exist, for it is impossible for people to understand good without evil. 'God wishes it to be so', he wrote, otherwise 'Why did he in the very beginning make a prince of demons who would corrupt and destroy everything?' Lactantius explained that if God were to exclude evil, then he would at the same time eliminate virtue — for in a world without alternatives, freedom of choice would not be possible. And so, because evil cannot possibly proceed from God, he necessarily created the Devil.[10] Thus, God incites the Devil to evil, but does not do evil himself.

This was about as good as it could get. The questions were answered and, although God created the Devil so that mankind could be tempted, his ruling in the Old Testament was still clear enough: 'Thou shalt not suffer a witch to live'.[11]

Other questions that loomed large were related to the Devil's appearance. If the witches and sorcerers were so obviously his slaves, then they must know him; they must know what he looks like. The medieval bishops excused their own lack of knowledge because they had never themselves been tempted by evil. But it was necessarily incumbent on them to find out so that Satan might be recognized when seen. He was of course a dark fallen angel, but Pope Gregory had described him as a goat-like satyr with horns and hooves. Alternatively, he was thought to be dragon-like and scaly, with claws. The route to a definitive answer was presumed once again to rest in the writings of the early Church Fathers. But this time the churchmen were not so fortunate in their searching.

Among the works consulted were those of Athanasius, the Bishop of Alexandria from AD 328. Athanasius had been responsible for compiling the final short list of gospels and epistles for the New Testament canon, and had also produced one of the most influential works of diabology, entitled *The Life of Anthony*. Plainly, Athanasius was the man to trust for an authoritative description of the Devil. But as it transpired, his description was not what the clerics were seeking. According to Athanasius, the Devil was an enormous giant who was 'prince of the power of the air' and could change his shape at will. In describing the immediate satanic image, Athanasius wrote: 'From his mouth proceed burning lamps, and hearths of fire are cast forth. The smoke of a furnace blazing with the fire of coals proceeds from his nostrils. His breath is coals, and from his mouth issues flames'.[12] Undoubtedly, a huge giant belching fire and smoke would be easy enough to recognize. But since no such creature had ever been seen, and given that the Devil was able to take on any appearance he wanted, the Athanasius document proved to be no help at all.

Another alternative was perhaps the 5th-century *Gospel of Bartholomew*. This also carried a description of Satan, derived from the notion that the apostle Bartholomew had actually seen him. But it was of no better use, and was clearly based on the Athanasius version of a 4,800-foot giant: 'He was sixteen hundred yards long and forty yards broad. His face was like a lightning of fire, and his eyes like sparks, and from his nostrils came a stinking smoke. His mouth was like the cleft of a rock, and a single one of his wings was eighty yards long'.[13] In the final event, no one was any the wiser, and the various dragon or goat-like depictions of the Devil continued much as before.

The Horned One

During the general excitement concerning sorcerers and Devil worshippers in Continental Europe, it was equally the case that England was a Catholic country during the Middle Ages, and thereby subject to papal law. In June 1162, King Henry II had appointed the churchman Thomas Becket to the post of

Archbishop of Canterbury. But from the outset, Becket went out of his way to oppose the King at every opportunity. The worst of the disputes was over a matter of Church regulation, which considered clerics to be exempt from sentence and punishment by secular law courts for criminal actions. Henry proclaimed that, in his view, churchmen who committed crimes should be handed over to the lay courts for trial like anyone else. But Thomas Becket opposed this, and so did the Pope. Maintaining his right to decide the law of his own realm, Henry then forfeited Becket's estates, and the discredited archbishop fled to France.

After eight years and a threat from Pope Alexander to have King Henry excommunicated, Becket returned to England. He not only renewed his hostility towards the King, but also denounced many of England's churchmen, whereupon the exasperated Henry expressed the plea, 'Who will rid me of this turbulent priest?' In a misguided attempt to gain royal favour, four knights hurried to Canterbury Cathedral where, on 29 December 1170, they slew Becket on the altar steps.[14] The unfortunate event had little or no effect on Henry's reputation or general popularity outside the Church, and he remained the most powerful king in Europe, but his dispute with Becket had been in vain. He was still subject to the Rule of Rome, and was instructed to pursue a course of persecution against heretics.

Given his vehement dislike of papal interference in matters of the English crown, King Henry took no such action, but he had heard discussion in his court about witches in the land. One of the favourite stories emanated from the recently deceased chronicler, William of Malmesbury, who told of a sorceress living in Berkeley. Said to be a practitioner of ancient divinations and unbounded debaucheries, she died after receiving an omen of doom from a jackdaw. At the witch's request, her children sewed her into a stag's skin and buried her in a stone coffin, bound with an iron chain. For two nights, while a choir of priests sang hymns around the grave, demons attempted to disinter the woman, but without success. On the third night, the Devil came on a great horse, yelling, 'I have come for the witch of Berkeley', and the woman cried out to him from the tomb. With that, the Devil wrenched off the chain, opened the coffin and tore apart the stag's skin. Then, throwing the sorceress onto his horse, the Devil rode away, and the witch of Berkeley was never seen again.

King Henry's chancellor Walter Map, Archdeacon of Oxford, was intrigued by such stories and, in 1182, he collated some in his *De Nugis Curialium*.[15] On the said authority of worthy report, Walter described the proceedings at witches' assemblies:

> About the first watch of the night, when the gates, doors and windows have been closed, the groups sit waiting in their synagogues, and a black cat of marvellous size climbs down a rope which hangs in their midst. On seeing it, they put out the lights. They do not sing hymns or repeat them distinctly, but hum through clenched teeth, and pantingly feel their way towards the place where they see their Lord.[16]

From whom Walter Map gleaned this strange information is unknown, but clearly certain practices of the rural folk had given rise to such tales. Indeed, it was very much the case that, in contrast to Christianity, there was still a widespread belief in the old gods and the forces of nature. Pastoral life was very much concerned with harvests, homefires, fertility, husbandry and the weather. It was an environment of high superstition, manifest in chants, potions, music, dancing, rituals and masquerades. Everything revolved around survival. It was said that fine things were never sought, but good weather was. Gold and riches were never attainable, but a rich harvest and enough surviving children might be possible if the gods were lenient.

Within the rites of this rural paganism, the principal male deity was not Satan, nor even singular. There were, in practice, twin fairy gods called the Oak King and the Holly King.[17] The Oak King was the designated Lord of the Greenwood, and was depicted with antlers. Dating from those times, and still enacted to this day, is the annual *Horn Dance* at Abbots Bromley in Staffordshire.[18] Along with other costumed figures are six antlered men, two of whom enter into combat in a ritual festival of the autumn harvest.

By way of strict identification, the ancient stag god of Gaul was Kerne, alternatively known as Cernunnos, the 'horned one'. As a god of fertility and abundance,[19] he was said to be born at each winter solstice, to marry the moon goddess at the Maytime feast of Beltane, and would die at the summer solstice. Thus, Cernunnos represented the continuing cycle of birth, death and rebirth — a base culture of all pagan belief. In inquisitional Europe, Cernunnos was vilified by the Church, along with Pan, the Arcadian god of the shepherds. Pan was usually portrayed as a goat-like satyr, and was another designated 'horned one'. But the bishops and friars associated horns and antlers directly with the Devil. For this reason, both goats and stags were regarded as being satanic.

From around 2800 BC the concept of a sacred goat had been introduced into ancient Egypt by the 2nd-dynasty Pharaoh Raneb in the Nile delta city of Mendes.[20] Commonly referred to as the Goat of Mendes, he was associated with ritualistic periods of study and contemplation outside of general toil. Such periods, based on the Greek *sabbaton* (to rest), were called 'sabbaticals' — a term still used in academic circles today. Hence, the Goat of Mendes became known as the Sabbatical Goat. In the esoteric tradition, his emblem was the five-pointed pentagram star of enlightenment — that is to say with two of the points uppermost (*see* opposite page 290). The other way about, with a single point uppermost, the pentagram was a goddess symbol, most significantly associated with Venus.)[21] Things changed, however, after Pope Gregory's 6th-century pronouncement that Satan had 'horns and hooves'. From that time, the upturned pentagram was classified as a diabolical image, and was thereafter proscribed by the Church as the ultimate symbol of the horned Devil.

Curse of the Serpent

Another courtier in the service of Henry II was the Essex statesman Gervase of Tilbury, a kinsman of the Earl of Salisbury. King Henry's father was Geoffrey Plantagenet of Anjou, and

Gervase was also of French descent from the House of Lusignan in Potiou, where King Henry's wife, Eleanor of Aquitaine, had her own court. In this regard, Gervase claimed descent from the legendary Mélusine, Lady of Lusignan.[22] From 1198, Gervase became the Marshall of Arles and, in the footsteps of Walter Map, collected stories of the region's folklore for his book of curious anecdotes, the *Liber Facetiarum*. In this work are many supposed eyewitness accounts of sorcerers and the Devil. Gervase wrote that men and women fly out at night over long distances above land and sea, so long as none makes the error of uttering the name of Christ, at which they would all plunge to the ground! 'They enter the houses of sleeping people and sit on their chests, causing nightmares and suffocation. They also suck their blood and steal infants from their beds'.

The popularity of such tales was confirmed by the Cistercian monk Cesarius of Heisterbach. He told of a knight in Liège who lost all his money, but had his fortune restored by renouncing God to receive financial assistance from the Devil. Apparently, it was only a short-term reprieve because the Blessed Virgin intervened and the knight was saved.[23] In his *Dialoguus Miraculorum* (a training manual for novice monks), Cesarius attributed thunderstorms, hail, howling wind, inundations, disease and unexpected noises to the machinations of the Devil.[24]

Such fanciful stories, as collected by those such as Map and Gervase, were entertainingly recounted from the pulpits, although presented by the churchmen as authentic accounts of diabolical sorcery and satanic practice. Resultantly, the concept of a widespread demonic cult evolved. Not least in the reckoning for demonizing in this regard was the ancestral family of Gervase himself, in particular the Lady Mélusine.

In 1387, Jean de Berry of the House of Valois commissioned his secretary Jean d'Arras to write a history of the family of Lusignan. He duly compiled *Le Noble Hystoire de Lusignan*,[25] which contained the *Chronique de Mélusine*. There is no doubt that this account was meant to be romantic in style, but the story had a traditional base, and Jean d'Arras cited an older version of the text written in Italian by a certain William de Portenach.[26]

The original legend of Mélusine came from the 8th-century region of the Loire Valley near St Étienne.[27] It gained a new popularity, however, when Gui de Lusignan, who claimed descent from Mélusine, became a 12th-century Crusader King of Jerusalem. Mélusine was, according to tradition, a shapeshifting demon with a serpent's tail and, like Satan himself, she had the wings of a bat. Unjustly cursed with these hideous attributes for imprisoning her faithless father, she had lived as a fountain fey in the forest of Poitou, and was eventually married to a noble young lord. But he had to promise never to see Mélusine on a Saturday. Overwhelmed by curiosity, the nobleman did chance to enter Mélusine's bathroom one Saturday, where he discovered the unfortunate reality of his demonic wife. Struck with surprise, he exclaimed, 'Ha! Serpent', whereupon Mélusine wished him farewell and flew out of the window. She then passed three times around the castle uttering a mournful and terrible cry: the *Cri de Mélusine*, said to have been heard thereafter whenever one of her family descendants was about to die.[28]

The enchanted Fount of Mélusine was located deep within a thicket wood at Verrières en Forez at a place called 'Lusina' — from which the original satanic connection was made. *Lusina* meant 'light bearer', and was identical to the Latin *lux fer*, rendered in transription as 'Lucifer'. In demonic terms, Mélusine was reckoned to be a *succubus*, a child of the Devil who preyed sexually upon men in their sleep. She was likened to Queen Lamia in the mythology of ancient Greece. Lamia was said to have been a mistress of the god Zeus, but was punished by the goddess Hera, who turned her into a scaly serpentine creature with a woman's face and breasts.

Pact with the Devil

In 1140, the Roman jurist Gratian had produced the *Concordia Discordantium Canonum* (Concord of Discordant Canons). This compilation of canon law emphasized the condemnation of heresy and magic, citing a framework for how these things were associated with Satan, and how magic constituted an absolute pact with the Devil.[29] Consequently, lynch mobs were locally empowered by the secular courts to seek out and execute heretics. Then in 1184, the bull *Ad Abolendum* of Pope Lucius III established a cooperation between State authorities and the Church in a campaign to root out diabolism. In that same year, the Council of Verona cursed all heretics and ordered them to be handed over to the secular authorities for capital punishment.[30]

Subsequently, in March 1199, Pope Innocent III issued his decretum *Vergentis in Senium*, which went so far as to pronounce heresy as treason against God. From that moment, sin and crime were officially linked by the joint provisions of Roman civil and ecclesiastical law. Those found guilty of heresy would, in the first instance, have all their possessions confiscated and their children subjected to perpetual deprivation.

In 1207 Pope Innocent announced: 'I am placed between God and man; lower than God but higher than man, the judge of all men who can be judged by none'. He then confirmed in the decree *Cum ex Officii Nostri*:

> Whatsoever heretic shall immediately be taken and delivered to the secular court to be punished according to law, all his goods also shall be sold ... The house in which a heretic has been received shall be altogether destroyed, nor shall anyone presume to rebuild it; but let that which was a den of iniquity become a receptacle of filth.[31]

The Fourth Lateran Council of 1215 later reaffirmed and substantially extended the legal provisions relating to heresy, blasphemy, diabolism and ungodliness. These new aspects of canon law were adopted into secular law by Holy Roman Emperor Frederick II in 1220. Henceforth, the punishment for any sin that constituted a pact with the Devil was death. In this regard, the ancient biblical law of the Old Testament book of Deuteronomy was considered appropriate:

If thy brother, the son of thy mother, or thy son, or thy daughter, or the wife of thy bosom, or thy friend which is as thine own soul, entice thee secretly, saying, Let us go and serve other gods ... Thou shalt not consent unto him, nor hearken unto him; neither shall thine eye pity him, neither shalt thou spare him, neither shalt thou conceal him. But thou shalt surely kill him.[32]

The Snares of Satan

In the 8th century, the Northumbrian liturgist Alcuin had asserted that 'He who accuses himself of his sins will not have the Devil for an accuser in the day of judgment'. The reference here was to an early practice that eventually became the *Sacrament of Penance* or, as more commonly known, 'Confession'. It had been assumed from the 4th century that the power to forgive extends to all sins, and that 'To his priests, God granted the authority to pardon without any exception'.[33] In earlier times, prior to the Church of Rome, the mood was not quite so forgiving. Around the year AD 200, the Christian apologist Tertullian expressed the view that there should only be one single forgiveness for certain grievous sins committed after baptism. In particular, he cited apostasy, murder and adultery, which he termed the Poisons of the Evil One. Tertullian maintained that if such a sin were committed again after a forgiveness, the perpetrator would have rendered himself a servant of Satan by having selected against God's law. Thus, a further repentance would be of no use to God, but of great satisfaction to his rival, the Devil.[34]

Shortly afterwards, in about AD 250, Cyprian, the Bishop of Carthage, wrote that 'Confession does not make a man free from the snares of the Devil ... otherwise we should never see in confessions those subsequent frauds and fornications and adulteries'.[35]

In constructing their systems of theology, the medieval clerics discussed at length the various problems connected with the *Sacrament of Penance*. They were practically unanimous in holding that confession was obligatory, for 'without confession there is no pardon ... no entrance into Paradise'. There were some who questioned the rights of priests to stand in the place of God as the judges and pardoners, but this debate was resolved by St Thomas Aquinas in the 13th century. He concluded:

> The institution of confession is necessary in order that the sin of the penitent might be revealed to Christ's minister. Hence, the minister to whom the confession is made must have judicial power as representing Christ, the judge of the living and the dead. This power requires two things: authority of knowledge, and the right to absolve or to condemn. These are called the Two Keys of the Church which the Lord entrusted to St Peter. But they were not given to Peter to be held by him alone, but to be handed on through him to others, else sufficient provision would not have been made for the salvation of the faithful.[36]

Clearly, this was only one man's personal opinion, based on his interpretation of Matthew 16:19 in which Jesus said to Peter, 'I will give unto thee the keys of the kingdom of heaven, and whatsoever thou shalt bind on earth shall be bound in heaven'. It was not much of a premise on which to claim that 13th-century priests somehow inherited a divine right of judgement from Jesus via Peter, but it was sufficient to gain inclusion in doctrinal application since no one else came up with a better idea.

It was the case however that, whereas matters of confession were of concern to Catholics, they were neither effective nor applicable in respect of those who might belong to other religions. Even other Christians who, from the days of the early Gnostics, followed traditions different from Catholicism, were excluded. In practice, such other groups were more inclined to support a more original form of Christianity based on the Nazarene customs of old Judaea, rather than those of latter-day Rome.

Given that the medieval Church of Rome considered itself to be the only true Church of God, all other branches of Christianity, along with Islām and Judaism were considered to be nests of pagans and sinners. If these religions did not represent God, there was only one possible alternative: they must be in league with the Devil. Thus, a Catholic war was decreed against these various opposition movements, and they were all classified as heretical.

In 1229, the Church formalized its related doctrine at the Synod of Toulouse, which established an ecclesiastical tribunal specifically charged with the suppression of heresy. A heresy is defined as 'a belief or practice contrary to the orthodox doctrine'. The term derives from the Greek *hairesis*, meaning 'choice'.[37] In this respect, what was forcibly being denied by the Church was the right of any choice, and a heretic was anyone who did not submit to the dogmatic Rule of Rome. The torture of heretics was granted papal sanction in 1252, and the trials were all held in secret. Victims who confessed to heresy were imprisoned, then strangled or burned, while those who made no such confession were given exactly the same punishments for their disobedience.

6

INQUISITION

Demonic Revels

In the Old Testament book of Job, there is mention of a large creature called a 'behemoth': 'Behold now behemoth, which I made with thee; he eateth grass as an ox. Lo now, his strength is in his loins, and his force is in the navel of his belly'.[1] As originally interpreted, the entry was thought to relate to a hippopotamus.[2] But with a more specific identification, the 'behemoth' appears in the *Book of Enoch* as the male land counterpart of a female sea-dragon called the 'leviathan':

> And on that day were two monsters parted, a female named Leviathan, to dwell in the abyss of the ocean over the fountains of the waters. But the male is named Behemoth, who occupied with his breast a waste wilderness named Duidain on the east of the garden where the elect and righteous dwell.[3]

There has long been a theological dispute as to whether the behemoth actually was a hippopotamus, or whether perhaps it was an elephant. St Thomas Aquinas had his own theory in the 13th century. He wrote in his *Commentary on Job* that 'behemoth (the elephant) was representative of the Devil'. In support of his reasoning, St Thomas continued:

> The demons frequently appear to man in the likenesses of beasts. God foresaw this and gave them the ability to take such figures of bodies to fittingly represent their condition ... Among all earthly animals, the elephant excels in size and strength ... So the Lord describes the Devil using the metaphor of an elephant ... Because

72

behemoth eats grass and other things of this kind, like
the ox, this is an image of where Satan feeds, because he
delights in the dominion of the earthly things.[4]

Having decided that the biblical behemoth was a manifestation of
the Devil, St Thomas then referred to Job 40:16, which states that
'his strength is in his loins, and his force is in the navel of his
belly'. This, he maintained, was indicative of the fact that the
Devil has intercourse with mortal women. Hence, the children are
the servants of Satan — more cunning than normal children on
account of the demoniacal influence to which they were exposed
in their pre-natal condition.[5]

From these wholly unfounded words of the revered saint,
it was determined that witches' gatherings were plainly where
such diabolical performances took place. These synagogues of
evil were demonic orgies where the wanton women engaged in
sex with the Devil.[6] Indeed, it was held in France that there was
evidence of this from long before in 1022, when a trial of heretics
had taken place in Orléans. They were accused of conducting
their orgies in an abandoned building, where they adored the
Devil, who appeared in the form of a great beast. It was said at the
trial that the children conceived at these demonic revels were
always burned eight days after their birth.

The good news for people at large was that such goings-on
could only take place at night, for no demon could appear during
the daytime. It had long been known from a 4th-century hymn
of the Roman poet, Prudentius:

Tis said that baleful spirits roam
Abroad beneath the dark's vast dome;
But, when the cock crows, take their flight
Sudden dispersed in sore affright.[7]

The given reason for this was that the rites of Satan had to cease
when the rites of the Holy Church began. The morning prayers of
Matins and *Lauds* were recited at dawn, and were known as the
Gallicinium, meaning 'cock crow'. It was reckoned that the cock,

as a herald of the dawn, was hated by Devil worshippers since the clapping of his wings made their spells ineffectual. Thus it was that, to prevent wandering demons entering the churches at night, iron cocks were placed atop weathervanes at the highest points of the steeples.[8]

Daughters of Darkness

The notion of heresy was not a new innovation of the1200s. It had existed as a concept from the earliest days of formalized Christianity by way of a divergence of belief patterns. The Church of Rome, as established by Emperor Constantine in the 4th century, focused more on the missionary preachings of St Paul (as in his New Testament epistles) than on the original Gospel teachings. The recognized Fathers of the movement in the centuries before Constantine drew a clear distinction between the Pauline philosophies and those of Jesus which they considered rather too Jewish. This particular form of Christ's Nazarene Jewishness emerged from the Qumrân tradition in Judaea, and from a community known as the Essenes, to which the Nazarenes were attached. The Hebrew chronicler, Flavius Josephus, explained in his 1st-century *Antiquities of the Jews* that the   essential difference between the Essenes, and the Pharisees and Sadducees of Jerusalem, was that the Essenes 'live the same kind of life as do those whom the Greeks call Pythagoreans'.[9] The community cultures of these three main philosophical groups were distinctly different in many respects, and Josephus described that the Essenes had 'a greater affection for one another than the other sects have'.[10]

Although Paul was equally as Jewish as Jesus, his missionary life was spent beyond Judaea in the more general Mediterranean world, heavily influenced by customs of the Greek and Roman gods. As a result, whereas Jesus was a promoter of Essene philosophy, St Paul became 'a promoter of Jesus', to the extent that he created a new religion with Jesus as its earthly godhead — a religion which, in AD 44, first became dubbed Christianity in

Antioch, Syria.[11] With its primary regions of support being Alexandria and Carthage in North Africa, the Pauline doctrine was assimilated in Rome to become the official religion of the Empire. Hence it was that subsequent writers rebuked those Christians who followed the original Nazarene model. The Church Fathers proclaimed them heretics, and accused them of a variety of satanic practices. Writing of them back in the 2nd century, Bishop Irenaeus of Lyon declared in his *Adversus Haereses* (Against Heresies):

> They practise also magical arts and incantations; philtres also, and love potions; and have recourse to familiar spirits, dream-sending demons and other abominations, declaring that they possess power to rule over, even now, the princes and formers of this world; and not only them, but also all things that are in it. These men, even as the Gentiles, have been sent forth by Satan to bring dishonour upon the Church so that, in one way or another, men hearing the things which they speak, and imagining that we all are such as they, may turn away their ears from the preaching of the truth.
>
> They declare the Adversary is one of those angels who are in the world, whom they call the Devil, maintaining that he was formed for this purpose, that he might lead those souls which have perished from the world to the supreme ruler [Satan]. They describe him also as being chief among the makers of the world.[12]

Tertullian of Carthage had also written a lengthy treatise, entitled *Prescription Against Heretics*, and was equally assured that the Devil was instrumental in subverting the said heretics' understanding of the scriptures:

> Nor do I risk contradiction in saying that the very scriptures were even arranged by the will of God in such a manner as to furnish materials for heretics, inasmuch as I read that there must be heresies, which

there cannot be without the scriptures. The question will arise: By whom is to be interpreted the sense of the passages which make for heresies? By the Devil of course, to whom pertain those wiles which pervert the truth, and who by the mystic rites of his idols vies even with the essential portions of the sacraments of God. He too baptizes some (that is his own believers and faithful followers) ... He, in the kingdom of Satan, sets his marks on the foreheads of his soldiers.[13]

Hippolytus, a 2nd-century elder of the early Christians in Rome, also produced a similar treatise, entitled *Refutation of all Heresies*. In line with the others, he held the Devil personally responsible for corrupting the minds of Christians outside the Pauline movement:

Now these heretics have themselves been sent forth by Satan, for the purpose of slandering before the Gentiles the divine name of the Church. And the Devil's object is that men hearing (now after one fashion, and now after another) the doctrines of those heretics, and thinking that all of us are people of the same stamp, may turn away their ears from the preaching of the truth.[14]

In the course of all this, a new thrust of heretical accusation emerged when it occurred to the writers that the concept of *Original Sin* must have some part to play in the way men's minds were being diverted from what they considered the truth. Eve might have been misguided by the serpent, but it was actually she who had seduced Adam into her evil ways. Eve was the culprit. By virtue of this, women must be the primary instigators of heresy because of their wicked seduction. Another round of writing therefore appeared, led in the first instance by Tertullian. He set the scene for women's lack of grace when compared to the essential purity of men. He suggested that, when the fallen angels came to earth and mated with the daughters of men, the angels imbued them with lust and carnal desire. They taught them to follow the ways of the serpent, and how to heap ornaments from the Devil's head onto their own bodies. Addressing women in general, Tertullian continued:

> Do you not know that you are each an Eve? The sentence of God on this sex of yours lives in this age; the guilt must of necessity live too. You are the Devil's gateway; you are the unsealer of that forbidden tree; you are the first deserter of the divine law; you are she who persuaded him whom the Devil was not valiant enough to attack. You destroyed so easily God's image: man. On account of your desertion, even the Son of God had to die.[15]

Cyprian of Carthage followed this lead by explaining that women aspire to seduce and corrupt men by the way they dress; and they adorn themselves for the Devil, against the wishes of God:

> For God neither made the sheep scarlet or purple, nor taught the juices of herbs and shellfish to dye and colour wool, nor arranged necklaces with stones set in gold. And with pearls distributed in a woven series or numerous cluster, wherewith you would hide the neck which He made, that what God formed in man may be covered, and that may be seen upon it that which the Devil has invented in addition.
>
> You have polluted your skin with a false medicament; you have changed your hair with an adulterous colour; your face is violently taken possession of by a lie; your figure is corrupted; your countenance is another's. You cannot see God since your eyes are not those which God made, but those which the Devil has spoiled. You have followed him; you have imitated the red and painted eyes of the serpent.[16]

It was soon after this that women were precluded from any further activity in the front line of the Church, as is still the case in Catholic doctrine today. But, prior to that, women had run educational missions for the Christian movement, as well as being ordained deacons of the pre-Roman Church. Bishop Clement of Alexandria, in his 2nd-century *Commentary on 1-Corinthians*, wrote that the apostles worked in the company of women, who were their 'sisters and co-ministers'. Origen of Alexandria, when writing about Paul's assistant, Phebe, stated that women were 'instituted as deacons in the church'. Even today's *Catholic Encyclopedia* relates to Phebe as having been a *diakonos* (deaconess). It maintains, 'There can be no question that women were permitted to exercise certain definite functions in the Church, and were known by the special name of *diakonoi* or *diakonissai*'.[17] The Roman senator, Pliny the younger, had written in AD 112 about female deacons. A later Council of Nicaea transcript from AD 325 also discusses the one-time ecclesiastical role of a deaconess, as did Epiphanius of Salamis (AD 315–403), St Basil of Caesarea (AD 329–379) and numerous others.[18]

Notwithstanding such records, and in view of the fact that women were now perceived as 'instruments of the Devil', Tertullian led the way for what eventually became the ruling of the Church of Rome:

> These heretical women; how audacious they are. They have no modesty. They are bold enough to teach, to engage in argument'.[19]
>
> It is not permitted for a woman to speak in church, nor is it permitted for her to baptise, nor to offer, nor to claim to herself a lot in any manly function, nor to have say in any sacred office.[20]

A thousand years later, when the Church persecution of heretics became fully operational after the 1229 Synod of Toulouse, women were placed once more in the firing line as the true instigators of sorcery and diabolical behaviour. The thought process was explained in the 13th-century *Summa Theologica* of the Catholic patron St Thomas Aquinas. He wrote that the Devil's greatest sin was his impossible aspiration to be like God.[21] It was for this reason that he envied Adam, who was created in God's image, which necessarily determines that the Devil does not have the likeness of a man. But the Devil was not alone; there was another creature who was different from man, and therefore also not like God. This was the creature who had seduced Adam and caused him to sin, and she was called 'woman'. Thus, it was claimed that women were the daughters of darkness, the seductive emissaries of the Devil.

A Church of Malignants

The heretics the Church feared most were not individuals, but those who were banded in large influential groups, posing a real threat to the ecclesiastical establishment. The first of these groups to create a major problem at the onset of the 13th century became known as the Waldensians. Originating in about 1173 as the Poor Men of Lyons, their founder was an opulent merchant called Pierre Valdès. He gave away his wealth and property, and began to preach the concept of poverty as a route to perfection in life.[22] Unable to obtain permission to preach from the Archbishop of Lyon, Valdès and some colleagues went to Rome in 1179 to seek the blessing of Pope Alexander III. But the idea of poverty for churchmen was the last thing on the Vatican agenda, and Alexander forbade them to continue their preaching in this regard. Ignoring the explicit directive, they persisted with their unorthodox mission back in France and Bohemia. This led, at the Council of Verona in 1184, to Pope Lucius III proclaiming them punishable heretics because of their unacceptable 'contempt for ecclesiastical power'.

Another charge laid against the Waldensians was that they had dared to translate the Gospels into French from their *Vulgate* Church Latin. Such a thing was expressly forbidden, and not surprisingly because the orthodox teaching (supposedly from the Bible) often bore little relation to what the scriptures actually stated. Since the Valdès translation was literal, he discovered that a multiplicity of doctrines, rites and ceremonies, which had been introduced into the Catholic religion, had no foundation in the Bible, and in some cases were even condemned in the New Testament. He maintained in particular that the *Doctrine of Transubstantiation,* as enforced by the Court of Rome, was 'a most pernicious practice of idolatry'. (The doctrine maintains that the eucharistic bread and wine of church ceremony actually constitute the body and blood of Christ.) Valdès announced publicly that the expectation of Christians to worship a mere consecrated wafer as if it were God, was a clerically contrived nonsense.[23] The Archbishop of Lyons became thoroughly indignant since the honour of the papacy was at stake. Thus, the Waldensians were seen as a real danger to the supposed divinely sanctioned hierarchy of the Church.[24]

In the light of their predicament, Valdès and his followers gave up open preaching and began travelling from town to town, meeting privately with small local groups. In contrast to the Roman establishment, their preachers (called *barbas*) included both men and women. They had not, in the first instance, sought rejection by the Church but, since it was thrust upon them, the Waldensians became increasingly anti-Catholic. They scorned the need for saintly relics and customary icons of superstition, claiming that the Bible was not a prerogative of the bishops, but a public domain document from which anyone should be able to read in company.

In retaliation, the Roman Church authorities brought to bear numerous accusations of secret sacrilegious rites and diabolism. The Waldensians were said to abandon themselves to excesses of libertinism in their assemblies,[25] flaunting themselves for the Devil. The official Church view of the Waldensians was written for the Inquisition by a certain Reinerius Saccho, who reported on the movement to Pope Innocent III. In his *Summa de Catharis et Pauperibus de Lugdun,* concerning the 'sects of modern heretics', he wrote, 'The Waldensians say that the Romish Church is not the Church of Jesus Christ, but a church of malignants'. In his further charges, Saccho explained that the heirs of Valdès considered themselves the true representatives of the apostolic Christian faith; that statues and decorations were superfluous; that they claimed obedience to God, not to prelates of whom the Pope was the chief source of errors, and that no one is greater than another within the Church.

The Waldensians believed that the Pope and bishops were guilty of homicides because of the Inquisition and the Crusades, and that bishops ought not to have rights akin to royalty.[26] The declaration of proscribed heresy against the Waldensians was ratified by the Fourth Lateran Council in 1215, prior to which the Bishop of Strasbourg breathed vengeance and slaughter against them. Although Valdès narrowly escaped apprehension, eighty members of the movement, accused of Devil worship, were staked and burned alive in that city. In a later incident, 224 Waldensians were thrown into a communal fire at Toulon.

When Satan Fell

In chapter 1 we encountered the Bogomil heretics of Bulgaria, who defined the godhead *Trinity* as being 'God the Father and his two sons, Satan and Jesus Christ'. A favoured text of the Bogomils was a work entitled *The Secret Book of John the Evangelist*, more commonly known as the *Liber Secretum* (Secret Book). Quite different in style from St John's biblical *Apocalypse*, and of much later composition, it appears to have originated in the 7th century. In 1208, a copy was discovered by the Catholic Inquisition in the South of France, in possession of the Cathars of Carcassonne. A Latin annotation was added to this *Liber Secretum* manuscript, stating, 'This is the secret book of the heretics of Concoreze, brought from Bulgaria by their bishop Nazarius'.

The Cathars (from the Greek, *Katheroi*) were called the Pure Ones, an heretical sect who prevailed in the Languedoc region of Provence, having emerged from Italian and German beginnings in Lombardy, Tuscany and the Rhineland.[27] It was from Concoreze in Lombardy that the Bogomil leader, Nazarius, brought the *Liber Secretum* to the Cathars in Carcassonne. The

Cathars were notably ascetic people, whose principal doctrine asserted that the spirit was pure, but that physical matter was defiled. For this reason, they believed (in accordance with the New Testament Gospel of St John) that Satan was the Prince of the World.[28] The *Liber Secretum* of the Bogomils concurred with this, and the 1176 Cathar Council of St Félix-de-Caraman furthered the concept of an inexorable opposition between God and the Devil.

Following the Waldensian lead, the Cathars had translated the Bible into their own tongue, the *langue d'oc*. It was from this unique language that the Provençal region of Languedoc acquired its name. The black-robed Cathar *Perfecti* (as the leading ascetics were called) were wholly celibate, but they upheld the equality of the sexes, and were expressly tolerant of the Jewish and Muslim faiths. Even the noble Counts of Toulouse, who governed the region, were censured by the papacy for affording Jews positions of public office. The immediate followers of the *Perfecti* were called *credentes* (believers). Throughout Languedoc, they ran an exemplary society with its own welfare system of charity schools and hospitals. Consequently, the non-Cathar population benefited greatly from their altruistic efforts. But, as far as the Church of Rome was concerned, the Cathars posed a far greater threat than the Waldensians.

The *Liber Secretum* is presented as a supposed conversation between St John and Jesus Christ. In the course of this, John asks, 'Lord, before Satan fell, in what glory abode he with thy Father?' The said response reads:

> And he said unto me, In such glory was he
> that he commanded the powers of the heavens
> ... And he saw the glory of him that moveth
> the heavens, and he thought to set his seat
> above the clouds of heaven and desired to be
> like unto the Most High.[29]

A further question is then posed by John: 'When Satan fell, in what place dwelt he? Jesus replied:

> My Father changed his [the Devil's] appearance
> because of his pride, and the light was taken
> from him. And his face became like unto heated
> iron, and his face became wholly like that of a
> man. And he drew with his tail the third part of
> the angels of God, and was cast out from the seat
> of God and from the stewardship of the heavens.
> And Satan came down into this firmament, and
> he could find no rest for himself, nor for them
> that were with him.

The text continues with an account of how it was not God, but the Devil who created Adam and Eve. This differentiation of the sexes (introducing both man and woman) was said to be the reason why the angels became divided in Heaven. It is not clear to what extent the Cathars of Languedoc might have upheld the Bogomil philosophy in this respect, but they certainly did subscribe to the view that God was the Lord of the heavens, whilst the Devil was Lord of the material world.[30] This concept is evident in the Cathar *Book of the Two Principles*, which describes the coeternal character of existence: the celestial realm of the God of goodness, and the bad corporeal world governed by Satan.[31]

Everything in the Cathar belief system argued against the devilish cult of the Prince of Darkness, and promoted a strict allegiance to the Lord of Light. But, for all that, the Church decreed that they were satanists because they did not adhere to the doctrine of physical resurrection as preached by St Paul and the bishops. Neither did they condone the use of sacramental bread and wine, nor even baptism by water. In the Cathari view, all physical matter was corrupt and had no place in holy ritual.

The Cathars also disputed the Catholic notion of Hell, claiming instead in their tenets that Hell was the material experience of life on Earth:

> The evil god, Satan, who inspired the malevolent
> parts of the Old Testament, is the Lord of this world,
> of the things that are seen and are temporal, and

especially of the outward man which is decaying, of the earthen vessel, the body of death and the flesh which takes us captive under the law of sin and desire. This world is the only true purgatory and hell, being the antithesis of the world eternal ... Christ's peace and kingdom are not of this world. Men are the result of a primal war in heaven, when hosts of angels, incited by Satan to revolt, were driven out and were imprisoned in terrestrial bodies created for them by the Adversary.[32]

In practical terms, the Cathars were simply nonconformists, preaching without licence, and having no requirement for appointed priests or the richly adorned churches of their Catholic neighbours. St Bernard, the Cistercian Abbot of Clairvaux, asserted that 'No sermons are more Christian than theirs, and their morals are pure'.[33] They believed in God and the Holy Spirit, and recited the *Lord's Prayer*, but their convictions were wholly unorthodox by comparison with the avaricious pursuits of Rome. In contrast to the generally subjugative climate in Western Europe, Languedoc society was markedly more tolerant and cosmopolitan, as well as being economically and commercially stable.[34] But all this was to change when papal troops arrived in the foothills of the Pyrenees.

According to King Philippe II of France, the Cathars were abominable heretics, and the document *Contra Haereticos* asserted that they indulged in the worship of Satan.[35] In view of this, Pope Innocent III admonished them in 1208 for iniquitous behaviour. Then, in the following year, an army of 30,000 soldiers invaded Languedoc under the command of Simon de Montfort. They were deceitfully adorned with the red cross of the Holy Land Crusaders, but their purpose was immeasurably different. They had been sent, at papal command, to exterminate the Cathars, whose popularity was so widespread that the Vatican edict of annihilation referred not only to the ascetics themselves, but to all who supported them. This included most people of the region. The military commanders consulted the papal legate Arnaud

Amaury, Abbot of Cîteaux, as to how they might differentiate between the Devil worshippers and any Catholic residents. His reply was, 'Kill them all; God will know his own'![36]

In allusion to the Languedoc centre at Albi, the savage campaign was called the Albigensian Crusade. The Cathars were charged with all manners of blasphemy and sexual deviance. Contrary to the accusations, the witnesses brought to give evidence spoke only of their Church of Love and devotion to the ministry of Jesus. Nonetheless, the slaughter went on for thirty-five years, claiming more than thirty-thousand lives. The territory was ravaged, crops were destroyed, towns and cities were razed, and a whole population was put to the sword.[37] In one of the worst episodes, the entire citizenship of Toulouse was decimated, when Cathar and Catholic alike — men, women and children — were slaughtered regardless. The culmination was a hideous massacre at the Cathar seminary of Montségur, which the Archbishop of Narbonne referred to as the Synagogue of Satan. There, in March 1244, more than 200 hostages were rounded up and burned alive.

Hounds of the Lord

The forerunner to the Catholic Inquisition had been established by Pope Gregory IX as the Holy Office in 1124. Two years later, King Louis VIII of France decreed that 'Persons excommunicated by the diocesan bishop, or by his delegate, should receive meet punishment (*debita animadversio*)'. In this respect, the burning of heretics was already regarded as prescriptive, and a decree of the Synod of Toulouse relates to death at the stake as in keeping with that requirement.

In Italy, the *Imperial Rescript for Lombardy* of 1224 is seemingly the first law in which death by fire was formally sanctioned. But, prior to that, burnings were common in Germany, and Waldensians and Cathars had already been burned in France.[38]

The Inquisition was codified in an instrument prepared by the 1229 Synod of Toulouse, with its superintendents to be appointed by prerogative of the Pope. In 1232, the Dominican Order of the Friars Preachers was placed at the head of the Tribunal of Inquisition, thereby gaining them (as a word-play on their Dominican style) the widely used identification, *Domini Canes* (Hounds of the Lord).[39]

An early campaign initiated by Gregory was against some fisherfolk of Friesland in the Netherlands. They were said to worship the Devil under the name of Asmodai who, as we saw earlier, was the demon that was reckoned to have befriended King Solomon. The inquisitors claimed that Asmodai had been seen and recognized in the semblance of a duck or a goose, or sometimes as an ordinary youth with whom the witches danced! When they kissed him, they were enveloped within his realm of darkness, whereupon they gave themselves up to debauchery.[40]

Soon afterwards, Pope Gregory sent the priest Conrad of Marburg to Germany, with unlimited powers to root out satanists and 'bring them to the faggots' (the blazing stick bundles). Conrad was so enthusiastic that he found witches and sorcerers everywhere. This incited personal rebellions against him by the Archbishops of Cologne, Treves and Mayence. But Conrad had his authority direct from the Pope, and even began proceedings against these high-ranking churchmen. He commissioned the Dominican priors of Regensburg, Friesach and Strasbourg as his primary enforcers. Wherever Conrad appeared the fires were lit, and a great many innocent people fell victim to his fanatical regime. The Archbishop of Mayence wrote a letter of complaint to Pope Gregory, but to no avail. He was avenged, however, when Conrad was ambushed on the road and slain by a band of angry noblemen on 30 July 1233. Resultantly, the Inquisitor General was proclaimed a martyr to the holy cause and canonized as a saint.[41] Gregory then instructed his inquisitors to be ever more vigilant and increasingly vigorous in suppressing the Devil worshippers. The Catholic Inquisition had truly begun.

There now existed a body of law that, under the initiative of the papacy, placed the punishment of the faith's enemies under exempt jurisdiction. Having begun in Germany, the Inquisition then extended into Aragon. Gregory announced subsequently, to the archbishops and bishops of France, that he was relieving them of their burden by choosing the Dominicans and some Franciscan friars to combat heresy. In principle, two inquisitors, with equal powers, were placed in charge of each tribunal. In Burgundy, from 1237, the Grand Inquisitor was Robert le Bougre, with the Dominican prior of Besancon as his enforcer. In one single day, Robert consigned 180 people to the flames in the region of Champagne.[42]

As well as straightforward heresy, the inquisitors showed a keen interest in prosecuting cases of sorcery and idolatry. In 1258, despite the inquisitors' requests to be granted such jurisdiction, Pope Alexander IV declared that the Inquisition should deal only with cases of sorcery that 'savour of manifest heresy'.[43] But Gratian's 1140 *Concordia Discordantium Canonum* had linked the two in any event, and the more recently published *Glossa Ordinaria* had explicitly associated *maleficium* (as in magical practice) with heresy.[44] The first historically recorded burning of an individually defined witch occurred soon afterwards at Toulouse in 1275. The judicial sentence was passed by the inquisitor Hugues de Baniol. In a crazed and tortured condition, the 65 year-old woman, Angèle of Labarthe, confessed to having given birth to a monster with a wolf's head, conceived by way of intercourse with the Devil.[45]

Whenever an inquisitor came to a supposed heresy-ridden district, the inhabitants were summoned to appear before him. The parish priest and secular authorities were required to present accusatory information gleaned from various informers, and the charges were presented to the judges. After that, the trials began. The inquisitors had four methods of extracting confessions: 1) The fear of death, whereby the stake awaited. 2) Incarceration and the denial of food. 3) Visits from supposedly released men, who would attempt to use friendly persuasion. 4) Torture by various means. (A favoured initial method of torture was to turn the accused on a slow wheel over burning coals. Even witnesses were placed on the wheel to compel the required testimonies against their friends and neighbours.)[46]

The inquisitorial procedure was a departure from all previous and traditional forms of accusation or denunciation. According to the new ruling, which differed from customary Roman law, the judge could bring suit against any individual who might even vaguely be the object of a rumour. The accused was not permitted to know the witnesses for the prosecution, and was thus deprived of any opportunity to challenge and confront them. The right of appeal to the Apostolic See was emphatically denied by the 1231 statute, *Excommunicamus*, of Pope Gregory IX, which established the Tribunal of Inquisition.[47] The defendant was then required to submit to any demand made by the inquisitors, who were granted extraordinary powers of torture and incarceration to overcome any stubbornness presumed to emanate from the diabolical will of Satan.

7

THE BURNING TIMES

Treacherous Wiles

In 1275 Jacopo de Voragine, Archbishop of Genoa, produced his famous work concerning the lives of a great many saints. Entitled *The Golden Legend*, it was a perfect opportunity to make strategic use of the Devil by showing how the various holy men were able to overcome his treacherous wiles with ease. No matter how cleverly disguised (from a beggar woman, to St James himself), the saints were always able to spot him in a moment:

> On a time, the holy man St Dominic woke in the church of Bologna, and the Devil appeared to him in the form of a friar. And St Dominic supposed that he had been a friar, and made him a sign that he should go to rest with the other friars. Then St Dominic lighted a candle at the lamp, and beheld him in his face. And he confessed that he was the Devil.[1]

At no time in any of the stories is the Devil presented as being in any way formidable. In fact, he is an amusingly sorry character, never achieving his goals, and forever being outwitted by those cleverer than himself. The sign of the cross defeats him at every turn, and the hooded monks fill him with dread. On one occasion, he fled from drinking in a town, crying, 'I may no longer abide here, sith they with the great hoods arise'. This was all good propaganda for the friars of the Inquisition, but it made absolutely nothing of their perceived satanic enemy.

In the same period, and in complete contrast, a diabolic and fearsome image of the all-powerful Satan was being projected as the secular courts and ecclesiastical tribunals proceeded against witchcraft with great severity. Torture was employed, and burning at the stake became the legal punishment for those who were reckoned just to have 'seen' the Devil. In *The Golden Legend*, however, the saints Nicholas, James, Dominic, Francis of Assisi, Thomas Becket and numerous others were each said to have seen the Devil and conversed with him. But they were not regarded as witches or sorcerers for having seen him, since they were God's appointees acting in the service of the Church.

That said, it was a fact that being a churchman (as distinct from being a canonized saint or appointed inquisitor) provided no automatic exemption from accusations of abominable diabolism. Bishop Peter of Bayeux was charged in 1278 for using sorcery against various high-born aristocrats. King Edward I of England then brought an action of *maleficia* against Walter Langton, Bishop of Lichfield and Coventry. The charge stated:

> For some time past, it has come to our attention that our venerable brother ... has been commonly defamed and accused, both in the realm of England and elsewhere, of paying homage to the Devil and kissing his posterior.[2]

High Priest of Satan

The chief Inquisitor for Toulouse in 1307–23 was Bernardo Gui, the notorious Dominican Prior of Carcassonne, as featured in the Umberto Eco novel and subsequent 1986 movie, *The Name of the Rose*. Bernardo's best known treatise, *Practica Inquisitionis Heretice Pravitatis* (Conduct of the Inquisition into Heretical Wickedness), lists his interrogation techniques in the form of instructions for his inquisitors. The objective was to get the defendants so confused that they ended up confessing to heresy without any intention. A key question in the sequence was: 'Will you then swear that you have never learned anything contrary to the faith which we hold to be true?' Plainly, it was quite impossible for anyone honestly to swear such an oath. Any person, even Bernardo Gui, was bound to have learned other things quite naturally in the ordinary course of life. But that would not mean necessarily that such things were believed. So the defendant could not swear to never learning things beyond Church doctrine. If he answered, 'Yes, I have heard other things', he was in real trouble. But if he said 'I have never learned anything contrary to the faith', he was equally at risk because the inquisitor would know he was lying. Having taken the victim to this point, Bernardo's instructions continue:

> Then trembling as if he cannot repeat the form, he will stumble along as though speaking for himself or for another, so that there is not an absolute form of oath and yet he may be thought to have sworn. If the words are there, they are so turned around that he does not swear and yet appears to have sworn. Or he converts the oath into a form of prayer, as 'God help me that I am not a heretic', or the like.
>
> When further hard pressed he will appeal, saying, 'Sir, if I have done amiss in aught, I will willingly bear the penance, only help me to avoid the infamy of which I am accused through malice and without fault of mine'. But a vigorous inquisitor must not allow himself to be worked upon in this way. He must proceed firmly till he make these people confess their error.[3]

In that same year of 1307, when Bernardo Gui was appointed in Toulouse, the military Order of the Temple of Solomon, better known as the Knights Templar, came under inquisitional fire in France. Originally founded in Jerusalem by Hugues de Payens (a cousin and vassal of the Comte de Champagne), the Bishop of Chartres had referred to the knights in 1114 as the *Milice du Christi* (Soldiers of Christ). Having been front-line ambassadors for the Crusader King Baudouin II, they had returned to France in 1127 at the direction of their patron, the Cistercian abbot St Bernard de Clairvaux. They were to attend a grand Council at Troyes, chaired by the Cardinal Legate, having brought a wealth of treasure and valuable documents from the excavated vaults of the ancient

Temple of Jerusalem. St Bernard was concerned that the Vatican authorities were intent to sequestrate the manuscripts, if not the treasure as well, because the writings were known to contain first-hand information from old Judaea that contradicted 12th-century Church teaching. In this regard, Bernard wrote: 'The work has been accomplished with our help, and the knights have been sent on a journey through France and Burgundy, under the protection of the Count of Champagne, where all precautions can be taken against all interference by public or ecclesiastical authority'.[4]

Following the Council of Troyes, the Templars' rise to prominence was remarkably swift as they became engaged in high-level politics and diplomacy in Europe and the Middle East. Just a few years later, in 1139, Pope Innocent II afforded the knights international independence from obligation to any authority save himself. Irrespective of kings, cardinals, or governments, the Order's only superior was the Pope, and they were granted vast territories and substantial property from Britain to Palestine. The Templars became revered by all and, notwithstanding their Jerusalem wealth, large donations were received from far and wide. The *Anglo-Saxon Chronicle* states that, when Hugues de Payens visited England's King Henry I in Normandy, 'The King received him with much honour, and gave him great treasures in gold and silver'.[5] The Spanish King, Alfonso of Aragon, passed a third of his kingdom to the Order, and the whole of Christendom was at their feet. No price was too high to secure affiliation and, within a century of their return from Jerusalem, they were the most influential body the world had ever known. Being so well funded, the Templars established the first international banking network, becoming financiers for the Levant and for practically every throne in Europe.

By 1306, the Order was so powerful that King Philippe IV of France viewed them with the utmost trepidation. He owed a great deal of money to the knights and was practically bankrupt. He also feared their political might, which he knew to be far greater than his own, especially since they were allied to Pope Boniface VIII. In 1296 Boniface had issued the bull *Clerics Laicos*, which forbade the clergy to give up ecclesiastical revenues or property without permission from the Apostolic See. His primary target was King Philippe IV, who was excommunicated for levying illegal taxes against the clergy.[6] Philippe then arranged for his chief minister, William de Nogaret, to have the Pope assassinated. His successor, Pope Benedict XI, also met his end in mysterious circumstances, to be replaced in 1305 by Philippe's own candidate, Bertrand de Got, Archbishop of Bordeaux, who duly became Pope Clement V. With this new French Pope seemingly under his control, Philippe drew up his list of accusations against the Knights Templar, and the easiest charges to lay were those of heresy and diabolism.

Since Boniface had been associated with the Order, Philippe demanded that he be 'stricken from the list of popes as a heretic, his bones disinterred, burned, and the ashes scattered to the winds'.[7] At the same time, Philippe accused Bishop Guichard of Troyes of doing homage to Satan, and imprisoned him for using magic against the Queen, Jeanne de Navarre.

An extended judicial inquiry followed, culminating in 1311, in which Pope Boniface was tried posthumously by Philippe's own inquisitors for entering a pact with the Devil.[8] This gained the Pope an entry in Dante Alighieri's *Divine Comedy*, wherein Boniface is destined for the *Malebolge* pit of the Eighth Circle of the Inferno. Completed in 1321, this epic Italian poem represents the Middle Ages view of the three realms of the dead: Paradise (for the righteous), Purgatory (for the imperfect), and Hell (for sinners). The first gate of Hell in the poem is marked with the warning, '*Lasciate ogne speranza, voi ch'intrate*' (Abandon all hope, ye who enter here).[9]

On Friday 13 October 1307, King Philippe's henchmen struck, and Templars were seized, with their accomplices, throughout France — a total of 15,000 captives in one day.[10] They were then 'handed over to the brethren of St Dominic, who were the most expert torturers',[11] and the Inquisition was instructed to assemble and examine the guilty, employing torture if necessary. The captured knights were imprisoned, interrogated, tortured and burned. Paid witnesses were called to give evidence against the Order and some truly bizarre statements were obtained.

The knights were accused of a variety of practices deemed unsavory, including necromancy, sexual perversion, abortion, blasphemy, Devil worship and the black arts. Once they had given their evidence, under whatever circumstances of bribery or duress, the witnesses disappeared without trace. On 19 October that year, 140 Templars were ritually tortured by the Grand Inquisitor, Guillaume de Paris, as a result of which thirty-six perished. The variously applied tortures were recorded as the thumbscrew, the rack to dislocate limbs, crushing by lead weights, teeth wrenched out, wedges driven beneath fingernails, and oil-basted feet roasted over the fire.[12]

The prevailing Grand Master of the Templars, Jacques de Molay, was seized with other key officers in 1308, subsequently to be interrogated by inquisitors at Chinon Castle in the Loire. But at this point in the story it becomes clear that, despite his presumed allegiance to King Philippe, Pope Clement V was not in favour of the proceedings. This was revealed in a document, now known as the *Chinon Parchment*, recently found in the Vatican Secret Archive.[13] Unknown before its discovery in 2001, the letter from Clement relates to the interrogation of Jacques de Molay and his colleagues by the Inquisition. Addressed to Philippe, and dated 20 August 1308, it explains that, following Clement's inquiry into the validity of the charges laid against the knights:

> We hereby decree that they are absolved by the Church, that they are restored to communion and that they may receive the holy sacraments ... While we were absent you turned your mind to the Knights Templar and their property. You have even gone so far as to incarcerate them, and what pains us most is that you have not released them. On the contrary, we have heard that you have done more, inflicting in addition to their imprisonment further suffering.[14]

This protest by the Pope was formalized by the previous bull *Subit Assidue* of 5 July 1308, in which Clement accused the French inquisitor, Guillaume de Paris, of failing to advise the papal authority of the arrests. But, unfortunately for the Templars, the Pope's words were completely disregarded by the King of France and the inquisitors. Clement, with his new See at Avignon, was not in a position to enforce the terms of his decree, and his cardinals in Rome were powerless against the despotic French monarch.

Consequently, some while later, at the Council of Vienne in 1312, Pope Clement tried another liberal strategy. He formally terminated the Templars' chivalric status in an attempt to have Jacques de Molay and the other prisoners handed over to the papal curia for a more comfortable house arrest. By this means, he figured that an official trial could be conducted under his own jurisdiction, and that the knights would be reprieved in due course. But it was to no avail, and the heated debate became so protracted that, during the course of it, Clement V drew near to his death.

King Philippe did not waste another moment, and had Jacques de Molay and his companions removed to an island on the River Seine. Irrespective of the *Chinon Parchment*, the hostages were said falsely to have formally been denounced by the Pope.[15] Then, without further trial, Jacques de Molay was proclaimed a 'high priest of Satan' and burnt at the stake with his colleagues on 18 March 1314.[16]

Invocations of Hell

To that point in the early 14th century, the formal Inquisition had been directed specifically against heretics — those whose religious beliefs were in contrast to orthodox Roman doctrine, or those who challenged the absolute authority of the Church. But the line between heresy and other sacrilegious practices was often difficult to determine, and it was not clear if Devil worship constituted a heresy under inquisitional law.

In England, the Bishop of Coventry had been brought to trial in 1303 for paying homage to an unnatural deity, but was found to be innocent. In 1324, Dame Alice Kyteler of Ireland (said to be the richest woman in Kilkenny) was accused of making magical ointments, poisoning her husbands and having sex with the Devil. In France, the Carmelite friar, Pierre Recordi, was brought to trial in 1329 for making wax and toad's blood images of women, and burying them under their thresholds as offerings to Satan. He was imprisoned for life. In 1335, Catherine Delort and Anne-Marie Georgel were tried in Toulouse for giving themselves to the Devil, who taught them spells to harm anyone they disliked.[17]

To cope with the anomalies of accusatory definition, Pope John XXII had widened the field of operation, and authorized the Inquisition to prosecute sorcerers, witches and ritual magicians. His bull, *Super illis Specula* of 1326, threatened anyone who made a pact with Hell and the practitioners of magical arts with the same penalties that were applicable to heresy. In a theological climate that displayed an increasing concern with the role and power of the Devil, certain procedures of ritual magic, involving invocations of Hell and maleficent beings, were now made subject to the criminal charge of *maleficia*.[18]

Implementation of the bull was a little slow to begin, since the inquisitors were unsure of precisely what constituted *maleficia*. An appropriate distinction was found, however, in 1388 when the Inquisition tortured a man who revealed the activities of a supposed Waldensian sect near Turin. He admitted that they worshipped the 'great dragon of The Revelation, who was called the Devil and Satan'.[19] They claimed him as 'the creator of this world, who on Earth is more powerful than God'.[20] This plainly was the difference: a heretic was one whose relationship with God differed from Church convention, whereas a witch did not acknowledge God at all, but was reckoned to worship Satan instead. The assimilation of various forms of magical arts and heresy was further enhanced in 1398, when the theology faculty of the University of Paris proclaimed that acts of magic, or superstitious practices seeking results beyond what might be expected from God and nature, were accomplished through an implicit or explicit pact with the Devil. This, it was determined, amounted to apostasy, and thus heresy.[21]

Notwithstanding the hardships of the Waldensians during that period, they persisted as an operative movement despite a further century of continued persecution. In 1451, the epic verse, *Le Champion des Dames* by Martin Le Franc, recounted the nobility and deeds of many women throughout history. When detailing the Waldensian women, the poem recalled how the Church had regarded them as perverted instruments of the Devil, condemning them as witches.[22] They and their men had been totally eradicated in Provence, but managed to survive elsewhere until they joined the 16th-century Protestant Reformation. Resultantly, the Waldensian Church is extant to this day as a member of the Ecumenical Council of Geneva and the World Alliance of Reform Churches.

Filth of the Devil

The 14th century was a period of great strife and general disorder in Britain and Continental Europe. A severe change in weather patterns had moved from three centuries of global warming in the Medieval Warm Period to a significant cooling in the northern hemisphere. Crops failed, animals died in their millions, and the catastrophic Great Famine struck the countries of Europe. Consequently, the scarcity of food resulted in widespread hunger and malnutrition. With the nation's sheep decimated, England's wool manufacturing ground to a halt, and the failure of exports led to the collapse of the Flemish weaving industry.

As if that were not enough, a dispute over heritable rights and territorial interests ensued between the Plantagenet King Edward II of England and Charles IV of France. This led to the Battle of Crécy in 1346, which protracted into the Hundred Years' War. Then, just two years later, came a typhoid epidemic and pestilence that targeted sheep and cattle. This was followed immediately by the bubonic plague of the Black Death, carried by rat-borne fleas on trading ships from China and Asia. In Britain and Europe, the plague claimed the lives of nearly half the population during a period called the Great Mortality.

The rural peasant classes were severely affected to the extent that even the meagre supplies of grain that were imported from unaffected countries never reached them. Their farms were devastated, and fish were scarce in the rivers. They prayed for deliverance; they used whatever herbs and potions they could muster to combat disease; they huddled in groups around community fires at night to share their sorrows and keep warm, and they were denounced by the Church as the very sorcerers and black witches who had summoned the filth of the Devil to contaminate the world!

In the course of this, a new definition of sorcerers' gatherings (previously called Synagogues of Satan) entered the vocabulary of Western Europe. Henceforth, these ritualistic conventions became known as Sabbats. The earliest accounts of a Witches' Sabbat come from the region of Toulouse in 1355.[23] In a large-scale witch trial, out of sixty-three persons accused of making pacts with the Devil, eight were handed over to the secular arm to be burned, and the rest were imprisoned, either for life or for a good many years. Under the duress of torture, two of the condemned, both elderly women, confessed that they had assisted at Sabbats, where they had worshipped the Devil and been guilty of hideous indecencies with him. Furthermore, they were compelled to admit that they had eaten the flesh of infants, whom they had carried off by night from the custody of their nurses.[24]

The term 'Sabbat' is generally associated with the familiar Jewish reference to Saturday, the seventh and last day of the week. It is said to represent God's day of rest, given as the *Sabbath* in the Genesis Creation account, and formally established in the subsequent laws of Exodus.[25] In practice, however, the custom had its historical origin in ancient Mesopotamia, where the *Sha-bat-um* defined the monthly feast of the full moon.[26] In the Akkadian language of Mesopotamia (Iraq), the term *sha-at-um* meant 'a passing',[27] and related to the completion of a sun cycle — in effect a year. The term for a lunar passing (the completion of a month) was *sha-bat-um*. From this, although differently applied to a week, rather than a month, derived the Israelite biblical term *Shābath*.

Calendars prior to Roman intervention were generally lunar, rather than solar, and were based upon moon cycles. The moon's waxing and waning were easy for all to see, whilst new moons and full moons were very discernible as well as being regular. Thus, there were thirteen 28-day moons to the year, not twelve months as in modern calendars. In rural Britain and Western Europe, this lunar calendar was perpetuated by the villagers in conjunction with the solar cycle. The whole was seen as a rotating wheel — a progression of birth, life, decline, death and rebirth of the seasons. Within this cycle were four key festivals, falling on the solar equinoxes and solstices, with another four solar dates, called the Greater Sabbats, in between — all celebrated by rural communities at large.[28] Along with these particular festival events, the assemblies also included ritual observances on all nights of the full moon in accordance with the original Mesopotamian feasts of *Sha-bat-um* — a time to relax and revel at the divisions of the months.[29]

Death at the Stake

In the early 1400s, wholesale witch prosecutions were conducted from Berne in Switzerland by the secular judge Peter de Gruyères. In the Swiss canton of The Valais, 200 Devil worshippers were put to death, while at Briancon another 150 suffered execution.[30] Many supposed witches and sorcerers were killed by way of excessive water torture even before sentence was passed. In this method of interrogation, the victims were laid flat, with their nostrils compressed to prevent breathing, whilst water was poured continually into their throats. Described in the law book *Praxis Rerum Criminalium*, by the Flemish lawyer Joost de Damhoudère, it was known as being 'put to the question' and, to avoid drowning, the water had to be swallowed, causing severe stomach distension and immense pain.

In the ensuing centuries, alleged witches and sorcerers were executed in their thousands — sometimes hanged, strangled or drowned, but mostly burned at stakes, flamed in tar-barrels, or roasted on spits during a period which has since become known as the Burning Times. From the inquisitors' perspective, the wonderful thing about witchcraft, sorcery and *maleficia* was that just about anybody could be caught in the ever-widening net. For the legal authorities, the charge of Devil worship became an expedient substitute for criminal and political indictments. On many occasions, the very flexible and necessarily indistinct accusation was used to circumvent courtroom trial altogether. This convenient measure was brought to bear against some very influential figures in England, where witchcraft was ranked as an offence against the monarch and was, therefore, said to be treasonable.

Of all the historical characters who fell to the fate of the Burning Times, perhaps the best known is Joan of Arc, the famous Maid of Orléans. Born in 1412, Joan was the daughter of a Domrémy farmer in the French Duchy of Bar. In the following year, Henry V became King of England and, at the time of his accession, the Plantagenet war which had been waged for some years against France had subsided. Henry nevertheless decided to renew his Plantagenet family's claim to the French kingdom on the basis that his great-great-grandmother of a century before was the daughter of King Philippe IV of France.

King Henry, with 2,000 men-at-arms and 6,000 archers, swept through Normandy and Rouen, defeating the French at Agincourt in 1415. He was subsequently proclaimed Regent of France by the Treaty of Troyes. Then, with the aid of the faithless French Queen Isabau, he married the princess Katherine de Valois and set a course towards overthrowing her brother, the Dauphin. It transpired, however, that Henry V died two years later, as did King Charles VI of France. In England, the heir to the throne was Henry's infant son, whose uncles — the Dukes of Bedford and Gloucester — became overlords of France. The French people were necessarily concerned about their future prospects, but all was not lost for along came the inspired Joan of Arc. In 1429 she appeared at the fortress of Vaucouleurs, near Domrémy, announcing that she had been commanded by the saints to besiege the English at Orléans.

At the age of seventeen, Joan departed for the Royal Court at Chinon, along with the Dauphin's brother-in-law, René d'Anjou. Once at Chinon on the Loire, she proclaimed her divine mission to save France from the invaders. At first, the Court resisted Joan's military ambitions, but she gained the support of Yolande d'Aragon, the Dauphin's mother-in-law and mother of René d'Anjou. Joan was then entrusted with the command of more than 7,000 men, who destroyed the blockade at Orléans and overthrew the English garrison. Within a few weeks the Loire Valley was again in French hands and, on 17 July 1429, the Dauphin was crowned Charles VII at Reims Cathedral by Archbishop Regnault of Chartres.

Less than a year after her success, the Maid of Orléans was captured whilst besieging Paris, and England's Duke of Bedford arranged for her trial by Pierre Cauchon, the Bishop of Beauvais, who sentenced her to life imprisonment on bread and water. When Joan refused to submit to rape by her captors, the Bishop pronounced her an ungrateful sorceress. Charges were laid concerning her supernatural powers in battle, and her visions of saints were adjudged to be manifestations of diabolical spirits. She was condemned as a heretic for having short hair and wearing men's clothes during a sacrament. When asked whether St Michael had appeared to her clothed or naked, Joan did not answer the question. But an informer claimed that she had been seen dancing around a tree at Domrémy, and this was proof enough that she was indeed a Devil-worshipping witch! Without further trial, Joan was burned alive in the Market Square of Rouen on 30 May 1431.[31]

The Devil's Apprentice

In 1440, nine years after Joan of Arc's fate, the French nobleman Gilles de Retz was also tried for sorcery, being said to have made a compact with the Devil. Gilles is often cited as having been Joan's military commander, even her bodyguard, at the siege of Orléans. But he held neither of these posts. Joan's personal guard and master of horse was Jean d'Aulon, seconded to her by the Dauphin for her entire military career. According to the royal bursary record, Gilles de Retz simply led a detachment of 25 men-at-arms and 11 archers under Joan's ultimate command, and he was not associated with her at any personal level.[32]

Evidently, Gilles de Retz had kidnapped a clergyman named Jean le Ferron during a dispute at the Church of Saint Étienne de Mer Morte. This prompted an investigation by the Bishop of Nantes, during which the evidence of Gilles' extensive crimes was uncovered. Along with witchcraft and heresy, the charges laid against him were extraordinary; he was accused of torturing and murdering dozens, if not hundreds, of boys. It was claimed that a certain Francesco Prelati had promised Gilles that he could help him regain his misspent fortune by becoming a Devil's apprentice and sacrificing male children to him.

Numerous testimonies convinced the judges that there were adequate grounds for an establishment of guilt, as a result of which Gilles de Retz is now listed as the worst paedophile murderer of all time. It is reckoned that Gilles confessed to the charges as laid, but the trial transcript (which seemingly included testimony from the parents of missing children) was said to have been so lurid that the judges ordered much of it to be stricken from the record. Along with two accomplices, Gilles was excommunicated and strung-up at Nantes, above a burning pyre, on 26 October 1440.[33]

A recently published cache of fragmentary documents, believed to date from that year, purport to bear witness to Gilles' own state of mind as his execution neared.[34] Some scholars reckon the papers are not to be trusted; others hold them to be legitimate historical evidence. Either way, the debate continues, with historians and other academics still disagreeing over the extent of Gilles' guilt. Some are convinced that he was framed; others see him as the first recorded serial killer.

Probably, the full truth will never be known, but Gilles clearly had supporters and, when his rope broke and his executed body fell into the fire, it was snatched by some women and buried at a nearby Carmelite church. Two years later, King Charles VII of

France, whose cause Gilles had supported against the will of the bishops, granted *Letters of Rehabilitation*, stating: 'The said Gilles, unduly and without cause, was put to death'.[35] But weighed against this is the fact that a large number of skulls and young skeletons were reported to have been dredged from the moat of his castle. In view of the severity of the crimes, Gilles de Retz had been tried and convicted by three independent courts: 1) the Holy Inquisition and the Bishop of Nantes on charges of heresy and sorcery; 2) the Episcopal Court on charges of sacrilege and violation of ecclesiastical rights, and 3) by the Civil Court of the Duke of Brittany on charges of multiple murder. Separately, they each found him guilty as charged.[36]

8

FEASTS OF INIQUITY

Cult of the Damned

From about 1430, witchcraft was explicitly defined in a good many treatises, and was recognized as a distinctly identifiable cult. The punishments were individually affirmed, as were the methods for the detection and trial of witches. The cases were no longer sporadic, and were by no means exceptional, for witches were now regarded as an organized guild, marshalled by Satan to remove faith from the Earth.

There is no doubt that the responsibility for the spread of witch mania rested chiefly with the popes of the era. One after another, they countenanced and encouraged the belief, and not a single word emanated from any pontiff to discourage it. Successive popes called specifically on the Inquisition to detect and punish Devil-worshipping witches. In the first half of the 15th century, a series of papal bulls urged the Holy Office formally to proceed against magicians, diviners and satanists. In several addresses from 1434, Pope Eugene IV spoke in detail of those who made pacts with the Devil and offered demonic sacrifices. It was against the backdrop of the resultant sorcery trials that the notion of satanism truly began to crystallize. The practitioners of magical arts were said to have acquired their techniques by way of powers obtained from the Devil.[1]

In 1450, the noted German goldsmith and printer, Johannes Gutenberg, invented the movable-type printing press. From that time, mass-produced literature became possible, and satanic images moved into wide circulation.[2] The first book to be published on the subject of witchcraft was *Fortalitium Fidei* by Alphonsus de Spina, confessor to the Spanish King John of Castille. Published in about 1470, it discussed various types of demon, and explained how women were forever ready and

104

willing to submit to evil. Also detailed were unholy assemblies called Sabbats in the South of France. Consequently, a number of community gatherings were assaulted, and many women arrested and burned.[3]

The second book to appear on the subject (although written as early as 1435) was *Formicarius* by Johannes Nider, a Dominican professor of theology in Vienna. Published in 1475, this work also featured the Sabbats, and explained that the necessary trials, tortures and executions of witches were already taking place.[4] The guilty were said to have made pacts with the Devil by renouncing God in church, drinking the blood of sacrificed children, and subscribing to the iniquitous cult of the damned.[5]

Nider's opinion of women was itself diabolical, and he pronounced from the pulpits that 'Woman is more bitter than death'. He listed ten specific reasons why the cohabitation of men and women was a mortal sin, and classified marriage as a 'moral leprosy'. Although marriage ceremonies were officiated by the Church, it was determined that this was because there had to be some form of sanctification to weigh the balance of an institution that existed because of *Original Sin*. It was claimed that 'God permits the intervention of Satan's malefic agency through the marriage bed more than through any other medium, for the reason that the first sin was carried down through the marital act'.

John Geiler of Strassburg (the most influential preacher in Germany) explained that there would always be ten women to burn against one man because 'Woman is the door to the Devil, and the way of iniquity'. Various church officials and preachers of the day emphasized that malevolent witches, who flew through the air, copulated with the Devil and murdered unbaptized children, were cultish women who could turn their men into demons.

Nider wrote that the Devil appeared at the Sabbats in the form of a man, but the Dominican inquisitor, Nicholas Jacquier, asserted in 1458 that the Devil appeared in the manner of a goat.[6] Jacquier denounced witchcraft as the worst of all heresies, claiming that the Sabbats were the means by which Satan was establishing his kingdom on Earth. In one way or another, an alleged pact with the Devil was central to all charges of the crime of witchcraft, and the Inquisition was said to be waging God's war against Satan and the apostles of darkness.

In practice, the said goat-like appearances were seemingly correct, just as was the claim that the Devil appeared as a man, although strictly the other way about. The Masters of the rural Sabbats were indeed likened to devils. Among those recorded in Britain were Ould Birtles, his brother Roger, William Simpson, Thom Reid and William Soulis, who became Lord Hermitage in 1318. These men and their counterparts in other covens would each wear his own traditional costume, perhaps representing Kerne, the 'horned one', or maybe a satyr such as Pan. Often the Masters' costumes would take the form of a hideous black goat. In the Spanish Basque country, the term used to describe a Sabbat's venue was *akhelarre*, meaning 'goat pasture'.[7]

In England, France, and perhaps elsewhere, the requisite number of members in a coven seems to have been thirteen. The reason for this has never been fully ascertained. It was possibly related to the number of full moons in a year. Alternatively, some have suggested that it was to mimic the number of Jesus and his twelve apostles.[8] That there were often many more than thirteen at the Sabbats is not in doubt, but most were devotees of the sabbatical community, rather than members of the central coven itself. It was also the case that a number of covens and local communities would often conjoin for the revels.

A certain Estebène de Cambrue testified in 1567 that there were some meetings held only by the immediate coven members with no attendance by outsiders. They were called *Esbats*, and were more in the nature of business meetings, where those present would submit reports of 'all our acts and deeds betwixt the great meetings'.[9]

They were the days of a feudal regime that nailed everyday families to the soil and their trades, preventing mobility, while at the same time enforcing a high degree of economic and social uncertainty. In this environment, the feudal lords always retained the Right of Prehension — a privilege whereby they could carry away any animal, crop, or daughter, for their own benefit as desired.[10] Because of this, a man was never sure in what state he might find his home, family, workshop or farmstead at the end of a day. The rapacious barons would encroach regularly upon the peasants' fields and flout their traditional common rights. The peasants were often deprived of their privileges to fish and hunt for food, or to gather wood in the forests, in order that the wildlife and woodlands might be preserved for the sport of the nobles and churchmen.

Since this oppressive regime survived within a Church structured by way of authority from the Pope and the bishops (who technically owned much of the land), many of the rural folk and tenant farmers perceived Christianity as an evil regime. They considered the Christian God to be an obstructive force as far as they were concerned. He did not represent them or their dignity in any way, for he was the friend of tyrants and warmongers who lived in fine mansions and stone-built castles. The alternative deities of the country residents (those called witches by the Inquisition) were seen by them as opposers of this cruel establishment. They were not evil, but strong and supportive in a way that the Christian Church and its God had never been.

As Geiler had stated, there were about ten women condemned for witchcraft against every one man. Among those men was the elderly Pierre Vallin. In 1438 he was seized by the Inquisition in southern France and repeatedly tortured. His treatment was so severe that Pierre confessed to invoking Beelzebub, and said that he had served the Devil for 63 years. Following each enforced confession, he was again tortured until admitting to further accusations by the inquisitors. He had supposedly denied God, spat on the cross, eaten the flesh of children, and even sacrificed his own baby daughter. Since female witches were reckoned to copulate ritually with the Devil, Pierre was forced to agree that, in his particular case, the shapeshifting Devil that he knew took the form of a seductive girl. After many days of extreme torture, Pierre was answering 'yes' to all the accusations made against him. Then, at his trial, it was stated that he had made each of his admissions voluntarily. He was condemned as a heretic, an apostate and an idolater. All his possessions were confiscated, and he was then tortured again for a week whilst being forced to name some fellow conspirators. Given that valuable confiscations of wealth and property were expressly significant in order to fund the Inquisition, Pierre was pressured to give only the names of rich men, rather than poor.[11]

At much the same time in Germany, wealthy women were also placed under the hammer of discipline. They were said to be too extravagant in their devilish ornamentation. Town councils sat in judgment upon the number of gowns and other articles of apparel that ladies might possess without detriment to the community. Strict limitations were imposed on the allowable number of dresses and items of adornment. Maximum limits of expenditure were also fixed for each item. It was nevertheless deemed allowable for a woman to bathe once every two weeks!

The trains of women's dresses were described as 'the Devil's wagon — for neither men nor angels, but only the Devil has a caudal appendage'. John Geiler was responsible for much of the legal restraint, condemning women who might wear 'two dresses for a single day', and he lambasted 'those with long hair falling down over their shoulders'.[12] The greed of the Devil's pocket, he claimed, must not be appeased, for he frequents the market places disguised as a pedlar selling his wares. Meanwhile, at the poorer end of the scale, the peasant women were restricted to just one particular type of rough cloth for their outer garments.

In the course of these legislative measures, dancing was especially denounced. It was preached that 'The Devil is the head concertmaster at such entertainments, and the higher the dancers jump, the deeper their fall into Hell. The more firmly they hold on to each other with their hands, the more closely does the Devil tighten his hold upon them'.

Horns of the Church

Horned and antlered costumes might well have been a custom of the rural Sabbats, but they did not constitute a unique practice in this regard. Such disguises also had a history of use by the

Catholic priests. From 1445 comes an extraordinary account of a Church tradition which had been admonished by some bishops, but prevailed nonetheless:

> Priests and clerks may be seen wearing masks and monstrous visages at the hours of office ... They cense with stinking smoke from the soles of old shoes. They run and leap through the church, without a blush at their own shame ... and rouse the laughter of their fellows and bystanders in infamous performances with indecent gestures, and verses scurrilous and unchaste.[13]

Investigation of this long-standing New Year custom traces back to the 6th century, when St Caesarius of Arles had first referenced the same practice:

> Some dress themselves in the skins of herd animals. Others put on the heads of horned beasts, swelling and wildly exulting, if only they can so metamorphose themselves into the animal kinds that they seem to have entirely abandoned the human shape.

In 585, the Council of Auxerre had condemned all animal masquerades, such as that performed annually by the clergy at the New Year. Some decades later, in 668, Archbishop Theodore of Canterbury legislated in England that the donning of animal horns or skins constituted an evil transformation. The sentence to be imposed was 'a penance for three years, because this is devilish'.[14]

When Gregory I achieved the papal throne in 590, the bishops' debate in this regard was in progress. Gregory did not like his priests pretending to be 'goat-men with foul-smelling censers, distributing devilish charms'. He saw the practice as hideously pagan, tantamount to shapeshifting, and undoubtedly wicked. It is therefore perhaps not surprising that, when he redefined the Devil from his traditional role as a fallen angel, Gregory claimed that 'Satan has horns and hooves ... and a terrible stench'.

Albeit the Church hierarchy denounced the old clerical custom of the horned masquerade, it was not something that could effectively be policed. People in the towns and villages enjoyed the goat-men revels, and so the priests introduced them for a few extra days after each Christmas. The result was that, throughout the medieval period, when the Church set its sights against people who dressed up as goats, stags and other horned animals, it was in the first instance directing its displeasure against many of its own clergy.

When the Morality and Mystery Plays took shape as festival entertainment in the Middle Ages, the horned figure became a representation of Satan, who emerged as a popular character for the stage — often as the principal player.[15] He was the intriguer who, after his successful revolution against the Lord, had established his own empire in Hell. The premise was that 'without the Devil's intrigues, man's fall and later salvation by way of Jesus Christ would be impossible to portray'.[16]

These performances were conducted across Europe, from Rome to London, with England's other main centres being York, Chester, Coventry and Wakefield. In the context of these plays, Jacob Grimm (of 19th-century Brothers Grimm fame) explained that, in Teutonic Christmas performances, the satanic presence was seen as a wild figure named Claus.[17] He appeared as the mischievous alter ego of St Nicholas, in which event he became known as Old Nick — still a commonly used identification for the Devil today. Otherwise, in his own shape as a gift-bearing trickster, he was the *Satan Claus* who, by way of latter-day anagrammatical corruption, became the model for Santa Claus.

The Left Hand Path

Another early book to appear on the subject of witchcraft was *De Lamiis et Pythonicis Mulieribus* (The Witches and Diviner Women). Published in 1489, it was written by Ulrich Molitor, a professor of law at the German University of Konstanz.[18] In this work, Molitor made use of the Athanasius concept that the Devil was able to shapeshift into any form he wanted. He was therefore able to seduce women in the shape of an ordinary man, thereby making them his unwitting slaves by way of 'pacts' that bound them to him. Molitor's best known illustration from this book depicts such a scene but, despite the superficial disguise, the satanic features remain evident in the Devil's tail and clawed feet.

During the witch trials that followed in Britain, various women described the Devil they had met as being an ordinary sort of fellow. Jonet Barker said the Devil had appeared to her and two friends 'in the likeness of a trim, gentle man, and drank wine with them all three, and embraced Margaret Lauder in his arms at the drinking of beer, and put his arm about her waist'. Isobel Bardie recalled a similar drinking incident with mutual toasting, and Helen Guthrie said the Devil was a man with whom she had danced in a churchyard. Marie Lamont recalled a time when the Devil had joined her and some friends for bread and wine, after which he sang to them. And Elspet Bruce explained that the Devil had kissed all the women goodnight after an evening of pipe music, but he only shook hands with Kettie Scott because it was their first acquaintance.[19] Individually among these women, Helen Guthrie of Forfar became notorious in witch trial history. In an endeavour to protect her daughter, she aided the prosecutors by naming eleven others as witches, eight of whom were executed. But Helen did not escape; she was strangled, and her body burned to ashes in a barrel of tar.

Pacts with the Devil were regarded by the Inquisition as formal contracts, and were reckoned to be signed by witches on entering their master's service. In 1450, the anonymous *Errores Gazariorum* described that the Devil would draw blood from the left hand of an initiatory witch, and would write a sworn pledge between them with the blood, keeping the paper afterwards and setting his disciple on the evil 'left hand path'. Thus, the life energy of the witch was thereafter bound to Satan. The inquisitors' inspiration for this concept had originated with St Augustine of Hippo, who had written in the 4th century that the occult arts arose from pestiferous association with demons, 'formed by a pact of faithless and dishonourable friendship'.[20]

Despite the avid witch mania that flourished within the inquisitional environment, there were some who did not acknowledge the existence of witchery as a craft in its own right. Guillaume Adelin, the Prior of Saint-Germain-en-Laye, near Paris, had often preached against the reality of witchcraft, but in 1453 he made a surprising public announcement to support his opinion. In the Episcopal Chapel at Evreux, Guillaume admitted that he had himself worshipped Satan for a time, having renounced his faith in the Cross. This, he said, was how he knew witchcraft to be a delusion, because he discovered there was no such movement in the way it was customarily portrayed. He declared, however, that this same discovery had convinced him more firmly of the Devil's own reality. Since the clerics were so unashamedly committed to their notions about witchcraft, Guillaume deduced that they must have been fooled by the Devil, who had put the silly concept into their minds in his bid for domination of the Church.[21]

Also known as William von Edelin, the prior of Saint-Germain-en-Laye, as a Carmelite monk and professor, had taken part in the Council of Basle. Arraigned by the Inquisition in 1453 charged with heresy, he confessed to having 'done homage to the Devil', that he had joined an heretical group and had often attended their satanic assemblies. In spite of his abjurations, he was degraded by the ecclesiastical court for diabolism and imprisoned until he died.

Although there were no specific Bible-like testaments written in the name of Satan, he was viewed in a strict gospel sense as the 'prince of this world',[22] and therefore worthy of some recognition. Anne-Marie de Georgel (the first woman to be accused of ritual copulation with the Devil) had conceded as much in Toulouse when questioned by the Inquisition of Bernardo Gui in 1335.[23] How could one ignore such a powerful entity when the God of Heaven had abandoned ordinary people to become the friend of despots and torturers! In such an environment, Satan might well have been perceived as a figure of some possible support for the oppressed.

Within the various pagan traditions of early times, there were any number of gods and goddesses, some of whom had been venerated in Britain and Europe through the ages. Although the worshippers of these deities had long been regarded as heathens of one sort or another, it was not the case that their gods and goddesses were portrayed by the Church in any sense as black and evil as Satan. The reason was that the Devil was never a pagan entity; he was a product of Christianity itself. He was therefore a far more dangerous prospect since, unlike other deities who were easy to ridicule and dismiss, the Christian churchmen truly believed in him. To them, Satan was the bad god of Christianity, and they called him the Father of Lies.

Whether or not the horned figure of the rural Sabbats was ever meant to represent the biblical Devil is open to question. Those who admitted to this made their confessions under conditions of extreme pain and punishment. If indeed the name of Satan had ever been used at the assemblies instead of Kerne, Pan, or that of some other traditional figurehead, then it would have been appropriate enough in the original Hebrew sense of the word. Used in biblical times to identify prosecutors and magistrates, the word *satan* (also the given name of one of God's heavenly court) meant 'accuser'. In this context, the Masters of the Sabbats were undoubtedly accusing the Christian churchmen of being evil-doers.

The term 'witch' stems from the Old English *wicce* (as related to female enchanters and visionaries), and from *wicca* (used in respect of male practitioners).[24] The connection of witches to Devil worship was an attribution of the Church, but it was essentially incorrect, as were the clerics' variously related interpretations of the Bible. It was customarily taught from 1 Samuel 28:7–25 that King Saul of Israel consulted the 'witch of Endor' on the eve of the Battle of Gilboa. But in this regard, the Masoretic Hebrew uses the term 'diviner', and the *Vulgate* Latin refers only to 'a woman with a divining spirit'. There is no scriptural mention of her being a witch in any diabolical sense. The 'wise woman of Endor' was essentially an oracle with powers of divination. Even the concept of medieval witches using herbs and potions in their said devilish pursuits had a tradition that emanated from the earliest times. Genesis 30:14–16 relates that the wives of Abraham's grandson Jacob made use of mandrake as an aphrodisiac love-philtre. In his 1st-century chronicle, *Antiquities of the Jews*, Flavius Josephus explained that the Essenes of Qumrân were very practised in the art of healing, and received their therapeutic knowledge of medicinal roots from the writings of the ancients.[25]

Since most people of the rural classes were in some way connected to what was termed witchcraft in medieval times, there must surely have been good and bad in their number as in any widespread community. However, the one thing that none would ever dream of doing was to cause purposeful harm to those very aspects of their lives that were so important: the children, herds and harvests. Nevertheless, by specifying the evil practices charged against the witches — their intercourse with the Devil, their interference with childbirth, their sacrifice of infants, their power and malice in the infliction of pain and disease, and their destruction of crops and cattle — the popes and inquisitors were enabled to stress the malignancy of witchcraft in terms of its decidedly anti-Christian purpose.[26]

The Devil's Arts

During the time that elapsed from the 12th to the 15th century, there had been a considerable switch of emphasis from the original notions of heresy to the Church's concentration on matters of witchcraft. From the earliest 4th-century days of the Catholic Church, heretics had been evident. They were easy to define in that they were those who disagreed with certain doctrines established by the ecumenical councils and synods. They might perhaps have been Arians who did not uphold the *Trinity* ruling that the Father, Son and Holy Ghost were three persons in one. They might have been Nestorians who averred that Jesus was a man and not a divine agent. Or they might have been Gnostics, whose view of the faith was spiritually esoteric, rather than materialistic in accordance with the Roman ideal. There were also other groups who did not accept the doctrine of the Blessed Mary's perpetual virginity, or who argued against the orthodox interpretation of Christ's resurrection. Ultimately, there were the Waldensians who decried ecclesiastical opulence, and the Cathars with their dualist motivations. But what these groups had in common was that they were all Christians; they were simply not Catholics. This led the Church of Rome to presume that it had a right to monopolize the Christian faith by way of persecution and brutal enforcement.

By moving its sights towards witches, sorcerers and variously dubbed Devil-worshipping cults, the Church had actually changed its emphasis from punishing heterodox Christians to assaulting traditional pagan fraternities — or those which it assumed were so inclined. In practice, what had happened by the 15th century was that there were no heretical movements of the old style left to challenge, at least none that was in any way influential, since Catholicism was firmly in control of Christendom by that time. Without witches to prosecute, the Inquisition would have had little purpose and would have completely lost its momentum. Things changed once more, however, when it was brought to the attention of Pope Sixtus IV in 1478, that there were indeed others to consider; there were Jews and Muslims, a great many of whom were living in Catholic Spain. Thus a new impetus was gained with the implementation of a specifically defined Spanish Inquisition.

The wrath of this new institution was directed, in the first instance, against the men of those other religions who had adopted certain aspects of Christianity, to the degree that they might be considered partial converts. This was not accepted as being good news by the Vatican; in fact quite the contrary. The Catholic hierarchy decided that the Roman faith was actually endangered by this subversive infiltration. The semi-converted Jews were dubbed *Marranos*, and their counterpart Muslims (Moors) were called *Moriscos*.

In no part of Europe was the number of Jews so large as in Spain, and nowhere had they been more prosperous in trade, or reached such positions of eminence as physicians and counsellors at court. To take action against Jews who persisted in their ancestral belief was not within the jurisdiction of the Christian Church, which is why they had never been persecuted along with the so-called heretics. Canon Law was explicit in its ruling that the Jews were not to be molested in the practice of their traditional religion. But, as happened in Spain, from the moment that Jews and Moors embraced certain Christian rites, such as font baptism, or acknowledged their neighbours' Christian festivals, they became subject to ecclesiastical discipline.

These 'part conversions', as they were called, had resulted from a national wave of anti-Judaism, encouraged by the malicious preaching of the archdeacon Don Fernando Martinez. The violence had been especially bloody in Seville, Cordoba, Valencia and Barcelona, where synagogues were destroyed and hundreds massacred. Consequently, many of the Jews in Spain had become religiously flexible in order to appease the country's Catholic masters. But ultimately it was to no avail.

Clearly, it was going to be impossible for the inquisitors to prove cases of 'conversion' against the majority because they did not fall into that category. But, having cut its teeth elsewhere on the witches and sorcerers, the Inquisition had developed new methods. In instances where no evidence existed of any Christian attachment or affiliation, accusations were laid for offences based on criminal law, rather than being overtly religious in their application. That way, all the Jews and Moors could be hauled into the net and charged, as were the witches, with the sacrificial murder of children, 'whose blood they used in preparations for the purposes of diabolical sorcery'!

No country in the world was more concerned to maintain the pure Catholic faith than Spain. And no cause in all his realm was more important to King Ferdinand than his war against the Devil-worshipping enemies of the Church. Resultantly, no ecclesiastical organization was ever more unrestricted in its authority than the Spanish Inquisition. As distinct from the previously implemented Holy Office against heretics and sorcerors, the Spanish tribunal was established by appointment to the Spanish sovereign instead of the Pope. It was answerable to King Ferdinand alone, acting quite independently of Rome and the bishops.[27]

At the request of Ferdinand and Queen Isabella, Pope Sixtus agreed to the appointment of a Grand Inquisitor for the kingdoms of Castile, Leon, Aragon, Catalonia, and Valencia. The office was granted to the monarch's own senior confessor, the brutal Dominican monk Tomâs de Torquemada, whose appointment was subsequently confirmed by Pope Innocent VIII.[28] With Torquemada at its head, the Inquisition became, next to royalty itself, the dominant institution of Spain, and there was no power beneath the sovereign that dared to offer any resistance.

The crimes for which life imprisonment or death could be inflicted by the Spanish Inquisition included various Jewish and Islāmic practices, such as ritual washing in the daytime, abstaining from swine's flesh or wine, singing Moorish songs, using henna, possessing Arabic manuscripts, and indulging in mathematics or philosophy.

Pope Alexander III had forbidden the study of natural philosophy (the objective research of nature and the universe) back in 1163. This was partly because the Arabs, who were the foremost philosophers of the era, were considered infidels, and partly because there was nothing said about natural philosophy in the Bible. In the 13th century, the Franciscans and Dominicans had emphatically condemned all experiments in chemistry, physics and medicine. In 1380, Charles V of France promulgated stringent laws against the possession of furnaces, crucibles, retorts and other apparatus. Similar measures followed in Italy and Spain, where scientific adepts were classified as being the 'dreaded cohorts of Satan'. It was decreed that men who, in their attics and cellars, sought to dissect and understand God's work, were practising the Devil's Arts, and must have been instructed in them by the Prince of Evil himself. Mathematics was also looked upon with fear and, by the late 15th century, mathematicians were denounced as the greatest of all sorcerers.[29]

The horrors of the Spanish Inquisition were soon extended to Sicily, Holland and other Spanish dependencies in Europe, and then to the Spanish colonies of the New World. Rituals of public penance and execution, called *Autos-da-fe*, were conducted in Mexico, at Cartagena in Colombia, and at Lima in Peru, where the charges were mostly for diabolical magic and sorcery.[30] In Spain, the inquisitors also set their sights towards witchcraft — and the resultant oppression, with many thousands slain, was to last for more than two centuries. The unsuspecting prey were described as 'the most diabolical heretics who ever conspired to overthrow the Roman Church'.[31]

9

A DIABOLICAL DECREE

The Deadly Peril

In December 1484, Pope Innocent VIII issued the most comprehensive of all bulls concerning witchcraft. It was, he maintained, 'an heretical depravity in which people, influenced by the Devil, give themselves over to animals, causing children, herds and harvests to be ruined and perish'. This bull, *Summis Desiderantes Affectibus* (Desiring with Supreme Ardour), removed any hitherto restrictions that might have limited the inquisitors' powers. The notorious document of around 1,000 words was produced in response to questions posed to the papal chair by German inquisitors. It states, without any doubt or reservation, 'The current beliefs about demonic bewitchment are undeniable'.[1]

In order that Christians might recognize the Devil when they met him, Pope Innocent gave a detailed description to accompany the bull: 'He is humpbacked, black and hairy; he wears goatskins, has horns, carries a club, and is a sex fiend'![2]

It had come to the pontiff's attention that various regions teemed with people who, forsaking the Catholic faith, were consorting with demons: 'By incantations, conjurations and other iniquities, they are thwarting the parturition of women and destroying the seed of animals, the fruits of the earth, the grapes of the vine and the fruit of the orchard'. Men and women, flocks and herds were supposedly being afflicted by these diabolical sorcerers. Men could no longer beget, and women no longer conceive. Blaming the Devil's involvement, Innocent wrote:

> At the instigation of that enemy, they do not shrink from
> committing and perpetrating the foulest abominations
> and filthiest excesses to the deadly peril of their own
> souls, whereby they outrage the Divine Majesty.

In view of the perceived situation, the Pope authorized the Dominican inquisitors, Heinrich Kraemer and Jacob Sprenger, to hunt down these evil perpetrators, so as to bring them to trial and punishment. He called specifically upon the Bishop of Salzburg to ensure that his officers were not impeded in their work and, a few months later, ordered the Archbishop of Mainz to give them active support. In other documents, Innocent commended Sigismund, Archbishop of Austria, along with the Count of the Tyrol and others, for the aid they had rendered to Kraemer and Sprenger in their effort to crush the abominable cult. The burning of witches was thus declared an official policy of the Papal See, and inquisitors were required to carry out the instructions 'with untiring and merciless severity'.

Of all the documents which have ever been issued from Rome, whether imperial or papal, Innocent's bull caused more suffering than any other. He might have exercised his assumed pontifical infallibility in denying, or at least doubting, the credibility of a great many witnesses. But, in all cases, the flimsiest accusation was deemed an unquestionable assurance of guilt. A simple word from him would have prevented untold horrors, but neither he nor his successors expressed the slightest regret for the slaughter that followed. Anyone who opposed, or even dared to criticize, the regime was classified automatically with the said malefactors. A handwritten threat from the Pope was distributed, stating, 'All who endeavour to hinder or harass the inquisitors; all who oppose them; all rebels of whatsoever rank, estate, position, dignity, pre-eminence or privilege, will be made to suffer excommunication, suspension, interdict, and yet more terrible penalties, censures or punishments'.

At Satan's Command

Two years later, in 1486, Kraemer and Sprenger published the *Malleus Maleficarum* (Hammer of Witches), with the above papal bull as its Preface. In this regard, the bull gave full Vatican approval for the Inquisition, with permission to do whatever was

120

necessary to get rid of Devil-worshipping witches. Of these authors, Pope Innocent pronounced:

> Wherefore we decree and enjoin that the aforesaid inquisitors, Heinrich Kraemer and James Sprenger, professors of theology, of the Order of Friars Preachers, be empowered to proceed to the just correction, imprisonment and punishment of any persons, without let or hindrance ... correcting, mulcting, imprisoning, punishing, as their crimes merit, those who they have found guilty, the penalty being adapted to the offence ... without any right of appeal.[3]

Next to Innocent's bull, the *Malleus Maleficarum* is the most influential and nefarious proclamation the world has ever received on witchcraft. It became the principal casebook of sanctioned persecution, determining the progress and methods of the dreadful campaign for more than 200 years.

The *Malleus Maleficarum* asserted that, in the last quarter of the 15th century, the world was more given over to the Devil than in any preceding age, being 'flooded with all kinds of wickedness'. The document claimed that witches and sorcerers, 'whose father is the Devil', were bound together in an organized body of lust and destruction. Demons of both sexes swarmed at the meetings. Baptism and the Eucharist were subjected to ridicule, and the crucifix was trampled upon. It was further described that 'After an abundant repast, the lights are extinguished and, at Satan's command, there follow scenes of unutterable lewdness. It is common to all sorcerers and witches to practise carnal lust with demons'.

To support the said reality of these charges, the authors drew upon what they called their own 'extensive experience'. They declared that, in all cases brought before them during the previous five years, 'every victim confessed to having practised such abominable whoredoms'. Without exception, they had been burnt alive for their sins. Once again it was claimed that

Devil-worshipping witches were transported through the air; they killed unbaptized children and, to keep them out of Heaven, they ate the sacrificed bodies at the communal Sabbats.

The evil, but imaginative, work of Kraemer and Sprenger gave full details of the hideous threat posed by the practitioners of what was now being called 'satanic magic'. In line with Pope Innocent's bull, the *Malleus Maleficarum* asserted that the wretched satanists 'are to be put to torture to make them confess'. It also stipulated the inquisitorial powers in a manner which left no doubt that enforced confessions were allowable and that, whatever the circumstances, execution was inevitable:

> The method of beginning an examination by torture should be begun in this way: First, the officers prepare the implements of torture, then they strip the prisoner. The reason for this is lest some means of witchcraft may have been sewed into the clothes, for they often make such instruments, at the instruction of devils, from the bodies of unbaptized children, that they may forfeit the vision of salvation.
>
> And when the implements of torture have been dispensed, the judge, with other honest men zealous in the faith, tries to induce the prisoner to confess the truth freely. But if the prisoner refuses to confess, the judge bids attendants make the prisoner fast to the strappado or some other implement of torture. The attendants obey forthwith, yet with feigned agitation, appearing to be disturbed by their duty. Then, at the earnest request of someone of those present, the prisoner is loosed again and is taken aside, and once more persuaded to confess, being led to believe that by this means there can be an escaping of the death penalty.[4]

One of the devices for exposing guilt was described as a sheet of paper, reckoned to be the exact length of Christ's body. Inscribed with the words of the Cross,[5] it was to be tied on a witch before the ordeal of torture was applied. The test of carrying a red-hot iron was also recommended, but it was to be introduced with caution, as it was a trick of the Devil to cover the witches' hands with a magical salve to protect them from pain.

Since the inquisitors were all men, it was determined that satanism must be a form of depravity linked to 'the insatiable wantonness of women'. It was explained that loose women were seduced into sex with the Devil, thus paving their way to become witches. The theory was that men and women had dichotomous natures in that, whilst men were sexually calm, women were over-sexed. Men were good; women were evil. Men were God-fearing; women were witches: 'All witchcraft comes from carnal lust, which is in women insatiable … Wherefore, for the sake of fulfilling their lusts, they consort even with devils'.[6] The authors insisted that the very word *femina* (woman) derived from *fe* and *minus*, relating to *fides minus*, meaning 'less in faith'. Women spend much of their time spinning, it was claimed, 'which proves the crooked nature of their deceit'!

The document also states that it was perfectly reasonable for a judge to promise a witch that her life will be spared, but that he could later excuse himself by passing her to another judge who had not made such a promise. Then, having established the fact that the carnal desires of women were responsible for the downfall of men, it was conceded that the gullible men should be punished as well.

The *Malleus Maleficarum* is divided into three parts, the first two of which deal with the curse of witchcraft as established in the Bible, as well as with its diabolical nature. The third lays down practical rules for inquisitional procedure — whether the trial be conducted in an ecclesiastical or a secular court. Owing to its mass reproduction by the lately developed printing press, the work exercised tremendous influence. It contained nothing that was especially new, but it did fraudulently profess to have been approved by the University of Cologne, and it was sensational in the stigma it attached to satanism as a worse crime than heresy or blasphemy. The subject at once began to attract attention, even in the world of letters, and it generally inflamed the public imagination.[7] In contrast to the deceptive entry in the book concerning its academic approval, the Faculty of Theology at Cologne had actually condemned the work as both unethical and illegal. But, despite this, it received unequivocal sanction from Pope Innocent, and a royal patent from Maximillian, the Holy Roman Emperor.

Within thirty years from 1487, twenty print-runs of the *Malleus Maleficarum* were published, and another sixteen revised editions were printed between 1574 and 1669. It was substantially used as a judicial casebook for the detection and persecution of witches, and the interrogation procedures were clearly described, as a step-by-step guide, for the judges. The work even asserted that women who did not cry and admit their abominations must automatically be presumed guilty. It stressed that all witches have evil intentions and are inspired by the Devil, arguing that, because the Devil has the power to do astounding things, witches necessarily exist to help him. To combat this, it specified the rules of evidence and the canonical procedures by which suspected witches should be tortured and put to death. As a result, tens of thousands of people (primarily women) were judicially murdered for no other reason than perhaps having a strange birthmark, living alone, having a pet, being mentally ill, or for the cultivation of medicinal herbs.

The *Malleus Maleficarum* specially cautioned the judge not to conclude his examination too quickly, for the reason that 'Unless God, through a holy angel, compels the Devil to withhold his help from the witch, she will by the Devil's help maintain a stubborn silence, not only against questioning but against all torture. And even if her silence is at last broken, it will be only to assert her innocence falsely, for some witches, with the Devil's help, would sooner be torn limb from limb than confess any of the truth'. It was therefore instructed:

> She should first be stripped and searched, for witches often prepare instruments of witchcraft out of the limbs of unbaptized children, which they sew into their garments, hide in their hair or

even in unmentionable places in order to gain the
Devil's help in withstanding the pleas of honest
men and acquiring strength to resist the torture.[8]

The mood of this villainous, and now infamous, book is summed
up in its statement that witches usually deny their involvement in
witchcraft, even maintaining that they do not believe in it. But,
the *Malleus Maleficarum* declares, 'The greatest heresy is not to
believe in witchcraft'. To plead ignorance was counted as a crime
in itself, and the wording of the interrogation procedure made
it plain that, once charged and brought to trial, there was to be no
possible means of escape.[9]

Although the *Malleus Maleficarum* did not explain individual
methods of torture in any great detail, it was made clear that,
even if guilt were ascertained, there was still a requirement for a
full confession. In this respect, a variety of devices were put to
use. A principal item of equipment was the rack — a long table on
which the accused was tied by the hands and feet, then stretched
by rope and windlass until all joints were dislocated. To this were
added rollers covered with sharp spikes. These were placed
under the hips and shoulders, and the victim rolled back and
forth over them. There was the thumbscrew, an instrument for
disarticulating the fingers; pincers to tear out the fingernails;
adjustable iron boots to crush the legs and feet, and metal jackets
lined with protruding blades. This and other devices were
inscribed with the motto *Soli Deo Gloria* (Glory be only to God).
In addition there were branding irons and horsewhips, pins and
wedges to be jammed beneath the nails, and assorted contrap-
tions for suspending the accused head-down with weights
attached. Additionally, for the women, an accused witch's hair
might be soaked in spirit and set ablaze, or sulphur was burned
into her nipples and armpits.[10]

As we saw in chapter 5, the Benedictine abbot Regino of Prüm
had criticized the popular belief that certain abandoned women
were the hideous night riders of the ancient goddess Diana of the
Wild Hunt. But disregarding Abbot Regino, the inquisitors
Kraemer and Sprenger obtained their contrary information from

125

Gratian's 1140 *Concordance of Discordant Canons*, and from an earlier regulation (*c.*900) called the *Canon Episcopi*. In this regard, the *Malleus Maleficarum* stated:

> It is also not to be omitted that certain wicked women, perverted by the Devil and seduced by the illusions and phantasms of demons, believe and profess that they ride in the night hours on certain beasts with Diana, the heathen goddess, and an innumerable multitude of women, and in the silence of the dead of night do traverse great spaces of the Earth.[11]

Prior to inquisitional times, Diana the Huntress, goddess of the Greenwood, was never regarded as having anything to do with sorcery. But she did represent the self-empowered woman, which was reason enough for the Church to condemn her tradition — as in the 906 *De Ecclesiasticis Disciplinis*.[12]

Whether or not related to Diana, stories of flying witches were a major feature of all prosecutions. As early as 1460, pictures were printed representing women riding through the air, straddling tree-stocks, broomsticks and goats, or carried by demons. Taught by the Devil, they were reckoned to make a magical flying ointment from the ashes of a toad fed on the blood of murdered children. Other ingredients included seven different herbs, each gathered on a different day of the week. The Heidelberg court preacher, Matthias Widman, who proclaimed that witches should be subjected to 'an abundance of fire, without mercy', said there were many reports of women flying on sticks and goats. They were even said to change their own shapes into the forms of animals when journeying to organized Sabbats. The Dominican theologian, Thomas de Chantimpré, told of the young daughter of a Count of Schwanenburg, who was carried every night through the air, managing to elude the strong hold of a Franciscan friar who kept trying to pull her back.[13]

Although the *Malleus Maleficarum* had an enormous impact in Continental Europe, it was of little consequence in England, where it was not published until ninety years after its original release. It was also the case that English churchmen did not display the same hatred for women as professed by their European counterparts. Even when the British witch trials did eventually begin, they arose as a result of the Protestant Reformation, not as part of the Catholic Inquisition.

Number of the Beast

At the onset of the 16th century, some 500 years from the millennium, a new round of debate ensued concerning the Antichrist. As we have seen, the book of The Revelation applies the description 'Satan and the Devil' to a seven-headed red dragon with seven crowns — a clear identification of the seven kings of Rome whose standard bore a red dragon.[14] Subsequently, although retaining its 'seven heads', the dragon is said to have acquired additional crowns, one for each of its ten horns, and is further identified as the beast of blasphemy.[15] At the time when St John wrote The Revelation (around AD 90), *ten* Roman emperors had reigned since 44 BC, following the original *seven* kings. It is possible that they were regarded as the horns of the imperial beast, although this interpretation is by no means certain.[16] Establishing separately the appearance of yet another beast, St John then wrote:

> And I beheld another beast coming up out of the
> earth; and he had two horns like a lamb, and he
> spake as a dragon ... And he causeth all, both small
> and great, rich and poor, free and bond, to receive a
> mark in their right hand, or in their foreheads ...
> Let him that hath understanding count the number
> of the beast, for it is the number of a man, and his
> number is six hundred threescore and six.[17]

Since it was given that the number 666 related to 'a man' (clerically interpreted as the Antichrist who supported the satanic beast), suggestions concerning his identity had been put forward from distant times. The application of early Hebrew *gematria* (a substitution of numbers for their corresponding letters) revealed the name of Nero Caesar. However, since Emperor Domitian was reigning at the time of the book's compilation in Greek (not Hebrew), the strategic application of a Greek form of *gematria* rendered the name of Domitian. It was also discovered that the first six Roman numerals, written in descending order, produced DCLXVI: the number 666.

Over and above these explanations, some extremely complex mathematical equations were produced to give a variety of possible solutions. Also there have been suggestions based on notions of cosmic energy and earth currents. For example, 666 is said to be the numerically evaluated polar opposite to the spiritual energy of water, which is numbered 1080.[18]

As it transpired, the evaluators of the 16th century had no more success in deciphering the number than their predecessors had at the millennium. The majority opinion was that St John had a Roman emperor in mind when he wrote the verse in question, and was most likely referring to Domitian, the brutal persecutor of Christians at that time. However, 16th-century Catholic doctrine professed that the day of the Antichrist was still at hand. On that basis, no one was expecting Domitian to return from the dead, and so the numerical problem remained unsolved.

Oddly, the 'mark of the beast' was never directly associated with the Devil's Mark, which inquisitors sought to find branded on the witches, and the number 666 did not feature as an aspect of the witch trials. But, following the Protestant Reformation, a new theory was developed concerning the Antichrist and, as we shall discover, was once again associated directly with Rome.

In modern times, there has been an interesting development on this front. Although The Revelation was written in the late 1st century, the oldest known manuscript copy dates only from the 4th century. But in 1895 some fragments of an earlier text were unearthed at Oxyrhynchus in Egypt.[19] Only in very recent years have classics scholars at Oxford University been able to read the badly discoloured papyrus using advanced imaging techniques. Fortunately, the verse in question is legible. Written in Greek, it does not state 'six hundred threescore and six' in words as do later texts, but gives the 'mark of the beast' as a three-digit number. From this it is ascertained that the more original entry in The Revelation was not 666 at all, but 616.[20]

A Council of Witches

Apart from numerous trial records, there is not much literature that recounts the first-hand experiences of those who were accused and tortured during the Inquisition. A good example of how the system worked is extant, however, from the pen of 55 year-old Johannes Junius, the Burgomaster of Bamberg. The account emanates from 1628 as a direct result of the tribunal established in Germany by Kraemer and Sprenger.

In line with the *Malleus Maleficarum*, the slightest rumour, whether true or false, was sufficient cause for an indictment by the Inquisition. Junius fell foul of this ruling because he was suspected of having attended a witches' gathering. He denied this emphatically although, in his mayoral role as a burgomaster, he had naturally attended many public meetings. Accused, nevertheless, of sorcery, he responded that he was wholly innocent, had never in his life renounced God, had no correspondence with the Devil, and knew nothing of the crime with which he was charged. But witnesses were found to corroborate the indictment, one of whom insisted that Junius had been seen with a grassmaid who turned into a demon. On another occasion, he was said to have been in the proximity of a goat, who must have been the Devil himself. He was also found to have a small blemish on his left side, and this was determined to be the mark of a diabolical pact with Satan.

Following a series of tortures, including thumbscrews, leg-screws, the strappado and the rack, Junius was forced to confess that a particular Town Council meeting in the Bamberg electoral chamber was, in reality, a coven of witches. Also that, whenever he wished to travel, he would fly on the back of a great black dog that was 'raised in the name of the Devil'.

REVELATION OF THE DEVIL

church of Fairford depicts him carting souls in a wheelbarrow, and a carving at Worcester Cathedral portrays him with a bag full of souls on his back. The theory was that souls of the damned were physically collected by Satan and taken to Hell. Legend had it that St Medard, a canon of Picardy, had caught the Devil sneaking away with a bag of souls, but he crept up behind and slit open the sack to let the poor captives free:

> Away went the Quaker; away went the baker.
> Away went the friar, that fine fat ghost,
> Whose marrow Old Nick had intended to prick,
> Dressed like a woodcock and served upon toast.

> Away went the nice little Cardinal's niece,
> And the pretty grisettes, and the dons from Spain.
> And the *Corsair's* crew, and the coin-clipping Jew,
> They scampered like lamplighters over the plain.[23]

In much the same way as horseshoes, ordinary shoes were also considered to be a deterrent against the Devil. Old shoes were often secreted in chimneys to prevent his access by that route. Thus it was the case that, whereas the fearsome Devil of the Inquisition was thought to be insurmountable by any ordinary means outside Church intervention, the Devil of many people at large (especially the English country folk) could plainly be deceived and outwitted. This appears to draw a firm distinction between the everyday perception of Satan and the revered horned deity of the rural Sabbats, despite the ecclesiastical combining of the two characters.

It was indeed the case that, in many respects, the Devil was regarded more as a figure of ridicule than a formidable prince of evil. At a time when many in Britain and Europe were pulling away from the Catholic belief system, the Devil remained significant in terms of his malevolence, but had become idealized as a material presence. He was therefore not invulnerable, and fewer people were actually terrified of him. In Germany, a traveller arrived at a town during a carnival, but was unaware of

132

the festivity. On seeing the Devil chasing a woman, he assaulted the costumed man with an axe and killed him. Charged with murder, he pleaded in court that he honestly thought he was saving the woman from the Devil.[24]

Albeit the majority of people in Italy, France and Spain were locked into Catholic perceptions of the Devil as the omnipotent Antichrist, a great many in Germany, Holland and England saw him as an assailable character who could be duped and overcome with relative ease. This appears to be somewhat anomalous, given that the *Malleus Maleficarum* came out of Germany, whilst Holland (a dependency of Spain) was beset with the Spanish Inquisition. But it might well account for why so many people admitted so readily to having seen the Devil in a variety of forms and guises. A German miller was reckoned to have tied the Devil to his water-wheel; a farmer was said to have cheated the Devil in a land deal by selling him sterile ground, and a tailor supposedly saved himself from Hell by making the Devil a fine new suit.

It was the case, however, that this light-hearted interim view of the Devil was not to last for long. Everything was soon destined to change with the advent of the Protestant Reformation. Despite all the Catholic Church had achieved with the Inquisition and the *Malleus Maleficarum*, the Devil had still not reached his diabolical prime on the social stage. In fact, his story was barely under way, and the darkest hours of his dreadful tradition were yet to come.

10

SATANIC REFORMATION

Teeth of the Beast

In the early 1500s, the Church's endeavour to hold people in fear of the Devil was wearing a little thin. The Europeans were far more troubled by the friars of the Inquisition, while in Britain the Devil was viewed more as a nuisance than a threat. The myriad pictures and descriptions of him, from a fire-breathing dragon to a goat-like satyr, were so diverse that there was nothing remotely plausible in any of them. Not only had the *Malleus Maleficarum* and other propagandist works entered the public domain by way of the printing press, but so had numerous less serious pamphlets and theatre programmes. In many of these, the Devil was portrayed in comical cartoons that mocked the inquisitional powers.

It was, nonetheless, essential to the bishops that evil was personified in a trepidatory manner. Something more scary was now required to hold the people in thrall, something more fearsome and hideously supernatural — the representation of a devilish threat in an earthly form that might terrify people as a recognizable physical entity.

In *The Histories* of the Greek scholar Herodotus, from the 5th century BC, there is reference to an Indo-European tribe called the Neurians, of whom Herodotus related:

> The Greeks and Scythians who live in Scythia say that once a year every Neurian becomes a wolf for a few days and then reverts to his original state. Personally I do not believe this, but they make the claim despite its implausibility, and even swear that they are telling the truth.[1]

In reality, the ancient Neurians did nothing more than to don wolfskins at their annual festivals, but the concept was appealing enough to find its way into subsequent Greek and Roman mythology. In AD 8, the most significant mention of the wolf-man phenomenon appeared in the *Metamorphoses* of Ovid. When considering the Creation and Ages of Mankind, Ovid's work relates to Lycaon, a King of Arcadia who presented Jupiter (who did not eat flesh) with a feast of meat, thereby affronting the god, who turned Lycaon into a wolf:

> With rabid mouth he turned his lust for slaughter
> Against the flocks, delighting still in blood.
> His clothes changed to coarse hair, his arms to legs.
> He was a wolf, yet kept some human trace,
> The same grey hair, the same fierce face.[2]

The donning of wolfskins appeared quite often in old folklore, along with the premise that the wearer's nature could be transformed to become as wolf-like as his appearance. In the Nordic *Volsunga Saga*, the characters Sigmund and Sinfjölti come upon the home of a sleeping skinner deep in the forest, whereupon each of them throws one of the man's wolfskins onto his back. At this, the nature of the original animals becomes evident and the companions howl like wolves, being quite unable to remove the skins. Once back in the forest, they discover that they have acquired the strength of many men and begin to slaughter wayfarers, biting their throats with impunity.[3]

In view of the Devil's uncertain image, the concept of wolf transformation became very attractive to the Christian churchmen, especially since the wolf had been used as a predatory example in the New Testament gospels. Matthew 7:15 states that Jesus said, 'Beware of false prophets which come to you in sheep's clothing, but inwardly they are ravening wolves'. Also, in Matthew 10:16: 'Behold, I send you forth as sheep in the midst of wolves; be ye therefore as wise as serpents and harmless as doves'. Although this Bible entry established the serpent as a creature of wisdom, rather than as something satanic in accordance with customary doctrinal interpretation, it also introduced the adversarial wolf. In practice, the wolf had only been suggested figuratively as an enemy of sheep, but since the Christian 'flock' were likened to sheep, the wolf became a symbolic enemy of the Church. The concept was further supported by another Jesus quotation in Luke 10:3: 'Go your ways; behold, I send you forth as lambs among wolves'. In the light of this, the shapeshifting ability of the Devil and his disciples, as promoted long before by Athanasius, was brought into play, and the inquisitors introduced the werewolf.[4]

Apart from a notional, but essentially unfounded, fear of wolves, there was nothing that associated them directly with anything devilish, and there was nothing in their nature or appearance which could be so ascribed. Even when the *Lay of the Werewolf* had appeared in the 12th-century writings of Marie de France, there was nothing unduly dark about the character. The story was of an unfortunate baron who, on being betrayed by his wife and her knightly lover, was destined to live in the woods as a wolf called Bisclavaret. On gaining the friendship of a noble king and welcomed into his court, the wolf-man was enabled to take revenge on the dishonourable knight, as a result of which he regained his manhood.[5]

In formulating its theories about witchcraft, the inquisitional Church had dubbed a number of animals, including goats and stags, with supernatural or unholy significance. But although these creatures had horns and might be portrayed as somehow malevolent, the animals were not fearsome in themselves. The predatory wolf was a far better candidate and, to support the ideal, the inquisitors moved beyond the New Testament gospels, harking back to pronouncements of the Old Testament. The book of Leviticus 26:22 states as a godly decree to the Israelites, 'I will send wild beasts among you, which shall rob you of your children and destroy your cattle, and make you few in number'. Then again in Deuteronomy 32:24: 'I will also send the teeth of beasts upon them'.

Both of these biblical citations were detailed in the *Malleus Maleficarum* to establish the case against witches,[6] but it was in the latter of the two entries that the Church found its most strategic inspiration: 'the teeth of beasts'. Since teeth are not among the natural weapons of man, there was something frighteningly attractive about the concept of portraying the shapeshifting Devil in such a way. It was decided, however, that a better strategy was to apply this transformational ability to Satan's most diabolical emissaries rather than to himself. That way, there could be any number of werewolves on the prowl.

Many wild animals, especially fanged creatures, are, by virtue of their strength, cunning ways and carnivorous habits, naturally avoided and treated with some reserve by humans, but that does not make them in any way dark, dangerous or devilish. By contrast, a man or woman with the ability to turn into such a beast, with obvious harmful intent, becomes a very scary prospect. It was deemed to be the stuff of nightmares, and the Church made good use of this potential. The official definition of a werewolf was laid down by the Catholic antiquarian and compiler of devotional books, Richard Verstegan. He wrote:

> The werewolves are certain sorcerers who,
> having anointed their bodies with an ointment
> which they make by instinct of the Devil, and
> putting on a certain enchanted girdle, do not
> only into the view of others seem as wolves,
> but to their own thinking they have both the
> shape and nature of wolves'.[7]

Being an essentially nocturnal creature, the wolf is dubbed with its own lunar significance and, by virtue of the Sabbats, werewolves were reckoned to assume their wolf-form on nights of the full moon, when there is witchcraft and sinister uncertainty in the air. Henri Boguet, the notorious 16th-century Witchfinder of Burgundy, claimed that, when it came to a werewolf's prey, there was no distinction between men, women or children. They did not even have to commit any particular act to encourage a werewolf's anger. Similarly, it was determined that anyone who entered the Devil's service could become a werewolf. One poor girl was burnt alive at the stake by Boguet simply because she was thought to have turned into a wolf whilst hiding behind a bush.

Boguet boasted of having burned 600 werewolves and, within the 1500s alone, there were no fewer than 30,000 werewolf trials in France, notwithstanding the rest of Europe. In large measure, these trials implicated either gypsies or poor people from the rural regions. It was reckoned that such folk of rude habits, who wandered in the woods and wild places, might naturally fall into evil ways. The main connection made by the inquisitors between gypsies and werewolves was their mutual association with silver, the element of the moon. This was said to be deadly to the werewolf who, when in the wolf state, could only be killed with a silver blade or bullet. Similarly, to gain the trust and avoid the curse of a gypsy, one was supposed to divest oneself of any silver as a mark of submission. In time, once the Inquisition had become inactive, the tradition was continued symbolically by way of a single coin: 'crossing the palm with silver'. For this, the woman gypsy would respond with her art of *dukkering*, a Romany word that defines a skill of fortune telling through reading one's body-signs. It was said to have been a form of bewitching inherited from ancient Egypt, where Wepwawet was the sacred wolf-god of Lycopolis.[8]

Consigned to the Devil

Owing to the high costs of the Catholic Inquisition, the Dominican friar Johann Tetzel implemented a lucrative scheme in 1517 to enhance the Vatican coffers. It concerned the forgiveness of sins, which had hitherto been expiated by means of penances such as fasting, repetition of the *Rosary* and other acts of repentance. Tetzel's new concept replaced these traditional penalties with Indulgences — formal declarations of guaranteed absolution, that were available for cash. Approved by decree of Pope Leo X, the sale of Indulgences soon became a source of considerable revenue for the Church.

For centuries, the orthodox clergy had suffered a series of outrageous measures imposed by an avaricious hierarchy that was becoming ever more corrupt. Through it all, they had upheld successive Vatican dictates with as much loyalty as they could muster, but the trading of Christian salvation for money was more than some could tolerate. The practice was, therefore, openly challenged. In October 1517, an Augustinian professor of theology at the University of Wittenberg in Germany, nailed his written protest to the door of his local church. It was an act of formal objection that was destined to split the Western Church permanently in two. On receiving a papal reprimand, he publicly set fire to it and was excommunicated for his pains. His name was Martin Luther, and his fellow 'protesters' became known as Protestants.

Luther's attempt to reform a particularly unwholesome Church practice quickly gained international support. This gave rise to a widespread Reformation movement, with the establishment of an alternative Christian society beyond Roman control. Despite all Vatican attempts to heighten and expand the authority of the Catholic Church, the Protestant Reformation completely undermined the authority of the Holy Roman Empire as the nations of Europe polarized and divided. Germany, for instance, separated into a predominantly Protestant north and a Roman Catholic south.

As the people settled into their separate Catholic and Protestant camps, it seemed likely that inquisitional pursuits might decline with the new establishment. But the Protestant Reformation had absolutely no impact on witch-hunting activities. In fact, it enhanced the previous effort with even more vigorous rulings. Martin Luther argued that all witches should be burned for having made their pacts with the Devil. They were, he said, an important battalion in the vast legion of enemies that the Devil was assembling against the Protestant Church.[9] Luther saw the Devil everywhere. He detested the Catholic Church so much that he regarded Pope Leo as the Antichrist: an emissary of Satan himself. As a direct result of this denominational hatred within Christianity, the Spanish Inquisition against Jews and

Muslims was extended to include Protestants in Spain and the Low Countries.

Luther was adamant that the Devil existed as a physical entity with the Catholic Church in his service. He therefore knew that he would be constantly watched in his Protestant endeavour by the Evil One, and was always prepared to be confronted. On one occasion he reckoned that he saw the Devil grinning at his work in Wartburg Castle, and was said to have thrown his inkstand at him.[10]

As a result of the fast-growing Lutheran influence, popular belief in the power of the Devil, as exercised through witchcraft and other magical practices, was developed beyond all measure. Naturally, Luther did not appeal to any papal bull; he looked only to the Bible, and it was because of the biblical command, 'Thou shalt not suffer a witch to live',[11] that he advocated the extermination of witches. His opinion of satanic interference was not, however, confined to the world of witchcraft; Luther imagined the malign influence to exist in the ordinary affairs of everyday life. His series of *Teufelsbucher* (Devil's Books) related how it was that such things as fine dressing, dancing, party-going, sex and extravagant food were all vices that resulted from succumbing to the will of the Devil. But even beyond frivolity and extravagance, Luther reckoned that, as the biblically cited 'prince of the world', the Devil must be instrumental in all things. In this regard, he insisted, 'The bread which we eat, the drink which we drink, the garments which we wear, the air and whatever we live by in the flesh is under his dominion'.[12]

In England, the most significant consequence of the Reformation was the formal rejection of the Pope's authority, and his replacement as Head of the English Church by King Henry VIII Tudor. In 1563, the *Thirty-Nine Articles* of the Anglican Protestant faith were subsequently enacted by Henry's daughter, Queen Elizabeth I. This formally established the independent Church of England, for which Elizabeth was excommunicated by Rome in 1570. Scotland's secession from a somewhat limited vestige of papal control occurred a little earlier in 1560, with the establishment of the Presbyterian Kirk under the influence of the

140

reformer John Knox, a one-time chaplain to the Tudor Court. The Presbyterian movement had emerged from the teachings of the French theologian, John Calvin, who formulated his Calvinist branch of the Protestant Reformation in the footsteps of Martin Luther. In 1541, Calvin's *Ecclesiastical Ordinances* were enacted in Geneva, Switzerland, and were later interpreted for implementation by the National Kirk of Scotland.

It was within the environment of this newly developed anti-Catholic structure that the Devil moved truly into his prime. The 16th-century Protestant view of Satan was far more dreadful than that of the Catholics had ever been. The inquisitors had used the Devil as an efficient object of strategy in their campaign against heretics, sorcerers and witches. But the Protestants, especially those of the more zealous Calvinist branch, truly believed in him. Consequently, rather than being a peripheral figure linked to witchcraft, Satan became a principal player in the daily affairs of all people's lives. 'The gates of Hell are opened', wrote William Chub in *The True Travaile of All Faithfull Christians*, 'and the floods of Satan hath overflown the whole world'.

Compiled in the reign of England's King Edward VI (1547–53) was the *Catechism of Prayer* by Thomas Becon, chaplain to Archbishop Cranmer of Canterbury in the new English Church. It embodies an evaluation of the Devil's position in the Protestant belief of the era:

> It is not unknown how great, how mighty, and of what puissance the kingdom of Satan is, which, as St Peter saith, 'goeth about like a roaring lion, seeking whom he may devour'; which Satan, in the holy scriptures, is termed 'the prince and god of this world, the ruler of darkness' ... There is no ravening wolf that so earnestly seeketh greedily to devour his prey, as the enemy of mankind; that old serpent, who hunteth and studyeth, every moment of an hour, how he may destroy and bring to everlasting damnation mortal men, that they might fall from the favour of God, and have

their portion with him in that lake that burneth
with fire and brimstone. As this god of the world,
I mean Satan, is a great king and a mighty prince,
and strongly ruleth in the children of unbelief
and in the vessels of wrath, so is his kingdom
ample and large ... The Devil is our arch-enemy,
and above all other seeketh our destruction.[13]

In terms of *Original Sin*, there was little difference between the
Catholic and Protestant beliefs at that time. Article IX of the
constitutional *Articles* of the Anglican Church states: 'The flesh
lusteth always contrary to the spirit; and therefore every person
born into this world deserveth God's wrath and damnation'.
In pursuance of this theme, the point is made in Article XVII that
a certain elect, as chosen by God, will be delivered from curse and
damnation. But, it was added:

For curious and carnal persons, lacking the Spirit
of Christ, to have continually before their eyes
the sentence of God's predestination, is a most
dangerous downfall, whereby the Devil doth
thrust them either into desperation, or into
wretchlessness of most unclean living.

The theory of 'predestination' determined (in contrast to free will)
that God's advance decisions regarding the destiny of individuals
were cemented and unchangeable. This aspect of belief, whereby
God would arbitrarily damn one person and save another, was
sufficient for the Protestant Church to maintain social control.
Those who did not submit to the will of God, as presented and
upheld by his ministers, would be consigned to the Devil.

Meanwhile, the Catholic Church had formalized its *Sacrament
of Penance* (Confession) at the Council of Trent in Northern Italy.
This protracted event lasted from 1545 to 1551 in order to
determine the doctrines of the Church following the Protestant
separation. The notion that supports Confession, as determined
by the Council, states: 'The Lord principally instituted the

142

Sacrament of Penance when, being raised from the dead, he breathed upon his disciples saying, Receive ye the Holy Ghost. Whose soever sins ye remit, they are remitted unto them; and whose soever sins ye retain, they are retained'.[14] The sacrament is said to embody two primary actions:

1. That of the penitent in presenting himself to the priest with a self-accusation of sin.

2. That of the priest in pronouncing absolution and imposing satisfaction.

It is considered to be a judicial process in which the penitent is the accuser, the accused and the witness, whilst the priest pronounces judgment and sentence. The grace conferred is seen as a deliverance from the guilt of sin and, in the case of mortal sin, from eternal punishment.

The significance of this ruling was its complete contrast to Protestant opinion that there was no forgiveness and no prospect of salvation, except for those of a chosen elite. In some cases, the elite members were converts from the Catholic clergy but, in the main, they were a new breed of appointed ministers. Either way, the inference was that God had chosen them to lead the new holy mission. Everyone else was a presumed child of the Devil, in consequence of which a new Inquisition was born as the witch craze of Europe moved into Britain.

In parallel with this Protestant mania, new decrees emanated from the Catholic establishment. The *Constitutio Criminalis Carolina* of the Holy Roman Empire in 1532 emphasized the power of the Devil and his responsibility for sin in the world. This imperial penal code decreed that sorcery throughout the Empire should be treated not just as heresy, but as a criminal offence. If a supposed witch was deemed remotely capable of inflicting malice or injury upon any person, irrespective of whether such injury had actually been committed, then by virtue of capability alone the suspect was to be burnt at the stake. The Protestant Reformation was perceived by the Vatican as a great wave of apostasy — the filtration of a new heresy into the Catholic lands.

143

This prompted Pope Paul III to establish a central inquisitional tribunal of six cardinals in Rome. Operative from July 1542, it was to be the final court of appeal for trials concerning faith, and the 'court of first instance' for cases reserved to the Pope.[15] By this means, the Holy Office of the Inquisition (*Romano Inquisito*) was reaffirmed as the Supreme Sacred Congregation of the Roman and Universal Inquisition. At that stage, the papal bull *Licet ab Initio* declared the new Roman Inquisition to be the 'supreme tribunal for the whole world'.[16] Then in 1572 Augustus, Elector of Saxony, imposed the penalty of burning for every kind of magical practice, including simple fortune telling.[17]

A Realm of Vice

A significant aspect of emergent Devil lore, during this formative period of the Protestant movement, was the manner in which his image changed in people's minds. Martin Luther had envisioned the Devil in such a way that (although not as simplistic as the vulnerable Satan with his barrow-load of souls) he was still a challengeable figure at whom he could hurl his inkstand. He wrote of how there was a certain familiarity between them, even conversational disputes. But, in terms of true evil, Luther found the dark embodiment of the biblical Antichrist in the person of Pope Leo X, and considered the Church of Rome to be the ultimate kingdom of Hell.

Martin Luther died in 1546 — just twenty-five years after his Catholic excommunication, and even fewer years after the composition of his alternative Mass and the birth of the Protestant Church. Within the body of his followers, and those who progressed the new movement, were many who viewed the Devil in a far more sinister light. To them, he was not so much a personal figure of any kind, but the abominable representation of sin itself. They identified Satan in much deeper psychological terms as the ultimate lord of temptation, who governed the world of vice, lust and greed.[18] Indeed, all pleasures and extravagances were considered devilish by the hard-line Protestant leaders who succeeded Martin Luther. In the realm of their preaching, the Devil became the ultimate prince of Hell, not just a fallen angel as in earlier diabology, but a brooding black menace with whom no other evil could compare. His heart was said to be icy cold, and his torment so vile that only those who forsook every pleasure in life could possibly hope to escape the snare of his immorality on Earth, as well as for ever in death.

The rigorously strict regime of the puritanical Protestants was exaggerated on the European stage because the movement was born during the late era of the High Renaissance, when flamboyant art and architectural design were flourishing as never before. Everything was colourful, ambitious, extravagant and entertaining. Above all, the Renaissance had set a uniquely creative scene, thereby constituting the greatest of all Protestant sins in its attempt to emulate God. From a Catholic environment in which Raphael, Michelangelo, Bramante and Romano developed the harmony of classical art to its highest form, had emerged a widespread sect of uncompromising religious devotees who condemned it all. Disavowing even the mainstream ecclesiastical structure of the Anglican Church, the Puritans (as they became known) despised every technological advancement of the Renaissance, prizing austerity and their own bland interpretation of godliness above everything.

The puritanical hatred of art and design appears to have emanated from the very outset when Martin Luther and his original protesters stood against the extreme hypocrisy of the popes and cardinals of the era. Not least among these was Luther's worst enemy, Giovanni de Medici, who had gained the throne as Pope Leo X.

Despite all the cultural wonders of the Renaissance period, it was undoubtedly the case that, whilst artistically creative on the one hand, it would have been perceived by some pious monks and other devout clergy as spiritually destructive on the other. In this respect, Pope Leo was the epitome of all that had ever been levelled by the Inquisition against witches and sorcerers in terms of their lustful pursuits. Leo ran a lucrative brothel in Rome, with a quarter of the courtesans' property and income made over to the Church. Ignoring the Vatican's celibacy rule, he had a number of illegitimate sons and, according to the Florentine statesman, Francesco Guicciardini, he was 'excessively devoted to the flesh', to which Francesco added, 'especially those pleasures which cannot, with delicacy, be mentioned'. Other accounts state, 'He was much given to idleness, pleasure and carnal delights'. But, alongside his profligate lifestyle, Leo was also the generous patron of Raphael and Michelangelo.[19]

None of this was in any way new to Martin Luther, and the corrupt selling of Indulgences proved to be the final straw for him. Leo's predecessor, Pope Julius II, had three daughters and even issued a bull to establish his St Peter's whorehouse on 2 July 1510. Like others before him, Julius was notorious for what were called his 'hectic activities amongst prostitutes and boys'.[20] Again, however, he was an enthusiastic patron of the arts, and commissioned Michelangelo to paint the famous Sistine Chapel ceiling in the Vatican. It is perhaps not surprising that the breakaway Protestants directly associated the artistic Renaissance with the extraordinary papal behaviour, so that aesthetic mastery was regarded by them as equally diabolical.

In the earlier times of Pope Innocent VIII, the Archbishop of Canterbury in England had become so embarrassed by what he termed 'all manner of shameless and riotous living' that he confronted Innocent on the matter. But the Pope was more concerned with implementing the Spanish Inquisition, and dismissed the Archbishop, stating, 'It is so widespread among the priests and the curia, you will hardly find one without his concubine'. In that era, the in-house courtesans of the papal court were endowed with their own high status, and many of them used their positions to exercise their own intellectual abilities in a society that would otherwise have denied such rights to women.[21] The most renowned mistress of Rodrigo Borgia, who became Pope Alexander VI in 1492, was Vannozza dei Cattanei. She gave him four children, including the much maligned Lucrezia Borgia.[22] Vannozza was followed as the Pope's young concubine by Giulia Farnese, the fifteen year-old granddaughter of Pope Innocent VIII.

The goings-on in Vatican life were so constantly interspersed with sexual scandals that the papal regime was dubbed a 'pornocracy'. In 1534, Giulia's brother Alessandro became Pope Paul III, and was nicknamed Cardinal Petticoat by virtue of his numerous mistresses. One of these was another Lucrezia, who bore him three daughters, along with a courtesan named Masina. These women lived in the greatest of papal luxury, with mansions, vineyards and all manner of wealth lavished on them.

As far as Martin Luther was concerned, the sheer hypocrisy of Catholicism was the root of all evil. No seat could be closer to the Devil than the papal throne, and no place more a semblance of Hell than Vatican City itself. Always conscious of his monastic background within that establishment, Luther was constantly plagued by a fear that the Devil was after him. 'Early this morning', he wrote in his journal, 'when I awoke, the fiend began disputing with me. Thou art a great sinner, said he, to which I replied, Canst not thou tell me something new, Satan?'[23]

Through such writings, Luther created a concept which, in later times, became popularly identified as 'the Devil within' — a notion that was widely promulgated by the Puritan sect in its doctrine that people are inherently wicked and can do nothing about it. Given that people's minds and bodies were said to be the residences of Satan, they must do nothing to make his life in any way satisfying or pleasurable. This was to be achieved through lives of personal deprivation, free from extravagance, ambition, and devoid of pleasures. By this means, it was reckoned that the Devil would be made to suffer in his lodgings.

The mainstream Anglican High Church of Tudor times, from the latter 1500s, took a middle-ground stance in its Protestant outlook, retaining a good deal of the Catholic colour. But the austere Puritans gained considerable strength alongside, and were soon destined to control the nation. When that time came, the self-righteous ministers proved to be as hypocritical as the Roman clergy, and were equally brutal in their treatment of those who took any form of stance against them.

11

INFERNAL PURSUITS

Vow to the Devil

The laws of England had included references to witchcraft from the 9th-century Saxon days of King Alfred the Great, but the connection was never made directly between witchcraft and Devil worship in those times. Satan did not feature in the English culture of the period — not for the native Britons, nor for the integrated Anglo-Saxons. The formative legal citations of the era were mainly related to customary rural practices, given as 'the worship of heathen gods, and the sun or moon, fire or flood, water, wells or stones, or any kind of wood or trees'.

The preserved 'heathen god' cultures were essentially those of the Celtic and early Romano Britons, whereas the Anglo-Saxon kings had, by that time, become Christianized. But, when their forebears had first entered Britain as invaders from Northern Germany in the 5th century, the Angles and Saxons had their own gods such as Woden and Thunor, so it was always the case that the old gods of Britain were foreign to them. But although the races were largely amalgamated as Christians 400 years later in Alfred's time, the traditions of British gods like Taranis and Esus still persisted in some regions, along with remnant Saxon beliefs in Woden and others. Additionally there were the great lords of the greenwood such as Kearne, the horned one, and the stag-god of the *Caille Daouine* in the northern forests of Caledonia.

The Christianized Anglo-Saxons approved of none of these deities, and considered those who followed the ancient customs to be witches. But they did acknowledge that certain powers could be attributed to the old gods, and the invocation of such powers was declared to be witchcraft. An early proclamation in this regard was issued at Grately, Hampshire, by King Athelstan in about 932. His law decreed:

> And we have ordained respecting witchcrafts, and
> lyblacs [sorcerers], and morthdaeds [murderers]: if
> any one should be thereby killed, and he could not
> deny it, that he be liable in his life. But if he will
> deny it, and at threefold ordeal shall be guilty; that
> he be 120 days in prison; and after that let kindred
> take him out, and give to the king 120 shillings ...
> that he evermore desist from the like.[1]

In their consideration of presumed witchery that might affect the crops and harvests, the Christian churchmen of the Saxons had their own spells, rituals and incantations to restore fertility to the land. A related Saxon spell from the 10th century begins: 'Here is the remedy whereby thou mayest restore thy fields, if they will not produce well, or where any uncanny thing has befallen them, like magic or witchcraft'.[2]

Although witches were admonished in later times for concocting plant remedies, the earliest known English medical manual contains a series of recommended herbal 'prescriptions for divers ailments', with directions for their manufacture and application. Prepared by a Saxon physician named Bald, and based on medicines from the days of King Alfred, it contains numerous recipes that were a part of everyday life in the 10th century.[3] But eventually, when the witch-hunts began a few hundred years later, they were all classified by the Church as potions of illegal sorcery.

Emanating from that same 10th-century era is the first known English reference to the Devil in connection with afflictions and disease. The Saxon bishop, known as Wulfstan of Winchester, identified that,

> From the Devil comes every evil, every misery, and
> no remedy. Where he finds incautious men, he
> sends on themselves, or sometimes on their cattle,
> some terrible ailment, and they proceed to vow
> alms by the Devil's suggestion, either to a well or to
> a stone, or else to some unlawful things.[4]

Blood for Satan

During the next 500 years, there were some instances when witches were blamed for individual crimes or unfortunate events as determined by the *Law of Athelstan* and its revisions. In a typical late 10th-century example, a woman and her son were tried for driving spikes into the image of a man. The woman was taken and drowned in the River Thames at London Bridge, but the son escaped and was outlawed. In 1337, a man was charged with disobeying legal instruction by not delivering the Devil as a manorial court witness in Hatfield, Hertfordshire. Given the Devil's failure to appear before the judge as summoned, the case was dismissed![5] It was not, however, until as late as 1566 that England's first major trial of witches was held at Chelmsford in Essex. Whilst the nation's Protestants had been subdued by the short-term Catholic monarchy of Queen Mary I (known as *Bloody Mary*) in the 1550s, the puritanical clergy had forged their own course, setting their sights against defenceless women in order to formulate and assert their own methods of social control.

The Chelmsford witch trial was an unprecedented historical landmark, which established the legality of courts accepting unsupported evidence from well-rewarded children. It also introduced the notion of Devil's Marks — blemishes or bodily imperfections, often as small as flea bites, that served to reveal and identify witches. These 'marks' were later referenced in the work, *De Confessionibus Maleficorum et Sagarum* (Of the Confessions of Warlocks and Witches), by the German theologian Peter Binsfeld in 1596. Binsfeld was the Catholic Bishop of Trier, and was not convinced by the Protestant theory of Devil's Marks. But, more generally, the European inquisitors accepted the idea since it was another way of proving the association between witches and the Devil. Binsfeld's writings were rather more concerned with extracting confessions by way of torture, and he claimed that, however violently enforced, such confessions should always be believed.[6]

Unlike the sorcery trials in Europe, the Tudor witch trials of Elizabethan England (following the era of *Bloody Mary*) focused on charges of *maleficium*, not heresy, and convicted witches were hanged rather than burned. Burning at the stake was rare in England except for cases of treason. Torture of the inquisitional style was not used in interrogations, although certain procedures for testing witches were in themselves deadly. These tests included water immersion, as originally prescribed by Pope Nicholas in 886. With hands and feet bound (often a thumb tied to a toe), the innocent sank and drowned in the moats, rivers and ponds, whereas, in a 'no win' situation, those who floated and survived were necessarily guilty and were executed.

Beyond the Elizabethan realm, in Scotland, torture and burning did become commonplace for a time. In 1594, Alesoun Balfour was accused of trying to murder the Earl of Orkney by means of witchcraft because she was found to have possessed a piece of wax. Taken to Kirkwall Castle, she was kept for 48 hours in the 'caspie claws' — vice-like frames for crushing the legs. Her husband was pressed beneath 700 pounds of iron bars, her daughter tortured with 'pilliwinks' (thumbscrews), and her son received 57 hammer blows to saw-edged wedges driven into his joints. The guilty party in the murder plot turned out to be the Earl's own servant, Thomas Paplay, who was duly executed. But Alesoun was strangled and burned all the same, even though a subsequent court hearing ruled her to have been innocent. Other similar events occurred in places like Inverkip, Paisley and Kirkaldy, where victims were covered in pitch, stood in tar-barrels and set ablaze.[7]

The primary accused at Chelmsford in 1566 had been Elizabeth Francis. She was said to have learned witchcraft from her grandmother, who taught her to renounce God, and to give of her blood to Satan. The incarnation of Satan was reckoned to be Elizabeth's spotted cat. Each time the cat did his owner a favour, Elizabeth was said to have cut herself and allowed him to lick her blood. At her wish, *Satan* was reckoned to have killed her unwanted child and made her husband lame.[8] In time, Elizabeth gave the cat away to an elderly woman called Agnes Waterhouse. She was charged in court with pursuing a similar course, willing *Satan* to kill the pigs, geese and cattle of her neighbours in return

151

for drops of her blood. She then had the cat kill her husband. Testimonies at the public hearing grew ever wilder, and it was claimed that the devilish cat would sometimes turn into a toad, or into a great dog with horns.[9]

The trial result was that Elizabeth Frances was sentenced to a year in prison, but old Agnes Waterhouse was hanged. Later, in 1579, Elizabeth faced further accusations of malevolent sorcery, and was this time strung on the gibbet with several other women. Then, in 1589, three more women (Joan Cunny, Joan Upney and Joan Prentice) were hanged for owning familiar pets, whereby they relinquished their souls to the Devil. Joan Prentice was reckoned to be in the service of Satan, whom she first met in an almshouse in the shape of a ferret. The trial transcript explains:

> Between the feasts of All Saints and the birth of
> our Lord God, the Devil appeared unto her in the
> almshouse aforesaid about ten of the clock in the
> night time, being in the shape and proportion of
> a dunnish coloured ferret, having fiery eyes. And
> the said examinate being alone in her chamber,
> and sitting upon a low stool preparing herself to
> bedward, the ferret standing with his hinder legs
> upon the ground and his forelegs settled upon
> her lap ... To whom this examinate, being greatly
> amazed, said 'In the name of God, What art
> thou?' The ferret answered 'I am Satan; fear me
> not, my coming unto thee is to do thee no hurt
> but to obtain thy soul'.[10]

Likewise, the diabolic familiars of Joan Cunny were said to have been two black frogs named Jack and Gill, and Joan Upney possessed a mole and a toad. Witnesses testified that each of the satanic creatures had, by the Devil's will, 'slain men, women, and children, and had committed very wicked and horrible actions, divers and sundrye times'. Thereupon, sentencing the witches, 'the judge proceeded, and pronounced the sentence of death against them, as worthely they had deserved'.

The Devil Within

A key aspect of the witch trials that followed was that the Devil was always presented as a physical entity. He featured either as an individual character in a variety of guises, or by way of representative pets and other creatures that were reckoned to embody his demonic spirit. This was a very useful device for the prosecutors in that it enabled the Devil to be present in any number of locations at the same time. It meant that just about any pet could be adjudged as a familiar spirit and blamed for all manner of local tragedies and unfortunate incidents.

By contrast, the Devil, as applied to a more generally enforced Protestant theology outside the witch persecutions, was described as a hideous unseen force whose intervention induced and encouraged crime. Thomas Cranmer, Archbishop of Canterbury until 1566, claimed that the unseen Devil could enter peoples' minds to introduce sinful thoughts and notions of evil. In this respect, the 'Devil within' posed a tremendous threat against which people's only recourse was the strength of their faith, the constant study of their Bibles and their frequent, regular attendance at the churches and chapels, where the Devil could not inflict his will. Cranmer blamed this unseen inner Devil for every adversity, and listed in his *Catechisms* the numerous afflictions suffered at the Devil's command, including 'sadness, sorrow, trouble of conscience, faintness of heart, sickness of the body, poverty, slanders, despising, reproaches, persecutions, battle, sedition, hunger, pestilence and all plagues'. The Devil's agency was in no way considered a theological puzzle to be debated. It was preached as a demonstrable certainty to be recognized and confronted, and the havoc he wreaked on Earth was only too evident.[11]

It was asserted, nevertheless, that the Devil, in his ultimately personal form, was as cited in the New Testament epistle of 1 Peter 5:8, which states, 'Be sober, be vigilant; because your adversary the Devil, as a roaring lion, walketh about, seeking whom he may devour'. In this regard, it was common at the time to portray the gateway to Hell as the mouth of a great lion.

The perception throughout the Protestant movement was that the doorway which afforded Satan's re-entry into the world, from the confines of the abyss, had been opened for him by the evil Catholic Church. In his work *The Practice of Prelates*, the Lutheran reformer William Tyndale described how the Pope had 'put down the kingdom of Christ, and hath set up the ministers of Satan'. He further explained:

> The kingdoms of the Earth and the glory of them, which Christ refused, did the Devil proffer unto the Pope; and he immediately fell from Christ, and worshipped the Devil, and received them.[12]

Thus it was that, when Elizabethan England was under threat from Catholic Spain in 1588, the courtier Anthony Marten described the invading Spanish Armada as the work of 'the beast from the bottomless pit'.[13]

King Philip II of Spain had been married to Queen Elizabeth's elder sister, Mary Tudor, who had reigned before her for a few years (1553–58). Despite the separation of the English Church from papal control by her father, Henry VIII, Mary was an ardent Catholic and had taken up the Spanish cause against Protestants in England. She had almost 300 religious dissenters burned alive, including Archbishop Cranmer. Following her early death at the age of forty-two, the merchant classes of Elizabeth's subsequent reign joined forces with the Dutch Protestants to suppress Spain's international commercial pretensions. The response was King Philip's Armada, a great sea invasion that was successfully repelled with the considerable help of inclement weather.

In criticising the Catholic-led Renaissance, Thomas Cranmer's chaplain, Thomas Becon, had asserted that 'people are but pilgrims in the world, who bring nothing into it, and ultimately can take nothing out'. Thus it was that things belonging to the world were not of God; they were the possessions of Satan. 'To love the world', wrote Becon, 'is to be God's enemy'.

It was upon such principles that the extremes of Puritan austerity were eventually based. With Catholicism finally ejected as a national belief system from Britain, sinful places like theatres and alehouses, along with pastimes such as sports and dancing, were declared to be Satan's back-doors into society. They were said to 'mock at religion and abuse the holy scriptures'. In the days of William Shakespeare, the theatre was said to be 'the schoolhouse of Satan, and the chapel of ill-counsel'. Playwrights were identified with the mind of the Devil, conceiving their seductive deceptions, whilst the playhouse was deemed the Devil's equivalent of a church, wherein the players were 'the limbs, proportion and members of the Evil One'.[14] Human senses were provided, claimed the Puritans, 'so that man might hear the scriptures and see God's justice'. But senses lulled by pleasurable experience were vulnerable to diabolic invasion: 'The Devil tickles our senses, especially by way of poetry which slippeth down like sugar'. The only way to resist his temptations was to avoid all inclination to pleasures, entertainments and earthly delights.

Lord of the Dance

In 1562, the French Protestants (Huguenots) rose against their Catholic monarchy, and the ensuing civil struggles, which lasted until 1598, became known as the Wars of Religion. The House of Valois was then in power, but the contemporary Regent of France was the Florentine, Catherine de Medici. She was the niece of Pope Clement VII, and was largely responsible for the hideous Saint Bartholomew's Day Massacre of 24 August 1572. On that ill-fated day, which began a wave of Catholic mob violence against the Protestants, more than 3,000 Huguenots were slaughtered in Paris, while another 12,000 were killed elsewhere in France. This clearly delighted Pope Gregory XIII, who sent a personal note of congratulation to Catherine's court. During the next two months, similar massacres took place in Toulouse, Bordeaux, Lyon, Bourges, Rouen, and Orléans. The overall number of Huguenot victims is unknown, but the total is presumed to be close to 100,000.

In the wake of this outrage, Jean Bodin, a jurist and member of the Parlement de Française, wrote that Catherine de Medici was the most evil of satanists, who had performed a diabolical ceremony known as the Black Mass. This unholy rite was said to be similar to the gruesome Mass of Saint-Sécair,[15] a ritual performed in Gascony with the purpose of causing death to an enemy. Such Masses could only be said in ruined or abandoned churches where bats, owls and toads were resident. Better still if Christian congregations had been terminated and forbidden there because of some terrible event. At the stroke of 11 o'clock pm, the corrupt priest, with his illicit mistress as an attendant, would begin to recite the Mass backwards, invoking the name of Satan, and being sure to finish at the last stroke of midnight. The eucharistic host would be triangular and black, and instead of wine there would be polluted water from a well in which an unbaptized child had been drowned. The priest would then make the sign of the cross with his left foot on the ground before him, and would pronounce the name of the victim who, it was believed, would soon waste away and die.[16]

This destructive type of Mass was no invention of the era, but a long-standing custom which originally had nothing to do with Satan. Priests of the orthodox Roman Church had for centuries used death-dealing wax figures when saying malicious Requiem Masses to dispatch their enemies' souls to Hell, rather than deliver them from its pains.[17]

In December 1579, Jean Bodin wrote to the president of the Parlement de Paris to warn him and the magistrates about Catholic sorcerers and the Devil. There were many pamphlets at the time, claiming that sorcerers were harmless, and Bodin's intention was to have these writings denounced in law. He wrote that he wished to alert readers of such literature to the fact that 'there is no crime that could be more atrocious or deserve more serious punishment'. He asserted that he wished to speak out against those who 'try by all means to rescue the sorcerers through printed books'. Moreover, he insisted that 'Satan has men in his grasp who write, publish and speak, claiming that nothing said against sorcerers is true'. Unfortunately for Bodin, his campaign backfired. Many wondered how he knew so much about the Devil, and why he was so curious if he was not himself involved with witchcraft. The State prosecutor ordered the Lieutenant General of Laon to search Bodin's home for evidence, but there was nothing to be found. Subsequently, in 1580, Bodin published his book, *La Démonomanie des Sorciers* (The Demon Mania of Sorcerers), claiming that 'A sorcerer is one who, by commerce with the Devil, has a full intention of attaining his own ends'.[18] Regarding the necessity for rooting out devilish witchcraft, he asserted:

> Now, if there is any means to appease the wrath of God; to gain his blessing; to strike awe into some by the punishment of others; to preserve some from being infected by others; to diminish the number of evil-doers; to make secure the life of the well-disposed, and to punish the most detestable crimes of which the human mind can conceive, it is to punish with the utmost rigour the witches.[19]

Of the witches' assemblies and Sabbats, Jean Bodin wrote, 'The places where sorcerers meet are remarkable and generally distinguished by some trees, or even a cross'. Ancient cromlechs and granite dolmens were favoured sites in France, as they were in England. Also popular venues were the market crosses of English towns.[20] One of these was Banbury Cross in Oxfordshire, which was torn down by Puritan witchhunters in 1650 (the present cross having been later erected in Victorian times). A seemingly odd chord is struck by the fact that the cross was a Christian monument built in Saxon times, but it was demolished by ardent Christians because it had become a place of pagan congregation. At the Maytime festival, an elected girl, representing the Earth goddess and decorated with magical rings and bells, would gallop her white horse through the fields in the hope of increasing their fertility. She would then complete her ride at the Cross, being led into town amid music and general merrymaking:

Ride a cock horse to Banbury Cross,
To see a fine lady upon a white horse.
Rings on her fingers and bells on her toes,
She shall have music wherever she goes.

As given in 1589, a 'cock horse' was a straight stick of broom placed between the legs and ridden in a skipping and leaping fashion, as if on a horse.[21] It was referred to as the witches' broomstick, as might be the handle of a broom, and was the origin of the concept that witches rode upon broomsticks (or broom-staves), although not upon complete brooms as so commonly portrayed, and they certainly did not fly in the air.

Banbury Cross is not the only pagan rural song to survive as a children's nursery rhyme. Many of these popular lyrics have pagan derivations, especially the best known Ring Dance which swirled around the tree that bore the most sacred fruit of the moon goddess, the Mulberry:[22]

Here we go 'round the mulberry bush,
The mulberry bush, the mulberry bush.
Here we go 'round the mulberry bush,
So early in the morning.

This particular dance was of an especially imitative variety, usually performed by children who would enact various sexual functions as they swung around the tree. Today, the words have all been changed beyond the first verse, with references now to washing clothes and sweeping floors. But the original words and actions were far from innocent, for this dance was an unabashed rustic fertility rite.

In Scotland, the Aberdeen witches, thirteen of whom were executed in 1597, were accused of devilish dancing around the Market Cross and Fish Cross of the town. They were also charged with being 'under the conduct of thy master, the Devil, dancing in a ring' around a great stone at the foot of Craigleauch Hill.[23]

Such dances were processional to begin, in a follow-the-leader style, with the Devil figure at the front.[24] Once at the stone or cross, the Devil would lead them around it in a ring, becoming the 'ring leader'. He would then close up behind the last, 'taking the hindmost', to complete the continuing circle.

Of all the ritual practices which the Church condemned, the Ring Dance was among the most detested. In his *Discourse des Sorciers*, Henri Boguet, Grand Justice of the district of Saint Claude in Burgundy, likened the dancing of witches and gypsies to the hideous revels of the fairies, whom he called 'devils incarnate'.[25] This type of dance was possibly based on that of Apollo and the Muses from Greek mythology, but it also had a tradition in Christianity.

Among the most respected theologians of the Catholic Church in the late 4th century had been St Augustine of Hippo. Renowned for his numerous epistles and philosophical writings, Augustine wrote about a Ring Dance that he reckoned was directly attributed to Jesus and his Apostles.[26] He recorded every aspect of the dance and its related chant, from start to finish, as it had appeared in the 2nd-century *Acts of John*. Sections of the ritual were eventually read at the Second Council of Nicaea in 787, shortly before King Charlemagne became Holy Roman Emperor. An extract from the *Acts of John* reads:

> He [Jesus] gathered all of us together and said, 'Before I am delivered up unto them let us sing an hymn to the Father, and so go forth to that which lieth before us'. He bade us therefore make as it were a ring, holding one another's hands, and himself standing in the midst he said, 'Answer Amen unto me'. He began to sing an hymn and to say 'Glory be to the Father'. And we, going about in a ring, answered him, 'Amen'.[27]

From that point, the dance continued through a lengthy sequence of chanting between Jesus in the centre and the others circling around him. Whether or not this apocryphal portrayal is historically factual or not is of no consequence; its importance lies in the fact that such dances were performed in those times, as had been recorded in the *Acts of John*.

In this respect, it was not so much that the latter-day witches and moon cultists had taken over an originally Christian tradition, but rather more that the cultures had grown in parallel, with similar rituals from early times. It was the Roman Church which had changed the rules from the 4th century, when Emperor Constantine established a hybrid style of Christian faith which had very little to do with the customs and conventions of the religion whose name it purloined. Consequently, when the Ring Dance was performed in the Middle Ages, with costumed figures (sometimes representing hobgoblins such as Puck or Robin Goodfellow) at its centre, it was perceived as a wholly pagan event by the unenlightened bishops of the day. It was seen to be representative of a witches' coven because there were thirteen participants in all, with one in the centre and twelve in the ring. What never occurred to the inquisitors was the fact that Jesus and his immediate fraternity had constituted their own coven of himself and the twelve delegate apostles. Such groups of thirteen were not invented by medieval witches, as the inquisitors imagined, they were a relic of the time-honoured lore of many kindred cultures.

Irreconcilable War

In 1584 Reginald Scott, an English justice of the peace in Kent, took up the cause against the witch persecutors, refuting the idea of any diabolic influence in his treatise *The Discoverie of Witchcraft*. 'If witches could cast successful spells', he asked, 'then why do they not all live in a grand style? Instead, so many of them lead lives of misery, ultimately coming to the gallows'. He thus held that the prosecution of those accused of witchcraft was contrary to the dictates of reason as well as of religion, and he placed the responsibility firmly at the door of the Church. He noted that no woman could be truly safe from an accusation of witchcraft, stating, 'Neither can any avoid being a witch, except she lock herself up in a chamber'.[28] Scott was, however, an exponent of juggling and performance magic in his own right, even producing

160

a book of magic tricks that became a standard reference work for stage magicians. Consequently, his theory concerning witches was soon discounted because he was himself a conjuror, and many copies of his book on the subject were publicly burned.

Soon afterwards, in 1589, Dr Dietrich Flade, an eminent jurist and chief judge of the Electoral Court at Trier in Germany, revolted from the ranks of orthodoxy. After having sentenced many people to death, he admitted that it was all unreal. The confessions forced out of the victims of his torture chamber, he claimed, were either the result of madness or the necessity to confess anything and everything in order to shorten their fearsome ordeal. But when Flade expressed this doubt, he was immediately arrested by the authority of the archbishop, and charged with having sold himself to Satan. Thus, he was subjected to the same tortures that he had described, until he confessed everything that his interrogators suggested.[29] At length, he was strangled and burned, to become the highest-ranking official ever convicted and executed for witchcraft and Devil worship.

Meanwhile, from the camp of the persecutors, the most curious work of Protestant demonology was the 1587 *Theatrum Diabolorum* by Sigmund Feyerabend, the Heidelberg publisher of the famous Lutheran Bible. The *Theatrum* is a voluminous collection of essays by Martin Luther's followers concerning the ways of the Black One. In a section written by a Reverend Hocker, it is explained that the number of vices that could be attributed to devilish interference was 2,665,866,746,664, while others put the figure at not less than ten thousand billion![30]

John Calvin had said, 'Whoever shall now contend that it is unjust to put heretics and blasphemers to death will, knowingly and willingly, incur their very guilt'. He wrote in detail of the 'irreconcilable war' that must constantly be waged against the Devil, who 'plots to ruin and extinguish Christ's kingdom'. So forceful and consistent were such decrees from Calvin and others of the extreme Protestant movement that, for the longest time, their various church groups were focused almost entirely on withstanding the satanic influence. This had the effect of putting people in fear of their every action, their every word and their every thought — for they knew that the Devil reigned on Earth and was in control of everything that happened. People were taught that their greatest misfortune was to have been born into an evil world that separated them from God. Their only hope, if any existed, was to lean wholly on the instruction of the preachers — those of the ministerial elite, who were the only ones whose recommendations for personal salvation God might possibly take into account.

12

WAY OF THE DEVIL

Father of Lies

From just about any perspective, the early Protestant arguments concerning the Devil were almost impossible for people to comprehend. In the first instance, it was preached that there was no greater power than God. Thus, it was determined that the Devil could only exist with God's blessing. On that basis, the Devil was said to be a chosen instrument of God's purpose. By obeying the will of God (in effect the will of the clergy), there should be no need for people to fear the Devil. But the Devil ruled the world in any event, because it was the very place where God's retribution was waged, and he had put the Devil in charge. Hence, there was no escape. The very fact of being born into the world meant that God was already serving his punishment, with the people as Satan's quarry. It was therefore to be expected that such things as pain, poverty, misfortune and despair were the natural manner of existence, and it was the duty of churchmen to make these things felt with severity.

This truly was the age when 'fire and brimstone' preaching began. Not only did the 16th-century Protestant followers have the power of the Devil to consider, but also the unmitigated wrath of God. They were taught that there was no way they could earn the love of God since, by the very nature of their earthly existence, they did not, and could not, deserve it. All effort to appease him was futile since he had created them to exist in sin, rendering them unworthy of his consideration. He would select only his chosen elite for the grant of his mercy. The best that others could do was to obey the preaching elite, to pray earnestly and, above all things, to abandon physical lust and material gratification in the hope that God might possibly notice. Whereas the Catholic Church promoted a view of confession, repentance and forgiveness, there was no such ideal in the hard-line Lutheran belief that rectified actions and penitence had any effect. Just one sin, just one foot out of line, were enough to secure eternal damnation without recourse or reprieve. There was only one way to stand any possible chance of salvation, and that was not to make a single wrong move, or have a single wrong thought, ever.

The greatest fear of the Protestant 'divines' (theologians) was that the Devil was clever enough to convince people that he did not exist, or perhaps to persuade them that he was at least ineffectual as an influence on their lives. According to Puritans like John Olde, in his work *A Short Description of Antichrist*, Satan was the 'father of lies'. Nobody could be believed (except, of course, the ministers) because all human thoughts and actions were products of the Devil in the evil world that he alone ruled: 'It is the policy and practice of the Devil, the father of lies, to lay siege against the truth of God'.[1] In this environment, the events of everyday life were all perceived to be contrivances of the Devil, who secured his mastery with tricks and deceitful illusions. There was no way to circumvent this, for it was the reality of mortal existence, to the extent that even the best considered actions were not sanctioned or authorized by God. In the 1590s, this view was elaborated in the puritanical writings of William Perkins of Christ's College, Cambridge:

> Most common people think that good meaning will save them; but a man may profess any religion, and have good meaning, and yet not know one step to the kingdom of Heaven, but remain the vassal and slave of Satan. For a man may have outward civil justice and civil policy, and mean well, yet still be the servant of the Devil.[2]

The distinction between 'good and bad meaning' was, in the view of the clerics, a straightforward one. While it was people's destiny to suffer, and to do so praising God for the privilege, there were those who sought alternatives to make their lives more pleasant by way of various games, pastimes and entertainments. But such things were declared to be in defiance of the Will of God, and were therefore the Way of the Devil. It was also considered ungodly to seek or take advice from anyone but the churchmen. Hence it was that elderly family members, who might be deemed wise through experience, and would naturally be consulted for their opinions, stood the greatest chance of being condemned by the clerical regulators as oracles, witches, wizards and diviners. Being elderly or experienced in the ways of the world did not, in the eyes of the Church, make one morally or socially wise. On the contrary, each year of life rendered one more capable of sin and deception; each additional breath from the foul air of the Devil's belly enabled one to lie more expediently, and each night that passed imbued the soul with an increasing darkness — a fact proven by the waning eyesight of the aged, who were the 'jugglers of Satan's wiles'. William Perkins maintained that 'All diviners, charmers, jugglers, and all wizards, commonly called wise men and wise women', were guilty of witchcraft and deserved to be hanged.[3] In his *Discourse of the Damned Art of Witchcraft*, Perkins asserted that, 'because witches have renounced God ... and have bound themselves, by way of other laws, to the service of the enemies of the Church, then death must be justly assigned since, in God's view, a witch may not live'.[4]

In line with Martin Luther's opinion, the Protestant belief centred on an idea that the institution fronting the Devil's wicked campaign on Earth was the Church of Rome. The papal office was declared to be that of the Antichrist, and the pomp and ceremonies of his Church were the seductive trappings of the Devil. John Olde declared that popish beliefs were the 'doctrines of devils', and the Pope was 'the Devil's vicar and successor, or else the Devil himself'.

Although the Anglican Church maintained an episcopal hierarchy, its ceremonies and ritual were generally abandoned at local community level in favour of solemn preaching. Vestments, altars, sanctified objects, candles, music, crucifixes, flowers and any form of ornamentation were discarded by the local parsons, and the chapels became thoroughly bland, cold and austere. It was from this practice of a perceived 'purity' in approach (as opposed to High Church idolatry) that the term Puritan was coined by outsiders, almost in mockery, for this most extreme branch of the Protestant movement.

Despite the Protestant hatred of all things Catholic, there was a commonality of opinion in that both groups considered women to be the primary source of evil at Satan's behest. After all, it was Eve who had been seduced by the serpent, not Adam. He had subsequently been the victim of Eve's wiles, but the seed of transgression was that of the woman. A pamphlet, entitled *The Devil Incarnate*, described the female body as a 'snare of Satan', while another tract, *The Reign of the Devil*, described the treacherous nature of the female mind.[5] The point was made, however, that the greater fault might well rest with Adam, since he had been deceived by a mere woman, whereas Eve had been seduced by the incredible power of Satan himself.[6] This led many to concede that both men and women were equally depraved by sin, and equally at risk from the temptations of the Devil. It was agreed, nevertheless, that the sins of pride and vanity were essentially feminine weaknesses. A resultant work in 1583 by the reformer Philip Stubbes, entitled *Anatomie of Abuses*, contained a near repeat of what Cyprian of Carthage had written in the 3rd century concerning the Devil's face-paints and the depravity of female dress: 'Women aspire to seduce and corrupt men by the way they dress, and they adorn themselves diabolically against the wishes of God'.

Slaves of the Devil

In Scotland, the witch trials commenced in the middle 1500s and, within the space of 100 years, about 1,000 people were executed, 85 percent of whom were female. The most notable trials involved a number of people from East Lothian who, in 1590, were accused of witchcraft in St Andrew's Auld Kirk, North Berwick. With 70 implicated defendants, the North Berwick trials continued for two years, and the accused included Francis Stewart, Earl of Bothwell, on a charge of high treason for plotting with others to murder King James VI of Scots by means of sorcery. They were said to have wrapped a wax image of the King in a stolen piece of his clothing, and burnt it. They also baptised a cat with the name of the King and threw it into the sea. The Grand Master of the coven, John Fian, was reckoned to have opened a locked church with a hand cut from a corpse on a gibbet, and had then performed an abominable service to the Devil.[7] The list of accusations at the North Berwick trials was seemingly endless.

Confessions were extracted by torture, and several people were convicted of having used witchcraft to create a storm in an attempt to sink the ship on which King James and his bride, Anne of Denmark, had been voyaging. The records maintain that one of the accused captives, Agnes Sampson, was fastened to the wall of her cell by a witch's bridle — an iron facial strap with sharp prongs forced into her mouth. When Agnes was eventually brought for interrogation, she had been kept without sleep for many days, and resultantly admitted to 53 separate indictments before being strangled and burned. Agnes was pressed into admitting that she knew the Devil and, when describing him, she confessed:

> The Devil was clad in a black gown, with a black hat upon his head ... His face was terrible, his nose like the beak of an eagle; great burning eyes. His hands and legs were hairy, with claws upon his hands, and feet like the gryphon.[8]

In 1597, a few years after the North Berwick trials, King James wrote a treatise entitled *Daemonology*, concerning witchcraft and the Devil. Raised as a Presbyterian of the Scottish Kirk, James was absolutely convinced that witchcraft was a Devil-worshipping cult, and that witches held nocturnal gatherings to pay homage to their despicable leader. He saw the practice as a complete reversal of the Protestant behaviour with which he was familiar, and endeavoured to persuade the many sceptics of his court that witches truly did exist:

167

> The fearful abounding, at this time in this country, of these detestable slaves of the Devil, the witches or enchanters, hath moved me to dispatch in post this following treatise of mine, not in any way to serve for a show of my learning and ingine, but only, moved of conscience, to preasse thereby, so far as I can, to resolve the doubting hearts of many; both that such assaults of Satan are most certainly practised, and that the instruments thereof merit most severely to be punished.[9]

James was entirely certain that witches' circles and their conjurations were able to raise malevolent spirits.[10] He referred his readers specifically to the earlier work, *La Démonomanie des Sorciers* by Jean Bodin, where they would find 'many examples of witchcraft collected with great diligence'. Bodin's writing had an enormous influence in fomenting the terrible witch craze that raged with such intensity in Scotland thereafter, as well as in England and Europe.[11]

The mood of the era was well suited to an exorcism fever among certain members of the Protestant clergy, even though Martin Luther had abhorred this originally Catholic tradition, and hated anything that even hinted at ecclesiastical magic.[12] The cult of the Virgin Mary, and the astonishing cures associated with her numerous shrines, were examples cited by Luther of the Church of Rome's own endorsement of magic and superstition. But, despite the Lutheran view, cases of demonic possession provided an ideal way for the Puritan ministers to demonstrate their influence and thereby exert their authority. Perhaps the best known exorcist of the 1590s was John Darrel, who specialized in expelling demons from children and young adults in middle England. Eventually, however, one of the said demoniacs gave evidence against Darrel, insisting that the minister had concocted the whole fiasco of his exorcism as an elaborate deception for a large crowd of spectators. In 1599, Darrel was charged with fraud and brought before the court of John Whitgift, Archbishop of

Canterbury. Found guilty and condemned, he was stripped of his privilege, removed from the ministry and briefly imprisoned. Subsequently, it was decreed that the office of an approved Protestant exorcist required the grant of a particular licence from the Anglican Church authorities.[13]

Puritanical exorcisms took many forms, among the favoured of which was to beat the possessed person about the body so hard and consistently that the Devil was made too uncomfortable and was compelled to depart. At the other end of the scale, for pastors well versed in the scriptures, a scholarly debate might be conducted with the Devil, forcing him into the embarrassment of surrender and departure because of his lack of biblical knowledge! Either way, the object of the exercise was that of a public performance that was reckoned to provide 'a better lesson than any pulpit sermon'.

The Christian philosopher, Samuel Clarke, documented an exorcist's alleged conversation with the Devil in his work, *The Lives of Thirty-Two English Divines*. The case concerned the minister Robert Balsom, who heard the voice of Satan emanating from a demoniac's neck. 'He is mine!', exclaimed the Devil to the gathered crowd; 'If God would let me loose upon you, I should find enough in the best of you to make you all mine'. Balsom responded, 'But thou art bound Satan!'. Then turning to the crowd, he continued, 'What a gracious God have we, that suffers not Satan to have his will upon us'.[14] Numerous possession narratives of this type (often presented as lengthy accounts) were preached and passed around in pamphlets in order to demonstrate how the Devil could be confronted by way of godly intellect and the courage of devotional faith. By this means, the ministers became greatly revered and gained significant individual levels of social control.

The Devil was thought to be lurking everywhere at that time — in every unfortunate circumstance, in every undesirable action, in every impious thought, and in every unpleasant event. His power of temptation had no equal and, since he was uniquely empowered by God to spare no unscrupulous device in testing people's faith, there was no way to know when, where or how he might make his approach. He was portrayed as an unprecedented trickster, who might appear in any place in any guise. In this respect, the preachers made good use of St Paul's New Testament letter to the Corinthians, wherein he stated that, in a realm where false apostles and deceitful workers abound, 'even Satan himself is transformed into an angel of light'.[15] People must therefore be vigilant in watching for him at every turn. On one occasion, the mathematician Thomas Allen visited a colleague in Hertfordshire, and left his pocket watch (a recent invention) on a shelf in his quarters. Later, the housemaids reported that they had been afraid to find the Devil ticking in Allen's room, but had managed to capture him with tongs, and had thrown him out into the moat to drown him!

During the course of this Devil mania, a demonic literary figure called Mephistophilis appeared in 1592 by way of a German legend, entitled *The Historie of the Damnable Life and Deserved Death of Doctor John Faustus*. It was subsequently adapted by the Elizabethan writer Christopher Marlowe for his English play, *The Tragical History of Doctor Faustus* (posthumously published in 1604). The story is of how Faustus sells his soul to the Devil in order to gain power and knowledge. A moralistic tale, it relates how the nature of a person who chooses material gain over spiritual belief will decay, as a result of which he will lose his soul.[16] On one occasion, the devil Mephistophilis, when conjured by Marlowe's Dr Faustus, appears in the habit of a Franciscan friar.[17]

There is a striking resemblance between the original source title for Marlowe's play, *The Historie of the Damnable Life and Deserved Death of Doctor John Faustus,* and that of an anonymous pamphlet, 'News from Scotland': *Declaring the Damnable Life and Death of Doctor Fian,* published in London during the previous year. As detailed above, Dr Fian was the master of the North Berwick witches, believed to have plotted the death of King James VI of Scots.

On 30 May 1593, Christopher Marlowe was stabbed to death at a London meeting house in Deptford, having been arrested a few days earlier, charged with atheism and released on bail. The full details of his murder remain a mystery, but appear to have been related to his work for the Elizabethan Secret Service.[18] That apart, the Puritan evangelist Thomas Beard had his own view on the matter. Since Marlowe was a playwright, he was obviously in the service of Satan, and had deserved to die a damnable death! In 1597 Beard wrote in his work, *The Theatre of God's Judgements*, that Marlowe was 'a playmaker, and a poet of scurrilitie ... a transgressor of God's commandments, who received the admirable judgement of God'.

Rampant Power

The latter 16th century was very much an era of sensational Protestant literature. Illustrated pamphlets and leaflets were widely available concerning items of newsworthy public interest, and top of the list for popularity were accounts of violent crimes and murders. No matter whether these were premeditated actions or passionate deeds of impulse, and irrespective of the details as logged in official trial reports, the press centred its portrayals on the Devil as the constant protagonist.[19] Not only were people terrified of the Devil, but it seems that the avid readers of these regular bulletins actually wanted to be terrified. This suited the religious pastors since the pamphlet narratives served to heighten what they were preaching, and the ways of the Evil One were kept to the forefront of everyday news. Crime was a sin, and criminals were seduced into their wrong actions by the temptations of Satan. Thus, all crime was perceived to be the result of diabolic agency, which lured ordinary people into demonic acts by selling their souls to the Devil. Everyone was therefore a potential criminal, whose only route to avoidance was to resist all temptations as determined by the preachers.

Social records of the period indicate that the number of premeditated murders was proportionately low in comparison with those committed on violent impulse by one member of a family, or community group, against another. Many of these brutal assaults would not have resulted in murder if the physicians of the day had been more competent in treating the injured victims.[20] But such things were not mentioned in the pamphlets, whose sensational accounts were contrived to relate all such crimes to hideous schemes and planned motivation. In the majority of explanations, the Devil appeared as an actual character in the plot and, whatever the reality of the situation, it was always the Devil who made them do it: 'Then did the Devil entice them straight to murder, death and blood'.[21]

Over and above the bulletins and other literature relating to actual events, a great many ballads were also composed and widely distributed. Sometimes these were fictional or based on items of traditional folklore, but very often they were a different form of documenting the same desperate crimes. It was not uncommon for three or four separate ballads to be written in respect of the more notable murders and suicides. Once again, however, the inclusion of the Devil was essential to the lasting popularity of the lyrics. Always he was seen to lure, trick and entice his victims into injuring or killing themselves and others, as in the case of *The Poor Man in Essex*:

> See, quoth the Devil, vengeance doth
> pursue thee every hour.
> Go cursed wretch, quoth he,
> and rid away thy life.
> But murder first thy children young
> and miserable wife.[22]

Supplied with a wealth of such printed information, people were assured that the Evil One reigned supreme, and God was no comfort to them, for he was a terrible avenger intent to punish all who lived in Satan's world. The result was that people's greatest fear was a mistrust of themselves and the persistent threat that they might unwittingly stray out of line. Martin Luther had written that the Devil 'stuck closer to a man than his habit or his shirt, even closer than his skin'.[23]

In the context of this uncertainty, men were continually warned to keep a close eye on the women of their households.

Females were far more susceptible to diabolic influence and, in line with the Catholic perception, Protestant teaching also diagnosed the insatiable lust of women to be the most common snare of evil. Throughout the Italian-led Renaissance and the ensuing Northern Renaissance, the traditional connection between sin and the female form had been sidelined in a liberated world of sculpture and pictorial art which took female nudity to a level not seen since classical times. But this practice was soon curtailed by new Catholic rulings at the Council of Trent in the middle 1500s.[24] Prohibitions were subsequently enforced, and a new breed of specially trained artists called 'figleafers' came into being. Their function was to overpaint extant artwork, even the paintings of great masters like Michelangelo, Titian and Dürer, on an international scale, with strategically placed leaves and gossamer veils.[25] Much of their obliterative work remains on the paintings today, often applied to male nudes as well as female, despite interim partial restorations which have still left many of the spurious overpaintings intact.

Seemingly exempt from the ruling in both the Catholic and Protestant environments were depictions of witches who, from the early 16th century, were often portrayed revelling without clothes. It was not so much the Church's view that the naked female body should not be seen in the world of pictorial art. More to the point was the opinion that, when it was seen, it should be related directly to sin and devilish behaviour.

Throughout the length and breadth of Christendom, whether Roman or Lutheran, creative free will was overshadowed by trepidation as people became servile and hesitant against the rampant power of Satan and the merciless God whom he served. Rights to personal opinion were overwhelmed in matters of morality on which only the churchmen ruled. Whereas medieval Christianity had been very much a collective faith, people were newly conditioned to become isolated in the wrap of their own temptations. The Devil stalked his prey relentlessly from the cradle to the grave. He set his sights on vulnerable individuals, and was ready to inflict his malicious will at any opportunity. No one was safe from the prospect of his grasp, and the jaws of the eternal abyss were a figment of everyday belief as people strove earnestly to obey the pastoral rules in order to avoid diabolic invasion by the inexorable Prince of Darkness.

The Abominable Web

By way of intense rivalry, a Devil-centred competition raged between the Catholic and Protestant factions, and the Church of Rome was clearly incensed that its primary figurehead of threat and control had been hijacked by the opposition. The Catholic bishops sought, therefore, to prove that satanic activity had increased significantly because of the Protestant Reformation. Then, in their Counter Reformation campaign, the gypsies of Europe were dragged firmly into the witchcraft net by the inquisitors. Any person with no fixed place of residence was regarded with suspicion because an itinerant lifestyle was perceived as a means by which to evade Church authority.[26] Gypsies lived outside the towns and villages, and were thought to be very mysterious. Many gained temporary employment as woodcutters or splitters (stave-makers), as a product of which such trades, along with those of the pedlars, horse dealers and animal trainers, became subject to an all-embracing blanket excommunication by the Church of Rome. At the same time, a new style of Christian mythology was promoted in propagandist tales such as eventually found a revival two centuries later in Brothers Grimm nursery stories like *Hansel and Gretel* and *Little Red Riding Hood*. In their original form, stories of this type were tactically designed to make children fearful of straying into the woods, where child-eating werewolves and witches might lurk — wild places that were the domain of gypsies and wicked woodcutters, where the Church was unable to wield any regulatory influence.

Other affronts said to be perpetrated against the Church by itinerant people were such things as palmistry and fortune telling, which were reckoned to deny the unforeseen will of God. The most hideous outrage said to be committed by gypsies was the fact that they wore rings in their ears. This was clearly a mark of heresy, just as Joan of Arc had been charged with having magical rings in her possession. They used gypsy rings, said the inquisitors, 'as a means of storing spells', while even their homes were supported by spoked wheels, which plainly identified the defiant nature of the Devil. Those skilled in the use of herbal remedies were denounced as the 'brewers of dark wizardry', while ventriloquists were undoubtedly in commune with satanic forces, being the 'mouthpieces of demons'. In 1602, Henri Boguet, the Witchfinder of Burgundy, wrote in his *Discourse des Sorciers*, 'It was good to hunt down our comedians and minstrels, considering that most of them are wizards and magicians'.[27]

Once gypsies and entertainers had been hauled into the abominable web of Devil worship, the field was opened even wider, so that just about anyone could be charged with heresy and sorcery. In this regard, midwives were among those specifically targetted, since the Catholic Church considered childbirth to be a defilement of both the mother and the child.[28] Midwives were first blacklisted in the 1486 *Malleus Maleficarum*, which stated that they 'surpass all others in wickedness'.[29] Consequently, women who died in childbirth were denied Church burial because they were unclean. It was decreed that midwives were clearly witches because they were the upholders of the sinful act, in addition to which they used herbal potions for the relief of maternal pain, and had the audacity to defy the clergy in this respect. New mothers had to undergo a humbling readmission to the Church by way of 'churching', whereby they were not allowed into consecrated places until blessed by a priest and given permission. The infants were separately cleansed by Church baptism, prior to which they existed only in sin.[30]

By the close of the 1500s, the outburst of satanic fever had reached hitherto unprecedented levels, and variously classified Devil worshippers were being burned in their thousands throughout Christendom. The campaign was ferocious in the extreme, with an ever-increasing emphasis on the demonic sexuality of women. Every arrest led to torturous interrogation;

every interrogation led to a confession; every confession led to an execution, and every execution proved beyond doubt that the Devil was being thwarted if not overcome. There was no question that everyone was guilty of sin; the Church of Rome had always asserted this. Meanwhile, the Puritans knew that their very existence on Earth constituted a vulgar affront to God and the Church, no matter how well they tried to behave.

13

DEGENERATE ASSEMBLY

Devil in the Vault

Following the childless death of Queen Elizabeth in 1603, King
James VI of Scots also became James I of England, being
Elizabeth's closest living relative by way of an earlier
Tudor/Stuart marriage.[1] Thus, England's monarchy moved from
the Tudor dynasty to that of the Royal House of Stuart, which had
reigned in Scotland from 1371. Whereas Elizabeth was the
Protestant founder of the Anglican Church, James had been
raised as a Presbyterian of the Scottish Kirk. His Calvinist views
were far more strict than those of the Anglicans but, when he met
with extreme Puritan leaders at Hampton Court Palace, he
threatened to 'harry them out of the land, or do worse' unless
they conformed to the Anglican Rule.[2] As the new Head of the
Church of England, James was adamant that the recognized
ecclesiastical structure and the *Book of Common Prayer* should be
acknowledged. Surprisingly, given his own sober religious
upbringing, he stated that the Puritan assemblies were as far
apart from his kingly beliefs as were God and the Devil. 'When I
mean to live under a presbytery', he added, 'I will go into
Scotland again. But while I am in England, I will have bishops
govern the Church'. In order to bring some regularity to religious
teaching, the ultimate result of this Hampton Court conference
was the King James English translation of the 1611 Authorized
Version of the Bible (KJV), which became the standard Protestant
Christian edition thereafter.

The nature of the dissenting Puritan clergy, as against the
mainstream Protestants, was epitomized by a London merchant
named Barbon, who gave regular sermons as a pastor for the
Puritan cause. Tall and very thin, he became known as 'Praise-
God Barebones'. As with all Protestants, he hated the Church of

Rome but, along with other Puritans, he also despised the Church of England. To the Puritans, it was unacceptable that the Anglican clergy wore colourful vestments, bowed in the name of Christ, and performed ceremonies with altars, candles and all the remnant trappings of the previous Catholic establishment. Barebones would deliver his sermons in the chapels and meeting halls for hours at a time, yelling fearsome threats of Hell-fire and damnation. He believed that people should be sternly governed by the ministry, insisting that he had been specially chosen by God, and that anyone who disagreed with him would 'burn for ever in Hell'.[3] Eventually, when the Puritans of Oliver Cromwell took over the Westminster Government, dissolving Parliament and abolishing free elections in 1653, Barebones was appointed to the replacement Nominated Assembly of selected 'godly men'. In the event, his immoderate presence was so loud and forceful that Cromwell's governing Assembly was mockingly referred to as the *Barebones Parliament*.

Early in the reign of James I, the explorer, poet and colonial governor, Sir Walter Raleigh, a favoured courtier of Queen Elizabeth, was arrested in 1603 and imprisoned in the Tower of London. He was accused and tried as a suspected conspirator in a Catholic plot to depose King James. In reality, Raleigh was neither Catholic nor Protestant. He had helped defend England against Catholic Spain, but was a well-known atheist which, to the parliamentary churchmen of the early 17th century, meant that he was a satanist. As such, he must therefore be in league with the Catholics, who were led by the papal Antichrist. A philosophical group, to which Raleigh had belonged with the late Christopher Marlowe and others of the literary and scientific fraternities, became dubbed the School of Night. Its members were said to perform iniquitous rituals of Devil worship in the tradition of Renaissance satanists such as Leonardo Da Vinci and Michelangelo! Since the monarch was the Head of the Church, with James being far more devout than Elizabeth had been, atheism was regarded as a treasonable offence in that it was tantamount to anarchy. At Raleigh's trial in Winchester Castle Hall, the Attorney General, Sir Edward Coke, accused him of pursuing 'a devilish policy ... the most horrible practices that ever came out of the bottomless pit of the lowest Hell'.[4]

Sir Walter Raleigh languished in prison for many years after sentence, and was finally executed in 1618. Meanwhile, King James had been the personal focus of an actual Catholic assault on 5 November 1605. As well as standing firm against the Puritans, James had also announced that he had 'no need of papists', as a result of which a gang of angry Catholics planned to blow up the King and his ministers in Parliament. Fortunately, the Gunpowder Plot was discovered and averted at the last, but the failed attempt brought the Devil firmly into the public arena with numerous pamphlets and sermons — for who else could possibly have masterminded such a heinous campaign? The official account of the event, called *The King's Book*, laid the blame squarely at the Devil's feet, proclaiming the plot as 'an outbreak of Hell on Earth'. A pamphlet, entitled *The Arraignment and Execution of the Late Traitors*, classified the perpetrators as being of the 'synagogue of Satan', and Guido (Guy) Fawkes, who would have lit the gunpowder fuse, was said to have been the 'Devil in the Vault'.[5] In a subsequent broadsheet, entitled *The Powder Treason*, the plot was described as having been 'propounded by Satan, founded in Hell, and confounded in Heaven'. The Bishop of Chichester noted that the Devil, by his agents, devised at one secret blow to destroy the King, princes, nobility and the clergy in the Westminster House of Lords.[6]

Ministers of the Fiend

At more than a century since the appearance of the inquisitional *Malleus Maleficarum*, a new edition concerning witchcraft and its relationship with the Devil emerged in 1608. Compiled by the Italian monk Francesco Maria Guazzo, it was entitled *Compendium Maleficarum*.[7] Guazzo was a monk of the Milanese Congregation of St Ambrose, whose ambition was to improve the moral life of women and promote the permanent institution of virgins (*de institutione virginis*) by way of cloistered nunneries.

179

In his explanatory Preface to the *Compendium*, Guazzo gave his own considered impression of the Devil:

> When he sees men of weak and timid mind, he takes them by storm. When he finds them dauntless and firm, he becomes as it were a cunning fox to deceive them, for he has a thousand means of hurting us, and he uses countless methods, superstitions and curious arts to seduce men's minds from God and lead them to his own follies. And all these he wondrously performs by means of illusions and witchcraft.[8]

The *Compendium* explains that, although the Devil has various means of inflicting injury, 'so there are effective remedies by which these harms may be met and dispersed when recognized'. It therefore seeks, by way of numerous documented examples, to illustrate how Satan makes his presence felt, and lists certain treatments and cures for those who have been corrupted by his evil. A central focus of the text is the nature of witchcraft, and specifically itemized are the eleven undertakings allegedly necessary to participate fully in the witches' Sabbat. Included are detailed descriptions of sexual activities with seductive demons, men with *succubi*, and women with *incubi*.[9] The witches, claimed Guazzo, 'rejoice and dance around a fire in the presence of Satan, who appears on his throne in the form of a hideous black goat'. Also featured are said aspects of ritual, such as offerings of black candles, satanic baptism, feasting, frenzied dancing and the notorious sabbatical rite of the *osculum infame* (kissing the Devil's hindmost).

According to the allegations and enforced confessions in trial records of the Inquisition, witches would give the 'kiss of shame' at the beginning of the Sabbat, after the Devil had read out the names of his followers present. The same was reported at the North Berwick witch trials in Scotland, when the *osculum infame* was said to be an act of both homage and penance:

And seeing that they tarried over long, he at their coming enjoined them all to a penance, which was, that they should kiss his buttocks in sign of duty to him.[10]

The worshippers were said to approach the Devil 'awkwardly, with grotesque and obscene mops and mows, sometimes straddling sideways, sometimes walking backwards', in order to perform the 'impious and lewd ritual' as part of the rite of admission.

In brief, the eleven articles of diabolic faith, which constitute the solemn and complete binding to witchcraft, were given by Guazzo as:

1. Candidates conclude an express compact with the Devil, by which they devote themselves to the service of evil.

2. They explicitly withdraw their allegiance to God, and renounce him.

3. They cast away, with contempt, the holy rosary, and trample upon the cross.

4. They vow obedience and subjection to the Devil, and bind themselves to blasphemous oaths, swearing to do no good work, but to obey the will of Satan.

5. They promise to strive with all power to induce others into the detestable service of the Devil.

6. They receive a sacrilegious baptism by the Devil, with sponsors to instruct them in evil sorcery.

7. They cut pieces from their garments, and tender them to the Devil as tokens of homage.

8. They stand within a circle, drawn by the Devil on the ground, where they confirm their satanic loyalty.

9. They request the Devil to strike them from the book of Christ, and to inscribe them in his own black book.

10. They promise the Devil offerings of child sacrifices once a fortnight, and swear to torment mankind with plagues and tempests.

11. They heap curses on the saints, and receive a secret mark on their bodies from the Devil as a branding of enslavement.[11]

Hermann Thyraus, the Jesuit Provincial of the Rhine, had written about such things a few years earlier in his *De Spirituum Apparitione*. His opinion, along with that of Guazzo, was very much the norm among Catholic demonologists and Protestant divines of the era. It was asserted that to differ from the clerical views of the Sabbat was 'mere obstinacy and foolhardiness ... for all the wisest writers on philosophy agree on this matter'. In making his case for the orthodox opinion, Thyraus wrote:

> It is so rash and inept to deny these things, that to adopt this attitude you must needs reject and spurn the most weighty and considered judgements of the most holy and authoritative writers. Nay, you must wage war upon man's sense and consciousness, whilst at the same time you expose your ignorance of the power of the Devil and the empery that evil spirits may obtain over man.[12]

The main item of occasional disagreement was the matter of whether the Devil appeared in person at all the Sabbats, or whether he was sometimes represented by the Grand Master in costume — most commonly as a black goat. Either way, it was reckoned that those present were the 'bond slaves of Satan', and the Masters were the incarnate ministers of the Fiend, 'devoted to his service, and acting under his direction by the inspiration of Hell'.

There was no disagreement, however, in respect of the Devil always being male. His carnal abominations at the Sabbats were conducted with women whose compliance was understood by the very fact of their presence. There were many reports at the witch trials of hideous infant monsters being born as a result of ritual intercourse with Satan. None was ever reported seen as described by any judge or inquisitor, but the production by witnesses of earwigs or toads in court was deemed enough to confirm and prove the reality of such charges.

Pursuing Henri Boguet's obsession with the satanic Ring Dance, Guazzo made reference in the *Compendium Maleficarum* to the practice at the Sabbats, explaining:

> The rites are performed with the utmost absurdity in a frenzied ring, with hands joined and back to back. And so they dance, throwing their heads like frantic folk, sometimes holding in their hands the candles which they have before used in worshipping the Devil'.[13]

Subsequently, in 1653, Dr Henry More of Christ's College, Cambridge, also wrote about Ring Dances in his theological treatise, *Antidote Against Atheism*. He explained that the dancers often performed their revels around mulberry bushes, and that stone circles were used, along with large rings that appeared mysteriously overnight in the grasses.[14] These so-called 'fairy rings' seem to have been not unlike some of today's enigmatic crop circles. In 1678 an intriguing English woodcut, in a Hertfordshire pamphlet entitled *Strange News*, depicted the Devil mowing an oval design in a crop field.

In apparent confirmation of Guazzo's assertion that children were ritually baptised at sabbatical assemblies, Jeanette d'Abadie, a confessed witch of the Pyrenees, declared in 1609 that children were often baptised by the Devil at witches' Sabbats. If anyone new to the Sabbat had already received a Christian baptism, this had to be formally renounced by the candidate and by any previous sponsors. The newly affirmed witch was then given an alternative name by the Devil, who assigned new sponsors to instruct them in the ways of diabolic sorcery. This practice was confirmed by many others, including a certain Gentin le Clere at his trial for wizardry at Orléans in 1614. He said that he and fifteen companions had been baptised by 'a monstrous goat, whom they called *l'Aspic*'.[15] It was also the case that marriages were conducted by the sabbatical Grand Masters in denial of the presumed sole authority of the Church.

Infected with Evil

As a direct and immediate reaction to Guazzo's *Compendium Maleficarum*, Pierre de Lancre, a French judge of Bordeaux, conducted a major witch-hunt in 1609, burning seventy people at the stake in Labourd. He expressed the view that sorcerers and witches were an organized, antisocial force, and a danger to the established order.[16] In his *Portrait of the Inconstancy of Witches*, he divulged the requirements of those at the Sabbats:

> To dance indecently, eat excessively, make love diabolically, commit atrocious acts of sodomy, blaspheme scandalously, avenge themselves insidiously, run after all horrible dirty and crudely unnatural desires, keep toads, vipers, lizards, and all sorts of poison as precious things, love passionately a stinking goat, caress him lovingly, associate with and mate with him in a disgusting and scabrous fashion. Are these not the uncontrolled characteristics of an unparalleled lightness of being and of an execrable inconstancy that can be expiated only through the divine fire that justice placed in Hell?[17]

In contrast, Friedrich von Spee, a Jesuit theologian and professor at Wurzburg University, was a noted opponent of trials for witchcraft, and spoke out strongly against them. Having acted as a confessor to hundreds of accused witches as they went to the stake, he was among the first openly to denounce torture as a means of obtaining information. Condemning the brutal techniques of the inquisitors, he wrote in 1631:

> The result is the same whether she confessed or not ... She can never clear herself. The investigating body would feel disgraced if it acquitted a woman. Once arrested and in chains, she has to be guilty by fair means or foul.[18]

Despite the Church's uncompromising attitude towards sorcery and satanic witchcraft, a good many priests and other churchmen were themselves condemned during this period. Pierre de Lancre claimed that the clergy of the Basque country were 'infected with satanism'. He identified five priests who had attended Sabbbats, one of whom paid the Devil two-hundred crowns and confessed the oath which he swore to him: 'I put myself wholly in thy power and in thy hands'.[19]

The Curé of Peifane was said to have accomplished the ruin of a highly respected and virtuous lady parishioner, the Dame du Lieu, by resort to sorcery, and was burned alive for it by the Parlement de Grenoble. In 1611, the priest Louis Gauffridy of Accules, near Marseilles, was burned by the Parlement de Provence for seducing Madeleine de la Palud at the confessional by way of magical breathing. It was said that, whilst in prison, his examiners found three Devil's Marks on the priest's body,[20] but it is not entirely clear to what extent the priest might actually have been guilty.

Gauffridy had known Madeleine since she was twelve, when she became his pupil. As she grew, he became infatuated with her and swore that if he, as a priest, could not marry her before God, then he would 'wed her before the Devil'. He told her that he was the Prince of Magicians, and vowed always to protect her.[21] Frightened by this talk of the Devil, Madeleine left her father's house and took refuge with the Ursuline sisters of Marseilles. But Gauffridy made arrangements to become her personal confessor, and the nuns were soon convinced that Madeleine was in Satan's power. In time, one of the sisters, Louise Capeau, jealous of the priest's favouritism for Madeleine, ensured that stories of his satanic power reached the ears of the Inquisitor for Provence. Gauffridy was duly seized, and word was soon out that the Prince of the Magicians had been captured. When Louise was asked by the tribunal where the Devil might reside that he could have such control over the accused, she pointed directly at him, saying, 'I see him plainly there at Gauffridy's ear'. The confessor's fate was thus sealed and, whatever his motive or actions might truly have been, he was burned alive at Aix.

A particularly sensational case was that of Urbain Grandier, a priest of Loudun in the French department of Vienne. The accounts of his trial in 1632 relate that, by wiles of the Devil, he had used magic to seduce seventeen nuns at the Ursuline convent of Loudun. Jeanne des Anges, the Mother Superior, testified that Grandier had taught them witchery and introduced them to the Devil. Jeanne and the nuns were publicly exorcised on many occasions, with reports that they contorted their bodies disgustingly and yelled obscenities to the detriment of Grandier. Although notably profligate in the town, Grandier had never once visited the convent, but he was accused of inflicting his spiritual presence by way of sorcery from a distance, and the unfounded malice against him was extraordinary. Given that Jeanne des Agnes was reputed for making up stories, Grandier was not punished severely in the first instance, although dismissed from his post by the Tribunal of Poitiers. A civil trial then found him innocent of all charges, but another session convened by Cardinal Richelieu determined that Grandier had indeed made a pact with the Devil. He even had the signature of Satan on a document, written backwards in an unknown language! The court found the priest guilty, and he was burned at the stake in 1634.[22]

A very evident feature of these cases, and many others like them, is that they emanate almost entirely from Capuchin,

Carmelite, Franciscan and Ursuline convents in southern France, but very rarely from neighbouring Spain. There appears to have been a distinct difference between the passive nuns of the Spanish sector and their wayward French sisters in nearby Provence. All accounts indicate that the latter were mercenary in their spites and jealousies of each other and those around them.[23] When testimonies on behalf of the various priests are considered, it seems that there was often more devilry in the women than in their accused confessors, and the convents were notorious in their scandals. In environments of extreme repression, the French nuns would regularly endeavour to outdo their companions with individual tales of sexual encounters with visitors. But they would extricate themselves from personal responsibility with explanations of being overwhelmed on such occasions by the Devil. When particular situations became publicly heightened, the man to blame for bringing the Devil into a nunnery was nearly always a priestly confessor or some other member of the clergy. It is therefore impossible to know the full truth of cases like those of Gauffridy and Grandier, but seemingly there were faults and indiscretions on both sides, and being a conventual or otherwise local priest was plainly a dangerous occupation.

One of the few unfortunate cases to emanate from Spain was that of Magdalena de la Cruz, a Franciscan nun who entered the convent in Córdoba. She acquired an extraordinary reputation for sanctity and, following lengthy service, was elected abbess. But then, some years later, she fell seriously ill and was taken prisoner by friars of the Inquisition, with charges of witchcraft laid against her. Under whatever conditions of duress, Magdalena confessed that, when she was twelve, the Devil had appeared to her, and had bound her to him for forty-one years. With a decade of this pact still to be completed, she was incarcerated for the rest of her life.[24]

Following the affair at Loudun, three successive conventual directors at Louviers were charged with using magical arts and having 'dealings with the Devil'. The friars of the Inquisition seemed to delight in torturing and burning their priestly cousins. But, as the *Desmarets et Histoire de Madeleine Bavent de Louviers* explains, the unscrupulous nuns did not always escape without punishment. At the age of eighteen, Madeleine Bavent accused Mathurin Picard and Father Thomas Boulle (the director and confessor respectively of her convent at Louviers) of taking her to a witches' Sabbat. Whilst there, she described how she had been married to the Devil and committed sexual acts with him on the altar. Other nuns then alleged their similar experiences, and demonstrated the devilish influence by way of unnatural contortions and words of an unknown tongue. Satan, they claimed at the trial in 1647, had led them (in the guises of Picard and Boulle) into his realm of debauchery and copulation with demons. Consequently, both of the men were tortured, during the course of which Picard died, but the original case brought by Madeleine Bavent was not proven. Boulle was nevertheless burned alive in the market square, by virtue of a public outcry against him, and the wretched Madeleine was exorcised and imprisoned for the rest of her life in an underground dungeon.[25]

Plight of the Witches

Among the best remembered of all England's witch trials was that of the Lancashire witches of Pendle in 1612. Records of the proceedings, as documented by Thomas Potts, Clerk to the Justices, provide a good example of the lunacies of the witch craze era.[26] This mass trial of seventeen alleged witches was the largest in England to that date, and created a considerable stir throughout the northern counties.

Many unfortunate folk lived in the desolate forest region of Pendle Hill — uneducated and existing in abject poverty. Among them were two eighty year-old women: Elizabeth Southernes (known as Old Mother Demdike) and Anne Whittle (known as Old Chattox). Thomas Potts wrote of the blind widow Demdike that she was 'the rankest hag that ever troubled daylight'. Old Chattox, he described as 'a withered, spent and decrepit creature'.

Together with her daughter, Elizabeth, and some grand-children, Demdike lived in squalor at an old ruin called Malkin

188

Tower. Chattox lived nearby, in equally dire conditions, with her daughters Alizon and Bessie. They all survived by begging for money or meagre supplies, but the two families were not on the best of terms with each other. The trouble began when Bessie of the Chattox clan stole some oatmeal from Malkin Tower, at which Alizon of the Demdikes lodged a formal complaint with the local magistrate, Roger Nowell. When Bessie was charged with theft, she accused Old Mother Demdike of practising witchcraft. In retaliation, Alizon then levelled the same charge against Old Chattox, and soon the various members of each faction were accusing each of their opposite numbers and their associates of satanic practices.

Roger Nowell had been appointed specifically by King James to uphold the royally implemented regulation that witchcraft was a capital offence. It was a situation ready-made for the mood of the era, and the foolish rustic families had brought the trouble upon themselves. Also implicated with Demdike, Chattox and fourteen others, was the nearby resident Alice Nutter. The farcical trial centred on testimonies about a devil named Tibb and a talking black dog. But charges of evil cursing, bewitching, grave robbery and diabolical murder also came into the reckoning as the testimonies became ever wilder and more imaginative. The result was that ten of the said witches, including Nutter, Chattox and two children, were taken to the Lancaster Castle gallows and hanged. Others were pilloried or imprisoned, and Old Demdike died, before execution, in her cell.

* * *

At this stage, it becomes increasingly evident that there were particular differences between the notions of witchcraft and sorcery in Continental Europe, and those in Britain. In Europe, the majority of cases were specifically related to heretical actions and satanic practices that were either politically or sexually driven in their motives, whether real or imagined. In Britain, apart from some limited high-level involvement by those such as the 'Wizard Earl' of Bothwell in Scotland, the witch craze was more concerned with rural covens, or those individuals and families of a poverty-stricken rustic underclass whose strange behaviour was considered somehow threatening. They were said to be in communion with the Devil, and were feared as malevolent creatures who cast spells and made curses to harm those around them. Sometimes their alleged activities included black magic aspects of a voodoo nature, such as pin-sticking or burning wax images. They were reckoned to fly at night, and were often portrayed around fires, brewing vile potions in their cauldrons. This is the popular image which, during the days of the King James persecutions, William Shakespeare used so well for the three weird sisters in his Scottish play, *Macbeth*. The one common factor, however, was that (whether the culprit indicted for witchcraft was a wayward French nun or a miserable English crone) the ultimate cause of their diabolical behaviour was always the same. In every instance, the instigator was the Devil.

An English witch of the dejected crone variety was theatrically portrayed at court to King James in the play *The Witch of Edmonton*, following its London opening at Drury Lane in 1621. Described as a tragic comedy, it was based on the true story of one Elizabeth Sawyer, who was hanged at Tyburn that year after imprisonment in London's Newgate Gaol for selling her soul to the Devil. Wretched, shunned, disgustingly poor, half paralysed, and accompanied only by her ragged black dog, she was seen on stage gathering sticks for her fire, whilst receiving hateful words and vicious blows from those around. Just as it was in Elizabeth's life, the stark realism was depicted in the play, but there was no sympathy from the audience. Each time Elizabeth appeared, they hissed and booed at the sorry old hag and her plight.[27]

Elizabeth Sawyer was not in real life, nor in theatre portrayal, associated with any assembly or coven. But, in the main, such witches were reckoned to have their own community groups with organized ritual gatherings. The common perception of the goings-on at witches' Sabbats was related by way of a contemporary English treatise. It does seem, however, that the content of this work was extracted mainly from the 1608 *Compendium Maleficarum* of Francesco Maria Guazzo:

190

They are carried out of the house, either by the window, door, or chimney, mounted on their imps ... Thus brought to the designed place, they find a great number of others arrived there by the same means; who, before Lucifer takes his place in his throne as king, do make their accustomed homage, adoring and proclaiming him their Lord, and rendering him all honour. This solemnity being finished, they sit to table where no delicate meats are wanting ... The *incubi* in the shape of proper men satisfy the desires of the witches, and the *succubi* serve for whores to the wizards.

At last before Aurora brings back the day, each one mounts on his spirit, and so returns to their respective dwelling place ... When the assembly is ready to break up, and the Devil to dispatch them, he publisheth this law with a loud voice, 'Revenge yourselves or else you shall die'. Then each one, kissing the posterior of the Devil, returns upon their aiery vehicles to their habitations.[28]

14

SATAN'S REBELLION

The King and the Devil

For twenty-two years, King James I of England (VI of Scots) battled against pressures from the Anglican Parliament and other Christian establishments. Apart from being the King of England, Scotland and Wales, he was also King of Ireland, an intrinsically Catholic domain. Hence, with three major Christian denominations to consider, an amount of religious toleration was necessary, but this was not welcomed by the sectarian Anglicans or those of the Presbyterian and Puritan movements. In upholding the Acts of Uniformity in respect of the *Book of Common Prayer*, James had upset the hard-line Catholics and prompted the unsuccessful Gunpowder Plot. As for the unbending National Kirk elders in Scotland, they were more than displeased by James's concept of a moderate Scottish Episcopal Church, which was neither Anglican, Presbyterian, nor Catholic.

Queen Elizabeth had been largely autocratic, and had ruled without too much parliamentary reliance. The expensive wars and navigational exploits of her reign had put the English Crown into considerable debt, and James was obliged to implement higher taxation. The politicians agreed to this, but with the proviso that such new measures should only come into force by Act of Parliament. Being more familiar with the traditions of Scottish kingship, James disagreed with this restriction, claiming that he was not answerable to his own appointed ministers, but to God and the Nation. Opposing him in this regard were the parliamentary Anglicans. Having become separated from papal control, the bishops wanted independence under their senior figurehead, the Archbishop of Canterbury, and did not hold with the King's inheritance (as established by Henry VIII and Elizabeth I) that the monarch was Head of the Church.

During his English reign, James continued to expound his concerns about witchcraft and the Devil, as described in his Scottish *Daemonology*, and the witch trials persisted throughout the realm. Satanic interference was a common subject of discussion at the royal court in London, as recorded by the Middle Temple lawyer, Sir Simon D'Ewes, who outlined various incidents of said diabolic activity in his journal. On one occasion, he wrote that many of the ships in Plymouth harbour had been wrecked by a violent storm. It was subsequently reported that the Devil was personally responsible, and had been witnessed at the scene in the guise of a black dog![1]

Following a severe stroke and fever, King James died in 1625, to be succeeded by his son as King Charles I. His immediate concern was to rid the administration of the parliamentary subversion that had plagued his father. But the fast-growing Puritan sect had risen to prominence in Westminster, and was now wholly nonconformist. They stood against all forms of Anglican episcopacy and monarchy, claiming that the King had no divine right to be the head of either the Church or the Nation. The scene was now set for the anarchic dissenters to break with all tradition by associating the King himself with Devil worship.

At the outset of this demonizing campaign, accusations were laid against those closest to King Charles. These focused in particular on George Villiers, the Duke of Buckingham, whose religious beliefs were largely undefined, although he did have a Catholic mother. Buckingham had been the closest of all courtiers and personal friends of Charles' father. But he was charged by the Puritans with being a satanic emissary who, in league with his mother, a witch, and by the express will of the Devil, had caused the death of King James with sorcery.[2] He was further accused of causing a terrible thunderstorm over London, and of practising the black arts to manipulate King Charles into the Devil's service, giving rise to the chant:

> Who rules the Kingdom? The King.
> Who rules the King? The Duke.
> Who rules the Duke? The Devil.

Buckingham's astrological adviser, John Lambe, was identified as a despicable magician, and was mercilessly stoned and lynched in the street by a London mob in 1628.[3] Buckingham was stabbed and murdered two weeks later in Portsmouth by the Puritan army officer, John Felton, as eventually part fictionalized in the Alexander Dumas classic novel, *The Three Musketeers*. Shortly after the assassination, Felton admitted his crime publicly, expecting to be well received. But instead he was arrested and taken before magistrates, who sent him to London for interrogation. Given that his effort did not achieve the anticipated reaction, Felton presumed that he must somehow have been duped into action by evil powers, and declared before his execution that he had acted 'at the instigation of the Devil'.

Prior to his coronation, Charles had married Henrietta Maria of France, the sister of King Louis XIII. But, since she was a Catholic, it was impossible for her to be crowned with her husband in an Anglican ceremony. In his *Histrio-Mastix* (1633), William Prynne, a formidable Puritan opponent of the Anglican and Catholic establishments, laid a heavy assault against the abominable behaviour of Charles and Henrietta Maria, because they regularly danced at court masques and pastorals. In preparation for things soon to come on the political stage, Prynne denounced all forms of dancing and entertainment, along with their 'swarms of lustful spectators, whose unchaste, unruly lusts are apt to be inflamed with every wanton gesture, smile, or pace'. Dancing, he asserted, was 'a pomp and a vanity of this wicked world; an invention, yea, a work of Satan'. It was, he insisted, 'the Devil's procession that leads men to Hell'.[5]

From the start of King Charles' reign, the high-handed Anglican ministry was felt to be too distant and aloof by large sectors of the community, and the locally preaching Puritans gained a certain amount of public support. Charles I, nonetheless, perceived them as potentially dangerous insurgents, in consequence of which he lent his personal allegiance wholly to the Church of England. As a result, the Puritans restricted Parliament's financial grants and subjected the King to their express demands. Accordingly, Charles dissolved his Parliament in 1629, raised his own finances by way of grants and loans from the wealthy gentry, and successfully managed national affairs by himself for the next eleven years.

Devilish Designs

In the course of this, the King's alliance with William Laud, Archbishop of Canterbury, annoyed the Scottish Kirk and led to the Bishops' Wars of 1639–40. These were sparked by Laud's endeavour to introduce Anglican practices into Presbyterian Scotland, and the financial requirements of the conflict caused Charles to reconvene Parliament. This so-called Short Parliament of April and May 1640 was a worthless exercise, as was the ultimately fatal Long Parliament convened in the following November. Being quite unwilling to assist the Anglican national community, the Westminster Puritans abolished the King's Council of the Star Chamber, executed the royal advisor, Viscount Strafford, and produced the infamous *Grand Remonstrance* — a list of complaints against the King and his 'devilish designs'. These included such charges as 'diabolic apostacy' in his encouragement of the theatre.

From Tudor times, there had been significant unrest in Ireland, and in 1641 rebellion erupted in the north-eastern province of Ulster. The Irish Catholics had made a stand against the increasing number of English merchants who were taking over their towns and cities. On learning of the insurgency, Charles endeavoured to raise an army to quell the riots, but the politicians refused him the resources, fearing that he would turn his military force against Parliament. Charles sought to arrest five MPs for their obstructive behaviour, but the gates of London were locked against him, and the result was Civil War. Aligned against Charles and his supporters, the parliamentary army was led by the politically ambitious countryman, Oliver Cromwell.

From that point, the Devil became a figurative weapon in the verbal and literary propaganda of each faction — the royalist Cavaliers against the parliamentary Roundheads. The Royalists issued a leaflet, entitled *The Devil Turn'd Round-head*, in which the Evil One was portrayed as a fanatical Puritan. In response, the Cromwellians published their pamphlet, *A Short, Compendious and True Description of the Round-heads and Long-heads*. Each accused the other side of being hand-in-glove with Satan as 'the seed and spawn of the Devil'.[6]

Other news bulletins, leaflets and ballads followed in a similar vein, so that Protestants at large, whether Anglican or Puritan, became more afraid than ever of diabolic control over their lives. The Puritan agitator, John Lilburne, then attacked Archbishop Laud for attempting to reintroduce altars and prayer books into local parish churches in an effort to promote Anglican style worship. He asserted that Laud was a servant of Satan, with King Charles being a victim of his power.[7] This had the effect of associating the Protestant archbishop with the Catholic Church, which was deemed satanic. A mischievous pamphlet, entitled *A Disputation Betwixt the Devil and the Pope*, then enforced the assertion by directly aligning the Anglican hierarchy with the papacy in Rome. Hence, Archbishop Laud was seen to be attached firmly to the forces of the Devil. It was maintained that, for the sake of Protestant progress and parliamentary reform, all mitres and popish books must be banished from England, and the pamphlet depicted Satan and the Pope debating the failure of their subversive tactics in the face of godly Puritan opposition.[8]

Another such publication, called *News From Hell*, reproduced a letter said to have been written by the Devil himself in the 5,661st year of his reign on Earth. Alluding to Archbishop Laud's attempt to introduce the Anglican *Book of Common Prayer* into Scotland, the Devil's letter congratulated the Pope for his skill in using the Anglican episcopate to set up a war between King Charles and his Presbyterian subjects.[9] This was closely followed in 1642 by another leaflet, *The Papists' Petition in England*, which contained an imaginary petition from papal devotees, along with details of yet another discussion between the Pope and the Devil. With Archbishop Laud portrayed as their appointed emissary in England, they debated how they might concoct a suitably damnable scheme to destroy the puritanical establishment.[10]

By virtue of these ludicrous fabrications, Archbishop Laud was impeached and imprisoned in the Tower of London on a charge of high treason. But the maliciously contrived pamphlets continued to appear, and there was no way that he could defend himself. His status as the Devil's accomplice had become so well cemented in the public imagination that the Westminster Puritans took a further step in declaring Laud to be none other than the Antichrist himself. He was finally brought to trial before the House of Lords in March 1644, with the prosecution led by the fanatical William Prynne. But, given the nature of the archbishop's very able defence, it was impossible to prove him guilty of treason, and the Lords adjourned without coming to a vote. The puritanical House of Commons then resorted to a Bill of Attainder, arrogating to themselves the right to nominate any crime they chose as high treason. Among variously cited misdeeds deemed treasonable, Laud had supported King Charles' *Book of Sports* (1633), which declared dancing and games to be lawful. He was therefore a devilish opposer of God's law! Condemned to death by the House of Commons, without the benefit of a further hearing, Archbishop William Laud was taken to Tower Hill and beheaded on 10 January 1645.

The Witchfinder

Eventually, after some further years of skirmishes and battles between the Royalists and Roundheads, King Charles was also executed in Whitehall, London, on 30 January 1649. Subsequent to a short period of Commonwealth, Oliver Cromwell then undertook to rule the nation by martial force alone. He established his Protectorate in 1653, and dissolved Parliament to facilitate his military dictatorship. The oppressive Puritan faction was now firmly in control of the whole country.

As the self-appointed Lord Protector, Cromwell presumed greater dictatorial powers than any king had ever known. Immediately, he sought to demolish the activities of the Anglican Church and, at his order, the *Book of Common Prayer* was forbidden, as were the celebrations of Christmas and Easter. Within the universities, his commissioners banned the teaching of mathematics, science, astronomy and natural philosophy, which were all considered demonic. Games, sports and entertainment were restricted; dissenters were tortured and banished; houses were sequestrated; punitive taxes were levied; theatres and inns were closed; freedom of speech was denied; adultery was made a capital offence, and mothers of illegitimate children were incarcerated. No one was safe, and any unwitting group of family or friends could be charged with plotting against a regime that empowered crushing fines and penalties to be imposed at will by the Cromwellian soldiers.[11]

Not surprisingly, the savage dictatorship gave rise to a widespread increase in witch-hunting pursuits. It was said that, during the Cromwellian era, 'the fire and cord were seldom at rest'. The Puritan masters gave no fair trial, nor showed the least mercy to any poor wretch upon whom could be pinned the faintest suspicion of having anything to do with witchcraft.[12] Prominent as a pre-Cromwellian accuser in this regard was the infamous, self-styled Witchfinder-General, Matthew Hopkins.

Hopkins was said to have become alarmed in 1644 by an outbreak of diabolism in his home town of Manningtree in Essex. 'That horrible sect of witches', he wrote, 'was convening at night in an area beside my house', where he heard them conversing with imps and swearing oaths to the Devil. Having managed to extract a confession from one of them (an aged, one-legged widow named Elizabeth Clarke), Hopkins pursued others, bringing thirty-six to the Essex Assizes. He then progressed into other counties: Suffolk, Norfolk, Huntingdonshire, Cambridgeshire, Northamptonshire and Bedfordshire. Unlike the regular civil authorities, who relied on specific charges being laid for investigation, Hopkins actively 'hunted' witches. During the period 1645–47 he brought nearly 250 suspected witches to trial, of whom around 100 were hanged.[13]

Along with his assistant, John Stearne, Matthew Hopkins terrorized the eastern counties. His notorious, although short-lived, career was conducted under cover of the Civil War, and he earned his money from local authorities by promising to free their communities of satanists. Hopkins made judicial use of the popular belief that witches had familiar animals (cats, hares, stoats and frogs), concentrating his effort very largely on laying charges against elderly women with pets. On many occasions, the women confessed that they had seen the Devil in the shape of a white dog, a black dog, or a boy with shaggy hair. One woman admitted, after torture by sleep deprivation, that she had been married to Satan for three years before discovering his secret. Also, since witches were said not to bleed when pricked at the point of their Devil's Mark, Hopkins made good use of his spring-loaded, retractable stiletto. Eventually, though, his days were numbered when John Gaule, the vicar of Great Staughton in Huntingdonshire, published his condemnation of Hopkins in a book entitled *Select Cases of Conscience Touching Witches and Witchcraft*. It was so well written and convincing that public opinion was aroused against Hopkins. In exposing the Witchfinder's methods, Gaule explained:

> Every old woman with a wrinkled face, a furrowed brow, a hairy lip, a gobber tooth, a squint eye, a squeaking voice or scolding tongue, having a rugged coat on her back, a skullcap on her head, a spindle in her hand, and a dog or cat by her side, is not only suspect, but pronounced for a witch.[14]

In response to this and other formal complaints made about him to the Norfolk authorities, Hopkins wrote his own pamphlet, *The Discovery of Witches*, in an attempt to explain and justify his actions.[15] Subsequent to that, he disappeared from the scene with no one knowing quite what became of him. Two centuries later, the parish register of Mistley in Essex was found to contain the burial entry of a certain Matthew Hopkins on 12 August 1647.[16] Since this date coincides with the Witchfinder-General's disappearance, it is presumed by many to be the record of his death, the nature of which remains unknown.

Conference with the Devil

The activities of Matthew Hopkins, although only semi-official, were supported from the outset by the 1645 publication *Lawes Against Witches and Conjuration*. In line with Hopkins' targetted subjects, this report makes much of the fact that witches have familiar spirits as animal pets, 'which appeareth to them sometimes in one shape, sometimes in another'. It also gives a general impression that witches were perceived as elderly, cursing hags.[17] As with the previously discussed witch of Edmonton, and the witches of Pendle, the portrayals are mainly of lone individuals or close-knit relatives, unlike the covens and community groups of the earlier medieval Sabbats. This was all very different to the way things were understood in Europe, where so many of the witches were said to be nuns and otherwise seductive young women, whether of the rural classes or the nobility.

Throughout this period, hardly any literature concerning witchcraft emanated from the Anglican Church. The reports from Britain are essentially products of the Puritan and Presbyterian movements. As such, the stories, whether true or false, follow the bland and colourless models of these sullen, black-garbed religious institutions. All notion of any romantically conceived portrayal was somehow lost as the world of sorcery became a perceived realm of crones and squalor. The peaks of its excitement rested in tales of isolated women and their familiars, who might cast spells upon their neighbours' chickens and cattle. Meanwhile, the more colourful model of the Catholic establishment was left to be reflected in the stories of inquisitional Europe. In terms of their popular entertainment value, these accounts focused on gypsy lore, werewolves and beguiling enchantresses. Across the board, however, a common factor that tied them all together was that, even as described in the English *Lawes Against Witches and Conjuration*, 'Witches have personal conference with the Devil'.

During the 1640s, the General Assembly of the Scottish Kirk passed a series of five condemnatory rulings against witches, thereby causing a sharp rise in the number of related trials and prosecutions. In alliance with the Privy Council, the Kirk's pursuit of those carrying on the craft of witchery was undertaken in the King's name against those accused of associating with Satan or his agents. Superstitions abounded within all classes of society, and diabolic molestation was a major concern of the era. Trials were conducted across the length and breadth of the land, most significantly in Aberdeenshire, the Lothians, Stirlingshire, Ayrshire, Galloway, Lanarkshire and Orkney. Foremost in substantiating the executions was the much cited entry from the King James Bible: 'Thou shalt not suffer a witch to live'.[18] But there was actually no such entry in the Old Testament from which the 1611 translation into English was made. The original Hebrew word, *chenaph*, did not translate correctly to 'witch'; it related more precisely to 'someone who acts wickedly'. It appears, therefore, to have been the case that the translators pandered to the King's known fear of witches, as made evident fifteen years earlier in his *Daemonology*. In this context, the 17th-century English Bible entry seems to have been made as a direct result of the prevailing witch-hunting craze, rather than providing any legitimate theological justification for the persecutions.

Some of the charges, for which women in particular were executed in Scotland, were based on the flimsiest of evidence. A number of people who had been resident near Janet Wishart's house in Aberdeen had, not surprisingly, died within a period of thirty years. For this, Janet was burned for being able to induce illness and death. Isobell Scudder was renowned as a keen and astute matchmaker. It was therefore determined that she was a sorceress who used evil spells to charm men. A woman in Fyvie was condemned for calling in a wizard who cured her sick cow. A woman of Irongray was sentenced by the Bishop of Galloway, and burnt in a tar-barrel because she had, on several occasions, correctly predicted the weather. Elspeth of Kirkcudbright was burnt alive because she had a pin in her roof beam that would cause a low milk yield in her neighbour's cows.

The total number of people accused of Devil attachment in Scotland between 1563 and 1736 appears to be around 4,000.

There are extant records giving the names of 3,212 individuals of whom 85 percent were women. The compiler of a carefully prepared article in the *Scottish Review* of October 1891 found details of 3,400 who perished in Scotland even before the 1700s. Many were midwives and, as was the case in inquisitional Europe, midwifery was classified as an aspect of witchcraft. Others were folk healers, an art that was deemed to be diabolical magic. The most common method of torture was sleep deprivation, because it led to hallucination and resultant confession, especially to descriptions of meetings with the Devil, and of entering into sexual relationships or pacts with him.[19] The number of witches hanged in England during that period is unknown because of poor record keeping, but it was in any event considerably higher than in Scotland.

Curse of the Undead

Throughout Europe, during the first half of the 1600s, notions of Satan and sorcery were flourishing just as in Britain. The Devil was no longer, in anyone's eyes, a figure who could be duped and ridiculed; he had achieved the status of a phenomenal power-lord intent to dominate the world. Thus, all disasters and calamities were said to be of his making.[20]

In 1618, the Thirty Years' War in Germany and the Low Countries had begun when Bohemian Protestants rebelled against Catholic Habsburg rule from Austria. They offered their crown instead to Prince Friedrich V, Elector Palatine of the Rhine. He was the nephew of the French Huguenot leader, Henri, Duc de Bouillon. On Friedrich's acceptance of the honour, the wrath of the Pope and the Holy Roman Emperor descended, and the conflict ensued until 1648. There was no concern for anyone's rights as entire regions were laid to waste by the foraging armies. During the strife, Bohemia's cause was joined by Sweden, along with Protestant factions of France and Germany. In time, the imperial territories were depleted to the extent that the Emperor retained purely nominal control in the Germanic states.

Just as with the English Civil War, the factions on either side of the European dispute claimed that the Prince of Darkness was leading the forces of the enemy, with a determination to bring everyone under his control. Never in all history had Satan been so prominent in the collective consciousness and, whether Catholic or Protestant, the people on either side of the conflict were respectively convinced that they were fighting the Devil.

At the same time, emerging quietly in the background, new philosophies were being born as science and logic began to break through the age-old barriers of religious theology. Led by rational men like the French mathematical philosopher René Descartes, followed by the German polymath Gottfried Leibniz and others, it was to become known as the Age of Reason. This was by no means an atheistic ideal, simply the application of a more balanced approach. Descartes was perfectly content with the idea that God created the world and its natural laws, but reckoned that he then left things to function of their own accord, without further intervention. On that basis, Descartes suggested that people should not keep blaming God or the Devil for their individual failures and adversities, but should begin to take personal responsibility for their actions.[21]

Suggestions of this type led eventually to the beginning of decline in satanic belief, and a generally calmer view of existence. For the time being, however, the Devil still reigned supreme and, once the Thirty Years' War was over, the Catholic Church looked to find new avenues of approach in the ongoing persecution of heretics and sorcerers. With the Devil fully at the zenith of his contrived existence by the middle 1600s, and a great many supposed disciples among the witches and gypsies, a new form of diabolical horror was introduced by the inquisitors to ride alongside the threat of werewolves.[22] Since Jesus was reckoned to have a host of heavenly angels at his disposal, it was decided that Satan was in need of more hostile emissaries, in order that the divine war could be properly waged and preached with a fearsome new gusto from the pulpits.

The main premise of Christianity was the promise of salvation, as achieved through subservience to the bishops, aligned with the perpetuation of a serene afterlife in a heavenly environment. But how could the alternative notion of Hell be portrayed on Earth in a manner that would scare the life out of tentative believers or reluctant worshippers? Somehow, Hell had to be given an earthly form, and what better than the concept of dead people who could not complete their dying because they were so hideously unclean − people who were, in fact, 'undead'. Such revenants, said the Catholic churchmen, had to roam the mortal world like lost souls, with no dimension of life or death to call their own, because they had managed to die without the blessing or consent of God!

The concept was good enough in part, but it was really no more scary than the idea of ghosts with a physical form. Something else was needed; these creatures had to become predators, like the werewolves, in order to make people fearful enough to lean wholly upon the Church for deliverance. So, what would all people, rich and poor alike, fear to lose the most if they were seeking salvation for their souls?

The answer to this question was found (as it had to be if the plan were to succeed) in the Bible. To be precise, it was found in the Old Testament book of Leviticus 17:11, which states: 'It is the blood that maketh an atonement for the soul'. It was therefore determined that the 'undead' creatures would be said to prey upon people's blood, thereby divesting them of the route to salvation.

If there was a problem to overcome in this regard, it was the fact that the Leviticus entry was an aspect of ancient Hebrew atonement law, which had little or nothing to do with Christianity. But a way was soon found to accommodate the law when the Church reasserted the *Doctrine of Transubstantiation*. In this rule of faith, every good Christian who partook of the eucharistic wine was said figuratively to be drinking the blood of Christ. This divine blood then became a part of his or her own body, and any creature which then extracted blood from such a person was reckoned to be guilty of stealing the blood of Christ! In this regard, the 'undead' revenants could be portrayed as antichrists endeavouring to devour the very life-blood of the Christian Saviour.[23]

Back in 12th-century England, the Augustinian chronicler, William of Newburgh, had mentioned occasions when the dead were said to return to terrorize the living. He identified these apparent fiends as being *sanguisuga* — a Latin term for 'bloodsucking',[24] although relating at the time rather more to ruthless extortion than sucking blood in the literal sense.

In 1645, the first book concerning the bloodthirsty 'undead' was produced by the Greek Catholic clerk, Leo Allatius. In his *De Graecorum Hodie Quorundam Opinationibus*, he told of the *vrykolakas* — a corpse taken over by a demon. This idea was relatively new to western Christianity, but the *vrykolakas* had persisted for some time in Greek folklore, and had already been recognized as a devil figure by the Eastern Orthodox Church. In 1657, the diabolical revenant was mentioned again by the French Jesuit, Fr François Richard, in his *Relation de ce qui s'est passe a Saint-Erini Isle de l'Archipel*.

In this context, the churchmen found their greatest inspiration. By bringing this satanic creature into play, they were enabled to redesign and embellish the character of the *vrykolakas* for a market that hitherto had never heard of him. In doing this, it was reckoned that such a devil figure could not possibly be seen to exist in the company of Christian artefacts. In consequence, a whole new mythology was born. The creatures could be repelled, it was decreed, by such devices as consecrated holy water, the eucharistic wafer and the crucifix.

Dating from as far back as the 9th century was an old Romanian and Hungarian practice designed to prevent the dead from walking. In the minds of the pastoral folk, a person who died was seen as having been cut down from life, as might be a tree or a crop. In this regard it was customary to lay a sickle upon the buried body to serve as a reminder that it could no longer stray into the mortal world. This perhaps accounts for the fact that *Death* (the Grim Reaper) has long been portrayed as a partially clad skeletal figure carrying a sickle or scythe.

This practice was applied especially to those who had died before their allotted time — maybe as the unfortunate product of an accident, murder or disease — and might awaken without knowing they were supposed to be dead! Such people, it was thought, were the most likely candidates to become the walking 'undead', along with those who died from suicide, alcoholism or, as the clerics insisted, those who had been illegitimately born. Just about anyone who might have died without the consent of God's own permission was destined to become a revenant, as were those buried in unconsecrated ground. Very often people died of plague or communicable infection, following which they were interred in a hurry, with no ceremony, so as to confine their disease within the earth. Such victims were expressly condemned by the Church, for to be buried without a priest in attendance was a certain route to a compact with the Devil.

In some ways, the nominal definition of the *vrykolakas* was similar to that of the werewolf which, in the Slovakian and Bulgarian traditions, had been called the *verkolak*. The Byzantine Church Serbians were the first to link the two demonic types together, referring to them jointly as *vlkoslak*.[25] This was all very good news for the 17th-century bishops, because the shapeshifting werewolf had a limited trepidatory function, especially in places like England where wolves were generally unknown, although some existed then to the north in Scotland.

The work of Leo Allatius was carefully devised so as to link the *vrykolakas* with the Devil-worshipping witches and gypsies. But it was not long before the concept was further expanded, and a new strategy enabled the Church to add a truly fearsome creature to the list of satanic emissaries. This, as we shall see, led to the demonic cult of the vampire.

15

THE DEVIL AND REASON

Son of the Dawn

Some years after the execution of Archbishop Laud, when the Anglican Church re-emerged from being suppressed during the Cromwellian Protectorate, the Protestant identification of the Antichrist reverted once more to the Pope. In this regard, the view of the English writer, John Milton, was Lutheran to the extent that he regarded the Catholic Church as a truly wicked enterprise. His 1659 *Treatise of Civil Power in Ecclesiastical Causes* states:

> Chiefly for this cause do all true Protestants account the Pope as Antichrist, for that he assumes to himself this infallibility over both the conscience and the scripture, sitting in the temple of God, as it were opposite to God, and exalting himself above all that is called God.[1]

Alongside this opinion, the Devil (as against the papal Antichrist) appeared with a somewhat unconventional persona in Milton's highly acclaimed *Paradise Lost.* Published in 1667, it portrays him without the wickedness of his familiar image. In this epic poem, Satan is no hideous goat or otherwise demonic entity, but returns to his original form as a fallen angel. Moreover, he is a fallen angel who assumes the mantle of a proud and heroic revolutionary. In this enterprising role, he seeks a route to salvation for those condemned, without reprieve, to the Catholic Hell that he knows so well. With the determination of an arch-rebel against authority, fearless and defiant in the face of a dominant force, Satan asks, 'Is there no place left for repentance; none for pardon left?' His character is dignified, and he is presented as a champion of liberty in the face of dogmatic oppression. The portrayal is a far cry from the malevolent Devil whose emissaries were being stalked and hunted by the intrepid witchfinders.

In chapter 2 we saw that, in Milton's *Paradise Lost*, Satan was identified with Lucifer, the 'day star', subsequently to influence popular perception of the Devil. This premise emanated from the Old Testament citation in Isaiah 14:12, with the 'day star' relating to the 'light bearer'. The biblical verse, in symbolic reference to the fall of King Nabonidus of Babylon, states, 'How art thou fallen from heaven, O day star, son of the dawn!' Milton's apparent error, in connecting this event with the fall of Satan, was not however of his own making. The connection had actually been drawn back in the 2nd century by the Church Father, Origen of Alexandria, in his *De Principiis*. Having confused Lucifer (*Lux-fer*) with Satan of his own accord, Origen then argued with himself about how the connection made no sense. After all, he posited, the day star named *Lux-fer* rises in the morning. But how can Satan rise in the morning? How can he be the light bringer if he is the Prince of Darkness? Origen then attempted to justify the mutual identification, but without any satisfactory result since his Luciferian concept was flawed from the outset.[2] Nevertheless, close to 1,500 years later, John Milton appears to have liked the idea and, in *Paradise Lost*, he referred to the heroic Satan as a paragon of brightness, personified by Lucifer, otherwise Venus, the day star.

There had, in fact, been an heretical movement called the Luciferians back in the 4th century, but they were nothing to do with the Devil except by way of Church inference. They were actually named after Lucifer Calaritanus of Cagliari in Sardinia, and were assaulted in a polemic of the contemporary Christian apologist St Jerome. In his treatise of AD 379, entitled *Against the Luciferians*, Jerome stated:

> It happened not long ago that a follower of Lucifer had a dispute with a son of the Church. His loquacity was odious and the language he employed most abusive. For he declared that the world belonged to the

Devil and, as is commonly said by them at
the present day, that the Church was turned
into a brothel.[3]

John Milton's sequel, *Paradise Regained*, deals essentially with the
temptation of Christ by the Devil, as given in the Gospel of Luke.[4]
The difference is that, in the Milton version, Satan is presented as
a 'son of God' in accordance with the Old Testament book of Job.[5]
Thus, the temptation sequence is portrayed as a dispute between
two of God's sons and, when Jesus wins the debate, Satan is
'smitten with amazement', and falls, 'struck with dread and
anguish', into Hell and the Gates of Abaddon.[6] As previously
discussed, the name Abaddon is sometimes used as an alternative
for Satan. But, in accurate compliance with the book of The
Revelation,[7] Milton identified Abaddon separately as the angel
of the bottomless pit — the ultimate guardian of the abyss into
which Satan was said to have been cast for his misdeeds.

Although clearly a Protestant with republican leanings, Milton
was not a hard-line Puritan, as evidenced by his contrary life as a
poet and musical composer, along with his strangely sympathetic
view of the Devil. He had, however, supported the Cromwellian
regime and was imprisoned briefly in 1659 for his propagandist
writings when the Protectorate was terminated.

Oliver Cromwell had died in 1658, when his despotic legacy
fell to his son Richard. Fortunately, Richard was not possessed of
his father's dictatorial ambition, with the result that it was not
long before the monarchy of Britain was returned. At that time,
John Milton was released as preparations were made for the 1660
coronation of King Charles II and the Restoration of the Royal
House of Stuart. Having been crowned in Scotland nine years
earlier, this flamboyant son of Charles I came to London from
exile in The Hague, to lead the nation in a new age of liberty
and toleration. Charles II was skilful, well-liked and perfectly
suited to the mood of the era. His primary concern was to afford
people considerable freedom after more than a decade of harsh
military oppression. In this respect, he allowed an abandoned
gaiety to prevail, reopening the inns, theatres and sportsfields,

while at the same time a new romantic spirit of learning and enquiry was born.

Charles II reformed the Anglican Church, and maintained a social realm wherein all religious denominations were equally accepted. Yet, despite these achievements, the obstructive Anglican politicians and clergy pursued their imperious course. No matter what the King thought, they had no intention of showing any forbearance towards other religious persuasions, particularly not to the Jews or Catholics. Moreover, because Charles was married to the Portuguese Catherine of Braganza, they insisted that he must have leanings toward the Church of Rome. Parliament therefore passed the restrictive 1673 and 1678 *Test Acts*, precluding anyone other than Anglicans from holding governmental or public office.

Nonetheless, Charles forged his strategy of liberal reform, with an intention to bring the philosophical Age of Reason (as perceived by the French mathematician René Descartes) into Britain. To this end, in 1662, he chartered the Royal Society of London. With founders such as Christopher Wren and Robert Boyle, later joined by Isaac Newton, Edmond Halley and other notable scholars, the Society remains the nation's foremost academy of science and natural philosophy to this day.

Another prominent writer of the era was the Bedfordshire missionary John Bunyan, who was also imprisoned by the Anglican hierarchy in 1660. The charge was that he had been preaching without a licence. Whilst in gaol, he completed his celebrated allegorical novel, *The Pilgrim's Progress*. In this work, concerning the adventures of a pilgrim named Christian, Bunyan introduced a devil called Apollyon. This was an alternative name for Abaddon (as given in Revelation 9:11), the same guardian of the abyss who was referenced by John Milton. When introducing this lord of the inferno , the Bible explains:

> And they had a king over them, which is the angel of the bottomless pit, whose name in the Hebrew tongue is Abaddon, but in the Greek tongue hath his name Apollyon.

In describing Apollyon for *The Pilgrim's Progress*, Bunyan wrote:

> Now the monster was hideous to behold; he was
> clothed with scales like a fish (and they are his pride);
> he had wings like a dragon, feet like a bear, and out of
> his belly came fire and smoke, and his mouth was the
> mouth of a lion.

During his exchange with the young pilgrim, Apollyon referred to God as the King of Princes, exclaiming, 'I hate his person, his laws and people!' He then hurled darts at Christian for half a day before the devout pilgrim wounded the adversary with his sword: 'And with that, Apollyon spread forth his dragon's wings, and sped him away, that Christian saw him no more'.[8]

John Bunyan's imprisonment by the Anglican bishops occurred by way of the Church of England's regained prominence as the primary religious institution in post-Cromwellian times. Attempting to defend his position as an unauthorized preacher, Bunyan explained in his confession to the Church commissioners how it was that talk of the Devil had first inspired him to become a brisk talker on religious matters. He described that it began when he heard two Baptist women conversing in a street in Bedford:

> Their talk was about a new birth, the work
> of God in their hearts; as also, how they
> were convinced of their miserable state by
> nature. They talked of how God had visited
> their souls with his love in the Lord Jesus,
> and with what promises they had been
> refreshed, comforted and supported against
> the temptations of the Devil.[9]

Prior to that, Bunyan had considered the Devil's temptations to be concerned with wickedness and crime, but he was fascinated by the women's perception of them being the cause of everyday enticements. The talk of salvation through Jesus was entirely new to him, for there had been no such ideal in the Puritan agenda. The message from the preachers had been only of God's wrath and damnation, with no hope of reprieve; there had been no mention of Jesus. What Bunyan experienced from the women's conversation was a refreshing new style of Christian evangelism, an unfamiliar concept that completely overwhelmed him.

To that point in his life, Bunyan had been a maker of pots and kettles, having also served for a while in the Cromwellian parliamentary army. But he was well enough educated and, after studying the new-found doctrine of the Gospels, he began to write religious books and preach. After some years, he was drawing bigger congregations than the parish churches, and the commissioners were infuriated. In the midst of a sermon, Bunyan was arrested and charged with holding unlawful meetings and conventicles, with the result that he was imprisoned for twelve years. Upon his release, King Charles II granted him a royal licence to preach, but his time behind bars had not been in vain. Along with other books, it had seen the birth of *The Pilgrim's Progress*, one of the great classical works in the English language.[10]

The Mark of Satan

During the religiously tolerant reigns of Charles II and his succeeding brother, James II, there were comparatively few witchcraft trials or related hangings in England — just eleven recorded cases in the twenty-five years from 1660 to 1685. In Presbyterian Scotland, however, the situation was rather different and the persecutions continued for a while, just as they had in the past. The best known and most fully documented of the English trials was that of the Lowestoft witches. In 1662, two elderly widows, Amy Duny and Rose Cullender of Suffolk, were sentenced at the Lent Assizes in Bury St Edmonds for bewitching seven children. Amy was said to be able to turn into a toad!

The historical importance of this particular case is that certain irregular witness statements for the prosecution, newly referred to as 'spectral evidence', were allowed by the judge, Sir Matthew Hale, Lord Chief Baron of the Court of Exchequer. Without this record as a necessary legal precedent, the infamous American witch trials in Salem, Massachusetts, thirty years later, would never have taken their course to so many unjustified hangings. Just as eventually happened in Salem, it was reported of the said bewitched children of Lowestoft that, when three of them appeared in court, they 'fell into strange and violent fits, screeching out in a most sad manner'.[11]

The notion of 'spectral evidence', which became a short-term courtroom precedent, was based on a Bury St Edmonds ruling that 'anyone claimed by the child victims to have been encountered by them in a vision must automatically be presumed guilty of witchcraft in the manner envisioned'. It stemmed from the fact that the children, who were each prone to violent fits and tantrums, claimed they had seen Amy Duny and Rose Cullender shaking their fists and threatening them. They would then run to the places where they fancied the women had stood, and would begin 'spinning, and sometimes reeling, or move in other postures', demonstrating the evil contortions of the witches' aggressive torments.

One girl had seen a large mouse run across the hearth in her home; another had been approached by an annoying bee; another had seen a duck in a poultry house. These and other such ordinary events were each adjudged to prove how the two old women were using their devilish powers to terrify the children from a distance. One of the girls brought a nail into the court; another brought a handful of pins, and each claimed to have vomited these items. This was clearly evidence of a most diabolical nature, for nails and pins were undoubtedly items of the most abominable sorcery! To cap it all was the ultimate evidence: When asked to read from the New Testament, the children were quite unable to say the name of Jesus Christ, but they could read the name of the Devil loud enough. In conclusion, the judge and all the court were fully satisfied to give a guilty verdict, and the two old women were hanged, still protesting their innocence with their last breaths.[12]

A key item of evidence at this trial related to the matter of Devil's Marks, as previously mentioned in respect of the French priest Louis Gauffridy. The Bury St Edmonds court transcript relates that when the two women were brought before Justice of the Peace, Sir Edmund Bacon,

> He gave order that they should be searched; whereupon this deponent with five others … coming to the house of Rose Cullender, did acquaint her with what they were come about, and asked whether she was contented that they should search her. She did not oppose it, whereupon they began at her head, and so stripped her naked … Upon narrower search, they found in her privy parts three excrescencies [small growths].

Superficial bodily imperfections, whether moles, warts or other common blemishes and minor growths or depressions, were crucial to those of the witch-hunting profession. Warts were the favourite and, wherever placed on the body, whether on face, hand or foot, were reckoned to be teats implanted by the Devil, whereby the witches would suckle their imps and familiars. But imperfections in whatever form, no matter how minor and insignificant, were classified as Devil's Marks.

In 1661, pupils of the French visionary nun, Antoinette Bourignon of Lille, confessed that the Devil had given them each 'a mark for their pledges to him', with new marks granted for each new promise of their loyalty. The inquisitional theory was that such marks represented the very sign and personal seal of Satan. As mentioned in respect of Matthew Hopkins, it was said that, when pricked, a Devil's Mark would not bleed; neither would the bearer feel any pain. The marks were often found to be as tiny as flea bites, hidden beneath the hair on any part of the body, or out of sight within bodily orifices. Thus it became the practice for priests, ministers, inquisitors and court officials to shave captive witches and investigate them minutely for any sign of their traffic with evil.[13]

214

Robert Kirk, a minister at Aberfoyle in Scotland, wrote in 1691 that he had found a witch with such marks concealed in the roof of her mouth. When pricked, he claimed, 'the marks revealed themselves as toads or bats'.[14] Shortly afterwards, the Franciscan friar, Ludovico Maria Sinistrari, wrote in his *De Daemonialitate*:

> The mark is not always of the same shape or figure; sometimes it is a hare, sometimes a toad's leg, sometimes a spider, a puppy or a doormouse. It is imprinted on the most hidden parts of the body ... With women it is usually on the breasts or her privy parts. Now the stamp which imprints these marks is none other than the Devil's claw.[15]

Setting the scene for the investigation of such marks in England was the *Country Justice Guide* for magistrates. Prepared in 1618 by the Cambridgeshire lawyer and member of Parliament, Michael Dalton, it explained, 'These Devil's marks be often in their secretest parts, and therefore require diligent and careful search'. Subsequently published in London, the *Guide* became an official document of legal authority, empowering justices to conduct full pre-trial body searches with an express focus upon the female genitalia, 'lest even perchance a familiar imp might be hidden there'.[16]

Puritan ministers soon latched onto this regulation, and in 1627 the pastor Richard Bernard stated, in his *Guide to Grand Jury Men in Cases of Witchcraft*, that the Devil's Mark might be found anywhere, 'and since it is likely to be in very hidden places, the search must be diligent'.[17]

The convent novices of Lille had said that, in their case, 'the Devil branded some part of them with an iron awl'. Searching and probing women's bodies for these marks became an intrinsic part of the witchfinding process, to the extent that the most expert 'prickers' (as the investigators were called) formed their own regular 'trade guild', attached to the Kirk in Scotland. Among the most notorious of 'prickers' in Scotland were John Kincaid of Trenent, John Balfour of Corhouse, John Dick and, most infamously, Paterson of Inverness, who turned out to be a woman disguised in men's clothing.[18]

In terms of final execution after sentence, England and Scotland were by no means exempt from the same epidemic of cruelty as in Europe, although witches were usually hanged or drowned, rather than burned. The *Country Justice* proclamation did, however, cite the legality of burning for cases where death or bodily harm had been inflicted by Devil-worshipping witches:

> To use or practice witchcrafts, enchantment, charm, or sorcery, whereby any person shall be killed, pinned, or lamed in any part of their body, or to be counselling or aiding thereto, is felony. By the ancient common law such offenders are to be burned.

In every Scottish kirk there was a box into which the names of suspected witches could be dropped secretly by anyone who bore some personal grudge or malice against another. To be suspected was to be accused, and to be accused was a certain route to interrogation and sentence. One man in Leith suffered extreme tortures. His legs were crushed in iron frames, and wedges were driven beneath his finger and toe nails until he finally confessed, as required, that he knew of several hundred witches who had gone to sea in a sieve and raised a tempest!

The Black Mass

Earlier, we saw that the Regent of France, Catherine de Medici, was described as an evil satanist who had performed a diabolical ceremony known as the Black Mass. From that time in the latter 16th century, nothing further is known to have been recorded about such a rite for more than 100 years. The next event of any note in this regard occurred in 1678, when the renegade Abbé Etienne Guibourg and a certain Catherine Deshayes (known as *La Voisin*: 'the neighbour') were said to have performed a

Black Mass in Paris. It was commissioned by Françoise-Athénaïs, Marquise de Montespan, the mistress of King Louis XIV.

Catherine Deshayes was of petit-bourgeois stock, and ran a beauty parlour specializing in chemical cosmetics and potions. She was also an astrologer, credited with magical powers, and had a high-ranking clientele, whose coaches with armorial bearings were often seen at her premises in the Rue de Beauregard. Police reports confirm that, alongside her various dispensaries and laboratories, was a large room, like a chapel, hung wall-to-wall with black. There were upturned crosses, an altar draped with a black cloth, and black candles around. Catherine, along with her apothecary, had been conspiring with corrupt priests, illegally to obtain consecrated hosts (eucharistic wafers) in order to perform satanic rituals that would aid her clients in their marriages, extra-marital affairs and other sexual liaisons. As a clandestine abortionist, she was able to acquire the necessary human fat to make the black candles as required for the unholy Mass, and she manufactured specially prepared poisons for the dispatching of unwanted husbands or troublesome admirers.

In January 1678, the Marquise de Montespan applied to Catherine Deshayes for a Black Mass in order to secure her position as King Louis' favourite mistress. The ceremony was conducted by Abbé Guibourg, whilst the Marquise, clasping two black candlesticks, lay on her back, naked across the altar, with her legs over the side and the priest stood between her knees. Blood from an aborted foetus was mixed with wine, and the chalice was placed on her body, whilst a suplication for the woman's desire to dominate the King's bed was made to the Evil One.[19] It is not clear who reported the Mass to the authorities, but the resultant criminal investigation led to the imprisonment of Guibourg and the execution of Catherine Deshayes, who was burned at the stake for poisoning and sorcery.[20]

The occult significance of the orthodox Catholic Mass dates back to the 6th century, and magical outcomes were believed possible by the clergy. The Vatican's liturgical book of the *Gelasian Sacramentary* asserts that Masses can bring good weather or rain as required; they can protect travellers embarking on journeys, and can ward off diseases in people and cattle. Catholic Masses were even performed to bless ships, and to render farm tools more effective. In later 17th-century times, when Masses were used for unauthorized magical purposes, they were seemingly conducted by corrupt churchmen in the service of the Devil.

Following the Guibourg Mass, a great many tales emerged of how priests were using desecrated hosts and black chalices in the worship of Beelzebub. The Mass readings were said to be conducted by the Goat of Mendes from a black Devil's *Missal* bound in wolfskin, and the rituals progressed into frenzied orgies.[21] The theory was that, at Black Masses, everything was done in opposition to the recognized procedures: crosses were upside-down or broken, candles were black, censers contained hallucinogens, and the litany was recited backwards. The ceremony was always conducted over a naked woman, who lay upon a black-draped altar.[22]

Rituals involving homage to the Devil, with the trappings of the orthodox Mass employed, had been described by the inquisitor Paolo Grillandi in his 1525 *Tractatus de Hereticis et Sortilegiis*, shortly before the time of Catherine de Medici. It was postulated by some that the Black Mass was performed as a symbolic redemption of women from the curse of Eve that Catholicism had thrust upon them.[23] But, as the stories became more exaggerated, accounts of sacrificial virgins and children ensued, with over fifty French priests executed in the 1680s for sacrilege, wizardry and sexual abuse. But to whatever extent these Black Mass descriptions might have been true, they were essentially the practices of an heretical cult of unfrocked or renegade clergymen, and had nothing whatever to do with conventionally perceived witchcraft.[24]

Hypocritical Integrity

As the teeth of the Age of Reason bit ever more deeply into the social culture, it became increasingly difficult for the Catholic

218

Church and various Protestant Churches to maintain the concept of divine miracles. New miracles were emerging before people's eyes in the shape of scientific discovery and the explained laws of Nature. Scepticisms, such as were prevalent in the days of Galileo, were giving way to revelatory knowledge and an understanding of life's real magic. In the wider scheme of things, beyond the closed doors of the Black Mass and the secret doings of certain occultist groups, the old perceptions of malevolent wizardry were in fast decline as sorcerers and theologians became gradually more impotent. The days, when miracles were the product of supernatural intervention or unaccountable providence, were being superseded by a culture that sought its answers from Nature and Reason. Within this environment, the concepts of God and the Devil prevailed, although with a lessening influence on people's daily lives. But the notion of witchcraft was doomed as talk of Sabbats and the like faded into eventual obscurity.[25]

The tide was initially turned by a notable case in 1670, when the provincial parliament of Normandy condemned a dozen women, young and old, to be burned at the stake. Their crime was determined as 'Attendance upon the Witches' Sabbat'. But an appeal was resultantly taken to the Crown, and Louis XIV was persuaded to spare their lives on condition that they should leave the kingdom and never return. Astonishment and indignation greeted this exercise of royal clemency, and the court officials sent a grave petition to the King:

> Your parliament have thought it their duty on
> occasion of these crimes, the greatest which
> men can commit, to make you acquainted with
> the general and uniform feeling of the people
> of this province with regard to them; it being
> moreover a question in which are concerned
> the glory of God and the relief of your
> suffering subjects, who groan under their fears
> from the threats and malevolence of these
> people; on the loss of goods and chattels, and
> the deaths from unknown diseases, which are

219

often the consequence of their menaces, all of
which may easily be proved to your Majesty's
satisfaction by the records of various trials
before your parliaments.[26]

But Louis was not convinced. During the twenty-seven years of
his reign to that point, he had heard and seen enough in this
connection, as had his younger cousin Charles II in England
after the Lowestoft fiasco. The time had come to regulate such
proceedings, and King Louis made his stand. He could find no
proof whatever of malevolence causing any loss of goods and
chattels, nor inflictions of disease. Even if such were to have been
the case, they were hardly the greatest of crimes, and would not
warrant the death penalty. After all due consideration, the King's
final decision countermanded the highest court of Normandy,
and the women were all pardoned by royal decree.

Beyond the familiar accusations of malevolent sorcery, so
many of the pleasures associated with witches' assemblies — the
dancing, feasting, revelry and sexual adventures for which
countless victims had been hanged, drowned and burned, were
now becoming aspects of everyday life. If these things were truly
embodied in the agenda of Satan, as had been claimed, then
people (having come through the constraints of Puritanism and
active Inquisition) were now living their lives in the manner of a
constant, all-embracing Sabbat. In this context, the stalwart
churchmen might well have considered that Satan had finally
won the day, but those like Isaac Newton and Voltaire were to
disagree. In their view, Reason was winning over and above
centuries of dogmatic assertion based on nothing but a desire to
hold society in thrall. It was now the case that people's minds
and bodies were being liberated from the long-term constraints of
clerical dominion. In the course of this, alchemists and conjurors
were being transformed into respected scientists and doctors.
Demonic possessions, such as afflicted the nuns of Loudon
and Louviers, were now being medically redefined as mental and
physical disturbances caused by the sedentary confines of the
cloisters.[27]

There was, however, a dark aspect to consider as the realities of the past in sanctified establishments became ever more evident with the new openness of society. It became commonplace, as a required procedure, for births within convents to be announced, formally registered and legally declared. Controlling the nunneries of Provence was the Noble Chapter of the Canons of Pignan. There were sixteen canons in charge of the region's nuns, and in one year the office of the Provost received sixteen individual declarations of pregnancy. Similar incidents occurred throughout the conventual establishments, and it transpired that the holy sisters had learned in their training to accept the births as 'a necessary accident of our profession'.[28] From the late 1600s, it became the practice to put the unrequired infants out to nurse with peasant families who were ready to adopt them. But it emerged that, prior to that time, the rate of infanticide within nunneries had been extraordinarily high. For centuries, countless innocent young lives had been terminated in order to preserve the hypocritical integrity of the Church.

16

A FIENDISH TRANSITION

A Priestly Fraud

A premise of the latter 17th-century Age of Reason was that, in matters of philosophical and behavioural understanding, the application of logic would supersede enforced dogma. And so it did in many respects. It was also the case that individual reasoning made use of intuition as well as logic. The net result was a greater freedom of expression in word and deed, which led to a great many differences of opinion as people reasoned their ways in and out of situations rather than following strictly governed principles. Unlike fixed rules and regulations, the logic and intuition of one person were not necessarily the same as those of another; they were subject to interpretation by way of individual circumstance and desire. Hence, reasoning could lead to an ideal of service or, in contrast, to an outlook of greed. Either way, it was vastly different to past situations of religious obligation, and people were quick to grasp their opportunities. On one side of the scales, this induced a wealth of discovery and enlightenment. But on the other side it engendered a considerable moral laxity in those who felt that a freedom to choose was a permit to misbehave.

In this environment, the Devil had no established position or fully identified purpose. He was still lurking offstage, but was generally ignored and needed a new realm of operation. Having been a fallen angel, who had become a horned satyr, a winged dragon, a hideous monster and a black goat with claws, his image had lost all credibility. He had been the Prince of the World and the Lord of Temptation, a subject of Middle Ages ridicule and of Reformation fear. But through all this, even in his darkest days, it was not so much the Devil himself that filled people with trepidation; it was the power of his malign influence as portrayed by the Church establishments. The Devil's temptations led to sin, but so many sins of yesteryear — the dancing, singing, feasting, drinking, theatre-going and sexual promiscuity — were now commonplace. Even the bishops and clergy had become more open and flexible in their approach. In any event, Catholics, who perhaps pushed the boundaries a little too far, could always confess and receive absolution. But, whether Catholic or Protestant, a good many people were now crossing the line of responsibility, especially those of the wealthy upper classes, and it was destined to be some while before the unabashed fever of liberation settled back to a more reasonable norm. Meanwhile, it was for many an age of excess, as notions of acceptability moved almost from one extreme of behaviour to the other.

In all of this, few ever thought to ask, Where is the Devil? There were, of course, still religious movements and plenty of devout people who remained on a straight and narrow path, but even they were substantially freed from the dogmatic constraints of the witch-hunting years. They could now pursue their beliefs and various forms of worship without fear of retribution from their own guiding masters. In the new scheme of things, they were now God's children, and the figure of Jesus had been brought to the fore after centuries of being almost forgotten. There was now a Saviour at hand, and life in the church communities became a good deal more comfortable.

From the early days of persecuting heretics, the Catholic inquisitors and Puritan divines had long focused their concepts of satanism on the witches who, along with gypsies and others, were reckoned to be the Devil's primary disciples. But things had changed beyond any recovery of such concepts. Gypsies were no longer viewed with unnecessary suspicion, and the days of the witch-hunt were officially over. Hence, in theological terms, the Devil was back in his original role as the biblical tempter of Jesus — a lone antagonist who had lost the debate, just as John Milton reminded people in his *Paradise Regained*. The timing of this work, published in 1671, was absolutely perfect.

In Holland, the prosecution of sorcerers and witches had been abolished as early as 1610. In Geneva, Switzerland, the trials ceased in 1632, and Queen Christina of Sweden issued her proclamation of termination in 1649. Since then, as we have seen, the majority of prosecutions for sorcery, witchcraft and Devil worship had been in France and Britain. It was therefore a ruling of significant impact when, in July 1682, King Louis XIV signed the edict that ended judicial proceedings against witches in France.[1] No longer was there any risk of a death penalty for soothsayers, magicians or enchanters, unless of course, like anyone else, they had committed a crime that otherwise demanded it. Murder by poisoning was the most common cause of such sentencing in France at that time.

Witch prosecutions in England were also made illegal from 1682.[2] But despite this, some unauthorized interrogations continued for many more decades in the rural areas and remote places where superstitions continued to flourish. As late as 1760, Joseph Baretti of the Society of Antiquaries wrote that in Honiton, near Exeter, a ducking stool was still in use for trying witches, and that beliefs in sorcery and Devil worship remained extant in the Devonshire region.[3] The ducking stool was a means whereby suspected witches were lowered into water on suspended chairs. This form of undignified testing was also used as a method of humiliation for women regarded as public nuisances — those who committed offences such as prostitution, or women called 'scolds' who caused disturbances of the peace. Unruly men were instead placed in pillories or the stocks.[4]

The problem that sceptics of witchcraft had faced for the longest time was that to write or speak against the existence of the cult was open to court mockery and likely prosecution. The fears were so strong that anyone who did not believe in witchery was necessarily perceived as a witch trying to throw others off track. Those who made such attempts did so on the basis of citing mercy and charity. But this had caused its own difficulties, since the rationale was founded on the same Christian principles supposedly upheld by the witchfinders. For as long as the Devil was accepted as a fact, and that his purpose was to undermine the Christian faith, it was impossible to argue that there were not heretics and sorcerers on his side. There must therefore be Devil worshippers, and it was clearly the job of true believers to seek them out.[5]

In contrast to this, it was widely understood from the 1680s that witches did not exist. Prosecutions ceased, apart from some isolated incidents where laws were flouted, or where old superstitions remained extant in some lower levels of jurisdiction. It was also asserted by many notable scholars that even the Devil did not exist. In 1685 the Dutch physician, Anton Van Dale, wrote in his *De Oraculis Ethnicorum* (Pagan Oracles) that everything concerning the Devil had been 'a priestly fraud'.[6] This paved the way for the Dutch theologian Balthasar Bekker, who published his *De Betoverde Weereld* (Enchanted World) in 1691. In a formidable attack against the Inquisition and its wicked ensnaring of innocent victims, Bekker sought to prove that the Devil was irrelevant. Moving God back into centre-stage position, Bekker wrote:

> I will restore the glory of the power and
> the wisdom of this Sovereign Master of the
> world, inasmuch as he has been robbed of it
> so as to give part to the Devil. I will banish
> from the world this abominable creature to
> shackle him in Hell.[7]

The underlying principle of this and other such writings was not implicitly to deny the Devil's existence, but to deny the long-standing premise that he was in control of people's lives. Bekker's treatise, although welcomed and influential on a wide scale, was admonished by some churchmen outside Holland, but was highly acclaimed by philosophers and reformists. Voltaire wrote that Bekker was the 'great enemy of eternal Hell and the Devil'.

A few years later, in 1699, Christian Thomasius of Halle University, a founder of the German Enlightenment, admitted his own error in having condemned a witch to death. He came out boldly against the practice, denying that there was any possibility of anyone making a compact with the Devil, since he was not a reality. And so it was that, by the late 17th century, Satan was on his own — manoeuvred, without emissaries or disciples, into a twilight zone of incompetence where he was no longer an object of universal fear.[8]

Spirit of Evil

From the time that King Louis XIV made his investigation of the said Normandy witches in 1670, it had become evident that Devil worship in the manner of its speculation since the 1486 *Malleus Maleficarum* was a fabricated myth. But that did not mean that Satan could not have worshippers and disciples, for there were still those who asserted his existence and elected to believe in his powers. Furthermore, they declared that he could be invoked in person, and supplicated for his intervention. It was precisely this contention by certain occultists in France that gave rise to the Satanic Mass rituals as seemingly begun in Paris by Abbé Etienne Guibourg and Catherine Deshayes in 1678.

Whilst the world was pushing the Devil aside from the mainstream culture, he was now available to be adopted by a very corrupt branch of society that could use its presumed diabolic connection for nefarious purposes. Notwithstanding that belief in the Devil was waning, there were still many who upheld the 'spirit of evil' as a concept. Unlike the earlier innocent victims of prosecution, or those who had striven to resist temptation, these 17th-century satanists were prepared to submit themselves fully to wickedness, debauchery and crime on a ceremonial scale. Material science had provided new knowledge concerning hallucinogens and chemical intoxicants, so that apothecaries and unfrocked priests were in a position to perform impressive feats of apparent sorcery and conjuration with significant expertise.

People's minds, although now released from immediate fear in terms of demonic intrusion, still carried memories of the sinister hooded monks, tortures and black dungeons of the Inquisition. They were enjoying their new-found liberation, but many were inclined to consider the notion of a dark side — a prevalent force of evil that was far more threatening than spiteful witches or sex-crazed nuns. In this regard, the epitome of evil might just as well be called *Satan* as by any other name. If there truly were priests and conjurers who might, by way of rites and incantations, have a controlling access to such a malevolent force, they would present a very scary prospect. Alternatively, if one were to associate with them, gaining access to their resources, then personal ambitions and desires might be fulfilled by way of diabolical process. It was just such an inclination that brought the Marquise de Montespan to the chapel in the Rue de Beauregard. Her intention was to have black magic secure her position as the King's favourite, but many others used such Masses for the purposes of murder and various acts of hate and revenge.

All the wicked practices, hitherto wrongly attributed to witches and gypsies, now came into play as a reality. As previously cited, over fifty French priests were executed in the 1680s alone, for sacrilegious crimes of violence and sexual abuse, whilst many more were imprisoned. At the same time, a most striking characteristic of the era was that murder by poison increased at an alarming rate, and the principal practitioners were women.[9] A key player in this regard was the beautiful Marie-Madeleine d'Aubray, the Marquise de Brinvilliers. She and her lover poisoned her father and two brothers, although the attempt on her husband failed. When incriminating papers were found, the Marquise fled from France to England, and then to Flanders. Arrested eventually in Liège and taken to Paris, she was tortured, tried, beheaded and burned. During her interrogation, she declared, 'Half the people of quality are involved in this sort of thing and, if I cared to talk, I could ruin them'.[10] It was as a result of this trial in 1676 that King Louis established a special court of satanic investigation under the commissioner of police, Nicholas de La Reynie, who arrested Abbé Guibourg and Catherine Deshayes two years later.

In her citation regarding 'people of quality', the Marquise was undoubtedly correct. The related police archive suggests that many of those involved in the iniquitous Mass rituals, with their sexual debauchery and associated crimes, were women of noble and other high rank. Involvement with their covert societies was plainly an expensive business, and very much an elite playground of the rich and titled. In 1679, Anne-Marie Mancini, the Duchesse de Bouillon, was questioned by La Reynie. She was suspected of being a cult devotee, and of attempting to poison her husband to inherit the estate. She denied the poison charge, but admitted to being a frequent visitor at a house in Villeneuve where Satanic Masses were conducted. In establishing his new department, which became known as the *Burning Court*, La Reynie became very unpopular with the women of high society, and was feared to the extent that the Countess of Soissons fled to Belgium.[11] Among others whose coaches were seen at the Villeneuve house were the Duchesse de Duras and Princesse Marie-Louise de Tingry. Not surprisingly, given the notability of the parties concerned, a strong female opposition to the *Burning Court* made itself felt in Paris and Versailles, especially when La Reynie set his sights towards the King's own mistress, the Marquise de Montespan. Although Guibourg and Deshayes were arrested and sentenced, King Louis destroyed the incriminating documents relating to the Marquise, and dismissed her from court to prevent too much of a royal scandal. She then retired to seek refuge in the Convent of St Joseph.

Although the Devil had no particular physical image at that time, it was deemed necessary for his presence to be felt, and preferably seen, at the unholy Mass rituals. However, the Devil was actually a product of Christian demonology, and these ceremonies were not Christian. The priests therefore reverted to more ancient pagan concepts and, since the witches' Sabbats had long been associated with a satanic goat, the Egyptian Goat of Mendes became the most common portrayal by way of a costumed figure. Thus, the Devil's tradition was moved into a pre-Christian context to provide a tantalizing element of danger for the participants. Straying from their everyday lives in a Catholic environment, they were transported into a sinister, and somehow exciting, realm of the old gods.

In such a context, the door was opened to an idea that was in complete contrast to Christian dogma because, in pagan times, there were not only gods, but goddesses. It was therefore a great inspiration to the women who frequented these Masses for Satan to have a female companion, or indeed a female equal. Sometimes the Devil was personally identified as an androgynous character. The records of the Guibourg Mass make it plain that, in paying tribute to the Devil, the priest also made offerings to both Ashtaroth and Asmodai.[12] As we saw in chapter 1, Asmodai was an original prince of darkness and lust in pre-Christian times. Ashtaroth, however, was a woman — the wife of the ancient Canaanite god El Elyon. Alternatively styled Ashtoreth or Asherah, the name of this goddess features no fewer than forty-four times in the Old Testament.[13]

It is evident nevertheless, from the various trial records, that the Mass ceremony was itself no more than an entertaining stage play, enacted for the purpose of extracting exorbitant sums of money from a wealthy clientele for what was actually a profitable traffic in drugs. The scientific revolution of the era had led to a professional awareness of chemical compounds, and there were always chemists and apothecaries in the employ of Mass organizers such as Catherine Deshayes. With hallucinogens and sexual stimulants used in the mesmerizing rituals, the clients were satisfactorily seduced into parting with considerable sums of money in exchange for aphrodisiac love potions and toxic powders for effective poisoning.[14]

The Devil's New World

Ten years after the formal abolition of witch trials in England, the last major hearing for witchcraft in the English-speaking world took place in North America. It occurred in the village of Salem, Massachusetts, and has become especially well remembered by way of Arthur Miller's play and the resultant 1997 movie, *The Crucible*.

On 5 August 1620, the overcrowded ship *Mayflower* left Plymouth in the south of England, carrying Puritans to the east coast of America. Escaping what they perceived as the gaudy show of the Anglican Church, they sought to establish their own settlements in the New World, where the first successful English colony had been established in 1607. They had applied for a land grant in Virginia, but the *Mayflower* was blown off course and, instead, those who survived the perils of the voyage landed at Cape Cod, Massachusetts.

A group, since recognized as the Pilgrim Fathers, drafted the *Mayflower Compact* which laid down the basis for disciplined government and the rights of the settlers. Their appointed leaders were John Carver, elected as the Massachusetts Governor, along with William Bradford and Myles Standish. Considerable numbers of other Puritans followed across the Atlantic during the reigns of James I and Charles I, to the extent that sizeable colonies were established in the region that became known as New England.[15] The Native Americans acted as guides and taught the colonists woodcraft, trapping, hunting, how to make maple sugar and birch-bark canoes, and how to raise crops of maize and tobacco. They also introduced them to the turkey which, following the first truly successful harvest in the autumn of 1621, became the centrepiece of the annual Thanksgiving festival.

Just nine years before the Pilgrim Fathers had sailed from Plymouth, the Authorized Bible of King James had been printed in English,[16] and was readily available for Puritan interpretation, without Anglican interference, by the New England voyagers. Along with their Bibles, they also carried European books about sorcery, and were inclined to blame incidents such as failed crops and disease among their cattle and pigs on the spells of malevolent sorcerers. One view assumed that witches were isolated individuals, or belonged to small covens that harmed others for material gain. But the Puritan clergy insisted that they were members of an organized satanic cult, whose purpose was to destroy the pilgrim communities.

The most prominent clergyman to hold that view was Cotton Mather, who spoke of an 'army of devils' ready to strike at any moment in New England. He also believed that the 'redskin indians' were sorcerers and black magicians. There was no doubt in his mind that the heathen New World was Satan's kingdom.

'The Devil was very much alive in their midst', said Mather, who encouraged the settlers to fight a holy war against the powers of evil.[17] Thus, a law against witchcraft was passed in 1636, with the first execution occurring in 1648. The victim was Margaret Jones of Charlestown, who had some unconventional ideas about medicine. She disapproved of bleeding techniques and violent emetics, and preferred to work cures by means of herbal tonics and other natural prescriptions. This greatly offended the doctors, and the poor woman was tried for witchcraft, convicted, and hanged. The Colonial Governor, John Winthrop, wrote that, at the very hour of Margaret's execution, there was a great gale in Connecticut which blew down the trees, and he considered this to be an absolute demonstration of her guilt.[18] About the same time, a Massachusetts woman was hanged for witchcraft in Dorchester, and another in Cambridge.

The next case was somewhat startling on account of the victim's social position. A married woman like the aforementioned Margaret Jones would, in those early New England times, not be called Mrs Jones, but Goodwife Jones or Goody Jones. To be a Mrs or Mistress, a woman had to be the wife of an esquire, as a baronet might be regarded in England. One such man had been William Hibbins, the late diplomatic agent for the colony. His widow, Mistress Ann Hibbins, was the sister of Richard Bellingham, the Deputy Governor of Massachusetts. But in June 1656 this prominent lady was tried for witchcraft before Governor Endicott and the General Court.

One day she had seen two women, whom she knew to be unfriendly, talking in the street, whereupon she exclaimed that she was aware they were talking about her. Ann's guess was correct, and was duly reported to the authorities, whereupon she was accused of having 'supernatural insight which must have been imparted to her by the Devil'. Upon physical examination, Ann was found to be the bearer of a Devil's Mark, which automatically rendered her guilty, and she was hanged on Boston Common. The Rev John Norton exclaimed, after the event, that Mistress Hibbins was executed 'only for having more wit than her neighbours'.[19]

Within no more than a dozen recorded trials in the next thirty years, there were several acquittals, including the case of John Bradstreet of Rowley, who was accused of 'familiarity with the Devil'. He had confessed that, whilst reading a book of magic, he heard a voice questioning him. For this he was brought to trial and was destined to be found guilty of 'diabolic conversation'. But the jury in Ipswich decided that Bradstreet was lying, whereupon the court sentenced him to a whipping and a fine of twenty shillings for wasting everyone's time.[20]

Rather more disastrous was the 1688 case of the Goodwin children in Boston. An Irish Catholic woman named Glover was the laundress for John Goodwin's family, in which there were four children. One day the eldest child, Martha, aged thirteen, accused the Glover woman of stealing some items of linen. Glover responded with anger, and young Martha collapsed in a fit. The other children (aged eleven, seven, and five) then followed her example. In subsequent days, they pretended to be deaf and dumb; they barked like dogs and complained of being pricked with imaginary pins. It was even said that they 'flew around like geese'. Doctors and ministers, called in to investigate, agreed that the girls had been bewitched by the Catholic laundress. She was forced to confess that she had made a covenant with Satan, and was in the habit of going to meetings with him. Accordingly, she was found guilty and hanged.[21]

Around that time, Cotton Mather was collecting stories of witchcraft from home and abroad, writing essays such as *Enchantments Encountered: On New England as a home of the Saints and the plot of the Devil against her*. Others were *A Discourse on the Wonders of the Invisible World*, along with *Memorable Providences* and *An Hortatory and Necessary Address to a Country now extraordinarily alarum'd by the Wrath of the Devil*. In time, these various writings became embodied in his 1693 book *The Wonders of the Invisible World*. Meanwhile, however, Mather was using his research as the subject matter for his sermons.[22] Within the context of these public addresses, he gave details of the 1662 Lowestoft witch trial and the precedent of 'spectral evidence' as established by the English judge, Matthew Hale. The related

Tryal of Witches booklet was in circulation from England, and accounts of how the bewitched children shrieked, fainted and fell about in court were well known in Massachusetts. Thus it was that in 1692, when the persecution of New England witches reached a climax in the village of Salem, the scene was set for a major repeat performance. The Devil was bestirring himself; the fuel for an explosion was laid, and it needed but a spark to fire it.

In that year, Salem acquired a new minister, Rev Samuel Parris, who was disliked by many in the community. His young daughter Betty, aged nine, and mischievous niece Abigail, aged eleven, would meet regularly with other girls outside of the church congregations, and this was deemed very irregular by many of the villagers. Although generally quite young, some of the girls were in their teens, and a couple were young women of twenty. One of the group, a West Indian servant of Rev Parris, was named Tituba, and she amused the others with tales of the supernatural and imaginary spells.[23] The girls felt they should keep this sinful behaviour secret but, as time wore on in the superstitious climate of Salem, the strain took effect and two of the girls fell into seizures. Everyone assumed it was demonic possession, and Dr William Griggs said there was no natural explanation. He deduced that it was caused by the evil eye of a witch. Rev Parris then leapt into action, rousing the villagers against powerful witches who, at the behest of Satan, were intent to wreck the community:

> The Devil ... has decoyed a fearful knot of
> proud, forward, ignorant, envious and
> malicious creatures to list themselves in
> his horrid service by entering their names
> in a book by him tendered unto them.

Parris further commented, 'If ever there were witches ... here are multitudes'. In confirmation of this, Cotton Mather added his explanation based on the piety of Puritan New England: 'I think it no wonder. Where will the Devil show the most malice, but where he is hated, and hateth, most?'[24]

The first suspect was of course Tituba. She admitted that she must have bewitched the girls, and named her conspirators as Sarah Good and Sarah Osburn, who were not especially liked in the village. The girls of Tituba's circle immediately concurred, and the magistrates were convinced of a local conspiracy with the Devil. At this, more of the girls became sick with supposed demonic seizures, and a number of arrests followed. The girls then accused old Rebecca Nurse, who had opposed the Parris appointment as minister. She was charged not only with bewitching the girls, but with the murder of several youngsters who had died shortly before. Martha Corey, one of the few people to question the girls' obviously pernicious motives, was arrested, at which Tituba announced that Martha and Rebecca had also been her accomplices. By then, many of the Salem residents were accusing their neighbours of Devil worship without the slightest evidence or proof, and no one dared to object because opposition led to immediate arrest. Any woman who was in any way different to the deferential Puritan norm was classified as a witch, and long-standing squabbles between rival factions in the east and west of the village erupted in a frenzy of hatred.[25] One of the primary witnesses against the girls was seventeen year-old Mary Walcott, whose aunt had been complicit in teaching a supposed spell to Tituba.

In Boston, Cotton Mather prepared a document explaining the ministerial view of sorcery. He suggested legal procedures in which those possessed should be treated with all consideration and support, whilst the guilty must be treated decisively and harshly. In the light of the Bury St Edmonds precedent, he conceded that 'spectral evidence' should be acknowledged by the court, and that anyone claimed by the girls to have been seen by them in a vision was to be declared immediately guilty of witchcraft. Salem was perceived by Rev Mather and the ministers as a microcosm of the great universal drama in which God and Satan were struggling for supremacy, and the witches were the undoubted servants of Satan.[26]

Entirely reminiscent of the Lowestoft children in England, the malicious girls shrieked and fainted in court, pointing out new witches at random. As a result, 150 were imprisoned as a rampant witch mania prevailed. In all, twenty were hanged, including old Rebecca Nurse and the unmarried mother, Sarah Good. One man, Giles Cory, was pressed to death over two days with large crushing stones. Sarah Osburn died without a hearing, and Tituba was sold to a new slave master in Virginia.[27]

When the motives of the girls and the validity of 'spectral evidence' were eventually challenged by William Phipps, the new Governor of Massachusetts, no one in Salem shouldered the responsibility. It was maintained that all the prosecutors had been unwittingly manipulated and controlled by Satan. He had seduced them into believing that witches were truly at work and, with regard to the hangings, it was agreed that no one was to blame because the Devil had made them do it.

17

THE LIGHT OF LUCIFER

A Question of Belief

Notwithstanding that belief in diabolism had been substantially abandoned by the end of the 17th century, the Devil continued to feature in satirical writings and portrayals. Amid the general laxity of the era, there appears to have been a certain uneasiness about the comparatively fast rejection of long-standing traditions. On the surface, people were seemingly unconcerned about malevolent forces, but there was still an abiding fear. What if the scholars and authorities were wrong? In view of this continuing apprehension (largely fuelled by a disquieting awareness of occult societies), the Devil found his way into stories and plays that were often tinged with humour. It was, nevertheless, a different humour to that of the Middle Ages, which ridiculed the Devil; it was rather more a case of veiling what to many was a lingering, though perhaps unconfessed, trepidation.

Among the writers of these satirical works was the French abbot Laurent Bordelon, whose novel *A History of the Ridiculous Extravagancies of Monsieur Oufle* was published in 1710.[1] It dealt with the experiences of a man who read too many books about supernatural events and the Black Arts, but included a double-page tableau of Satan and a Sabbat that parodied a depiction from a century earlier by the Polish engraver Jan Ziarnko. The original work had been produced for Pierre de Lancre, the judge of Bordeaux, who launched the first major witch-hunt of 1609 in response to the *Compendium Maleficarum*.[2] Interestingly, the satirized image did not follow the earlier perception of wild, half naked, rustic revellers. The witches of 1710 were finely dressed women of quality with fashionable hairstyles, feasting at tables, with Satan suitably enthroned amid jesters, tumblers and other court entertainers. There is no doubt, from this and other contemporary works, that witches had not been forgotten, but their status had now been lifted into the higher echelons of those who were powerful even without any diabolic involvement. Since these influential women were of the educated class, onlookers deduced that, if such women truly believed in the Devil, and frequented his Mass ceremonies, there was a fair chance that Satan might exist after all.

At the opposite end of Paris society from the rich and titled women who visited the occultist centres, was a significant underclass of people who were vagrants and beggars. Among these were a great many women. To remove them from the streets, King Louis XIV founded the General Hospital for Women on the site of an old arsenal that had provided saltpetre for gunpowder. For this reason, the hospital became known as *La Salpêtrière*. Troublesome adolescents were enclosed in the 'correction section' for rehabilitation. Prostitutes filled the 'common section'. Women who were guilty of serious crime were quartered in the 'gaol section', and those who were mentally ill or subject to seizures were held in the 'insane section'. Some of these received treatment, while many were deemed incurable, and others were hostile and chained.

Although witchcraft was no longer a crime, it was common for the street women to solicit their real or imagined skills of divination. A good number of these presumed sorceresses, who would have been burnt or hung in earlier times, found their way into *La Salpêtrière*. Comte D'Argenson, the statesman and head of the Paris police in the middle 1700s, took a very close interest in these diviner-women.[3] Despite the regulations, he was not convinced that witches had never existed. The women were confined for creating disturbances of the peace, but D'Argenson perceived a dark, common motivation for their individual actions. He believed that the shadow of the Devil was still cast over the city, existing on the streets as well as in the palaces.

Meanwhile in England, an intriguing title to appear in 1726 was *The Political History of the Devil*, by the Presbyterian author and economic journalist, Daniel Defoe of *Robinson Crusoe* fame.[4] This is a curious work, in which Defoe discusses John Milton's

Paradise Lost, explaining why he considered it inaccurate, while at the same time expounding his own views on moral philosophy. Coming to terms with the problem of evil, Defoe ridiculed many popular notions about Satan, but took for granted the reality of his existence. He portrayed the Devil as an active participant in world history, blaming him for the horrors of the Catholic powers who served his interests. The premise, however, is not altogether satisfactory in that, to illustrate the Devil's responsibility for history's atrocities, Defoe discussed the said atrocities and then personally blamed the Devil for influencing those who caused them, as if that were in itself proof of his existence. In another of his works concerning demonology, Defoe wrote:

> With the pardon of all our modern unbelievers, who deny there is such a thing as the Devil or evil spirit in being, either in the world or out of it, I say with their good leave, I must take it for granted … Not only is there such a thing as the Devil, but also he has possession of several of his servants in human shapes.[5]

In the first part of *The Political History*, Defoe discussed the Devil in biblical terms, citing the nature and effect of the Evil One's influence on people at large. In the second part, he focused on contemporary government and how politicians were corrupted by the will of the Devil. He also stressed that the Devil has no permanent or visible shape, but is capable of achieving any appearance he desires to fulfil his purpose.

Within a British establishment that had largely forsaken such ideas about the Devil by that time, Defoe provides a good example of those religious stalwarts who continued to follow the original Lutheran and Calvinist models. Such views were not especially prevalent in England, but the Scottish Kirk maintained many of its traditional ideas. As a Presbyterian in England, Defoe suffered for his beliefs, being pilloried and imprisoned for a while after mocking High Church doctrines. But he emerged from his obsession with diabolism as an agent for the British Secret

Service,[6] and with the books *Robinson Crusoe*, *Moll Flanders* and *Roxana*, became recognized as the founder of the English novel.

Hell-Fire

Despite all the laws and changes of opinion concerning diabolic intervention in people's lives, there were still other possibilities to consider in the wider scheme of things. In view of revised scriptural teaching, people were getting more used to the idea that God was perhaps a caring deity who watched over the children of his created world. But this did not equate with the suffering caused by natural disasters that were not of man's own making. Surely it could not be God who wreaked havoc with storms, tempests, floods, plagues and earthquakes, causing loss of life, limb and property. There had to be another agency at work, and this could only be the Devil.

In the 2nd century, the Christian orator Tertullian had argued that lightning was the 'forked tongue of Hell-fire', maliciously wielded by Satan himself. Pope Gregory I then confirmed, in the 6th century, that the Devil had 'powers to control the weather'. Subsequently, the doctrine of the demonic origin of storms gathered strength so that thunder, lightning, wind, rain and hail were all reckoned to be of satanic consequence. Even after the Reformation, the same was accepted as an article of faith in the Protestant West.

A well-tried method of defeating the satanic onslaughts had long been the ringing of consecrated bells. Lengthy treatises were written on the subject of how bells could repel the Devil's tempests, because he could not withstand the holy chimes. But the tempests still occurred and the Devil continued to blast the world 'with the flapping of his wings'.

Another supposed means of thwarting the Devil's work were the idols of the *Agnus Dei* — individual pieces of wax blessed by the Pope's own hand, and stamped with the Lamb of God. They were held to be such a marvellous protection against storms that, in 1471, Pope Sixtus IV had prayed:

REVELATION OF THE DEVILL

> O God ... We humbly beseech thee that thou wilt bless these waxen forms, figured with the image of an innocent lamb ... that at the touch and sight of them, the faithful may break forth into praises, and that the crash of hailstorms, the blast of hurricanes, the violence of tempests, the fury of winds and the malice of thunderbolts may be tempered, and evil spirits flee and tremble before the standard of thy holy cross, which is graven upon them.

Sixtus had even issued a bull, reserving to himself the exclusive papal right to manufacture and consecrate the little waxen figures of the *Agnus Dei*. The mere touching of these Lamb of God representations was pronounced as sufficient to protect against fire and shipwreck, storm and hail, lightning and thunder.

Given that, in reality, neither bell-ringing nor magical wax effigies had any practical effect, it had been decided in the 16th century that perhaps the Devil was not working alone. Maybe he was employing witches to carry out his spiteful deeds with the weather. Since witches and gypsies were known to use bells in their own rituals, they were clearly immune in this regard. In contemplation of this, the English legal correspondent William West had written in the late 1500s:

> A witch or a hag is she which being deluded by a league made with the Devil through his persuasion, inspiration or juggling, thinketh she can design what manner or evil things soever, either by thought or imprecation, as to shake the air with lightnings and thunder, to cause hail and tempests, to remove green corn or trees to another place.

By the early 1700s, people were not entirely sure whether witches existed or not. But even if they did, witchcraft was no longer a punishable offence in its own right. It was evident, however, that newly suspected witches of the era were not the least interested in the weather; their motives in attending the Black Mass rituals were wholly centred on personal gratification and gain. Thus, the old speculation remained: If God was not causing the tempests, then they must be the work of the Devil. He must have found a way to close his ears to the bells. After all, St Paul himself had referred to Satan as the 'Prince of the Power of the Air'.[7]

It was not until 1752, when Benjamin Franklin sent a kite into the clouds, and drew lightning off its string, that the concept of meteorological demonology began to collapse. With Franklin's demonstration that lightning was the same type of electrical energy that crackled off a dry cat's back, the Devil began to lose his dominion over the weather. But there were still those in America who were prepared to uphold the old superstition at all costs. They called Franklin an 'archinfidel', and the magical iron rods which he invented to protect tall buildings from the Devil's wrath were deemed entirely blasphemous. The Devil could only do what God allowed him to do, and for Franklin to interfere with God's plan was sacrilege! Reverend Thomas Prince, pastor of the Old South Church in Boston, asserted in 1755 that a violent earthquake, which had shaken that city, was undoubtedly caused by Franklin's iron points. 'In Boston', he said, 'are more erected than anywhere else in New England, and Boston seems to be more dreadfully shaken'.[8]

It was a good while before churches consented in any number to be protected by the heretical device. The tower of St Mark's in Venice had been struck numerous times by lightning, and the powers of darkness appeared to have singled it out for special assault in spite of regular bell-ringing and the angel that adorned its summit. The tower was struck twice again after the lightning rod was invented, whereupon the authorities succumbed and a conductive rod was installed. In Austria, the church of Rosenberg was struck so frequently, and with such loss of life, that the people feared to attend services. Three times the spire had to be rebuilt, until the Devil was said to have been 'exorcised by an iron wand'.

Originally a Philadelphia printer, Benjamin Franklin was inducted as a Fellow of London's Royal Society on 24 November

1757 for his extraordinary work with lightning rods and electricity.[9] He also attracted widespread interest in France, where he was a regular attendee of the Académie Française and a welcome guest of the Royal Court.[10] Indeed, his connections were such that, despite the remnant of puritanical religious opinion against his scientific exploits, he became America's Ambassador to France in 1776. But, notwithstanding his achievements, certain American church groups were highly critical of Franklin's membership of an English society called the Knights of Saint Francis of Medmenham Abbey.[11] Located at West Wycombe in Buckinghamshire, the foundation was more commonly known as the Hell-Fire Club.

The formative Order had been located in St James's, near the royal palace in London, and was an undercover Jacobite cell in the Stuart campaign against the Hanoverian monarchy. The House of Stuart, under King James II (brother of Charles II), had been deposed by the Anglican Parliament in 1688. Then, following a period of reign by the Dutch prince, William of Orange, and King James's two daughters, the noble Electors of Hanover in Germany had assumed the British throne in 1714. The restrictive laws of this Georgian dynasty ultimately sparked the American War of Independence (1775–83), but Benjamin Franklin had been well ahead of the game, lining up support for America in France and from the Jacobite network in England. His Hell-Fire colleague, the prominent journalist John Wilkes, fought an ongoing press campaign for the rights of liberty, and was applauded by Franklin for the stand taken by his newspaper, *The North Briton*, in support of the American cause.[12] Not surprisingly, whilst gaining scientific and diplomatic accolades from their respective quarters, Franklin also came under heavy fire from the Georgian establishment, whose propaganda machine operated through Britain's colonial representatives in America. This fuelled a contrived notion that he was a scurrilous infidel, who meddled with God's laws by way of sorcery. Accusations of Devil worship and debauchery were then levelled against the Medmenham Order, giving rise to its dubbing as the Hell-Fire Club.

Concocted charges laid informally against the Hell-Fire members included all the familiar activities of the high-society occult chapels in Paris. In the old Abbey caves of West Wycombe, they were said to perform black magic and hideous satanic rites, even sacrifices. The most lurid descriptions were published long after the event by the parliamentary writer Nathaniel Wraxall. In 1815, he described a demonic cult that used 'inverted crucifixes, black candles and blood-red Mass wafers'. Such things were based, nevertheless, on hearsay alone, and there is not a scrap of evidence to support the contentions. All documentation concerning the politically sensitive activities of the Medmenham Order were destroyed by the Grand Master, Sir Francis Dashwood, shortly before his death in 1781.[13]

Prominent members, such as John Montagu, Earl of Sandwich, and Horace Walpole, Earl of Orford, were the first to admit that their colleagues were not necessarily paragons of moral virtue. Some were notorious libertines, and there is no doubt that society courtesans were admitted to the premises — but Devil worship was not on the agenda. At worst, the only items of any worth-while record appeared in respect of the formative Club when it was centred in London. *Applebee's Weekly Journal* of 6 May 1721 had reported that certain members 'ridiculed the sacred mysteries of religion, blaspheming and impugning the same in a manner very unfit to be here mentioned'.

In practice, the mask of diabolism actually suited the Club members, since it provided a sinister aspect that kept inquisitive people away from the Medmenham chapter house. Meanwhile, far removed from anything occult, Benjamin Franklin aided Sir Francis Dashwood in producing a revised Anglican *Book of Common Prayer*. This revision, with its Preface by Franklin, was later consulted by the Episcopal Church in America, when it became necessary to delete references to England's King and the Westminster Parliament, whilst making various other liturgical amendments.[14]

Referring to the regular women of the Medmenham fraternity (the 'nuns' as they were termed) and the casks of wine stored at the Abbey, Horace Walpole spoke of 'the nymphs and the hogsheads'. He also mentioned that the gardens of the West Wycombe estate had a shrine dedicated to the goddess Venus. Paul Whitehead, the secretary and steward of Medmenham, explained that the ceremonies of the Order were based on ancient Greek and Roman traditions, with Venus as the recognized *bona dea* (good goddess).[15] Acknowledging this as symbolic of the Order, the contemporary artist George Knapton, when painting Sir Francis Dashwood in a Franciscan habit, showed him along with a naked Venus. In a satirical representation of Bacchus, the god of wine, Knapton also introduced the face of Lord Sandwich peering through the friar's halo.

As the old Roman goddess of love and beauty, Venus was said to epitomize the precepts of the Order. But it was this affiliation that was largely responsible for the satanic association of the Medmenham monks, since Venus was referred to within the community by her Latin name of *Lux-fer,* the 'light bearer', which had been corrupted in biblical understanding to Lucifer. In this regard, Venus was the 'day star' that rose before the sun. Hence, it is clear that the romantically devised Hell-Fire Club had a distinctly pagan edge. But, beyond this, the Luciferian context of its proceedings was quite wrongly interpreted by later writers.

Lust of the Vampire

Although witch prosecutions and interrogations (involving pricking, ducking and the like) had been illegal in England from 1682, it was not until the *Witchcraft Act* of King George II in 1735 that the original 1541 Act of Elizabeth I, and that of James I in 1604, were fully and clearly revised with the substitute penalties laid down in law. The Elizabethan statute, which rendered witchery a capital offence, had decreed:

> It shall be felony to practise, or cause to
> be practised, conjuration, witchcraft,
> enchantment or sorcery, to get money
> or to consume any person in his body,

> members or goods, or to provoke any
> person to unlawful love, or for the
> despite of Christ or lucre of money, to
> pull down any cross.

In a significant relaxing of this old law, the 1735 Act confirmed that people were no longer to be executed for such actions, or for consorting with evil spirits. Instead, anyone who 'pretended' to call up spirits, cast spells or foretell the future, was to be punished as a confidence trickster, subject to fine and imprisonment.

By the 1750s, belief in the Devil had declined substantially. It only reared its head as a convenient premise when it suited those who sought the means to criticize some faction or other for involvements contrary to a recognized norm. Benjamin Franklin's electrical research and the activities of the Medmenham Order are good examples in this regard. The Anglican Church was very much in control at the spiritual level in England, but there were still dissenting movements who found the Church too adrift from the everyday concerns of working people, and were therefore popular as more accessible and sympathetic alternatives.

Foremost in this environment were the Methodists, whose ministers were inclined to uphold the old traditions of diabolic intervention. Their leader, John Wesley, believed firmly in witchcraft, and his followers took a keen interest in alleged cases of demonic possession. The ministers maintained a detailed correspondence on the subject, being the only Protestant movement in England to undertake exorcisms at that time.[16] In fact, Methodism achieved much of its popularity by adhering to otherwise dismissed satanic folklore in a society where many people, particularly in the rural areas, were still very fearful of the Evil One. As late as 1768, John Wesley declared that 'Giving up witchcraft was, in effect, giving up the Bible'. These days, however, it seems that, although Methodist catechisms make certain references to evil and sin, the Devil appears to have been sidelined as a specific figure of personal relevance.

Across the sea in Europe, the 18th-century Catholic Church was still toying with the notion of the 'undead' *vrykolakas*, as had been described by Leo Allatius. The threat of these wandering revenants was not scaring people in the way the bishops had hoped, and plainly needed some further development. Given that belief in the Devil had declined to such a degree, something more fearsome than the *vrykolakas* had to be introduced in support of his existence. Fortunately, the churchmen were in luck for, in the 100 years since Allatius, a parallel mythology had evolved in the Germanic regions. The creatures of this tradition were called *Nachtzehrer*, meaning 'night wasters'. They were said to be corpses who rose from their graves to feed upon other bodies, but also had the rather odd habit of chewing at their own extremities. When such presumed *Nachtzehrer* were found during the grave-huntings that went on in those times, it was customary to drive stakes through their mouths. This pinned their heads to the earth so they were prevented from their night wanderings.

It was soon adjudged by the clergy that these *Nachtzehrer* might be of some strategic use to the Church, and related writings began to emerge. These included *De Masticatione Mortuorum*, concerning the 'chewing dead', by theologian Philip Rohr, and *De Miraculis Mortuorum*, by the physician Christian Frederic Garmann.[17]

In the course of this, an Austrian military report, entitled *Visum et Repertum* (Seen and Discovered), was published in Belgrade regarding a series of murders in Serbia.[18] The man blamed by the villagers for these killings was an ex-soldier called Arnold Paole, who was recently dead and buried. But when his body was exhumed, it was said that his mouth showed signs of what appeared to be fresh blood.

Journalists in other parts of Europe took up the story and, in England, the field report was featured in *The London Journal* in 1732. Taken from the Serbian, the word used to describe the bloody-mouthed corpse, which must have 'risen to the world above', was *upire*. This was an old term, from the Balkan and Carpathian regions, meaning 'over', as in the similar English word 'upper'.[19]

In Prussia, it was also reported that some disinterred corpses showed signs of blood around their mouths. It transpired that this was a common symptom of death caused by pneumonic plague, when blood was expelled from the victim's lungs.[20] But already the churchmen were moving their brains into overdrive. The word *upire*, they determined, was not dissimilar to the Byzantine word *uber*, meaning 'witch'. Furthermore, these 'undead' *Nachtzehrer* must be stalking people at night in order to drain their blood.

In 1746, the French Benedictine abbot, Dom Augustin Calmet, published a treatise concerning these night-walking revenants. It was entitled, *Dissertations sur les Apparitions des Anges des Démons et des Esprits et sur les revenants, et Oupires de Hingrie, de Boheme, de Moravic, et de Silésie*. In this work, the term *upire* gained the variant form of *oupire*. In other translations, via the Slavonic words *vapir* and *vbpir*,[21] the *Oxford Etymological Dictionary* explains that (with an 'm' substituted for the letter 'b', as was common in consonantal switching) the word soon became *vmpir*,[22] By the middle 1700s, these bloodsucking disciples of the Devil were resultantly known as 'vampires'. Thus, Augustin Calmet's work became known by the short title, *A Treatise on Vampires*.

These newly devised fiends implanted a new dread in people's minds, and had the desired effect of making them lean far more heavily on the Church, which was the only perceived route to salvation. The vampires, it was said, could not be demolished by conventional means; only the power of Christianity could defeat these diabolical beings. They were portrayed as hellish demons and emissaries of Satan, who had to be exorcised and destroyed by the monks and clerics.

Another said ghoul of the era was the Bavarian *Blutsauger* (bloodsucker), who seemingly met his fate through not being baptized in life. The adoption of this creature was one of the Church's best conceived strategies to ensure that infants were taken dutifully to the font. This fiendish night stalker, as against the generally red-faced *Nachtzehrer*, was said to be very pale in colour, and it was from the *Blutsauger* legends that the notion of garlic arose as a vampire repellent.[23] Garlic was smeared around door and window-frames seemingly to prevent demonic access by a *blutsauger*. More realistically, it was thought to be a keen protection against plague. The Church was keen enough to accept garlic as an anti-vampire measure, alongside crucifixes and holy water, because garlic was not regarded as an item of herbal witch-craft as were many other plants.

If a *Nachtzehrer* or *blutsauger* did find its way into one's home, there were formally defined ways to check its authenticity — just in case a decomposing corpse was not enough for visual recognition! Firstly, it was reckoned that they cast no reflection in a mirror, since a mirror or water reflection was deemed to be the picture of one's soul. Given that revenants had no soul, it was impossible for them to have a reflection. It was, therefore, customary to cover mirrors or turn them to the wall when in the presence of a corpse, for it was thought that the mirror might harness the spirit of death, and cause another who looked in it to die.[24]

The second test of such a revenant was to check for any bodily shadow, for they were said to have none, especially if their shadow had been stolen or become separated during their lifetime.[25] One method by which shadows could become separated was if they had perhaps been nailed to a wall. Strange as it might seem, this actually was a practice on Romanian construction sites. By way of an inexplicable superstition, it was thought that to have a man cast his shadow upon a newly erected building, and then to drive a nail through the shadow's head would ensure the building's durability and longevity.

Numerous so-called vampiric events were placed on record in Central and Eastern Europe. They all concerned folk who had died and been buried, but who then returned to torment the people of their districts. There are long-winded accounts of corpses who stole milk, clothes, poultry and even children. And there are countless records of murders committed by the 'undead', or of their cattle rustling and, very commonly, rapings.

In Romania, vampires were referred to as *nosferatu*. They were said to be capable of creating other vampires by extracting their victims' blood, and that the creatures could be exorcised by way of stakes driven through their corpses.[26] But in all of this early

248

revenant folklore, there was little of anything which resembles the vampiric regime that became the stuff of popular Gothic Romance in later times. There was nothing enchanting enough to have prompted any long-standing mythology — just a collection of local superstitions, which enabled the authorities to fasten blame upon the dead, so as to avoid the bother of proper criminal investigation in the rural and poorer areas. All it took to satisfy the immediate requirement in each case was to unearth a body, stake it to the ground, sprinkle a few drops of holy water, whilst uttering some suitably impressive Latin, and God's justice was seen to be done.

Subsequently, in a climate of widespread plagues and Church propaganda, fear of the 'undead' grew to such fanatical proportion that a reworked version of the Arnold Paole report became a bestseller at the Leipzig Book Fair. Quite suddenly, the Church was in renewed business as a whole new genre of scary folklore was introduced. The premise behind the many emergent tales was not so much about saving victims, but rather more about destroying the devilish enemies of the Church, with crucifixes galore and gallons of holy water being the essential weapons in the dreaded undertaking against the sinister evil ones.

A widely publicized academic discussion, known as the 'Great Vampire Debate', then ensued within the universities. It was instigated by the theologian Michael Ranft, whose earlier work, *De Masticatione Mortuorum in Tumilis Liber*, had launched a direct attack against the existence of vampires. This had been followed by John Christian Stock's *Dissertio de Cadauveribus Sanguiugis*,[27] as an outcome of which the scholarly debaters came to the conclusion that vampire revenants were a myth created and upheld by Church-led superstition. But beyond the walls of academia, the story was rather different and, after so many years of clerical indoctrination, people began to blame all sorts of deaths, ills and infirmities upon vampires, making them scapegoats for any number of evils and misfortunes inflicted on behalf of the Devil. In consequence, it became common for graves to be raided and their occupants decapitated, with their hearts torn out and ritually burned. This desecration caused such a problem within families and local communities that, in 1755, Empress Maria Theresa of Austria was obliged to enact laws forbidding the practice. A full century later, in the middle 1800s, when vampire fever had soared into its next phase of high Gothic Romance, attractively boxed vampire killing sets were being sold. Each contained a flask of holy water, a tin of eucharistic wafers, a small pistol with silver bullets, a crucifix, a sharp peg and a mallet.

18

AN AGE OF HORROR

Tales From the Crypt

In the hundred years between 1700 and 1800, the French Texts Database identifies just 484 published books, treatises, essays and pamphlets concerning the Devil.[1] At less than five publications per year, this indicates a substantial decline in readership popularity of the subject. The French Revolution (1789–99) witnessed a particular, albeit temporary, reduction of interest in anything supernatural. People's minds were on current political and social affairs during a period when the Devil had no apparent relevance. He was all but forgotten, except by those revolutionaries who associated him with the aristocratic class against whom the Revolution was set — and, conversely, by those who took precisely the opposite view. The dogmatic theocrat Comte Joseph le Maistre maintained, for example, that the degeneracy of the revolutionaries and their disrespect for authority were directly attributable to the malice of the Evil One.

By the start of the 19th century, Satan was back in a very different form. This was not so much a personal return, but he had become the base element of a literary and theatrical culture that moved into realms of diabolical fantasy in a fashionable genre of Gothic horror and early science fiction. Britain and France jointly led the field in this regard, thereby cementing a cultural bridge of mutual interest while the countries were otherwise at loggerheads during the Napoleonic wars.

With the Industrial Revolution firmly under way, the rural life of England had changed for all time, as many of the long-prized trade skills became obsolete in the face of mass production. Communities were regrouped to accommodate an economically based social structure as the farm workers and craftsmen left their villages to work in the factories and mills. In this environment, opinions of what might be good or sinful changed almost overnight. Extravagance, parties and conspicuous consumption were no longer regarded as devilish vices; they were now prerequisites for the lifestyle of the burgeoning middle-class entrepreneurs, who sought to undermine the traditional aristocracy with competitive displays of wealth and industrial success.

There were, however, those of an emerging Romantic Movement who were appalled by what was happening. They were deeply distressed to see so much reward in the hands of those who reaped their returns with excellent manufacture, but did so at the expense of their workers — fellow countrymen, who were badly paid and lived mostly in overcrowded city squalor. Among the socially-minded critics was the artist and poet William Blake, who perceived industrialization not as a blessing, but as a new evil wherein the Devil reigned supreme as never before.

In the early 1800s Blake wrote and illustrated his epic poem, *Milton*. It concerns the writer John Milton, who returns from death to discuss with Blake the relationship between a living writer and his predecessor — the good and the bad of how things had changed, and the role of the philosophical mind in this process. As a preface to this work in 1804, Blake wrote a brief individual poem, beginning, 'And did those feet in ancient time walk upon England's mountains green'. Later set to music by C Hubert H Parry, it became the now famous song *Jerusalem*, in which the words of William Blake refer to the hellish workplaces of the Industrial Revolution as the 'dark satanic mills'.

Coinciding with this, the German polymath, Johann Wolfgang von Goethe, revisited the popular subject of Dr Faustus and Mephistophilis, as treated by Christopher Marlowe over 200 years before. Published in two parts (in 1808 and 1832 respectively), Goethe's play, entitled simply *Faust*, is far more complex than the original versions. Not unlike the biblical story of Job at its outset, the Devil figure (his name now spelt Mephistopheles) wagers with God that he can deflect the scholarly Dr Faust from his academic pursuits. Faust subsequently turns from his scientific and scriptural studies in an endeavour to further his learning by way of sorcery and magic. But, tortured through lack of success, he contemplates suicide, at which point the Devil comes to his aid. Initiating a blood pact, he promises to provide Faust with all that he desires during his life on Earth. In return, Faust must swear to serve the Devil forever after in Hell. Having sold his soul to the Black One, Faust learns eventually that fulfilling immediate desires at will does not constitute a satisfying existence. Instead, the rewards from gratifying pride and passion are short-lived and fraught with their own problems. Ultimately, he decides that material indulgence is no match for the pursuit of righteous learning. Consequently, he reverts to his original path and Mephistopheles loses his bet.

During this same era, the English poet Percy Bysshe Shelley was a very vocal opponent of the satanic tradition, writing *An Essay on the Devil and Devils* to express his views in 1820. In this work, he discussed the past difficulties faced by the Church in attempting to reconcile a world, created and super-vised by God, in which good and evil are equally apparent and inextricably entangled. Explaining his opinion of the persistent dilemma, Shelley wrote: 'The Christians invented, or adopted, the Devil to extricate them from this difficulty'.[2]

It was nonetheless still the case that, although the witch trials were confined to history, and the centuries of Church propaganda in this regard discredited, people at large remained fascinated by the concept of evil. Anti-Catholicism was widespread, not only in Britain, Germany and The Netherlands, where the Protestant cause was predominant, but in countries such as France, Italy and Spain, where the tortures of the Inquisition lingered in ancestral remembrance. If evil existed, then the Church had been its foremost protagonist, and much about the inquisitional era, even the Gothic architecture of the Middle Ages, was overlaid in people's minds with sinister implications. The old churches and monasteries of medieval Europe became ominous in the imagination, for they had been the haunts of brutal inquisitors such as Bernardo Gui, Conrad of Marburg and Tomás de Torquemada.

The onset of this groundswell of malignant imaginings had been pre-empted in England by Horace Walpole of the Hell-Fire Club fraternity. Back in 1764, he had published a suspenseful novel entitled *The Castle of Otranto*. Set in Italy at the time of the Crusades, it had a mysteriously supernatural ambiance, which began a popular literary genre that became known as Gothic Romance.[3] In 1794 another English writer, Ann Radcliffe, moved the concept forward with her book *The Mysteries of Udolpho*.[4] The scene for this brooding drama, with its scheming villain and persecuted heroine, is the South of France in 1584. It is replete with physical and psychological terror, crumbling castles and supernatural events, but it did not fulfil the ultimate objective of anti-Catholic opinion. This occurred two years later with Matthew Lewis' lurid tale of monastic debauchery, black magic and diabolism, entitled *The Monk*.[5] Published in 1796, and set during the Spanish Inquisition, it is a portrayal of depraved monks, sadistic inquisitors, demonic pacts, rapes and hypocritical nuns in the service of Satan. 'The monk', Ambrosio, falls victim to the repercussions of his own lust in the convents and is hauled before the Inquisition, but escapes by selling his soul to the Devil. Ann Radcliffe then followed this with her story *The Italian* in 1797.[6] This account of treachery in 18th-century Italy has its hapless protagonists ensnared in a web of deceit by a malignant friar, and dragged before the tribunals of the Holy Office in Rome.

The Final Terror

Scary as these books might have been, they were plainly not of any frightening consequence in the immediate daily scheme of things. Even if not entirely fictional, they were set in the past, and their readers were not likely to be seduced by malevolent nuns or hauled before torturous inquisitors by mad, black-hooded monks. The missing element was discovered by the English poet George Gordon, Lord Byron, who published his poem *The Giaour* in 1813.[7] Byron figured that what the stories lacked was a truly representative physical presence — not a servant of evil, but a personification of evil, just as the Devil was traditionally thought to have been. In this regard, Byron made use of the Church's concept of bodily resurrection, as had been promoted so vehemently in the New Testament epistles of St Paul.[8] He had stated that, when the time came for judgement, 'The dead in Christ shall rise first'.[9] But what if Paul had been wrong? What if the dead in Satan rose first? What if they did not wait for the Day of Judgement? What if they were around here and now?

An appropriate scene for this had already been set with the *vrykolakas, Nachtzehrer, Blutsauger, nosferatu* and *upires* — the hideous demons of the 'undead'. Following their combined classification as 'vampires' by Dom Augustin Calmet in 1746, a few poems alluding to the subject had been produced in the interim. A German poem entitled *Der Vampir*, by Heinrich August Ossenfelder, emerged in 1748. This was followed in 1797 with *Die Braut von Korinth* (The Bride of Corinth) by Goethe, prior to his publication of *Faust*. Then came the English poems, *Christabel* by Samuel Taylor Coleridge (1798), and *Thalaba* by Robert Southey (*c*.1800).[10]

Although these works each made reference to vampirism, it was Lord Byron who brought the hideous 'undead' to the forefront of presumed reality in *The Giaour*:

> But first on earth, as vampyre sent,
> Thy corpse shall from its tomb be rent;
> Then ghastly haunt thy native place,
> And suck the blood of all thy race.
> There from thy daughter, sister, wife,
> At midnight drain the stream of life;
> Yet loathe the banquet which perforce
> Must feed thy livid, living corse:
> Thy victims ere they yet expire
> Shall know the demon for their sire.

Byron's colleague, John Polidori, then wrote *The Vampyre* in 1819. This short story was the first work of English prose on the subject, and told of the mysterious aristocrat Lord Ruthven, who preyed upon the blood of innocent women. At this stage, the vampire was no longer a stinking revenant wrapped in a filthy linen shroud like the *Nachtzehrer*, but had moved into the realm of nobility, with a peculiar seductive charm.[11]

Another of the Byron/Polidori group was Mary Shelley (wife of the poet Percy Bysshe Shelley), whose own scary tale — created for her friends' amusement at a gathering near Geneva — emerged in print as the classic horror story *Frankenstein*, the first ever book of the science fiction genre. Other works, not necessarily associated with the horror movement as such, were equally considered Gothic by virtue of their dark undertones — stories such as Jane Austen's *Northanger Abbey* and Emily Brontë's *Wuthering Heights*.

Next on the vampire scene was the heraldist, playwright and librettist James R Planché, who recognized the potential for the stage. In 1820, his romantic Scottish drama *The Vampire, or the Bride of the Isles* opened at the English Opera House in London. It was based upon a play, similarly entitled *The Vampyre*, which had been staged the previous year in Paris by Charles Nodier. Also focused on the same theme was Heinrich Marschner's German opera *Der Vampyre*, which was performed in Leipzig in 1829. Subsequently, in 1841, the Russian writer Alexei Tolstoy published his story *Upyr*. Ten years later in Paris was performed the last dramatic play by Alexandre Dumas (of *The Three Musketeers* fame), entitled *Le Vampire*.

Then came the popular British series, *Varney the Vampire*, which appeared as weekly instalments in the 'penny dreadful' magazines. Later published in book form as *The Feast of Blood* in 1847,[12] James Malcolm Rymer's tale was of Sir Francis Varney, a Royalist in the 17th-century Civil War who was killed by Oliver Cromwell's soldiers, but continued his cause into the 18th century as a rather agreeable vampire. It was Varney who truly cemented the literary turning point from the grubby, stenching zombie of old European lore to the seductively normal figure who moved in polite company.[13] Here, at last, was the making of an image to which people could relate, as Varney emerged with elegance, flair and sex appeal. But he was deadly in his lustful pursuits:

> With a plunge he seizes her neck in his fang-like
> teeth; a gush of blood and a hideous gushing
> noise follows ... [later] All saw on Flora's neck a
> small puncture wound, or rather two, for there
> was one a little distance from the other.

In 1872, progressing the fast developing mood, the Irish lawyer J Sheridan le Fanu published a short novel concerning the female vampire *Carmilla*. This was another lurid tale which introduced more of the Gothic themes which have since become so familiar. Carmilla slept in a coffin; she had superhuman strength; she had become a vampire through being bitten by another, and was finally dispatched by a stake driven through her heart. Subsequently, in 1897, Britain's Poet Laureate, Joseph Rudyard Kipling, expanded the female vampire theme in his poem *The Vampire*. Then in that same year, the ultimate vampire appeared, and the Devil (or as close as needs be for the waiting market) was finally back in the pages of Bram Stoker's chilling novel, *Dracula*.[14]

The considered requirement to give the literary vampire an outwardly normal appearance was largely due to the fact that, by the late 19th century, the character of Satan had itself changed in the public imagination. To be truly seductive and enticing, in order to gather his disciples, it was figured by many that he would never have been hideous or grotesque. He would far more likely have appeared as a smart, alluring fellow.[15] And so it was that the diabolic vampire was moved into a realm of pseudo sophistication, whilst the fierce nature of the beast was hidden beneath his outward guise.

It had finally been recognized that true fear is not engendered by the notion of hideous dragons and mythical monsters that no one had seen, nor ever would see. The cruel monks of the Inquisition had provoked far greater trepidation than had imaginary demons. Not only was their brutality real, but they were men of the Church. They were the epitome of the Devil that lies within the human shell — an evil that can be found to exist where it should least be expected. This dark and brooding form of horror was the essence of Gothic vampire literature — a fear of the unknown Devil that hides beyond a veil of presumed innocence. In this context, the Devil need never be portrayed in person; his presence simply had to be felt, so that the nature of those he possessed was enough to convey his fearsome image. In the case of Count Dracula, who had been 'undead' for more than 400 years, his transformations to the vampiric state were sufficient to fulfil any devilish expectation. As the newly dubbed Prince of Darkness, he emerged as a more ferocious and predatory figure than any black goat or other perception of Satan had ever been:

> Never did I imagine such wrath and fury, even to the demons of the pit. His eyes were positively blazing. The red light in them was lurid, as if the flames of Hell-fire blazed behind them. His face was deathly pale, and the lines of it were hard like drawn wires. The thick eyebrows that met over the nose now seemed like a heaving bar of white-hot metal.

The author, Bram Stoker (1847–1912), was born in Ireland and attended Trinity College, Dublin, where he became president of the Philosophical Society and auditor of the Historical Society. In 1870, he graduated with honours in science and, after some time as a journalist, became the manager of Sir Henry Irving's Lyceum Theatre, London, in 1878. This was primarily a Shakespearean establishment, but it was here that, in the days before Irving and Stoker, James R Planché's play, *The Vampire*, had been staged in 1820, at which time the theatre was called the English Opera House. Immediately prior to the publication of Stoker's *Dracula* on 26 May 1897, the author led a four-hour dramatised reading from his book at the Lyceum. Unfortunately, fire swept through the theatre shortly afterwards, destroying all the *Dracula* costumes and props, and in 1902 the Lyceum was closed.

During the Irving/Stoker partnership, which persisted until Irving's death in 1905, Stoker had begun to write his watershed vampire novel in 1890, inspired particularly by J Sheridan le Fanu's tale of *Carmilla*. Compiling his book after the style of *The Moonstone* by Wilkie Collins, Stoker elected to tell the story through the eyes of various people, settling upon an intriguing presentation by way of a series of letters, journal entries and newspaper extracts. His working papers are now held at the Rosenbach Museum in Philadelphia, and from these it is evident that his originally intended character was to be an Austrian by the name of Count Wampyr.[16] But while in England at the public library in Whitby, Yorkshire, Stoker came upon an 1820 text concerning Romania, entitled *An Account of the Principalities of Wallachia and Moldavia*. It was written by William Wilkinson, a former British Consul in Bucharest, and it was from a reference in this work that Stoker's vision of the definitive vampire was born. It referred to 'A voivode [prince] Dracula', who led his troops across the River Danube to do battle with the Turks in the latter 1400s.[17]

This passage was a major inspiration for Bram Stoker, who immediately transformed his Austrian Count Wampyr to the Transylvanian Count Dracula. He also used the Wilkinson text to good advantage by ascribing its limited information to the words of his scholarly Dutch vampire hunter, Dr Abraham Van Helsing:

> He must indeed have been that voivode Dracula who won his name against the Turks over the great rivers on the very frontier of Turkey-land. If that be so, then he was no common man; for in that time, and for centuries after, he was spoken of as the cleverest and most cunning, as well as the bravest, of the sons of the land beyond the forest. That mighty brain and that iron resolution went with him to the grave, and are even now arrayed against us.

What appealed to Stoker was not just the wonderful ring of the name Dracula, but a note in the Wilkinson text which suggested that the name (in Romanian) meant 'Devil'. Subsequently, he learned that, more correctly, *Dracula* meant 'Son of the Dragon'.[18] Thus, the name was eminently suited to his character as a vampiric emissary of Satan. Historically, the 'dragon' styles had been used in 15th-century Romania by two Wallachian princes: Vlad II (*c*.1390–1447), who was called *Dracul*, and his son Vlad III (*c*.1431–76), known as *Dracula*. Wallachia was a Romanian province north of the River Danube and south of the Carpathian mountains. Bordering the north of Wallachia were Transylvania (a Hungarian domain in those times) and Moldavia, which lay to the east of the mountains, whilst to the east of Wallachia was the Black Sea, and to the south Bulgaria.

Although there is a nominal reference to Vlad in Francis Ford Coppola's 1992 film entitled *Bram Stoker's Dracula*, the name of this Romanian prince does not appear anywhere in Stoker's book. The extent of Stoker's knowledge of the historical Vlad III is, therefore, a matter of speculation. It is possible that he gleaned some information in this regard from the Hungarian professor Arminius Vambéry, whom he cites in his *Reminiscences of Henry Irving* as having met in 1890. But there is nothing in his *Dracula* notes to confirm that Vambéry was necessarily a source for the work. Nonetheless, it is interesting to see that (again in the words of the fictional Van Helsing) Stoker does make use of this man's name in the story:

> I have asked my friend Arminius of Buda-Pest University to make his record; and, from all the means that are, he tells me of what he [Dracula] has been. He must, indeed, have been that voivode Dracula who won his name against the Turks.

There is a good deal of evidence that Vlad III used the sobriquet *Dracula*, since it features in several 15th and 16th century historical sources, and in his own signatures.[19] But there is no reference to the fact that he was ever considered to be a bloodsucking vampire, whether in a literal or extortionate context. In practice, quite the reverse was the case and, to the

Romanian people, Vlad was a great national hero with a fine statue at Tirgoviste, and another by his castle ruin at Capîtîneni on the River Arges.

Even though *Dracula* was published in 1897, it was to be nearly a century before the Romanians became significantly aware of the connection between the fictional Count and their own historical Prince. This awareness only became fully evident after the 1989 fall of Soviet Communism, when Western literature found its way into the previously forbidden countries. This has now led to the legendary Count Dracula becoming a central feature of the expanding Romanian tourist industry. In real-life terms, Vlad-Dracula is remembered as a noted supporter of the peasant classes against the unscrupulous aristocrats — an upholder of law and order in turbulent times, and a vigilant defender of his Wallachian principality against the threatening might of the Ottoman Empire.[20] He is often cited in modern reference books as having been a brutal tyrant responsible for many atrocities, and indeed he was harsh and ruthless to the extreme. Records of the Turks and Germanic Saxons, who infiltrated the Romanian regions, tell that his favoured punishment for enemies of the State was to impale them on wooden stakes. On that account, he is often referred to as Vlad the Impaler.

Another intriguing reference from Stoker, relating to information received from Arminius, states with regard to Dracula:

> He was in life a most wonderful man: soldier, statesman and alchemist. Which latter was the highest development of the science knowledge of his time. He had a mighty brain, a learning beyond compare, and a heart that knew no fear and no remorse. He dared even to attend the Scholomance, and there was no branch of knowledge of his time that he did not essay.

The *Scholomance* (School of Solomon), located in the mountains near Hermannstadt in Austria, was referred to in *The Land Beyond the Forest* (1888) by Emily de Laszowska Gérard, a specialist in

Romanian folklore. Bram Stoker was well acquainted with her work, being a fellow correspondent for *The Nineteenth Century* journal. Regarding the *Scholomance*, Gérard wrote that this was considered to be 'a Devil's school, where the secrets of nature, the language of animals, and all magic spells are taught'.[21] Also important in relation to the work of Emily Gérard (who referred to Romanian vampires as *nosferatu*) was her 1885 essay *Transylvanian Superstitions*, which prompted Stoker to locate his Count Dracula in Transylvania, whereas the historical Vlad (although having his castle near the Transylvanian border) was actually a reigning dynast of neighbouring Wallachia. Gérard additionally confirmed the tradition that the *nosferatu* were capable of creating other vampires by extracting their blood, and that the creatures could be exorcised by way of stakes driven through their corpses — aspects that were well used by Bram Stoker in his novel.[22]

The Goat of Mendes

Although the *Compendium Maleficarum* idea of the Devil as a goat-like figure had moved into some obscurity (apart from his Satanic Mass representations), the image returned, almost by default, during the latter 19th century. From the middle 1800s, the French occultist Alphonse Louis Constant, who assumed the name Eliphas Lévi, wrote a number of works concerning transcendental magic. The best known of his compositions is entitled *Dogme et Rituel de la Haute Magie*. In this book, Lévi introduced the picture of a goat-like image, which he identified as *Baphomet* — a mysterious name, sourced by Lévi from Inquisition transcripts of the Knights Templar trials in the 14th century.

Creatively inspired as a composite figure, based on a variety of occult taditions and alchemical doctrines, Lévi considered his *Baphomet* to be the ultimate symbolic depiction of an hermetic absolute (*see* illustration on page xiv). Describing the figure's design and complexity in detail, Lévi wrote:

The goat carries the sign of the pentagram on the forehead, with one point at the top, a symbol of light, his two hands forming the sign of hermeticism, the one pointing up to the white moon of *Chesed* [Mercy], the other pointing down to the black one of *Geburah* [Severity]. This sign expresses the perfect harmony of mercy with justice. His one arm is female, the other male like the ones of the androgyn of *khunrath* [the art of hand mobility, handstands, etc.], the attributes of which we had to unite with those of our goat because he is one and the same symbol.

The flame of intelligence shining between his horns is the magic light of the universal balance, the image of the soul elevated above matter, as the flame, whilst being tied to matter, shines above it. The beast's head expresses the horror of the sinner, whose materially acting, solely responsible, part has to bear the punishment exclusively; because the soul is insensitive according to its nature and can only suffer when it materializes. The rod standing instead of genitals symbolizes eternal life; the body covered with scales is the water; the semicircle above it the atmosphere, the feathers following above the volatile. Humanity is represented by the two breasts and the androgyn arms of this sphinx of the occult sciences.[23]

The design of this *Baphomet* figure was based on a newly applied format of the ancient Egyptian Goat of Mendes. It was meant to be entirely magical, but not in any way sinister, and certainly not the Devil.[24] However, since the sabbatical goat of the witches had been deemed satanic, Lévi's enigmatic goat was well suited to diabolic portrayal. It has resultantly become one of the most used of all popular depictions of the Devil, as in the opening sequence of the 1968 Dennis Wheatley movie, *The Devil Rides Out*.

The secret of the name *Baphomet*, as used by Knights Templars in the Middle Ages, was eventually discovered in the 1950s by Dr Hugh Schonfield, a specialist in Middle Eastern studies and past president of the Commonwealth of World Citizens and the International Arbitration League. Dr Schonfield was nominated for the Nobel Peace Prize in 1959, and was the first Jew to make an objective translation of the Christian New Testament from the Greek into English — a work which has received the highest praise for its accuracy.[25]

In studying the scribal codes of the *Dead Sea Scrolls* in relation to aspects of the Old Testament, Schonfield came across one particular cipher that was well used, but very simplistic. The Hebrew alphabet has 22 letters, and the cipher exchanged the first 11 letters for the last 11 in reverse order. With the English alphabet this would mean that Z was substituted for A; Y for B; X for C, and so on. In Hebrew, this would be *Aleph* = *Tau*, and *Bet* = *Shin*, etc. Thus (as ATBSh), it was classified as the *Atbash* cipher.[26]

Knowing that the Templars had brought back many ancient manuscripts from the Holy Land in 1127, Dr Schonfield figured that maybe they had acquired a document which described the ancient Judaean cipher. This would perhaps have enabled the Knights to construct the word *Baphomet* which emerged during their trials. Consequently, he transcribed *Baphomet* into Hebrew, and then applied the *Atbash* cipher. It converted immediately into *Sophia* [Sofia] — the Greek word for 'wisdom'.[27]

The inappropriately dark application of Lévi's *Baphomet* (the sacred goat of wisdom) occurred in the early 1900s by way of misuse by the English occultist Aleister Crowley. A proponent of perverse practices, which he referred to as 'sexual magick', Crowley identified himself personally with Baphomet, and associated the figure specifically, though erroneously, with the 'lust of the beast'. Pursuing this imagined concept, he claimed: 'This Devil is called Satan ... The Devil is Capricornus, the Goat who leaps upon the loftiest mountains: the Godhead'. To this, Crowley added: 'We have therefore no scruple in restoring Devil worship'.[28]

19

THE EBBING TIDE

On Devil's Wings

Bram Stoker's account of the 'undead' Transylvanian nobleman brought many of the previous vampiric themes together, including Count Dracula's shapeshifting connection with another creature of the night: the bat. The association was not a specific allusion by Stoker to the vampire bat; in fact the reverse was the case. The latter actually derived its name from the 18th-century vampire treatise of Dom Augustin Calmet. This particular bat was named by the French naturalist Comte George de Buffon, Keeper of the *Jardin du Roi*, author of the *Histoire Naturelle* in 1765 and *Des Époques de la Nature* in 1778. Prior to these works, there had never been any association in any culture between vampires and bats. But since these particular South American nocturnal mammals fed upon the blood of sleeping animals, Buffon named them in accordance with the vampire tradition.[1] Stoker's *Dracula* concept was more directly related to the bat's wings that had so long been associated with Satan in his original role as a fallen angel.

During the era of Stoker and the Gothic movement, a revised concept of Satan was born. It reverted to the heroic image as created by John Milton in 1667, and stemmed from the artwork of William Blake in the early 1800s. Based on the notion that, in biblical terms, Satan was described in the Old Testament as a 'son of God', Blake and others of the Romantic period figured that the historical inquisitors and latter-day occultists were completely misguided in their demonic portrayals. Satan, they maintained, was not evil to begin. Neither was he in any way fiendish; he was an angelic member of the heavenly court, who fell from grace and was banished into the depths of the abyss. A not dissimilar scenario was presented in respect of the fictional

Count Dracula, who existed in the limbo realm of the 'undead', feeding on the blood of the living.

The 19th-century Romantics perceived a certain similarity between Satan and Dracula in that, whatever evil they committed (although not to be condoned) occurred in their desperate quests for individual deliverance. Lord Byron and others asserted that the Devil's outright wickedness was not biblical, but was 'invented' by the Church in response to Satan's justified revolt against a despotic God.[2] Thus it was that, from the time of William Blake, through to the era of Gustave Doré and other 19th-century artists, Satan was generally depicted as an athletic young man with angelic qualities, identifiable only by the replacement of his feathers with the night wings of a bat.

True evil, it was declared, did not emanate from the Devil. It was an aspect of the human condition, which never in all history had been more evident than in the terrible Catholic and Protestant establishments of the inquisitors and witchfinders. The ultimate devils of reality — those who had persecuted, tortured and burned innocent victims in the manner of Hell — had been the priests, ministers and friars of the Church. In more general terms, the idea that the potential for evil actually resides within the nature of mankind was treated in 1886 by Robert Louis Stevenson in *The Strange Case of Dr Jekyll and Mr Hyde*.[3] Recognizing that the worst designs of the Devil were those embodied in the evil side of personal natures, the French poet Charles Pierre Baudelaire wrote that 'In each person, two tendencies exist at every moment, one towards God and the other towards Satan'.

The notion that Satan originally had feathered wings, like any other angel of the Christian tradition, was taken up by Victor Hugo in his epic poem of the 1850s, *La Fin de Satan*. The poem relates that, during his contest with God after his fall, Satan lost a feather from his wing. The feather then transformed into a beautiful female angel named Liberty, who was empowered by Satan to strive against all evil and to destroy the infamous Paris prison of the Bastille. From Byron in England, to Hugo in France, there was a strong feeling among the Romantics that Satan's rebellion was perfectly legitimate because he was the opposer of unjust rules imposed by a tyrannical Church and the dutiful slaves of its relentless dominion.

Dance of Death

Another arena in which the position of the Devil was relaxed in the late 1800s was the world of music. The mood for change had begun in 1830 with the *Symphonie Fantastique* of the French composer Hector Berlioz. As one of the most important and representative pieces of the early Romantic period, the fifth movement of this symphony, entitled *Songe d'une nuit de Sabbat*, features a witches' Sabbat and Ring Dance (the *Ronde du Sabbat*). It also incorporates a musical parody of the *Dies Irae* (Day of Wrath), a 13th-century liturgical hymn of the Latin Church concerning the Mass of the Dead, along with a fugue which Berlioz described as representing a wild orgy. In recent times, the *Dies Irae* sequence was interpreted for the opening credits of Stanley Kubrick's 1980 horror movie, *The Shining*.

Still very evident in the 19th century was a long-standing hatred by the Church of a particular musical interval known as the *Devil's Tritone* or the *Diabolus in Musica* (the Devil in Music). In the Middle Ages, this tritone of the augmented fourth (or diminished fifth) was banned and cursed by the Catholic bishops, who insisted that it was capable of invoking the very Devil himself. In simple terms, it is an interval formed by three whole steps — as in: from F to B, containing the steps F–G, G–A and A–B — which produces a very tense and dissonant sound. The proof of its diabolic content was said to rest in the fact that three whole tones (a tritone) is six semitones. The churchmen insisted that these were directly related to the abominable number of the beast, '666'.

Beethoven had broken with tradition in this regard as early as 1805 in Act II of his opera *Fidelio*. To set the mood for the dark dungeon, the timpani of *Fidelio* are tuned a tritone apart, to A and E-flat, instead of the usual perfect fifths. In 1874, the tritone was more blatantly used by Saint-Saëns in his *Danse Macabre* (Dance of Death), wherein the top string of the solo violin is tuned down from E to E-flat. This creates a tritone with the open A-string, to represent the Devil tuning his fiddle for the dance. In more recent times, with the clerical restrictions long ignored by composers, the *Devil's Tritone* has been used in any number of instances, from a repetitive conflict motif in Leonard Bernstein's musical *West Side Story*, to the performances of the heavy metal rock band, Black Sabbath.

Synagogue of Satan

In 19th-century North America, just as in Britain and Europe, interest in the Devil as a physical character was waning fast. People throughout the West were increasingly conscious of a dark side of humanity, but religious teachers were hard-pressed to keep the old tradition of the Evil One alive. Whilst the Romantics were redefining Satan in such a way that any fear of Hell should be totally disregarded, the Church groups were in fear of losing their grip on society. Without belief in the Devil, there was every possibility that belief in God would also decline, as indeed it was in many quarters. The clergy were substantially threatened by the fact that so many people were now convinced that the Devil, if he existed, was embodied within themselves as a dark aspect of the human condition. A natural extension of that interpretation might well lead people to believe the same about God — that his spirit existed within everyone. This would then facilitate individual access to God without the need for priests to act as the authorized bridges in between. It could even cause people to become closer to God whilst becoming more distant from the Church. Thus it was deemed increasingly necessary for the clerics to press for the maintenance of a traditional belief in which God and the Devil were not spiritual elements of being, but material presences who were pulling the world against each other for their respective purposes of good and evil.

The very survival of the Christian Church was dependent on a notion of salvation from eternal damnation, but science and reason were causing such a concept to be questioned. In that critical environment, although the occult groups and pseudo-satanic societies were operating in direct opposition to the Christian establishment, they were also of considerable use to the clergy because they were keeping the satanic myth alive, albeit on a somewhat limited scale. Strategically designed Church propaganda in this regard led certain Christian factions to imagine that Devil worship was a truly widespread cult. Ludicrous charges of satanism and ritual sacrifice were levelled against many exclusive clubs and societies, not least of which vulnerable fraternities were the Freemasons, whose official policy was to ignore all contrary propaganda.

A primary exponent of satanic accusation in the late 1800s was a Frenchman named Gabriel Jorgand-Pages — better known by his pseudonym Léo Taxil. He became renowned as an ingenious hoaxer, managing to get beaches cleared on occasions by fake reports of shark attacks, whilst also fooling Swiss archaeologists about the existence of an entire Roman town at the bottom of a lake. He was prosecuted on numerous charges ranging from plagiarism to fraud but, whilst pursuing his unscrupulous career, Taxil was also a Freemason. When the embarrassment finally became too great for his lodge to withstand, Taxil was expelled from the fraternity in 1881, as a result of which he contrived an elaborate satanic hoax to discredit the Freemasons.

In the first instance, he imagined a women's masonic rite which he called Palladism, claiming that it was controlled from America by Albert Pike, the revered Grand Master of the Southern Jurisdiction.[4] Taxil's detailed descriptions of this supposed satanic rite were graphically sexual, and were said to have been imported into France by one Phileas Walder who, with the aid of Eliphas Lévi, had founded the Lodge of the Lotus. This duly enraged the Catholic hierarchy, who reacted with their own masonic condemnation. The impetuous Bishop Fava of Grenoble published a book on the subject, with its details extracted directly from Taxil. Other attacks soon followed from writers such as Archbishop Léon Meurin of Port Louis in Mauritius, who referred to Albert Pike as high priest of the Synagogue of Satan.

Having set this initial scene, Léo Taxil then changed his name yet again to write *The Devil in the Nineteenth Century* as a Dr Georges Bataille. This work further exaggerated the concept of masonic Devil worship, explaining how Albert Pike met secretly on Friday afternoons with a demon who would bring a winged crocodile to play the piano at his lodge meetings! Masonic documents were forged in France, along with staged photographs and drawings of supposed hideous goings-on in America. By that time, the *Palladian Rite* was reckoned to have bases established in Charleston, Washington, Rome, Berlin, Naples and Calcutta. Then, under his original pseudonym (as if to substantiate the work of the imaginary Dr Bataille), Taxil published a supportive text entitled *The Mysteries of the Freemasons Revealed*. A female demon named Bitruand was credited with the senior position of influence in France, and she was said to be the chosen grandmother of the Antichrist.

All that was needed to complete the hoax were the inside revelations of a reformed Palladian lodge member, and these appeared as the *Memoirs of an Ex-Palladist* by a certain Diana Vaughan. Again written by Taxil himself, this work revealed how, on Albert Pike's death, his American Grand Mastership had been passed to another in Rome. To give it weight and authenticity, the names of well-known masons in France, Italy and England were included as being part of the Palladian network.[5] It was all so convincing that even the *New Illustrated Larousse Encyclopedia* carried a two-column entry concerning Palladism and the *Palladian Rite*. In 1896 (still writing as Diana Vaughan), Taxil announced his greatest discovery: that Satan had his earthly headquarters deep within a cave on the Rock of Gibraltar!

At that stage, consternation arose within the Catholic Church, and the bishops began to wonder if they had been hoodwinked. An in-depth investigation into the affair was conducted by Arthur E Waite of the Theosophical Society who, although not a lover of Freemasonry, produced a devastating exposé of what he termed the *Pala Dium* in his book *Devil Worship in France, or the Question of Lucifer*.[6] One by one, Léo Taxil's fictions were unmasked, to be classified thereafter as 'an extraordinary literary swindle'.

At an international congress in Trent, Austria, on 26 September 1896, even the anti-masons became concerned. It was suggested that the said Diana Vaughan should be made to appear with proofs of her claims, at which point Taxil's collaborator, Charles Hacks, was forced to admit that she did not exist. A similar demand came from the Catholic newspaper *Universe*, which met with the same response. The Vatican Council was enormously embarrassed, since it was Taxil's original pronouncement about Palladism which had led to the 1884 encyclical *Humanum Genus* of Pope Leo XIII, wherein he discussed 'the strongly organized and widespread association called the Freemasons', stating:

> No longer making any secret of their purposes, they are now boldly rising up against God himself. They are planning the destruction of the Holy Church publicly and openly, and with this the set purpose of utterly despoiling the nations of Christendom ... We pray and beseech you, venerable brethren, to join your efforts with ours, and earnestly to strive for the extirpation of this foul plague.

Under extreme pressure, Taxil agreed to appear at the Paris Geographical Society on 19 April 1897, stating that he would bring Diana Vaughan with him. But he could not find a willing impersonator, so the days of his hoax were numbered. Ironically, a real Diana Vaughan did indeed exist, but she had nothing whatever to do with Freemasonry. Taxil had simply used her name after he met her once in Paris on a visit from the United States. She was actually a travelling sales representative for Remington Typewriters. Taxil arrived alone for the Geographical Society event, where he insisted (for the sake of his safety) that all sticks, umbrellas and the like should be left in the cloakroom. As his final joke, whilst seemingly awaiting Miss Vaughan's arrival, he collected cash from the attendees by raffling a portable Remington typewriter. In respect of Pope Leo's *Humanum*

Genus, Taxil stated that he had earned a good deal of money from 'the unknown idiocy of Catholics'. Then, before leaving the stage under an armed police escort, he announced publicly and for the press, 'The Palladium exists no more. I was its creator, and I have destroyed it'.[7]

The Unholy Rite

On a somewhat more credible front in 1896, a work entitled *La Satanisme*, by the French esoteric philosopher Henri Antoine Jules-Bois, described a diabolical rite which he called the *Vain Observance*. In essence, it focused on the use of some object or technique to obtain a result which, by its very nature, was impossible to achieve by the use of that object or technique. It was much like the papal concept of the *Agnus Dei*, a wax image of a lamb that was reckoned by the Vatican hierarchy to prevent storms. Associated with the discovery of the *Vain Observance* was evidence that consecrated eucharistic host wafers were still being stolen from French churches and that, behind the closed doors of Paris, there was a revived interest in the Black Satanic Mass.[8]

Maurice Renard, a French reporter for *Le Matin*, had written an article about the non-existence of such gatherings, but was then invited to attend one. He explained that the cellar-chapel, to which he was taken, was dark and arrayed with erotic murals. By the altar was an image of a goat trampling a crucifix, and around the altar were six large black candles of coal-tar and pitch. The renegade priest wore a red robe, and there were about fifty men and women in attendance. A naked girl was laid upon the altar, and the Satanic Mass was conducted over her, leading to an abandoned orgy of the worshippers.[9]

Various reports of similar events continued through the ensuing decades and, in 1940, the American occult reporter William Seabrook said he had witnessed Black Masses in London, Paris, Lyons and New York. His experiences were much the same as that of Renard. He described in his book, *Witchcraft: Its Power in the World Today*, the same scenes of broken crucifixes, scarlet

272

robes, black candles and bare-bodied girls draped on altars with chalices stood between their breasts.[10]

Some novelistic and cinematic portrayals of the Black Mass include the slaying by knife of the young woman on the altar. It might be that such a thing has taken place, but there is no record of it happening; neither was it an inherent aspect of the ritual since the woman was the focus of the ceremony and was deemed to be the very 'altar' itself. There is no complete record of a Satanic Mass, but eyewitness reports of numerous assemblies, dating onwards from the 17th century, indicate consistent similarities of ritual. All reported cases bear some likeness to the Guibourg Mass of the French royal mistress in 1678. As performances of wanton sexual activity in a ritualistic environment (which appears to have been the overwhelming purpose of the assemblies), they were all portrayed as grotesque parodies of the traditional Catholic Mass.

In 1903, Dr Gabriel Legué (noted for his discovery of the inherited neurological disorder *Tourette's Syndrome*) published some details of the Guibourg Mass in his *La Messe Noire*.[11] From a combination of this and other accounts, it is possible to reconstruct a fairly accurate portrayal of the litany and procedures of the assemblies. At the outset of the unholy rite, a naked woman was laid on a black-draped altar. From that point, she became the 'altar' for the purposes of the Mass. Along with the priestly celebrant and the woman, the other main participants included a boy and girl as servers, together with older acolytes who carried censers (traditionally containing henbane, thorn-apple and atropa belladonna). Various items of paraphernalia included black candles and a large image of Satan, if not a suitably costumed physical presence.

The black host was often a desecrated wafer stolen from a church, or sometimes a slice of rotting turnip, and the chalice contained red wine adulterated with hallucinogenic sundries. It was draped with a black veil and placed above or between the breasts of the 'altar'. During a series of versicles and responses, the priest involved the congregation in the rite, invoking their loyalty to the infernal master:

> Lord Satan, receive this host which I,
> thy worthy servant, offer to thee ... We
> offer the chalice of fleshly lust, that it
> may arise in the sight of thy majesty for
> our use and gratification.

Following a number of ritual performances with incense, bell- ringing, supplications to the Devil, and intimate groping of the 'altar' (the woman) by the priest, the ceremony was set to move into communal debauchery. The worshippers were called to remove their gowns and bare themselves before Satan's 'altar', on whose behalf it was pronounced:

> I am the root and stock of Lucifer, the
> bright and morning star. Come over to
> me all ye that desire me, and be filled
> with my fruits. Darkness shall cover
> me, and night shall be my light in the
> pleasure.

Along with an appropriately devised litany, a sequence of perverse activities then ensued between the priest, the child servers, the acolytes and the 'altar'.[12] Eventually, a satanic version of the *Lord's Prayer* was recited: 'Thy Will be done on Earth as it is in Hell ... etc.' The chalice was then placed aside, with the celebrant priest explaining: 'Lord Satan saith: In rioting and drunkenness I rise again. You shall fulfil the lusts of the flesh'.

After that, he would instruct all present to begin orgiastic revelling, 'without regard to privacy or relationship with their partners'. At length, the celebrant would raise the chalice, saying, 'Accept the chalice of voluptuous flesh in the name of the Infernal Lord'. With the rite concluded, he would then bless the congregation in the name of Satan, at which point they were dismissed.

During his 20th-century investigations in Britain, the English clergyman and occult researcher, Rev Montague Summers, wrote in 1946 from his experience:

The Black Mass today is sometimes celebrated in a cellar, but satanists have become so audacious and so strong in evil that the largest room in their houses is known to be permanently fitted up for these abominable mysteries. In one case the room is draped with black hangings and the windows are always shuttered with curtains drawn. The fact that the door is furnished with a Yale lock and key arouses no suspicion. Sometimes even a disused chapel is bought by a wealthy satanist and furnished for the ceremonial of the liturgy of the pit.

Regarding a particular Black Mass venue that he saw at Merthyr Tydfil in Wales, Summers described:

This back room was furnished as a chapel, and the altar, above which was suspended a pair of queer-looking horns, whilst odd objects ranged on the gradine, blazed with candles. Sometimes the altar is swathed in black velvet, and there are six black candles, three on either side of a crucifix. The crucifix is hideously distorted and caricatured ... Serge Basset [the French author, 1866–1917], who was taken to a Black Mass, observed that in the centre of the altar where a crucifix should be placed was squatting the monstrous figure of a half-human buck-goat, with staring eyes which flickered with red fire, whilst from the tips of its huge horns jetted a dull crimson flame.[13]

What emerges from studying the various accounts of Black Mass ceremonies in the 19th and 20th centuries is a clear indication that they were meticulously stage-managed to be entirely deceptive. People of means were attracted to them in the 1800s on the basis that they were privileged clients, selected to witness 'genuine ancient customs of Devil worship'. In England, this took place notably within a higher echelon of society — wealthy dissenters of the Church who sought danger and thrills within a strait-laced Victorian environment. But the price for that privilege was high, although the displays were often spectacular, being produced by experienced theatrical promoters. It was much the same in France, where the strong sexual emphases of the productions made them extremely popular, to the extent that they formed an integral part of the Paris nightlife industry. Even those who would not normally subscribe to such extravagance were seduced by the uniqueness of the experience. It was, in essence, vice and voyeurism dressed up as occult ritual, and the promoters made a great deal of money.[14]

The Devil Rides Out

By the close of the 19th century, there was no commonly held view of the Devil. Some believed in him; others did not. Some considered diabolic lore to be a mere superstition; others viewed the subject with all seriousness. Some ridiculed the Devil; others venerated him. But, whatever the case, people had moved into an era of personal choice, and there are few records of skirmishes between rationalists and believers at a street level. The new contest was now being waged above the crowd between scientists and the clergy. In this dispute which, by virtue of Charles Darwin and others, had brought the *Theory of Evolution* to the fore, the Church was largely involved with defending 'creationism' and the nature of God. There was little purpose in being overly concerned with the Devil since the world of science was not remotely interested in him. The Devil could only exist if God existed, so there was nothing in particular to debate unless the reality of God was upheld.

Aided by the growing popularity of Gothic Romance, some Catholic writers of the period used the field of novelistic fiction to hold the Devil in position, rather than do battle at an academic level. It was not difficult to sustain the notion of a dominant force of evil, since vice and corruption were prevalent in large measure — in the eyes of the Church at least. A notable work in this respect was *Les Diaboliques* (The Devils) by Jules Barbey d'Aurevilly. This collection of short stories from 1874 focused on vengeful women who committed acts of murder and extreme violence. The overall theme was that women are intrinsically evil, and fall easy prey to the devilish designs of pride, lust and hysteria.[15] But times had changed; this outmoded concept of the witch-hunting era was no longer acceptable, especially in France which was predominantly non-sexist after the Revolution. The work was deemed indecent and offensive, and the author was prosecuted. Not surprisingly, the prosecution drew inquisitive attention to the book, assuring its market success after the event, and *Les Diaboliques*, starring Simone Signoret and Véra Clouzot, was released as a cinema movie in 1955.

A key Church writer of the late 19th century in France was Abbé Brulon who, in his *L'explication du Catéchisme* (1891), levelled a significant assault against satanism and the Devil worshippers, who were determined to overthrow traditional religion. In following this course, he set his sights particularly against Freemasons, citing the presumed research of Léo Taxil's pseudo Dr Bataille.[16] He stressed that preparations were being made for the imminent coming of the Evil One. But, when Taxil was publicly discredited five years later, Brulon's credibility suffered as a consequence. He had impressed no one and, as a result of his writing, the integrity of the clergy was rendered more vulnerable than ever to challenge by the scientific community. Meanwhile, many children in the schools of Britain, France, Holland and Germany were being educated by rationalists, whilst also receiving separately taught lessons in theology. The received differences of opinion were perhaps confusing to them at that stage, but they were the first generation to be afforded any choice concerning what to believe. This had a significant impact on the Devil's perceived status as his tradition collapsed into the 20th century.

20

SATAN'S LAST STAND

The Great Beast

When Arthur E Waite began his investigation of the Léo Taxil hoax in his 1896 book *Devil Worship in France*, he opened by summarizing public opinion concerning the Devil at that time:

> If, a short time ago, that ultimate and universal source of reference, the person of average intelligence, had been asked concerning modern diabolism, or the question of Lucifer — What is it? Who are its disciples? Where is it practised? And why? — he would have replied, possibly with some asperity: 'The question of Lucifer! There is no question of Lucifer. Modern diabolism! There is no modern diabolism'. And all the advanced people and all the strong minds would have extolled the average intelligence, whereupon the matter would have been closed.[1]

Beyond the activities of a few occult sects, who sought to preserve certain lewd traditions and create contemporary pseudo rites on the pretence of their satanic authenticity, the Devil was of little mainstream consequence at the dawn of the 20th century. He was mainly evident in items of literature concerning Black Masses and diabolic ceremonies, which were the mainstay of his references as the century progressed. To whatever degree the reports of activities in this respect were true, they were always thoroughly anti-Christian, and yet the main promoter of the related writings was the Catholic Church! Interest in organized religion and church attendance had decreased significantly as a result of ongoing rationalism and scientific research. The bishops were desperate for an enemy — an adversary who could be confronted in the pursuit of salvation, so as to bring people back to the font and the altar. If not the Devil himself, they would have to make do with his disciples, just as they had done for centuries with the heretics and witches. But, for the most part, the club-like occultists of the day were secretive; they did not advertise their perversions or write descriptions of their rituals. The churchmen had to do this for themselves by creating publicity for the very enemy they sought to vanquish. Commenting in this regard, AE Waite wrote:

> The source of all our knowledge concerning modern diabolism exists within the pale of the Catholic Church; the entire literature is written from the standpoint of that Church, and has been created solely in its interests.[2]

Among the few occultists of the era who was forthcoming and wrote about his subject was the English mystic Aleister Crowley (1895–1947). As we have seen, he was perfectly open in stating, 'We have therefore no scruple in restoring Devil worship'. The *John Bull* periodical claimed in 1923 that Crowley was 'the wickedest man in the world'.[3] Pretentious and brash, Crowley founded a philosophy which he called *Thelema* (from the Greek relating to 'will' or 'purpose'). He wrote the rules of the philosophy, entitled *The Book of the Law*, and claimed that 'sexual magick' was the essential method for a person to reach a true understanding of the self. Written at a time when he was referring to himself as the *Antichrist* and the *Great Beast*, the main axiom of the book is: 'There is no law beyond Do what thou wilt'. It is geared to a premise, which states, 'Let Mary inviolate be torn upon wheels; for her sake let all chaste women be utterly despised among you'.[4]

279

In promoting his theory of depravity with no limits or boundaries, Crowley hit upon the attraction, for some, of the outrageous behaviour described by the inquisitors as being that of the witches. He took great delight in shocking British society by explicitly describing sexual promiscuity as a magical technique, declaring that 'Each individual has an absolute right to satisfy his sexual instinct ... The one injunction is to treat all such acts as sacraments'.

Although Crowley expounded the acceptable concept of Devil worship, his ego was such that he was in fact seeking veneration of himself as the Devil's apprentice. Or, by virtue of the diabolic titles which he bestowed on his own person, he might even have believed that he actually was the Devil.

The overtly sexual nature of Crowley's obsession was, in the opinion of the psychiatrist Sigmund Freud, precisely what the preoccupation with satanism had always been about in the minds of persecutors in the witch-craze era. Freud maintained in his 1923 work, *A Seventeenth Century Demonological Neurosis*, that the accounts of witches copulating with demons at nocturnal Sabbats were the result of heightened sexual repression in those doing the accusing and, more generally, in the society that was prepared to believe them.[5] Indeed, this was often the case in the minds of those who gave testimony — participants such as Catherine Deshayes, who confessed her role as hostess for the 17th-century Guibourg Mass.

It is this aspect of sexual repression, coupled with its resultant fantasy enactment, that appears to play such an essential part in what is termed 'modern satanic ritual'. Whether described by participants as 'magic', 'religion' or plain 'individualism', the practice has far more to do with self-indulgent submission to the 'devils within' than it has to worshipping the Devil as a separate personal entity. In much the same way, it was clearly perverse personal lust, not the Devil, that motivated the intimidating seductions of priests such as Louis Gauffridy, whilst driving Urbain Grandier and the nuns of Loudun into conventual debauchery, as so vividly portrayed in Ken Russell's related 1971 film, *The Devils*.

The Emergent Craft

Notwithstanding the black and expressly deviant nature of Aleister Crowley's dubiously conceived enterprise, a keen interest in ceremonial magic persisted within a 20th-century movement that grew apart from Christianity between the two World Wars. During this period, many people in England became otherwise spiritually inclined, pulling away from material values into a realm of more basic natural instincts. This led to a revised and updated form of witchcraft that became known as Wicca. The term originates from the Saxon verb *wicce* (feminine) or *wicca* (masculine), meaning to bend or yield, as do willow and wicker. Fronting this movement, and regarded as the founder of latter-day Wicca in the 1950s, was Gerald B Gardner, an amateur anthropologist and hitherto member of Crowley's fraternity. Gardner was initiated into a New Forest coven in the south of England, from which he drew his wiccan inspiration and departed from the dark side of Crowley's practices.[6] He wrote that the New Forest rites were fragmentary, but that he had added material from other sources to formulate a coherent system of rituals, which he called *The Book of Shadows*.[7]

Based on numerous aspects of long-term tradition, modern Wicca reintroduced many aspects of old lore, as previously discussed. It revived the customs of the Holly King and Oak King, reformulated the Sabbats into a combined solar and lunar calendar cycle, known as the Witches' Wheel, and focused attention on ancient rites, as had once been applicable to crops and harvests. Although the restructured witchcraft movement has nothing whatever to do with Satan or the Devil, it has created a new involvement with the horned gods of olden times, such as the medieval Kerne and the Arcadian Pan. Thus, in an emergent neopagan environment, it has restored the original satyr-style mythology with which our book began. More importantly for many, in the face of male-dominated Christianity, Wicca reintroduced the time-honoured cult of the Earth goddess, with high priestesses moving to the forefront of what became known as The Craft.[8]

Temple of Desire

What then of the Devil in current times? If modern witchcraft does not represent him, is there a cult or movement that does? It appears that there is. The Church of Satan (denounced and rejected by Wiccans) was founded in San Francisco by the former lion tamer and show-biz enthusiast, Anton LaVey, in 1966. This prompted a good deal of press and media controversy, which enabled LaVey to announce to the world that *evil* is simply 'live' spelt backwards, and that *devil* is 'lived' spelt backwards. Thus, he maintained, Evil and the Devil are just mirror images of life's reality. This anagrammatic manipulation only works, of course, when using the English written language, and is therefore a completely worthless proposition on any international scale.

The Church of Satan has its own *Satanic Bible*, published in 1969, and a book entitled *Satanic Rituals*, prefaced with the statement: 'The ultimate effect of shielding men from the effects of folly is to fill the world with fools'. Using an interpreted pentagram of Mendes as its sigil, the Church of Satan has an operative website that gives the late LaVey's intention as being to challenge the precepts of Christianity by way of satanic baptism and an alternative agenda. He stated, 'Rather than cleanse the child of *Original Sin*, as in the Christian baptism, imposing unwarranted guilt, we will glorify her natural instincts and intensify her lust for life'. The purpose is not to accept establishment oppression of natural instincts, and not to repress self-seeking motives, but to admit life's passions and work with them to achieve personal desires.[9] In essence, the Church of Satan is entirely hedonistic, and its precepts are concerned with the gratifying benefits of being wholly selfish and mercenary.

A spin-off from the Church of Satan, and now promoted as 'the world's pre-eminent satanic religious institution', is an organization called the Temple of Set. Again with its own website, the content explains that LaVey's Church was not truly satanic, and so 'the senior initiate invoked the Prince of Darkness in quest of a new Mandate'. On receipt of that mandate 'from that entity in his most ancient semblance as Set', the Temple was established in California in 1975. It is further described that 'The worship of Set is the worship of individualism', which the Church of Satan had interpreted to mean indulgence in all desires of the body and ego. But since many such desires are impulsive and destructive, the practices were often degrading rather than exalting. This seemingly led to tensions, and to the subsequent formation of the breakaway sect to advance the principles of the said 'higher self' by employing 'the colourful legacy of the Black Arts'.

The Devil on Screen

Beyond the world of occult societies and diabolical sects, which had little or no prominence in a mainstream environment, the Devil moved into a general obscurity during the 20th century. This did not mean that the fascination with evil was abandoned, only that supernatural matters had become divorced from perceived reality. People were taking a more objective approach to the subject and, the more removed they became from the Devil, the more his potential grew in the realm of fantasy, urged on by the increasing popularity of Gothic horror stories. The inquisitors and witchfinders, along with the demons and sorcerers of old lore, were now destined to become key players in the field of entertainment.

To begin, Satan was not featured as a principal character, as he had been in the Mystery Plays of the Middle Ages. His presence was sustained by way of transmitted evil in the portrayal of his emissaries. On the demonic front, the vampire was foremost in this regard but, although well established in Britain and Europe, the tradition of the malevolent 'undead' did not make its first newsworthy appearance in North America until the latter 19th century. Some of the early colonial settlers had taken their revenant beliefs with them to the eastern seaboard, in particular to the New England States, from where the first documented report of supposed vampiric activity emerged as late as 1888. It concerned the Stukeley family of fourteen children who began to die one by one. When six had died, the bodies were exhumed, and all but one were found to have been decomposing as expected. On that account, the better preserved daughter, Sarah, was blamed for the other deaths, and the corpses were all dealt with according to European custom, having their hearts cut out and burned. In real terms, this report was not vampiric in any way, but it brought the old lore of the dead affecting the living into play, following which other similar events followed in places such as Connecticut, Vermont and Rhode Island.[10]

In 1927 *Dracula* was brought to the London stage by the actor and playwright Hamilton Deane, whose Irish mother had been acquainted with Bram Stoker. This play was the first to introduce the Count's, now almost prerequisite, black opera cloak. Prior to that, the first Dracula based movie was the silent German film *Nosferatu: A Symphony of Horror*, released in 1922. Being an unauthorised adaptation of Stoker's novel, many details were changed, but it set the scene for a genre of vampiric and satanic movies that has continued through more than eight decades of popularity. America subsequently brought the subject to the silver screen, with the vampire played by Lon Chaney, in the 1927 captioned-stills film, *London After Midnight*. In that same year, the Hungarian exile Bela Lugosi introduced *Dracula* to the American stage with a forty-week Broadway production based upon Hamilton Deane's London play. Then, by special arrangement with Bram Stoker's widow, this was followed by Lugosi's screen role as the infamous Count in 1931. From 1958, Christopher Lee became a familiar Dracula in Britain's Hammer Films series, rivalling previously high transatlantic box office records when the original *Horror of Dracula* premiered at the Warner Theater in Milwaukee. Subsequent to that, the movie industry has never looked back, with films such as Francis Ford Coppola's 1992 production of *Bram Stoker's Dracula* harnessing one of the most popular of all filmable Gothic themes.

In many ways, it might be said that the screen has been responsible for protracting the Devil's own lease of life in modern times, especially since the 1950s when his entertainment value was recognized by the horror film industry. From that time, he has appeared in any number of guises. In 1957, the diabolic,

284

fire-snorting creature appeared with leathery wings and lacerating talons in *The Night of the Demon*. A decade later, Satan's brief appearance was suitably demonic in Roman Polanski's *Rosemary's Baby*. In that same year of 1968, the portrayal of the witches' Sabbat in *The Devil Rides Out* reverted, by way of Dennis Wheatley's novel, to the inquisitional ideal of an enthroned sabbatical goat. The theme of *Rosemary's Baby* is that the main character (played by Mia Farrow) becomes pregnant by Satan and has his child. A similar concept was used in *The Omen* (1976) in which the wife of the US Ambassador to England (played by Lee Remick) gives birth to the Antichrist. The theme was then repeated in director Richard Caesar's year-2000 film, *The Calling*.

Prior to that, in 1973, *The Exorcist* (from William Peter Blatty's novel) has a young girl possessed by the Devil — or more precisely by Pazuzu, king of the demons, whom we met in chapter 1. In Ridley Scott's fantasy movie, *Legend* (1985), a young man must stop the Lord of Darkness from destroying daylight and marrying the woman he loves. In *End of Days* (1999), Satan (Gabriel Byrne) visits New York in search of a bride, with only an ex-cop to prevent his success. Other films, with the Devil in modern guise, include *The Devil's Advocate* (1997), in which the Satan figure (Al Pachino) is a lawyer. Roman Polanski was back in 1999 with *The Ninth Gate*, in which the main character (Johnny Depp) is involved with an ancient book which can invoke Satan. *Constantine* (2005) has Satan (Peter Stormarre) as a white-suited man who leaves filthy footprints, and *Angel Heart* (2005) has the Devil (Robert de Niro) cast as the aptly named Louis Cyphre (Lucifer).

Threads of a Legend

In the 1980s, the American television broadcaster Giraldo Rivera hosted a series of programmes, discussing an alleged epidemic of Satanic Ritual Abuse. He estimated that there were over a million satanists in the United States, many of them linked in a highly organized secretive network. He connected Satan worship with various cases of child abuse, child pornography, and paedophilia in general. In making this claim, Rivera stated, 'The odds are that this is happening in your town'. Clearly (to whatever limited extent), the crimes to which he referred were indeed taking place, and a resultant hysteria broke out in many towns and cities. Allegations of satanic practice were directed towards all branches of society, from unruly teenagers to nursery school staff. Quite suddenly, there were satanists everywhere! Even Britain did not escape the new witch-hunt, and cases of Satanic Ritual Abuse (SRA) were reported in Rochdale, Nottingham and Orkney. In many instances the investigated cases turned out to be groundless, although some were plainly well-founded. But they produced no evidence of satanic involvement or Devil worship; they were straightforward performances of evil by sadistic criminals. Hence, although the term Satanic Ritual Abuse is still used for what appear to be offences with a ritualistic or cult-related motive, SRA is now more commonly defined as Sadistic Ritual Abuse.

In the wider scheme of things, beyond the confines of a few cultish movements that care to express devilish motivations, seriously or otherwise, the Devil has now moved very much into the background of social reckoning. Some Protestants of the old school endeavour to preserve traditional views of the Devil, and there are still a good number of believers in Satan, the Evil One. This is evident in the words of those such as Billy Graham of the Southern Baptist Convention in America. He stated in a 1994 *Weekly World News* article: 'When I hear people doubt the existence of the Devil, I shudder … The Devil is real, and that he is wielding an unholy power and influence there can be no doubt'.[11] But in the religious mainstream the subject is rarely one of debate, since there is really nothing to discuss. The Devil might remain a symbolic concept of evil but, for the majority, he is no longer a personal entity and has become largely inconsequential. On 23 December 1993, Rev David Jenkins, the Anglican Bishop of Durham, stated on the BBC Radio-4 programme, *The Moral Maze*, that the Devil was 'a powerful and historically significant Christian myth, which no longer seems real'.[12] But this is not a unanimous view of the Anglican hierarchy and, whilst the Devil might himself be consigned to a certain obscurity, a belief in demons and evil spirits persists in some quarters.[13]

The Ultimate Fall

On 7 December 1965, the Holy Office of the Supreme Sacred Congregation of the Roman and Universal Inquisition was changed in name to become the Sacred Congregation for the Doctrine of the Faith. Then, as recently as 1983, the Second Vatican Council confirmed the abbreviated style thereafter as the Congregation for the Doctrine of the Faith. According to Article 48 of the *Apostolic Constitution on the Roman Curia*, promulgated by Pope John Paul II on 28 June 1988: 'The duty proper to the Congregation for the Doctrine of the Faith is to promote and safeguard the doctrine on the faith and morals throughout the Catholic world. For this reason, everything which in any way touches such matters falls within its competence'.

The Roman Catholic Church still clings tenuously to a Middle Ages belief in the Devil but, when addressing the subject in 1972, Pope Paul VI was unspecific, stating only, 'It is all a mysterious realm, thrown into confusion by an unhappy drama about which we know very little'.[14] That apart, the role of the Devil still features in Catholic doctrine. In 1993, the *Catechism of the Catholic Church* was pronounced by Pope John Paul II, and later translated as a compendium in English as recently as 2005. It is published in full on the Vatican's own website. Article 597 — the penultimate and consolidating item of the *Compendium of the Catechism* (with the final Article 598 being simply 'Amen') — states unequivocally that the person of Satan remains alive and active in the eyes of Rome:

> Evil indicates the person of Satan who opposes
> God and is the deceiver of the whole world.
> Victory over the Devil has already been won
> by Christ. We pray, however, that the human

family be freed from Satan and his works. We also ask for the precious gift of peace and the grace of perseverance as we wait for the coming of Christ who will free us definitively from the Evil One.[15]

Although the Inquisition remains technically extant, albeit with a different name, the secular authorities of Christendom are no longer influenced in any way by the inquisitors. The Holy Office was the result of a deep-rooted belief in the Devil, but is now quite powerless, having been driven inside the walls of the Vatican. Meanwhile, baptism ritual retains its denouncement of 'the Devil and all his works', and exorcisms are still conducted. Father Gabriele Amorth, the senior exorcist for Vatican City, reported a few years ago that he had performed over 50,000 exorcisms, adding that Rome is exceptional, and 'there is more here because it is the centre of the Church, the most attacked place'.[16] More recently, Father Amorth made news headlines across the globe with his satanic opinion of JK Rowling's *Harry Potter* children's book series. The *Catholic News* reported on 4 January 2002 that Amorth stated in interview, 'Behind Harry Potter hides the signature of the king of darkness, the Devil'.[17]

Even more bizarre: On 20 March 2007, CBS Business News reported that the multinational company Procter & Gamble (manufacturers of consumer brands such as Pampers, Ariel, Crest, Fairy and Pantene) had won a jury award of $19.25m following a lengthy court battle over satanism. Rumours had been spread by agents of the direct sales competitor, Amway, that P&G's 'man-in-the-moon' logo was a blatant device of the Devil. The Amway representatives alleged that Procter & Gamble was run by Satan worshippers because a mirror image of three curled hairs of the moon-face logo revealed the number 666 — the given number of the beast in the book of The Revelation. Lies were even told of how the president of P&G had announced on television that a large portion of company profits was used to support the satanic movement. Needless to say, the District Court in Salt Lake City found in favour of Procter & Gamble but, in the interim, the company amended the logo slightly to appease the situation. To bother defending such a ludicrous accusation in court seems pointless in the modern age, but it does indicate a persistent trend of superstition within some consumer groups that was felt necessary to address. Many evangelical Christians were actually boycotting the company's products. Other such nonsensical assertions have followed. For example, the familiar corporate symbol of Apple Inc — an apple with a bite taken from it — has been fiercely attacked by fundamentalists as expressing the will of the Devil to eat the forbidden fruit of Eden!

The question of a conscious, malevolent entity that seeks to destroy individuals and the world has been objectively addressed by Rev Anthony David of Pathways Church in Southlake, Texas. In a recent sermon, *God and Satan in the 21st century*, Rev David discussed the high competitive drama in the long-standing Christian tradition. He made the point that it is all too common for some people to relinquish personal responsibility by claiming that the Devil is behind structural evils such as dysfunctional families, communities and nations — social breakdowns that lead to racism, sexism, homophobia, consumerism, poverty and war. Then there are life's horrific accidents, and natural occurrences like hurricanes and earthquakes, or diseases such as cancers and AIDS, along with matters of destructive choice leading to greed, betrayal, abuse, terrorism, murder and other crimes.

At an everyday level, although knowing consciously what is virtuous, there are always temptations to do the wrong things because they seem to embody reasonable gratifications, even if they might later be regretted. In some instances, such actions are treated (by those who wish to deny personal liability) as malicious interventions of the Devil, as if we are all hapless pawns in a predestined cosmic soap opera of conflict between good and evil. But, after 2,000 years of clerical subterfuge, the time has come for the horned Devil of old lore to be laid to rest, and for people to take charge by facing up to the devils within themselves. In this regard, the Satan of fabricated tradition is making his final stand, and now resides in the limited company of pseudo occult societies, fanatical priests who cling to the last vestiges of Inquisition, and in the minds of those who refuse to accept responsibility for their own shortcomings. The Devil's mythical career began with an imagined fall from grace, and is now concluding as the final journey of the Evil One takes him headlong into the ultimate darkness of oblivion.

A noticeable product of the 20th century, as the Devil plummetted into the void, has been his ultimate trivialization. For centuries in the past he was the celestial opponent of God, a formidable power-lord in the war between Heaven and Hell. It was deemed imperative to nominate Satan as the root of all evil, so as not to have any doubt of God's own motivation. But (as has not happened with God) the Devil has been shifted into a realm of comic-strips, fancy dress and plastic Halloween masks. He has become a marketing ploy for advertisers, who use him to convey images of pleasure and abandon. No longer symbolic of crime and the bestial lust of the Sabbats, the Devil of this modern culture has become a mischievous figure of fun, a scampering rascal, completely divorced from any overt moral or religiously motivated context.

Clearly, there are some branches on the fringes of today's Christianity which remain locked in a puritanical mind-set of the 1600s — a culture within which old fears and superstitions prevail as they did in the days of the witch-hunts. There are still some who sincerely believe in a personal Devil that wages his war of terror against God and mankind — a Devil who opposes all that is good and seeks to invade every aspect of earthly existence. In more general terms, however, beyond such remnants of a medieval belief system that facilitated a brutal control of people and their environments for hundreds of years, the Devil, for the majority, is now a defunct and best forgotten relic of a cruelly ignorant past.

NOTES AND REFERENCES

INTRODUCTION

1 Matthew 4:1-11.

2 Luke 4:1–13.

3 Matthew 24:21.

4 John 12:31.

5 Job 1:6.

6 'Where was God during the Virginia Tech Shootings?' Lillian Kwon, *Christian Post*, 19 April 2007.

7 Article 598, *Compendium of the Catechism of the Catholic Church*, Libreria Editrice Vaticana, 2005.

8 *Catholic Encyclopedia*, Robert Appleton Co, New York, NY, 1908, vol XI, under Original Sin.

9 Article published as 'Rome's Chief Exorcist warns parents against Harry Potter', in *Catholic News*, Catholic Telecommunications, Church Resources, Crows Nest, NSW, 4 January 2002.

Chapter 1: THE EVIL ONE

1 Job 1:6, 2:1.

2 Revelation 12:9, 20:2.

3 Matthew 12:24, Mark 3:22.

4 King James Version, Leviticus 17:7, Deuteronomy 32:17, 2 Chronicles 11:15, Psalms 106:37.

5 The consolidated Hebrew Bible (the *Tanakh*) did not appear in its currently extant form until the early 10th century AD. Onwards from the 8th century, a group of Jewish scholars, known as the Masoretes, had appended the *Masorah* (a body of traditional guideline notes) to the earlier texts. The purpose was to ensure a continuity of rabbinical teaching, rather than have the scriptures (especially the *Torah*: the first five Books of Moses) subjected to different oral interpretations. The oldest extant copy of the *Masoretic Bible* comes from AD 916, but the original manuscripts used by the Masoretes do not now exist.

6 *Jewish Encyclopedia*, Funk & Wagnalls, New York, NY, 1906, under Demonology.

7 Yuri Stoyanov, *The Other God*, Yale University Press, New Haven, CT, 2000, ch 3, pp 158, 173.

8 *Jewish Encyclopedia*, under Demonology.

9 Flavius Josephus, *The Antiquities of the Jews*, (trans, William Whiston), Milner & Sowerby, London, 1870, VI, 2:5.

10 James Hastings (ed), *Dictionary of the Bible*, T&T Clark, Edinburgh, 1909, under Demon and Devil.

11 Jeremy Black and Anthony Green, *Gods, Demons and Symbols of Ancient Mesopotamia*, British Museum Press, London, 1992, p 63.

12 Pazuzu was the demon who possessed young Regan McNeil in the Hollywood *Exorcist* film.

13 2 Kings 24:14.

14 The Hebrew *Book of Jubilees* was written by a Pharisee scribe in the 2nd century BC during the Maccabaean reign of John Hyrcanus in Jerusalem.

15 Rev George H Schodde (trans), *The Book of Jubilees*, Capital University, Columbus, OH, 1888; reprinted Artisan, CA, 1992.

16 Jubilees 10:1–14, 11:1–5.

17 David Freeman (ed), *Anchor Bible Dictionary*, Doubleday, Garden City, NY, 1992, under Satan.

18 1 Chronicles 21:1–14.

19 Geza Vermes, *The Complete Dead Sea Scrolls in English*, Penguin, London, 1997, p 161.

20 D. Freeman (ed), *Anchor Bible Dictionary*, under Satan.

21 Dualism, as reflected in evolutionary Christianity, is treated in depth in Yuri Stoyanov, *The Hidden Tradition in Europe*, Arkana/Penguin, London, 1995.

22 The precise dates of Zoroaster (Zarathustra) are unknown, but are generally thought to be around 1200 BC.

23 Ahura Mazda is also called Ormuzd.

24 Ahriman is also called Angra Mainyu.

25 Asmodai is alternatively known as Asmodeus or Ashmedai

26 The *Talmud* ('teaching') is essentially a commentary on the *Mishnah*, compiled originally in Hebrew and Aramaic and deriving from two independently important streams of Jewish tradition: the 'Palestinian' and the 'Babylonian'. The *Mishnah* – or Repetition – is an early codification of Jewish law, based on ancient compilations and edited in Palestine by the Ethnarch (Governor) Judah I in the early 3rd century AD. It consists of traditional law (*Halakah*) on a wide range of subjects, derived partly from old custom and partly from biblical law (*Tannaim*) as interpreted by the rabbis (teachers).

27 James H Charlesworth (ed), 'The Testament of Solomon' (trans, Dennis C Duling), in *Old Testament Pseudepigrapha*, Doubleday, Garden City, NY, 1983, vol 1, pp 935 ff.

28 *Jewish Encyclopedia*, under Demonology.

29 Revelation 16:14–16.

30 G Vermes, 'The War Scroll' in *The Complete Dead Sea Scrolls in English*, 1QM, XIII, p 177.

31 J Hastings (ed), *Dictionary of the Bible*, under Belial.

32 Jubilees 1:20.

33 2 Corinthians 6:14–15.

34 Rev Robert Sinker (trans), 'Testaments of the Twelve Patriarchs III' in *Ante-Nicene Fathers* (ed, A Cleveland Coxe, 1886), Eerdmans, Grand Rapids, MI, 1988, vol 8 (Belial rendered as alternative, Beliar). *See* also *Catholic Encyclopedia*, Robert Appleton Co, New York, NY, 1908, vol II, under Belial.

35 Five of the said nine Sybils are depicted in the 1509–11 ceiling frescoes of Michaelangelo at the Vatican's Sistine Chapel in Rome – namely the Delphic Sybil, the Erythraean Sibyl, the Cumaean Sibyl, the Persian Sibyl and the Libyan Sibyl.

36 Milton S Terry (trans), *The Sibylline Oracles*, Eaton & Mains, New York, NY, 1899, bk II, p 44:211.

37 At the order of Pope Damasus I, St Jerome translated the New Testament canon and the Jewish Old Testament into Latin. The whole become known as the *Vulgate* – a scriptural compilation that took its name from the phrase versio *vulgata*: 'the common version'.

38 *Catholic Encyclopedia*, vol 2, under Belial.

39 The *Damascus Document* was so called because of its references to a New Covenant said to have been made 'in the land of Damascus'.

40 G Vermes, 'The Damascus Document' in *The Complete Dead Sea Scrolls in English*, 4Q265–73, IV, p 130.

Chapter 2: GATES OF HELL

1 Luke 10:18.

2 The Genesis entry translated to 'sons of God' is rendered in Hebrew as *bene ha-elohim*. Since *elohim* is a plural noun, *bene ha-elohim* actually means 'sons of the gods'.

3 The mistranslation occurred because there was no single-word translation for *nephilim*, and the translators had been provided with 'giants' as a

possible alternative by Flavius Josephus in his 1st-century *Antiquities of the Jews*. He explained that these godly sons (the *bene ha-elohim*) 'begat sons that became unjust on account of the confidence they had in their own strength; for the tradition is that these men did what resembled the acts of those whom the Grecians call giants'. Josephus did not actually say that the *nephilim* were giants. Referring to the mythological Titans, he said only that their strength resembled 'those whom the Grecians call giants'. *See* F Josephus, Flavius, *Antiquities of the Jews*, bk I, ch III:1.

4 Zecharia Sitchin, *The 12th Planet*, Avon Books, New York, NY, 1978, intro, p vii.

5 G Vermes, *The Complete Dead Sea Scrolls in English*, scroll 4Q201, pp 513–14. Some Greek fragments of the *Book of Enoch* were previously found in Cairo in 1886, but the fullest rendition is a translation into Ethiopic, discovered in Abyssinia in 1773.

6 1 Enoch 6. *See* RH Charles (trans), *The Book of Enoch* (from Dillmann's 1893 edition of the Ethiopic text), Oxford University Press, 1906–1912.

7 Information concerning the origin of the *Septuagint* comes from a document of the era known as the *Letter of Aristeas*. It tells of how the pharaoh Ptolemy Philadelphus (285–247 BC) was advised by his librarian to have the laws of the Jews translated for his library, and that Aristeas was commissioned to ask the high priest, Eliezer, to send a body of scholars to translate their sacred scriptures into Greek.

8 Andrew Collins, *From the Ashes of Angels*, Michael Joseph, London, 1996, ch 1, p 10.

9 Also *see* André Dupont-Sommer, *The Essene Writings from Qumrân* (trans, Geza Vermes), Basil Blackwell, Oxford, 1961, ch 5, p 167

10 1 Enoch 10:16.

11 Daniel 4:13.

12 Daniel 4:23.

13 Jubilees 4:16–18.

14 Jubilees 8:3.

15 1 Enoch 20:20. The *Book of Jubilees* (written in much the same era as the books of Daniel and Enoch) also uses the term 'watchers' instead of *nephilim*.

16 G Vermes, 'The Damascus Document', Manuscript A, 2:17–19, in *The Complete Dead Sea Scrolls in English*, ch 5, p 124.

17 *The Secrets of Enoch* is generally referred to as 2 Enoch', as distinct from the *Book of Enoch*, known as 1 Enoch'.

18 2 Enoch XXXI. *See* 'The Secrets of Enoch: Creation of the World' in Willis Barnstone (ed), *The Other Bible*, HarperSanFrancisco, San Francisco,

CA, 1984, p 6.

19 *Ibid*, p 5.

20 As previously referenced in Isaiah 14:4.

21 Isaiah 14:12 – translation from the Hebrew Bible.

22 The Hebrew word *heilel* derives from the primitive *halal*, and is used 165 times in the Old Testament. Examples can be found in 1 Kings 20:11, Psalms 10:3, and Proverbs 20:14, and in each case (along with many others) *heilel* relates to boasting.

23 Elaine Pagels, *The Origin of Satan*, Random House, New York, NY, 1995, ch. 2, p 48.

24 John Milton, *Paradise Lost*, Jacob Tonson, London, 1730, bk 10, lines 425–26.

25 Nathan Bailey (ed), *Bailey's Universal Etymological Dictionary*, T Cox at The Lamb, Royal Exchange, London, 1721.

26 *Jewish Encyclopedia*, under Lucifer.

27 Matthew 12:24

28 Luke 11:15.

29 Mark 3:23.

30 'Gospel of Nicodemus' in W Barnstone (ed), *The Other Bible*, Christ's Descent into Hell VII, p 377.

31 This Psalms entry is repeated in Acts 2:27 of the New Testament: 'Because thou wilt not leave my soul in hell, neither wilt thou suffer thine Holy One to see corruption'.

32 Tertullian, 'Treatise on the Soul' in Rev Alexander Roberts and James Donaldson (eds), *The Ante-Nicene Fathers – The Writings of the Fathers down to AD 325*, T&T Clark, Edinburgh, 1867, vol III, ch LV.

33 *Jewish Encyclopedia*, under Sheol.

34 *Catholic Encyclopedia*, vol VI, under Hell.

35 Philippians 2:10.

36 Hippo, North Africa, is now Annaba in Algeria.

37 *Ibid*.

38 Matthew 16:18.

39 1 Enoch, sectn I, ch VI:3.

40 *Ibid*, ch VIII:6.

41 *Ibid*, ch IX:11–13.

42 *Ibid*, ch X:4–8.

43 Leviticus 16:10.

44 Leviticus 16:21–22.

45 Since this goat, with the sins of the people placed on it, was sent over a cliff or driven into the wilderness to perish, the word 'scapegoat' has come to mean a person, often innocent, who is blamed or punished for the sins, crimes or sufferings of others.

46 Phyllis Siefker, *Santa Claus, Last of the Wild Men*, MacFarland, Jefferson, NC, 1997, ch 4, pp 65–66.

47 1 Enoch, sectn II, ch LIV:1–6.

48 Genesis 4:22.

49 *Jewish Encyclopedia*, under Fall of Angels.

50 Romans 5:12.

51 John 14:30.

52 *Catholic Encyclopedia*, under Original Sin.

53 Genesis 3:3–4.

54 Genesis 3:24.

55 Z Sitchin, *The 12th Planet*, ch 13, p 371.

56 Christian and Barbara Joy O'Brien, *The Genius of the Few*, Dianthus, Cirencester, 1999, ch 6, p 136.

57 Genesis 3:3–6.

58 Genesis 2:17.

59 Genesis 3:17.

60 Genesis 3:22–24.

61 Genesis 3:16–19.

62 Genesis 3:16.

63 Rev A Roberts and J Donaldson (eds), *The Ante-Nicene Fathers*, vol III, 'De Corona' by Tertullian, ch III.2.

Chapter 3: CONFLICT WITH SATAN

1 Including 32 times in Genesis 1. Also Genesis 6:18, 9:15, 17:7, 50:24; I Kings 8:23; Jeremiah 31:33; Isaiah 40:1, along with numerous mentions in Ecclesiastes, Daniel and Jonah.

2 Genesis 3:3–4.

3 Genesis 3:22.

4 *Catholic Encyclopedia*, vol IX, under Devil.

5 *See*, for instance, the *Jerusalem Bible*, Darton, Longman & Todd, London.

6 Wisdom 2:24.

7 Genesis 16:7–12.

8 Genesis 19:1–3.

9 Numbers 22:21–35.

10 Judges 13:3–19.

11 Judges 6:11–22.

12 *Moses Apocalypse* XVI:1–3.

13 Both the *Moses Apocalypse* and the *Life of Adam and Eve* are translated in RH Charles (trans), *The Apocrypha and Pseudepigrapha of the Old Testament*, Clarendon Press, Oxford, 1913.

14 Life of Adam and Eve IX:1–2.

15 *Ibid*, XII:1–2.

16 Rev SC Malan (trans), *The Book of Adam and Eve* (from the Ethiopic text), Williams & Norgate, London, 1882. Also *see* 'The First Book of Adam and Eve: The Conflict of Adam and Eve with Satan' in Rutherford H Platt (ed), *The Lost Books of the Bible and the Forgotten Books of Eden*, New American Library, New York, NY, 1974, pp 3–59.

17 1 Adam and Eve LVII:2.

18 1 Adam and Eve LI:7.

19 1 Adam and Eve XLIV:5.

20 1 Adam and Eve XLIII:14.

21 1 Adam and Eve XLVIII:3.

22 Sir Ernest A Wallis Budge (trans), *The Book of the Cave of Treasures*, The Religious Tract Society, London, 1927.

23 Luke 22:3 and John 13:27.

24 Mark 3:23 and Luke 11:18.

25 For instance, Acts 5:3, 26:18, Romans 16:20 and 1 Corinthians 5:5.

26 Revelation 2:9.

27 Revelation 12:9, 20:2, 20:7.

28 *See* also Mark 8:33.

29 Romans 13:1–2.

30 A further entry in 2 John 1:7 states: 'For many deceivers are entered into the world, who confess not that Jesus Christ is come in the flesh. This is a deceiver and an antichrist'.

31 Leonard RN Ashley, *The Complete Book of Devils and Demons*, Robson Books, London, 1997, ch 1, p 15.

32 John Aylmer wrote *An Harborowe for Faithful and Trewe Subjectes* in 1559, to defend the monarchy of Elizabeth I against a newly emergent Puritan faction that opposed the concept of females in positions of authority and government.

33 Matthew 13:38–39.

34 Matthew 25:41.

35 Eusebius of Caesarea, *The History of the Church from Christ to Constantine*, Penguin, London, 1989, bk 3, ch 20, p 81.

36 Revelation 1:9.

37 For a detailed description of these codes and their operative use, *see* Barbara Thiering, *Jesus the Man*, Doubleday, London, 1992, passim.

38 From 753 BC, these kings were said to have been Romulus, Numa Pompilius, Tullius Hostilius, Ancus Marcius, Lucius Tarquinius Priscus, Servius Tullius and Tarquinius Superbus. The stories of these kings are in Titus Livius ('Livy' c.59 BC – AD 17), *Ab Urbe Condita* (From the Founding of the City) – vol I, Loeb Classical Library, Harvard University Press, Cambridge, MA, 1919; vol II, Bristol Classical Press, Bristol, 1998; vols III, IV, Loeb Classical Library, 1989.

39 Revelation 12:10.

40 Revelation 12:9.

41 Revelation 3:9.

42 Revelation 20:1–3, 8.

43 1 Enoch, sectn II, ch LIV:1–6.

44 Barbara Thiering, *Jesus of the Apocalypse*, Doubleday, London, 1996, intro, p vi.

45 Revelation 9:11.

46 Revelation 13:5–8.

47 Eusebius, *The History of the Church from Christ to Constantine*, bk 7, ch 25, p 241.

Chapter 4: A REIGN OF TERROR

1 Coptic was the colloquial language of Egypt until the late 9th century, when it was replaced with Arabic. The Coptic Museum in Cairo ascertained that certain words and the general terminology of the codices indicated that some were copies of older works originally composed in Greek.

2 James M Robinson (ed), *The Nag Hammadi Library*, Coptic Gnostic Project, Institute for Antiquity and Christianity, EJ Brill, Leiden, NL, 1977, tractate I (2) 4:30, p 31.

3 *Ibid*, tractate I (3) 33:20, p 44.

4 *Ibid*, tractates VII (4) 88:12, p 348; VII (4) 95:1, p 351.

5 *Ibid*, tractate IX (3) 47:6, p 412.

6 In AD 610, it is said that the Arabian merchant Muhammad ibn Abdallah received the recitation of *Al-Qur'an* as the directly communicated words of Allāh. Following Muhammad's death, the *Koran* was collated during the 2nd caliphate of Umar, and authorized by his successor, Uthmān (AD 644–56).

7 Koran 2:35–39.

8 *Life of Adam and Eve* XIV:3. Also *see* E Pagels, The Origin of Satan, ch 2, p 49.

9 Koran 2:208.

10 Koran 2:268.

11 Koran 5:91.

12 Koran 16:98.

13 CG Coulton (ed), *Life in the Middle Ages*, Macmillan, New York, NY, 1910, vol 1, pp 1–7.

14 Paul Carus, *The History of the Devil and the Idea of Evil*, Gramercy, New York, NY, 1996, p 167.

15 'Apocalypse of Peter' in W Barnstone (ed), *The Other Bible*, pp 532–36.

16 The full text of this work is given in Claude Carozzi, *Apocalypse et salut dans le christianisme ancien et médiéval*, Collection Historique, Aubier, Paris, 1999. Also *see* details in Michael Frassetto, *The Year 1000: Religious and Social Response to the Turning of the First Millennium*, Palgrave Macmillan, London, 2003.

17 This letter of Adso was written at the request of Queen Gerbera of France for clarification on the details of the rise and life of the Antichrist. It concludes: 'So, Your Highness, I your loyal servant, have faithfully fulfilled what you commanded. I am prepared to obey in other matters what you shall deem worthy to command'.

18 Records of the supernova of 1006 and the appearance of Halley's Comet in 1066 demonstrate that astronomical phenomena were noticed and recorded by 11th-century Europeans. *See* George W Collins II, William P Claspy and John C Martin, 'A Reinterpretation of Historical References to the Supernova of 1054 AD' in *Publications of the Astronomical Society of the Pacific* (PASP), Chicago, IL, July 1999, no 111, pp 871–80.

19 From Charles Pierre Baudelaire, *Le Joueur Généreux* (The Generous Gambler, 1864) in Frank J Finamore (ed), *Devilish Doings*, Gramercy Books, New York, NY, 1997.

20 Mark 3:22.

21 P Carus, *The History of the Devil and the Idea of Evil*, p 274.

22 Jeffrey Burton Russell, *A History of Witchcraft*, Thames and Hudson, London, 1980, ch 1, p 35.

23 Acts 13:9–11.

24 *Oxford Concise English Dictionary*, under Prayer.

25 *Catholic Encyclopedia*, vol XIII, under Rosary.

26 *Oxford Concise English Dictionary*, under Magic.

27 *Catholic Encyclopedia*, vol XI, under Occult Art, Occultism.

28 P Carus, *The History of the Devil and the Idea of Evil*, p 274.

29 Montague Summers, *The History of Witchcraft and Demonology*, Castle Books, Edison, NJ, 1992, ch 6, p 203.

30 For example, Matthew 10:8, 12:28.

31 Mark 1:34.

32 Justin Martyr, 'First Apology' in Rev A Roberts and J Donaldson (eds), *The Ante-Nicene Fathers – The Writings of the Fathers down to AD 325*, vol I, ch XIV.

33 P Carus, *The History of the Devil and the Idea of Evil*, p 280.

34 Justin Martyr, 'Second Apology' in Rev A Roberts and J Donaldson (eds), *The Ante-Nicene Fathers – The Writings of the Fathers down to AD 325*, vol I, ch VI.

35 Y Stoyanov, *The Other God*, ch 2, p 85.

36 *Catholic Encyclopedia*, vol V, under Exorcism.

37 *Ibid*.

38 M Summers, *The History of Witchcraft and Demonology*, ch 6, p 208.

39 Rev Alexander Roberts and James Donaldson (trans), *The Apostolical Constitutions*, The Ante-Nicene Christian Library, T&T Clark, Edinburgh, 1870, vol XVII, bk VIII, part 26, p 241.

40 Caesar of Heisterbach, *Caesarii Heisterbacensis Monachi Ordinis Cisterciensis Dialogus Miraculroum* (ed, Strange), Paris, 1851, vol I, sectn (distinctione) V, ch XI, p 291. This and other such tales can be found in *Translations and Reprints from the Original Sources of European History*, University of Pennsylvania Department of History, University of Pennsylvania Press, Philadelphia, PA, 1897–1907, vol II, no 4, pp 7–11.

NOTES AND REFERENCES

Chapter 5: PRINCE OF THE WORLD

1 Didache V:1–2. *See* in James A Kleist (trans), The Didache, Epistle of Barnabas, Epistle and Martyrdom of St Polycarp, Fragments of Papias, Epistle to Diognetus, *Ancient Christian Writers*, Paulist Press International, Mahwah, NJ, 1948.

2 Epistle of Barnabas, ch XX:1, in *Ibid*. (The Epistle of Barnabus was included in the 4th-century Bible of the *Codex Sinaiticus* and the 11th-century *Jerusalem Codex*, which also includes the Didache.)

3 *Catholic Encyclopedia*, vol XI, under Witchcraft.

4 P Carus, *The History of the Devil and the Idea of Evil*, p 308.

5 A full account of Priscillian's life is given in Henry Chadwick, *Priscillian of Avila: The Occult and the Charismatic in the Early Church*, Clarendon Press, Oxford, 1997.

6 Jacques-Paul Migne (ed), *Patrologiae Latinae Cursus Completus* (Patrologia Latina), Foucher, Paris, 1844–55, vol CXXXII:352. (The *Patrologia Latina* contains published writings of Latin ecclesiastical authors from Tertullian in AD 200 to Pope Innocent III's death in 1216.)

7 *The Corrector* appears in J-P Migne *Ibid*, vol CXL.

8 Jeffrey Burton Russell, *Satan: The Early Christian Tradition*, Cornell University Press, Ithaca, NY, 1987, ch 5, pp 112–13.

9 Origen, 'Against Celsus' in Rev A Roberts and J Donaldson (eds), *The Ante-Nicene Fathers – The Writings of the Fathers down to AD 325*, vol IV, bk VI, ch XLII.

10 JB Russell, *Satan: The Early Christian Tradition*, ch 6, pp 150–52.

11 Exodus 22:18.

12 Athanasius, 'Life of Anthony' in Philip Schaff and Henry Wace (eds), *Nicene and Post-Nicene Fathers*, Eerdmans Publishing, Grand Rapids, MI, 1997, Series II, vol IV, ch 24.

13 'Gospel of Bartholomew' in W Barnstone (ed), *The Other Bible*, ch IV, p 355.

14 The knights were Reginald Fitzurse, Hugh de Moreville, William de Tracy, and Richard le Breton.

15 Walter Map, *De Nugis Curialium* (trans, Christopher Brooke), Clarendon Press, Oxford, 1983.

16 Walter Wakefield and Austin P Evans, *Heresies of the High Middle Ages*, University of Columbia Press, New York, NY, 1969, p 254.

17 John Williamson, *The Oak King, the Holly King and the Unicorn*, Harper & Row, New York, NY, 1986, ch 5, pp 58–78.

18 The 'Abbots Bromley Horn Dance' (a 14 mile route) takes place on Wakes Monday – the day following Wakes Sunday, which is the first Sunday after 4 September. In practice, it is the Monday between 6 and 12 September, inclusive.

19 Richard Cavendish, *The Black Arts*, Perigee, New York, NY, 1983, ch 7, p 316.

20 Peter A Clayton, *Chronicle of the Pharaohs*, Thames and Hudson, London, 1994, p 26.

21 Manly P Hall, Masonic, *Hermetic, Qabbalistic and Rosicrucian Symbolical Philosophy – The Secret Teachings of All Ages*, Philosophical Research Society, Los Angeles, CA, 1989, p. CIV.

22 CC Oman, 'The English Folklore of Gervase of Tilbury' in *Folklore*, Taylor & Francis, London, vol 55, no 1, March 1944, pp 2–15.

23 JB Russell, *A History of Witchcraft*, ch 3, p 64.

24 P Carus, *The History of the Devil and the Idea of Evil*, p 283.

25 In 1478, the *Hystoire de Lusignan* was lodged with the Geneva Reserve of Rare and Precious Books.

26 Sabine Baring-Gould, *Myths of the Middle Ages* (ed, John Matthews), Blandford, London, 1996, ch 8, p 82.

27 The comlete story is given in Sir Algernon Tudor-Craig, *Mélusine and the Lukin Family*, Century House, London, 1932.

28 In the wake of this Mélusine account (published in Paris, Troyes, Lyons and Toulouse), numerous translations were made and, between 1478 and 1838, the tale became popular by way of editions from Geneva, Copenhagen, Prague, Augsburg, Strasbourg, Heidelberg, Nuremberg, Leipzig and Antwerp. Not only was Britain's House of Plantagenet quick to realize the importance of promoting a Mélusine descent, but other royal and noble houses (such as those of Luxembourg, Rohan and Sassenaye) also claimed this illustrious pedigree. *See* S Baring-Gould, Myths of the Middle Ages, ch 8, p 82. Also *see* Sir Iain Moncreiffe, *Royal Highness Ancestry of the Royal Child*, Hamish Hamilton, London, 1982, p 62, in respect of the ancestral heritage of Lady Diana Spencer by HM Albany Herald at Arms.

29 Y Stoyanov, *The Other God*, ch 5, p 235.

30 P Carus, *The History of the Devil and the Idea of Evil*, p 309.

31 Maureen Fiedler and Linda Rabben (eds), *Rome Has Spoken*, Crossroad Publishing, New York, NY, 1998, p 47.

32 Deuteronomy 13:6–9.

33 *Catholic Encyclopedia*, vol XI, under Sacrament of Penance

34 Tertullian, 'De Poenitentia' (On Repentance) in Rev A Roberts and J Donaldson (eds), *The Ante-Nicene Fathers – The Writings of the Fathers down to AD 325*, vol III, ch VII.

35 Cyprian 'On the Unity of the Church' in *Ibid*, vol V, item XX.

36 Thomas Aquinas, *Summa Contra Gentiles* (Summary Against the Gentiles – The Book on the Truth of the Catholic Faith against the Errors of the Infidels, *c*.1264 – ed, Joseph Rickaby), Burns and Oates, London, 1905, bk IV, ch 72.

37 *Oxford Concise English Dictionary*, under Heresy.

Chapter 6: INQUISITION

1 Job 40:15–16.

2 J Hastings (ed), *Dictionary of the Bible*, under Behemoth.

3 1 Enoch 60:7–8.

4 St Thomas Aquinas, *A Literal Exposition on Job*, Oxford University Press, Oxford, 1989, ch 40:10.

5 P Carus, *The History of the Devil and the Idea of Evil*, p 283.

6 JB Russell, *A History of Witchcraft*, ch 4, p 79.

7 Aurelius Clemens Prudentius, 'Hymn at Cock Crow' in *The Hymns of Prudentius* (trans, R Martin Pope), JM Dent, London, 1905.

8 M Summers, *The History of Witchcraft and Demonology*, ch IV, pp 119–20.

9 F Josephus, *The Antiquities of the Jews*, bk XV, ch X:4.

10 Flavius Josephus, *The Wars of the Jews* (trans, William Whiston), Milner & Sowerby, London, 1870, bk II, ch VIII:2.

11 The term 'Christianity' was first recorded in Antioch, Syria, in AD 44. *See* establishment of the Antioch Christian movement in Norman J Bull, *The Rise of the Church*, Heinemann, London, 1967, ch 3, pp 58–59.

12 Irenaeus, 'Adversus Haereses' in Rev A Roberts and J Donaldson (eds), *The Ante-Nicene Fathers – The Writings of the Fathers down to AD 325*, vol I, bk I, ch XXV:3, 4.

13 Tertullian, 'Prescription Against Heretics' in *Ibid*, vol III, ch XXXIX and ch XL.

14 Hippolytus, 'The Refutation of all Heresies' in *Ibid*, vol V, ch XX.

15 Tertullian, 'On the Apparel of Women' in *Ibid*, vol IV, bk I, ch 1:1.

16 Cyprian, 'On the Dress of Virgins' in *Ibid*, vol V, treatise II:14, 17.

17 *Catholic Encyclopedia*, vol IV, under Deaconesses.

18 J Wijngaards, *No Women in Holy Orders*, Canterbury Press, Norwich, 2002, app: The Texts, pp 156–205.

19 Elaine Pagels, *The Gnostic Gospels*, Weidenfeld and Nicolson, London, 1980, ch 3, p 60.

20 Tertullian, 'On the Veiling of Virgins' (De virginibus velandis) in Rev A Roberts and J Donaldson (eds), *The Ante-Nicene Fathers*, vol IV, ch 9.

21 St Thomas Aquinas, *Summa Theologica* (trans, Fathers of the English Dominican Province), R&T Washbourne, London, 1912, part 1:3.

22 *Encyclopedia Brittanica*, 11th edn, 1911, under Waldensians.

23 JP Perrin, *Histoire des Vaudois* (Geneva, 1619), English translation by R Baird and S Miller, Philadelphia, PA, 1847, ch 1.

24 William Jones, *The History of the Christian Church from the Birth of Christ to the 18th Century*, W Myers, London, 1812, 'History of the Waldenses and Albigenses', ch V.

25 Alain de Lille, *Ars fidei Catholicæ contra haereticos* (c.1190), ch II:l in J-P Migne (ed), Patrologiae Latinae Cursus Completus, vol CCX.

26 Reinerius Saccho, 'Of the Sects of Modern Heretics' – *Summa de Catharis et Pauperibus de Lugduno*, 1254 (trans, SR Maitland), in *Facts and Documents Illustrative of the History of the Albigenses and Waldensians*, CJG and F Rivington, London, 1832, pp. 407–13.

27 Y Stoyanov, *The Other God*, ch 4, pp 190–91.

28 John 12:31, 14:30, 16:11.

29 'The Book of John the Evangelist' in Montague R James (ed), *The Apocryphal New Testament*, Clarendon Press, Oxford, 1924.

30 Y Stoyanov, *The Other God*, ch 6, p 272.

31 Most of the Cathar literature was destroyed by the Inquisition, but the Rituel Cathare de Lyon is held at the Bibliothèque Municipale de Lyon. A French transcript of the *Nouveau Testament en Provencal* (ed, Cledat) was published in Paris, 1887.

32 *Encyclopedia Brittanica*, 11th edition, 1911, under Cathars.

33 Denis de Rougemont, *Love in the Western World* (trans, Montgomery Belgion), Princeton University Press, Princeton, NJ, 1983, p 78.

34 Y Stoyanov, *The Hidden Tradition in Europe*, ch 4, p 159.

35 Alain de Lille, *Ars fidei Catholicæ contra haereticos* (c.1190), ch I:lxiii in J-P Migne (ed), *Patrologiae Latinae Cursus Completus*, vol CCX.

36 Walter Birks and RA Gilbert, *The Treasure of Montségur*, Crucible/Aquarian, Wellingborough, 1987, part 2, ch 7, p 65.

37 Michael Baigent, Richard Leigh and Henry Lincoln, *The Holy Blood and the Holy Grail*, Jonathan Cape, London, 1982, ch 2, p 20.

38 *Catholic Encyclopedia*, vol III, under Inquisition.

39 P Carus, *The History of the Devil and the Idea of Evil*, pp 309–10.

40 Homer M Smith, *Man and His Gods*, Little, Brown, Boston, MD, 1952, ch VI:iv.

41 There are four major works concerning Conrad of Marburg: 1) ELT Henke, *Konrad von Marburg*, Marburg, 1861. 2) B Kaltner, *Konrad von Marburg and die Inquisition in Deutschland*, Prague, 1882. 3) A Hausrath, *Der Ketzermeister Konrad von Marburg*, Leipzig, 1883. 4) J Beck, *Konrad von Marburg*, Breslau, 1871.

42 *Catholic Encyclopedia*, vol VIII, under Inquisition.

43 Y Stoyanov, *The Other God*, ch 5, pp 236–37.

44 Currently published as David A Salomon, *The Glossa Ordinaria: Medieval Hypertext*, University of Wales Press, Cardiff, 2006. Also *see* Edward Peters, *The Magician, the Witch and the Law*, Harvester Press, Brighton, 1978, p 68.

45 P Carus, *The History of the Devil and the Idea of Evil*, pp 314–15.

46 *Catholic Encyclopedia*, vol III, under Inquisition.

47 Y Dossat, 'Les Debuts de l'Inquisition a Montpellier en Provence' in *Bulletin philologique et historique*, Paris, 1961, pp 561–79.

Chapter 7: THE BURNING TIMES

1 'The Life of St Dominic' in Jacobus de Voragine, Archbishop of Genoa, *The Golden Legend or Lives of the Saints* (1275), William Caxton, London, 1483; (ed, FS Ellis), Dent, London, 1900.

2 M Summers, *The History of Witchcraft and Demonology*, ch 4, p 138.

3 HC Lea (trans), *A History of the Inquisition of the Middle Ages*, Harper & Brothers, New York, NY, 1887, vol 1, pp 411–14.

4 Louis Charpentier, *The Mysteries of Chartres Cathedral*, Research Into Lost Knowledge Organization and Thorsons, Wellingborough, 1992, ch 8, p 69.

5 Michael Swanton (trans), *The Anglo-Saxon Chronicle*, JM Dent, London, 1997, Peterborough MS (E) 1128, p 259.

6 *Catholic Encyclopedia*, vol II, under Benedict XI, and vol XIV, under Toulouse.

7 *Ibid*, vol IV, under Pope Clement V.

8 JB Russell, *A History of Witchcraft*, ch 4, p 76.

9 Currently published as: Dante Alighieri, *Dante's Divine Comedy*, (illust, Gustave Doré), Arcturus Foulsham, Slough, 2006.

10 Desmond Seward, *The Monks of War*, Paladin/Granada, St Albans, 1974, ch V, p 202.

11 Charles G Addison, *The History of the Knights Templars* (1842), Adventures Unlimited, Kempton, IL, 1997, ch IX, pp 201, 204.

12 D Seward, *The Monks of War*, ch V, p 203.

13 *The Times*, London, 30th March 2002. The previously unknown *Chinon Parchment* was discovered by Dr Barbara Frale, a researcher at the Vatican School of Paleontology, on 13th September 2001. The parchment was published by E Baluze during the 1600s in *Vitae Paparum Avenionensis* (Lives of the Popes of Avignon).When questioned after the 2001 find by the Catholic daily paper *L'Awenire*, a Vatican spokesman said that, as far as the Vatican officials knew, the parchment had been lost in the early 19th century at the time of Napoleon.

14 *See* article: Barbara Frale, 'The Chinon Chart. Papal absolution to last Templar Master Jacques de Molay' in *The Journal of Medieval History*, no 30, April 2004, pp 109–34. Also *see* Adriano Forgione and Francesco Garufi, 'Templari: Assolti Con Formula Piena' in *Hera*, no 27, March 2002.

15 Bertrand Russell, *History of Western Philosophy*, Routledge, London, 2004, pp 469–70.

16 Accounts of the Templar Inquisition are objectively recorded in Malcolm Barber, *The Trial of the Templars*, Cambridge University Press, Cambridge, 2006.

17 Dennis Wheatley, *The Devil and All His Works*, American Heritage Press, New York, NY, 1971, pp 245–46.

18 Y Stoyanov, *The Other God*, ch 5, p 237.

19 Revelation 12:9.

20 R Cavendish, *The Black Arts*, ch 7, p 298.

21 Y Stoyanov, *The Other God*, ch 5, p 238.

22 The work is reproduced in Martin Le Franc, *Le Champion des Dames*, 1451 (ed, Robert Deschaux), Honore Champion, Paris, 1999.

23 R Cavendish, *The Black Arts*, ch 7, p 302.

24 *Catholic Encyclopedia*, vol XI, under Witchcraft.

25 Exodus 16:23 and 20:8–11.

26 Raphael Patai, *The Hebrew Goddess*, Wayne State University Press, Detroit, IL, 1967, ch 11, p 255. *Sha-bat-tu* derives probably from the Babylonian *sha-patti*: 'division of the month'.

27 Z Sitchin, *The 12th Planet*, ch 14, p 392.

28 In the cult of modern Wicca, from the 1950s, these festivals are classified as: *Samhain* (Halloween) – 31 October, *Yule* (Midwinter) – from 21 December, *Imbolc* (Oimelc) – 2 February, *Eostre* (Ostara) – *c.*21 March, *Beltane* (Bale-fire) – 1 May, *Midsummer* (Litha) – *c.*21 June, *Lammas* (Lughnasadh) – *c.*1 August, *Mabon* (Alben Elfed) – *c.*22 September.

29 These full-moon events have been called *Esbats*, from the French alluding to 'frolic'. *See* Margaret Alice Murray, *The Witch Cult in Western Europe*, Oxford University Press, Oxford, 1971, ch 4, p 97.

30 *Catholic Encyclopedia*, vol XI, under Witchcraft.

31 For a full account, *see* Regine Pernoud and Marie-Veronique Clin, *Joan of Arc* (trans, Jeremy du Quesnay Adams), Weidenfeld & Nicolson, London, 2000.

32 *Royal Financial Records Concerning Payments for Twenty-Seven Contingents in the Portion of Joan of Arc's Army Which Arrived At Orléans on 4 May 1429*, Historical Academy for Joan of Arc Studies, 2006 (ed, Paul Charpentier and Charles Cuissard), translated from 'Compte de Me Hémon Raguier' in *Journal du siège d'Orléans, 1428–1429: augmenté de plusieurs documents notamment des comptes de ville, 1429–1431*, H Herluison, Orléans, 1896.

33 Details of the accusations, the trial and the execution are given in Reginald Hyatte, *Laughter for the Devil: The Trials of Gilles De Rais* (1440), Fairleigh Dickinson University Press, Madison, NJ, 1984.

34 Georges Bataille, *Le Procès de Gilles de Rais* (Broché), Pauvert, Paris, 1977.

35 MA Murray, *The Witch Cult of Western Europe*, ch V, p 161; app IV, pp 276–79.

36 M Summers, *The History of Witchcraft and Demonology*, ch 1, p 34.

Chapter 8: FEASTS OF INIQUITY

1 Y Stoyanov, *The Other God*, ch 5, p 238.

2 One of the first works produced on the Gutenberg press in 1452 was the now famous *Gutenberg Bible*, a 1,300 page version of the Latin *Vulgate*.

3 Alphonsus de Spina, *Fortalitium Fidei*, Johann Mentelin, Strasbourg, *c.*1470.

4 Johannes Nider, *Formicarius*, Anton Sorg, Augsburg, *c.*1484.

5 LRN Ashley, *The Complete Book of Devils and Demons*, ch 3, p 106.

6 R Cavendish, *The Black Arts*, ch 7, p 308.

7 M Summers, *The History of Witchcraft and Demonology*, ch 1, pp 7, 10; ch 4, p 134.

8 *Ibid*, ch 1, p 40.

9 Margaret Alice Murray, 'The Devil's Officers and the Witches' Covens' in *Man*, Royal Anthropological Institute of Great Britain and Ireland, London, September 1919, vol, 19, pp 137–140.

10 Jules Michelet, *Satanism and Witchcraft*, Tandem, London, 1970, ch 4, p 37.

11 JB Russell, *A History of Witchcraft*, ch 4, pp 78–79.

12 Philip Schaff, *History of the Christian Church*, Charles Scribner's Sons, New York, NY, 1910, vol 6, ch 10.

13 P Siefker, *Santa Claus, Last of the Wild Men*, ch 4, p 68.

14 M Summers, *The History of Witchcraft and Demonology*, ch 4, p 134.

15 P Carus, *The History of the Devil and the Idea of Evil*, p 288.

16 Karl Friedrich Flögel and Friedrich W Ebeling, *Geschichte des Grotesk-Komischen*, H Barsdorf, Leipzig, 1887, pp 70–71, 119–20.

17 Jacob Grimm, *Teutonic Mythology*, Thoemmes Press, London, 1999, ch 17, pp 105, 115. Also *see* P Siefker, *Santa Claus, Last of the Wild Men*, ch 4, p 69.

18 Ulrich Molitor, *De Lamiis et Pythonicis Mulieribus*, Johann Prüss, Reutlingen, 1489.

19 MA Murray, *The Witch Cult in Western Europe*, ch IV, pp 113–14, regarding English and Scottish trials in the middle 1600s.

20 R Cavendish, *The Black Arts*, ch 7, pp 318–20.

21 P Carus, *The History of the Devil and the Idea of Evil*, p 318.

22 John 12:31, 14:20, 16:11.

23 HTF Rhodes, *The Satanic Mass*, Rider, London, 1954, ch 4, p 38.

24 *Concise Oxford English Dictionary*, under Witch.

25 F Josephus, *The Works of Flavius Josephus*, 'The Wars of the Jews', bk II, ch VIII:6.

26 *Catholic Encyclopedia*, vol XI, under Witchcraft.

27 For further reading on the subject, *see* Joseph, F Perez, *The Spanish Inquisition: A History* (trans, J Lloyd), Profile Books, London, 2004, and Helen Rawlings, *The Spanish Inquisition*, Blackwell, Oxford, 2005.

28 *Catholic Encyclopedia*, vol III, under Inquisition. Torquemada held the position until his death in 1498.

29 HW Smith, *Man and His Gods*, ch VI:vi.

30 Y Dossat, 'Les Debuts de l'Inquisition a Montpellier en Provence' in *Bulletin philologique et historique*, Paris, 1961, pp 561–79.

31 The Spanish Inquisition survived from 1478 to the beginning of the 19th century. It was suppressed by French authorities during the Napoleonic era (1808) and by Cortes of Cadiz (1813). It was re-established by Ferdinand VIII in 1813, but had no practical results, since the Inquisitor General did not resume his post. The last case of an execution by the Spanish Inquisition was that of a schoolmaster, Cayetano Ripoll, 26 July 1826, and the Inquisition was permanently suppressed by a papal decree of 15 July 1834.

Chapter 9: A DIABOLICAL DECREE

1 The 1484 bull of Pope Innocent VIII is translated in Heinrich Kraemer and James Sprenger, *The Malleus Maleficarum* (trans, Montague Summers), Dover Publications, New York, NY, 1971, pp xliii–xlv.

2 P Siefker, *Santa Claus, Last of the Wild Men*, ch 4, p 72.

3 HW Smith, *Man and His Gods*, ch VI:vii.

4 H Kraemer and J Sprenger, *The Malleus Maleficarum*, part III, question 14.

5 *Iesus Nazarenus Rex Iudaeorum* (Jesus of Nazareth King of the Jews), John 19:19.

6 H Kraemer and J Sprenger, *The Malleus Maleficarum*, part I, question 6.

7 *Catholic Encyclopedia*, vol XI, under Witchcraft.

8 H Kraemer and J Sprenger, *The Malleus Maleficarum*, part III, question 14.

9 P Carus, *The History of the Devil and the Idea of Evil*, pp 322–24.

10 HW Smith, *Man and His Gods*, ch VI:viii.

11 R Cavendish, *The Black Arts*, ch 7, p 304.

12 MA Murray, *The Witch Cult in Western Europe*, intro, p 12.

13 *British Educational Research Journal*, Routledge, London, vol 29, issue 2, April 2003, pp 175–87.

14 Revelation 12:3–9.

15 Revelation 13:1.

16 Augustus, Tiberius, Caligula, Claudius, Nero, Galba, Otho, Vespasian, Titus and Domitian.

17 Revelation 13:11–18.

18 John Michell, *Dimensions of Paradise*, Thames and Hudson, London, 1988, ch 1, p 18.

19 The *Oxyrhynchus Papyri* collection contains around 20 manuscripts of New Testament apocrypha: works from the early Christian period that were not ultimately approved in AD 397 for the New Testament canon.

20 Full details of the 'Oxyrhynchus Papyri Project' may be found on the Oxford University website.

21 George Lincoln Burr (ed), *The Witch Persecutions*, University of Pennsylvania History Department, Philadelphia, PA, 1897, pp 26–28.

22 Darren Oldridge, *The Devil in Early Modern England*, Sutton, Stroud, 2000, ch 2, p 16.

23 P Carus, *The History of the Devil and the Idea of Evil*, p 258.

24 RW Scribner, *Popular Culture and Popular Movements in Reformation Germany*, Hambledon Continuum, London, 1988, p 88.

Chapter 10: SATANIC REFORMATION

1 Herodotus, *The Histories* (trans, Robin Waterfield), Oxford University Press, Oxford, 1998, bk 4, item 105, p 270.

2 Ovid, *Metamorphoses* (trans, AD Melville), Oxford University Press, Oxford, 1986, bk I, p 8.

3 Jesse Byock (ed), *The Saga of the Volsungs*, Penguin, London, 1999, ch 8, pp 44–45. Also *see* S Baring-Gould, *The Book of Werewolves*, ch 3, pp 18–19.

4 Based on Ovid's tale of Lycaon, a medical condition in which people suffered from the delusion that they were wolves, caused the latter-day medical establishment to classify that condition as Lycanthropy. The noted Victorian essayist, Rev Sabine Baring-Gould, referred to this in 1865, stating that Lycanthropy 'truly consists as a form of madness such as may be found in most asylums'. *See* in Sabine Baring-Gould, *The Book of Werewolves*, Senate, London, 1995, ch 2, p 8.

5 Marie de France, *Lays* (trans, Eugene Mason), JM Dent, London, 1954, ch 8, pp 83–90.

6 H Kraemer and J Sprenger, *The Malleus Maleficarum*, part I, question 10.

7 *Oxford Compact English Dictionary*, under Werewolf.

8 Sir James George Frazer, *The Golden Bough*, Macmillan, London, 1907, ch 52, p 494.

9 JB Russell, *A History of Witchcraft*, ch 4, p 82.

10 P Carus, *The History of the Devil and the Idea of Evil*, pp 342–43.

11 Exodus 22:18.

12 D Oldridge, *The Devil in Early Modern England*, ch 2, p 24.

13 Thomas Becon, *The Catechism of Thomas Becon* (ed, Rev John Ayre for The Parker Society), Cambridge University Press, Cambridge, 1844, 'Catechism of Prayer', part IV, pp 149, 195.

14 John 20:22–23.

15 *Catholic Encyclopedia*, vol III, under Inquisition.

16 *Ibid*, vol XIII, under The Roman Congregations.

17 *Ibid*, vol XI, under Witchcraft.

18 P Carus, *The History of the Devil and the Idea of Evil*, pp 338–46.

19 Nigel Cawthorne, *Sex Lives of the Popes*, Prion, London, 2004, ch 15, pp 225–36.

20 *Ibid*, ch 15, pp 222–23.

21 Gaspara Stampa (1523–54), Veronica Franco (1546–91) and Tullia d'Aragona (1510–56) each made significant contributions to the poetry of the period.

22 Following Lucrezia, Pope Alexander's other children by Vannozza dei Cattanei were Giovanni, born in 1474, Cesare, born in 1476, and Goffredo, born in 1481.

23 P Carus, *The History of the Devil and the Idea of Evil*, p 343.

Chapter 11: INFERNAL PURSUITS

1 Oliver J Thatcher (ed), *The Library of Original Sources*, University Research Extension, Milwaukee, WI, 1901, vol. IV, pp 211–39.

2 John Earle, *Anglo-Saxon Literature*, Society for Promoting Christian Knowledge, London, 1884, ch III, p 76.

3 Penned by a monk named Cild, *The Leech Book of Bald* survives from around 940. The medical term 'leech' stems from the Old English word *læce*, meaning 'healer'. Details of this work and other medieval remedies are given in Stephen Pollington, *Leechcraft: Early English Charms, Plantlore and Healing*, Anglo Saxon Books, Swaffham, 2000.

4 *Ibid*, ch III, p 74.

5 A Calendar of Witch Trials is given in Richard Kieckhefer, *European Witch Trials: Their Foundations in Popular and Learned Culture, 1300–1500*, University of California Press, Berkeley, CA, 1976.

6 Peter Binsfeld, *Tractatus de Confessionibus Maleficorum et Sagarum*, Heinrich Bock, Trier, 1596.

7 Scotland's witchcraft trials are recorded in Hugo Arnot, *A Collection and Abridgement of Celebrated Criminal Trials in Scotland from 1536 to 1784*, William Smellie, Edinburgh, 1785.

8 Transcript: 'The Examination and Confession of Certain Witches at Chelmsford in the County of Essex, before the Queen Majesty's Judges, the 26th day of July, Anno 1566' in Alan C Kors and Edward Peters (eds), *Witchcraft in Europe, 1100–1700: A Documentary History*, University of Pennsylvania Press, Philadelphia, PA, 1972, pp. 229–35.

9 Also *see* details in Charles Williams, *Witchcraft*, Faber & Faber, London, 1941, pp 194–201.

10 *The Apprehension and Confession of three Notorious Witches* – Arraigned and by Justice condemned and executed at Chelmes-forde, in the Countye of Essex, the 5 day of Julye, last past, 1589.

11 Nathan Johnstone, *The Devil and Demonism in Early Modern England*, Cambridge University Press, Cambridge, 2006, ch 2, pp 29–31; ch 3, p 72.

12 *Ibid*, ch 2, pp 32, 54.

13 Anthony Marten, *An Exhortation to Stirre up the Mindes of all Her Maiesties Faithfulle Subjects to Defend their Countrey in this Dangerous Time, from the Invasion of Enemies*, John Windet, London, 1588.

14 N Johnstone, *The Devil and Demonism in Early Modern England*, ch 2, p 58.

15 The origin of this name and its saintly application are unknown.

16 JG Frazer, *The Golden Bough*, ch 4, p 53.

17 HTF Rhodes, *The Satanic Mass*, ch 15, p 128.

18 M Summers, *The History of Witchcraft and Demonology*, ch 1, p 1.

19 Jean Bodin, *La Démonomanie des Sorciers*, Paris 1580, recounted in George L Burr (ed), *The Witch Persecutions in Translations and Reprints from the Original Sources of European History*, University of Pennsylvania History Department, Philadelphia, PA, 1898–1912, vol 3, no 4, pp 5–6.

20 M Summers, *The History of Witchcraft and Demonology*, ch 4, p 114.

21 More lately (as a variant) called a 'hobby-horse': from the Old French hober: to 'move up and down'. Originally the hobby-horse (as against the cock horse) was a large covered frame with a horse's head, surrounding a festival dancer in the semblance of riding the horse. The hobby-horse is still used for Mayday celebrations in the Southwest of England. *Oxford Concise English Dictionary*, under Hobby-horse and Cock horse.

22 Robert Graves, *The White Goddess*, Faber & Faber, London, 1961, ch 4, p. 70; ch 23, p 410.

23 Margaret Alice Murray, *The God of the Witches*, Oxford University Press, Oxford, 1970, ch III, p 70; ch IV, p 112.

24 The Aberdeen witches confessed that, in their community, the devilish leader was called Christanday.

25 MA Murray, *The God of the Witches*, ch 4, pp 111–12.

26 *Ibid*, ch 4, p 111.

27 Acts of John 94–95, in MR James (ed), *The Apocryphal New Testament*, p 253.

28 The work is currently published as Reginald Scott, *The Discoverie of Witchcraft* (1584), Dover Publications, New York, NY, 1989.

29 HW Smith, *Man and His Gods*, ch VI:viii.

30 P Carus, *The History of the Devil and the Idea of Evil*, pp 345–46.

Chapter 12: WAY OF THE DEVIL

1 Gryffith Williams, *The True Church, shewd to all Men that desire to be Members of the Same*, London, 1629, p 556.

2 D Oldridge, *The Devil in Early Modern England,* ch 2, p 27.

3 *Ibid*, intro, p 7.

4 William Perkins, *A Discourse of the Damned Art of Witchcraft*, Cantrell Legge for the University of Cambridge, 1616. *See* also LRN Ashley, *The Complete Book of Devils and Demons*, ch 3, p 105.

5 D Oldridge, *The Devil in Early Modern England,* ch 5, p 93.

6 Richard Carpenter, *Experience, Historie and Divinitie*, Andrew Crooke, London, 1642, p 66.

7 D Wheatley, *The Devil and All His Works*, p 247.

8 M Summers, *The History of Witchcraft and Demonology*, ch 1, p 9.

9 King James VI of Scotland, I of England, *Daemonology*, Edinburgh 1597, Preface. The original is held at the Bodleian Library, Oxford. The work is currently published as: *James Stuart, King James's Daemonologie in the Form of a Dialogue, Divided into Three Books*, Godolphin House, Mandrake, Oxford, 1996.

10 King James VI, *Daemonology*, p 10.

11 FA Yates, *The Occult Philosophy in the Elizabethan Age*, ch VIII, pp 67, 91.

12 Peter Stanford, *The Devil: A Biography*, Mandarin, London, 1996, ch 8, p 156.

13 D Oldridge, *The Devil in Early Modern England*, intro, pp 12–13; ch 6, p 122.

14 N Johnstone, *The Devil and Demonism in Early Modern England*, ch 3, p 105. Also *see* Samuel Clarke, *The Lives of Thirty-Two English Divines*, William Birch, London, 1677.

15 2 Corinthians 11:13–14.

16 A later, and now better known, version of the Faustus legend was written by Johann Wolfgang von Goethe. His tragic play, entitled *Faust*, was published in two parts: 1) *Faust: der Tragödie erster Teil* [1806 – revised 1829], and 2) *Faust: der Tragödie zweiter Teil* [1832].

17 Frances A Yates, *The Occult Philosophy in the Elizabethan Age*, Routledge & Kegan Paul, London, 1983, ch XI, p 118.

18 Richard Deacon, *A History of the British Secret Service*, Grafton Books, London, 1982, ch 2 pp 51–52.

19 N Johnstone, *The Devil and Demonism in Early Modern England*, ch 5, pp 143–45.

20 JA Sharpe, *Crime in Seventeenth-Century England: A County Study*, Cambridge University Press, Cambridge, 1983, pp 123–28.

21 Extract from *A Warning for all Murderers*, The Roxburgh Collection, British Museum, London, vol 1, pp 484–85.

22 N Johnstone, *The Devil and Demonism in Early Modern England*, ch 5, pp 172–73. Extract from *A new ballad, shewing the great misery sustained by a poor man in Essex, his wife and children, with other strange things done by the Devil, c.1625*. Also *see* article on the subject: Michael MacDonald, 'Suicide and the Rise of the Popular Press in England', in *Representations*, University of California Press, Berkeley, CA, no 22, Spring 1988, pp 36–55.

23 Robert Muchembled, *A History of the Devil: From the Middle Ages to the Present*, Polity Press, Cambridge, 2003, ch 4, p 111.

24 *Ibid*, ch 2, pp 46–47.

25 Figleafing is especially evident in many paintings of Adam and Eve.

26 Jean-Paul Clébert, *The Gypsies* (trans, Charles Duff), Visita Books, London, 1963, pp 50–51.

27 R Graves, *The White Goddess*, ch 7, p 282.

28 The ruling came from the Old Testament book of Leviticus 12:2–8. Jesus' mother, Mary, conveniently escaped the doctrine since she had seemingly not committed the mortal sin which led to the conception, and was deemed for ever a virgin.

29 H Kraemer and J Sprenger, *The Malleus Maleficarum*, part I, question 6.

30 The 1552 *Book of Common Prayer* includes the ritual for 'The Thanksgiving of Women After Childbirth, commonly called the Churching of Women'.

Chapter 13: DEGENERATE ASSEMBLY

1 James IV of Scots had married Margaret Tudor, a daughter of Henry VII of England, in 1503.

2 AJ Patrick, *The Making of a Nation: 1603–1789*, Penguin, London, 1981, ch 1, p 10.

3 *Ibid*, ch 1, pp 11–12.

4 For further information on the subject, *see* Muriel C Bradbrook, *The School of Night: A Study in the Literary Relationships of Raleigh*, Cambridge University Press, Cambridge, 1936.

5 N Johnstone, *The Devil and Demonism in Early Modern England*, ch 6, pp 189–93.

6 *Ibid*, ch 6, p 196.

7 The book is correctly referenced by name in Roman Polanski's 1999 movie, *The Ninth Gate*, Also referenced in the film is the work, *Hypnerotomachia Polyphili*, printed in Venice by Aldus Manutius in December 1499. Written anonymously, there is dispute as to whether the author was Francesco Colonna or Leone Battista Alberti. It is, however, currently published as Francesco Colonna, *Hypnerotomachia Polyphili* (trans, Joscelin Godwin), Thames and Hudson, London, 2005. The book, with 174 exquisite woodcuts, presents an arcane allegory in which Poliphilo pursues an erotic fantasy through a dreamlike landscape, and is at last reconciled with his love, Polia, by the Fountain of Venus. It is one of the most important documents of Renaissance imagination and fantasy, and its woodcuts are a primary source for Renaissance ideas on buildings and gardens. Quite why it is referenced as a book about witchcraft in *The Ninth Gate* is a mystery. It is largely about the right of women to express their sexuality.

8 Francesco Maria Guazzo, *Compendium Maleficarum*, 1608 (ed, Montague Summers), Dover Publications, New York, NY, 1988, p iv.

9 *Succubus*: a demon who takes the form of a human female to seduce men. *Incubus*: a demon in male form that takes sexual advantage of sleeping women.

10 W Wright, *News from Scotland, Declaring the Damnable Life and Death of Doctor Fian*, London, 1592.

11 M Summers, *The History of Witchcraft and Demonology*, ch 3, pp 81–89.

12 *Ibid*, ch 3, p 93.

13 FM Guazzo, *Compendium Maleficarum*, bk I, ch XII.

14 Henry More, *Antidote Against Atheism*, London, 1653, p 232.

15 M Summers, *The History of Witchcraft and Demonology*, ch 3, p 84.

16 HTF Rhodes, *The Satanic Mass*, ch 3, p 34.

17 Pierre de Lancre, *Tableau de l'inconstance des Mauvais Anges et Demons: ou il est Amplement Traite des Sorciers et de la Sorcellerie*, Paris, 1613.

18 For the full record of these trials, *see* Friedrich Spee von Langenfeld, *Cautio Criminalis, or a Book on Witch Trials, 1631* (trans, Marcus Hellyer), University of Virginia Press, Charlottesville, VA, 2003.

19 R Cavendish, *The Black Arts*, ch 7, pp 311–12.

20 D Wheatley, *The Devil and All His Works*, p 227.

21 J Michelet, *Satanism and Witchcraft*, ch 17, p 124.

22 The subject of Grandier's trial is discussed in Aldous Huxley, *The Devils of Loudun*, Chatto & Windus, London, 1952. This book was adapted for the stage in 1961 by John Whiting (commissioned by the Royal Shakespeare Company). The play was then adapted for the movie screen by Ken Russell in his 1971 film *The Devils*.

23 J Michelet, *Satanism and Witchcraft*, ch 19, p 142.

24 M Summers, *The History of Witchcraft and Demonology*, ch 2, pp 69–70.

25 For full details of the affair, translated from the French, *see* Montague Summers (trans), *The Confessions of Madeleine Bavent (1652)*, Fortune Press, London, 1930.

26 Thomas Potts, *The Wonderful discoverie of witches in the countie of Lancaster: with the arraignment and triall of nineteene witches*, W Stansby for John Barnes, London, 1613; facsimile reprint: Carnegie Publishing, Lancaster, 2003.

27 Elizabeth's only confidant was the minister and Newgate Ordinary, Henry Goodecole. Following her execution, he wrote a pamphlet entitled *The Wonderfull Discoverie of Elizabeth Sawyer – a witch late of Edmonton: Her conviction, and condemnation, and death, together with the relation of the Devil's access to her and their conference together*, 1621.

28 Thomas Cooper, *Pleasant Treatise of Witches*, London, 1673.

Chapter 14: SATAN'S REBELLION

1 N Johnstone, *The Devil and Demonism in Early Modern England*, intro, p 7; ch 4, p 112.

2 *Ibid*, ch 6, pp 197, 202.

3 Lambe's story was recounted in *A Briefe Description of the Notorious Life of John Lambe*, London, 1628 – republished by Theatrum Orbis Terrarum, Amsterdam, 1976.

4 Thomas Birch, *The Court and Times of Charles I* (ed, RF Williams), Henry Colburn, London, 1842, vol I, p 446.

5 William Prynne, *Histrio-Mastix: The Player's Scourge, or Actors Tragedie*, London, 1633.

6 D Oldridge, *The Devil in Early Modern England*, ch 8, p 161.

7 N Johnstone, *The Devil and Demonism in Early Modern England*, intro, p 6.

8 *A Disputation Betwixt the Devil and the Pope: being a brief dialogue between Urban VIII, Pope of Rome, and Pluto, Prince of Hell*, London 1642.

9 *News From Hell, Rome and the Inns of Court: wherein is set forth the copy of a letter written from the Devil to the Pope*, London, 1641.

10 *The Papists Petition in England to their diabolical centre of impiety the Pope: or their glory, in a story, wherein they sit, and pumpe for witt*, John Hammond, London, 1642.

11 Sir Charles Petrie, *The Stuarts*, Eyre and Spottiswoode, London, 1937, ch 5, pp 216–17.

12 D Wheatley, *The Devil and All His Works*, p 251.

13 D Oldridge, *The Devil in Early Modern England*, ch 7, pp 154–55.
14 John Gaule, Select Cases of Conscience Touching Witches and Witchcraft, London, 1646.

15 Matthew Hopkins, *The Discovery of Witches: In answer to severall queries lately delivered to the Judges of Assize for the County of Norfolk*, Matthew Hopkins, Witch-finder, for the Benefit of the whole Kingdome, M. DC. XLVII.

16 William John Thorns (ed), *Notes & Queries*, 1st series, vol 10, London, 7 October 1854, p 283.

17 *The Lawes Against Witches and Conjuration – and some brief notes and observations for the Discovery of Witches. Being very useful for these times, wherein the Devil reignes and prevailes over the foules of poor creatures, in drawing them to that crying sin of witchcraft. Also, the confession of Mother Lakeland, who was arraigned and condemned for a witch, at Ipswich in Suffolke.* Published by Authority, Printed for RW, London, 1645.

18 Exodus 22:18.

19 The Survey of Scottish Witchcraft, with a fully comprehensive online database, is compiled by the Scottish History, School of History and Classics, University of Edinburgh, 17 Buccleuch Place, Edinburgh, EH8 9LN.

20 R Muchembled, *A History of the Devil: From the Middle Ages to the Present*, ch 5, pp 152–53.

21 *Ibid*, ch 5, pp 158–59.

22 P Carus, *The History of the Devil and the Idea of Evil*, p 30

23 J Gordon Melton, *The Vampire Book*, Visible Ink Press, Farmington Hills, MI, 1999, pp 55–56. The concept of bloodsucking demons dates back to ancient Mesopotamia in the 3rd millennium BC. The first such creature of literary significance appeared in Greek mythology. She was Lamia, a Queen of Libya and mistress of Zeus, who was punished by the goddess Hera and turned into a scaly four-footed creature with a woman's face and breasts. Subsequently, in Central and Eastern Europe, the idea became associated with an unholy cult of the living dead, but in Britain the tradition made a very slow start.

24 *Ibid*, fwd, p x.

25 S Baring-Gould, *The Book of Werewolves*, ch 8, p 115.

Chapter 15: THE DEVIL AND REASON

1 John Milton, *A Treatise of Civil Power in Ecclesiastical Causes: That it is Not Lawful for any Power On Earth to Compel in Matters of Religion*, Kessinger, Kila, MT, 2004.

2 Origen, 'De Principiis' in Rev A Roberts and J Donaldson (eds), *The Ante-Nicene Fathers – The Writings of the Fathers down to AD 325*, vol IV, bk I, ch 5:5.

3 'Against the Luciferians' in Philip Schaff (ed), *The Principal Works of St Jerome*, Christian Literature Publishing, New York, NY, 1892, pp 319–34.

4 Luke 4:1–13.

5 Job 2:1–2.

6 John Milton, *Paradise Regained*, W Taylor, London, 1721, bk IV:565–625.

7 Revelation 9:11.

8 John Bunyan, *The Pilgrim's Progress*, W Oliver, London, 1776, pp 91–97.

9 The details of Bunyan's life are covered in Robert Philip, *The Life, Times and Characteristics of John Bunyan*, Wm Carlton Regand, New York, NY, 1888.

10 Also recommended is John Brown, Minister of the Bunyan Church at Bedford, *John Bunyan, His Life, Times and Work*, Isbister, London, 1902.

11 Cotton Mather, the Governor of Massachusetts in 1692 at the time of the Salem witch trials, wrote of the Bury St Edmonds precedent in his book, Cotton Mather, *Wonders of the Invisible World*, reprinted: John Russell Smith, London, 1862, pp 111–20.

12 The full trial report (a reprint of 'A Tryal of Witches at Bury St Edmonds, March 10, 1665, before Sir Matthew Hale') is given in TB Howell (compiler), *The State Trials from the earliest period to the year 1783*, (Howell's State Trials), vol VI, pp 647–702. It is also fully discussed in Gilbert Geis and Ivan Bunn, *A Trial of Witches – A Seventeenth-century Witchcraft Prosecution*, Routledge, London, 1997.

13 JB Russell, *A History of Witchcraft*, ch 4, pp 80–81.

14 The writings are published as Robert Kirk, *The Secret Commonwealth of Elves, Fauns and Fairies*, NYRB Classics, New York, NY, 2006.

15 M Summers, *The History of Witchcraft and Demonology*, ch 2, pp 71–72.

16 The work is available in facsimile edition: Michael Dalton, *Country Justice* (1618 and London, 1630), The Legal Classics Library, Gryphon Editions, New York, NY, 1996.

17 Richard Bernard, *Guide to Grand Jury Men in Cases of Witchcraft*, London, 1627.

18 D Wheatley, *The Devil and All His Works*, p 249.

19 For details of the background to the Mass, *see* HTF Rhodes, *The Satanic Mass*, chs 12–14, pp 102–124.

20 A further account of the Guibourg Mass is given in Anne Somerset, *The Affair of the Poisons: Murder, Infanticide, and Satanism at the Court of Louis XIV*, St. Martin's Press, New York, NY, 2003.

21 R Cavendish, *The Black Arts*, ch 7, pp 326–27.

22 D Wheatley, *The Devil and All His Works*, p 230. Also *see* Montague Summers, *The History of Witchcraft and Demonology*, ch 3, p 87.

23 J Michelet, *Satanism and Witchcraft*, ch 11, p 82.

24 JB Russell, *A History of Witchcraft*, ch 7, p 130. Also *see* Janet and Stewart Farrar, *A Witches' Bible*, Phoenix, Custer, WA, 1996, part 2, p 318.

25 J Michelet, *Satanism and Witchcraft*, ch 21, pp 160–61.

26 John Fiske, *New France and New England*, Houghton Mifflin, Boston, MD, 1902, ch V, pp 133–34.

27 J Michelet, *Satanism and Witchcraft*, ch 21, p 163.

28 Jules Michelet, *La Sorcière* (trans, LJ Trotter), Simpkin Marshall, London, 1863, ch IX, p 301.

Chapter 16: A FIENDISH TRANSITION

1 R Muchembled, *A History of the Devil: From the Middle Ages to the Present*, ch 5, p 161.

2 P Carus, *The History of the Devil and the Idea of Evil*, pp 377–79.

3 The accounts of Baretti and other travel writers are recounted in Rosamond Bayne-Powell, *Travellers in Eighteenth-Century England*, John Murray, London, 1951.

4 In Germany the nun, Maria Renata, was beheaded in 1749 for owning herbs and casting spells on other sisters, and the very last judicial execution for witchcraft in Europe took place in Poland in 1793, when two old women were burned.

5 JB Russell, *A History of Witchcraft*, ch 7, pp 123–24.

6 Anton Van Dale, *De Oraculis Ethnicorum*, Amsterdam, 1685. Also *see* his *Dissertationes de origine ac progressu Idolalriæ*, Amsterdam, 1696.

7 R Muchembled, *A History of the Devil: From the Middle Ages to the Present*, ch 5, p 164.

8 P Carus, *The History of the Devil and the Idea of Evil*, pp 380–83.

9 HTF Rhodes, *The Satanic Mass*, ch 11, p 99.

10 D Wheatley, *The Devil and All His Works*, p 232.

11 HTF Rhodes, *The Satanic Mass*, ch 12, p 103.

12 *Ibid*, chs 10, p 90; 14, p 121.

13 Once in Exodus, once in Jeremiah, once in Micah, twice in Isaiah, three times in Deuteronomy, four times in 1 Samuel, five times in Judges, and twenty-seven times in the books of Kings and Chronicles.

14 Anne Somerset, *The Affair of the Poisons*, ch 8 pp 242–68.

15 New England, a region in the north-eastern corner of the United States, incorporates Connecticut, Maine, Massachusetts, New Hampshire, Rhode Island, and Vermont.

16 The complete story of this 1611 translation is told in Adam Nicolson, *Power and Glory*, HarperCollins, London, 2003.

17 C Mather, *The Wonders of the Invisible World*, p 74.

18 J Fiske, *New France and New England*, ch V, p 145.

19 Thomas Hutchinson, *The History of the Colony and Province of Massachusetts-Bay in New England*, Boston, MA, 1749–74, vol I, p 173.

20 Winfield S Nevins, *Witchcraft in Salem Village*, Northshore Publishing, Boston, 1892, p 34.

21 J Fiske, *New France and New England*, ch V, p 149.

22 'Introduction to The Wonders of the Invisible World by Cotton Mather, 1693', in George Lincoln Burr, *Narratives of the Witchcraft Cases, 1648–1706*, Charles Scribner's Sons, New York, NY, 1914, p 205.

23 D Wheatley, *The Devil and All His Works*, p 255.

24 John Putnam Demos, *Entertaining Satan*, Oxford University Press, Oxford, 1982, ch 9, p 305.

25 JB Russell, *A History of Witchcraft*, ch 6, pp 119–20.

26 Paul Boyer and Stephen Nissenbaum, *Salem Possessed: The Social Origins of Witchcraft*, Harvard University Press, Cambridge, MA, 1974, p 177.

27 P Carus, *The History of the Devil and the Idea of Evil*, pp 368–39.

Chapter 17: THE LIGHT OF LUCIFER

1 English translation: Abbé Laurent Bordelon, *A History of the Ridiculous Extravagancies of Monsieur Oufle*, J Morphew, London, 1711.

2 Pierre de Lancre, *Tableau de l'inconstance des Mauuaisanges et Demons*, Nicolas Buon, Paris, 1613.

3 R Muchembled, *A History of the Devil: From the Middle Ages to the Present*, ch 5, p 168.

4 Currently published as Daniel Defoe, *The Political History of the Devil*, AMS Press, New York, NY, 2003.

5 Daniel Defoe, *A System of Magic or a History of the Black Art*, Oxford, 1840, p 53.

6 Richard Deacon, *A History of the British Secret Service*, Grafton Books, London, 1982, ch 7, pp 83–94.

7 Ephesians 2:2.

8 HW Smith, *Man and His Gods*, ch VI:viii.

9 David T Morgan, *The Devious Doctor Franklin, Colonial Agent*, Mercer University Press, Macon, GA, 1999, ch 1, p 15.

10 James Breck Perkins, *France in the American Revolution*, Cornerhouse, Williamstown, MA, 1970, ch 7, p 140.

11 Geoffrey Ashe, *The Hell-Fire Clubs*, Sutton, Stroud, 2000, ch 9, pp 140–41.

12 Russell Phillips, *Benjamin Franklin: The First Civilized American*, Brentano's, New York, NY, 1926, ch 24, p 218.

13 HTF Rhodes, *The Satanic Mass*, ch 17, p 142.

14 Betty Kemp, *Sir Francis Dashwood*, Macmillan, London, 1967, ch 5, pp 144–57.

15 HTF Rhodes, *The Satanic Mass*, ch 18, p 149.

16 D Oldridge, *The Devil in Early Modern England*, ch 8, p 166.

17 Montague Summers, *The Vampire: His Kith and Kin*, K Paul Trench & Trubner, London, 1928, intro, p vi.

18 This report is fully transcribed in Paul Barber, *Vampires, Burial and Death*, Yale University Press, New Haven, CT, 1988, pp 16–17.

19 Derivative variations are used in today's English-language, in words denoting 'upper' (topmost) such as 'super', 'supervisor' and 'superintendent'.

20 P Barber, *Vampires, Burial and Death*, ch 6, p 42.

21 JG Melton, *The Vampire Book*, p. 626.
22 *Oxford Compact English Dictionary*, under Vampire.

23 JG Melton, *The Vampire Book*, pp 283–84, 288.

24 P Barber, *Vampires, Burial and Death*, ch 5, p 33.

25 JG Melton, *The Vampire Book*, p 467.

26 *Ibid*, p 573.

27 *Ibid*, p 288.

Chapter 18: AN AGE OF HORROR

1 R Muchembled, *A History of the Devil: From the Middle Ages to the Present*, ch 5, p 176.

2 P Stanford, *The Devil: A Biography*, ch 9, pp 203–204.

3 Horace Walpole, *The Castle of Otranto*, Oxford World's Classics, Oxford, 1998.

4 Ann Radcliffe, *The Mysteries of Udolpho*, Oxford World's Classics, Oxford, 1998.

5 Matthew Lewis, *The Monk*, Oxford World's Classics, Oxford, 1998.

6 Ann Radcliffe, *The Italian*, Oxford World's Classics, Oxford, 1998.

7 Giaour (correctly, *gavur*) is the Turkish word for 'infidel'.

8 For example, 1 Corinthians 15:13–16.

9 1 Thessalonians 4:16.

10 In England, the word 'vampire' did not feature in *Nathan Bailey's Dictionary*, published in 1721. The related word 'vamp' is given in modern dictionaries as 'a woman who uses sexual attractions to exploit men', but in *Bailey's* this same word is given as 'a kind of short stocking'. In the popular 1862 *Walker's Dictionary*, the meaning of vampire is given simply as 'a demon', whilst that word is itself listed as 'an evil spirit or devil'.

11 For some time after this, Lord Ruthven was taken up as a character by various magazine writers, with the concept of vampires being creatures of the night introduced in the middle 1800s.

12 James Malcolm Rymer, *Varney the Vampire – The Feast of Blood*, E Lloyd, London, 1847.

13 P Barber, *Vampires, Burial and Death*, intro. p 2.

14 Bram Stoker, *Dracula*, Archibald Constable, London, 1897.

15 HTF Rhodes, *The Satanic Mass*, ch 16, p 137.

16 Elizabeth Miller, *Dracula: Sense and Nonsense*, Desert Island Books, Westcliff-on-Sea, 2000, ch 2 p 72.

17 *Ibid*, ch 5, pp 187–88.

18 JG Melton, *The Vampire Book*, pp 573, 758–59.

19 Radu Florescu and Raymond McNally, *Dracula*, Robert Hale, London, 1973, intro, pp 9–10.

20 Succeeding the empire of the Seljuk Turks, the Ottoman Empire was founded *c*.1300. In 1452 the Ottoman Turks recovered Constantinople, which had long been the citadel of the East Roman Byzantine Empire. By the late 16th century the Ottoman domain extended from Hungary to Egypt and parts of Persia. Then a gradual decline followed until the establishment of the Republic of Turkey saw the end of imperialism in 1920.

21 R Florescu and R McNally, *Dracula*, ch 7, p 151.

22 JG Melton, *The Vampire Book*, p 573.

23 The English translation of *Dogme et Rituel de la Haute Magie*, is published as Arthur E Waite, *Transcendental Magic*, Samuel Weiser, York Beach, ME, 1896.

24 *See* 'Ceremonial Magic and Sorcery' in MP Hall, *Masonic, Hermetic, Qabbalistic and Rosicrucian Symbolical Philosophy – The Secret Teachings of All Ages*, p CI.

25 Hugh J Schonfield, *The Original New Testament*, Waterstone, London, 1985.

26 Hugh J Schonfield, *The Essene Odyssey*, Element Books, Shaftesbury, 1984, intro, pp 7–8, and ch 11, pp 66–68.

27 *Ibid*, app A, pp 162–165. *Baphomet* in Hebrew (right to left) is [*taf*] [*mem*] [*vav*] [*pe*] [*bet*]. Application of the *Atbash* cipher results (again right to left for Hebrew) in [*alef*] [*yud*] [*pe*] [*vav*] [*shin*] = 'Sofia'.

28 *Extracts from Aleister Crowley, Magick in Theory and Practice – Magick: Liber Aba, Book 4,* Castle Books, New York, NY, 1961, part 3, ch V.

Chapter 19: THE EBBING TIDE

1 JG Melton, *The Vampire Book*, p xi.

2 R Muchembled, *A History of the Devil: From the Middle Ages to the Present*, ch 6, p 192.

3 Robert Louis Stevenson, *The Strange Case of Dr Jekyll and Mr Hyde*, Oxford World's Classics, Oxford, 2006.

4 Albert Pike's 11-foot bronze statue, by the Italian sculptor Gaetano Trentaove, is located in downtown Washington, DC.

5 A complete edition of the work exists as Diana Vaughan, *Mémoires d'une Ex-Palladiste Parfait Initiée, Indépendant Publication mensuelle Cesi este un œuvre de bonne foi* (ed, A Pierret), Paris (undated).

6 A version of this work is now available as Arthur Edward Waite, *Devil Worship in France with Diana Vaughan and the Question of Modern Palladism*, Red Wheel Weiser, York Beach, ME, 2003.

7 The meeting was reported by Edmond Frank in *l'Illustration*, Paris, no. 2827, 1 May 1897.

8 HTF Rhodes, *The Satanic Mass*, ch 20, pp 171–75.

9 R Cavendish, *The Black Arts*, ch 7, p 337.

10 William Seabrook, *Witchcraft: Its Power in the World Today*, Harcourt Brace, New York, NY, 1940.

11 Gabriel Legué, *La Messe Noire*, Charpentier et Fasquelle, Paris, 1903.

12 Details of a Latin Black Mass, which originated in 17th-century France, are given in Aubrey Melech, *Missa Niger: La Messe Noire*, Sut Anubis, Northampton, 1986.

13 Montague Summers, *Witchcraft and Black Magic*, Dover, New York, NY, 2000, ch 7, passim.

14 HTF Rhodes, *The Satanic Mass*, ch 27, p 230.

15 R Muchembled, *A History of the Devil: From the Middle Ages to the Present*, ch 6, p 213.

16 *Ibid*, ch 6, p 205.

Chapter 20: SATAN'S LAST STAND

1 Arthur Edward Waite, *Devil Worship in France*, George Redway, London, 1896, ch I, p 1.

2 *Ibid*, ch II, p 22.

3 'The Wickedest Man in the World' in *John Bull*, Odham's Press, London, 24 March 1923

4 Aleister Crowley, *Liber AL vel Legis: The Book of the Law*, Mandrake, Oxford, 1992, ch III, item 55.

5 P Stanford, *The Devil: A Biography*, ch 14, p 267.

6 Details of Gerald Gardner's introduction to witchcraft are given in Gerald B Gardner, *Witchcraft Today*, I-H-O Books, Thame, 1954.

7 Accounts of these rituals and their inherent philosophies are given in J&S Farrar, *A Witches' Bible*, part 2, pp 1–275.

8 JB Russell, *A History of Witchcraft*, ch 9, p 154.

9 *Ibid*, ch 8, p 146.

10 JG Melton, *The Vampire Book*, p 11.
11 *Weekly World News*, American Media Inc, Boca Raton, FL, 18 October 1994.

12 P Stanford, *The Devil: A Biography*, ch 10, p 217.

13 Bishop Graham Dow, 'The Case for the Existence of Demons' in *Churchman*, The Church Society, Watford, issue 94/3, 1980.

14 Henry Ansgar Kelly, *Satan, a Biography*, Cambridge University Press, New York, NY, 2006, part V, ch 14, p 316.

15 Article 598, *Compendium of the Catechism of the Catholic Church*, Libreria Editrice Vaticana, 2005.

16 P Stanford, *The Devil: A Biography*, ch 10, p 215.

17 Article published as 'Rome's Chief Exorcist warns parents against Harry Potter', in *Catholic News*, Catholic Telecommunications, Church Resources, Crows Nest, NSW, 4 January 2002.

BIBLIOGRAPHY

Addison, Charles G, *The History of the Knights Templars* (1842), Adventures Unlimited, Kempton, IL, 1997.

Alighieri, Dante, *Dante's Divine Comedy*, (illust, Gustave Doré), Arcturus Foulsham, Slough, 2006.

Alphonsus de Spina, *Fortalitium Fideli*, Johann Mentelin, Strasbourg, c.1470.

Aquinas, St Thomas, *Summa Contra Gentiles* (Summary Against the Gentiles – *The Book on the Truth of the Catholic Faith against the Errors of the Infidels*), c.1264 – ed, Joseph Rickaby), Burns and Oates, London, 1905.

— *Summa Theologica* (trans, Fathers of the English Dominican Province), R&T Washbourne, London, 1912.

— *A Literal Exposition on Job*, Oxford University Press, Oxford, 1989.

Arnot, Hugo, *A Collection and Abridgement of Celebrated Criminal Trials in Scotland from 1536 to 1784*, William Smellie, Edinburgh, 1785.

Ashe, Geoffrey, *The Hell-Fire Clubs*, Sutton, Stroud, 2000.

Ashton, John, *The Devil in Britain and America*, Ward & Downey, London, 1896.

Ashley, Leonard RN, *The Complete Book of Devils and Demons*, Robson Books, London, 1997.

Baigent, Michael, Richard Leigh and Henry Lincoln, *The Holy Blood and the Holy Grail*, Jonathan Cape, London, 1982.

Bailey, Nathan (ed), *Bailey's Universal Etymological Dictionary*, T Cox at The Lamb, Royal Exchange, London, 1721.

Barber, Malcolm, *The Trial of the Templars*, Cambridge University Press, Cambridge, 2006.

Barber, Paul, *Vampires, Burial and Death*, Yale University Press, New Haven, CT, 1988.

Baring-Gould, Sabine, *The Book of Werewolves*, Senate, London, 1995.

— *Myths of the Middle Ages* (ed, John Matthews), Blandford, London, 1996.

Barnard, Leslie, *Justin Martyr, His Life and Thought*, Cambridge University Press, Cambridge, 1967.

Barnstone, Willis (ed), *The Other Bible*, HarperSanFrancisco, San Francisco, CA, 1984.

Bataille, Georges, *Le Procès de Gilles de Rais*, Pauvert, Paris, 1977

Bayne-Powell, Rosamond, *Travellers in Eighteenth-Century England*, John Murray, London, 1951.

Becon, Thomas, *The Catechism of Thomas Becon* (ed, Rev John Ayre for The Parker Society), Cambridge University Press, Cambridge, 1844.

Bernard, Richard, *Guide to Grand Jury Men in Cases of Witchcraft*, London, 1627.

Bettenson, Henry, *Documents of the Christian Church*, Oxford University Press, Oxford, 1950.

Binsfeld, Peter, *Tractatus de Confessionibus Maleficorum et Sagarum*, Heinrich Bock, Trier, 1596.

Birch, Thomas, *The Court and Times of Charles I* (ed, RF Williams), Henry Colburn, London, 1842.

Birks, Walter and RA Gilbert, *The Treasure of Montségur*, Aquarian, Wellingborough, 1987.

Black, Jeremy, and Anthony Green, *Gods, Demons and Symbols of Ancient Mesopotamia*, British Museum Press, London, 1992.

Bodin, Jean, *La Démonomanie des Sorciers*, Paris 1580.

Bordelon, Abbé Laurent, *A History of the Ridiculous Extravagancies of Monsieur Oufle*, J Morphew, London, 1711.

Boureau, Alain, *Satan the Heretic: The Birth of Demonology in the Medieval West*, University of Chicago Press, Chicago, IL, 2006.

Boyer, Paul, and Stephen Nissenbaum, *Salem Possessed: The Social Origins of Witchcraft*, Harvard University Press, Cambridge, MA, 1974.

— *Salem-Village Witchcraft: A Documentary Record of Local Conflict in Colonial New England*, Northeastern University Press, Boston, MA, 1993.

Bradbrook, Muriel C, *The School of Night: A Study in the Literary Relationships of Raleigh*, Cambridge University Press, Cambridge, 1936.

Brown, John, Minister of the Bunyan Church at Bedford, *John Bunyan, His Life, Times and Work*, Isbister, London, 1902.

Brown, Milton Perry, *The Authentic Writings of Ignatius: A Study of Linguistic Criteria*, Duke University Press, Durham, NC, 1963.

Bruyn, Lucy de, *Women and the Devil in Sixteenth Century Literature*, Old Compton Press, Tisbury, 1979.

Budge, Sir Ernest A Wallis (trans), *The Book of the Cave of Treasures*, The Religious Tract Society, London, 1927.

BIBLIOGRAPHY

Bull, Norman J, *The Rise of the Church*, Heinemann, London, 1967.

Bunyan, John, *The Pilgrim's Progress*, W Oliver, London, 1776

Burman, Edward, *The Inquisition: The Hammer of Heresy*, Sutton, Stroud, 2004.

Burr, George Lincoln (ed), *The Witch Persecutions*, University of Pennsylvania History Department, Philadelphia, PA, 1897.

— *The Witch Persecutions in Translations and Reprints from the Original Sources of European History*, University of Pennsylvania History Department, Philadelphia, PA, 1898–1912.

— *Narratives of the Witchcraft Cases, 1648–1706*, Charles Scribner's Sons, New York, NY, 1914.

Byock, Jesse (ed), *The Saga of the Volsungs*, Penguin, London, 1999.

Caesar of Heisterbach, *Caesarii Heisterbacensis Monachi Ordinis Cisterciensis Dialogus Miraculroum* (ed, Strange), Paris, 1851.

Camporesi, Piero, *The Fear of Hell: Images of Damnation and Salvation in Early Modern Europe*, Polity Press, Oxford, 1990.

Carozzi, Claude, *Apocalypse et salut dans le christianisme ancien et médiéval*, Collection Historique, Aubier, Paris, 1999.

Carpenter, Richard, *Experience, Historie and Divinitie*, Andrew Crooke, London, 1642.

Carus, Paul, *The History of the Devil and the Idea of Evil*, Gramercy, New York, NY, 1996.

Catholic Encyclopedia, Robert Appleton, New York, NY, 1910.

Cavendish, Richard, *The Black Arts*, Perigee, New York, NY, 1983.

Cawthorne, Nigel, *Sex Lives of the Popes*, Prion, London, 2004.

Chadwick, Henry, *Priscillian of Avila: The Occult and the Charismatic in the Early Church*, Clarendon Press, Oxford, 1997.

Charles, RH (trans), *The Book of Enoch* (from Dillmann's 1893 edition of the Ethiopic text), Oxford University Press, 1906–1912.

— *The Apocrypha and Pseudepigrapha of the Old Testament*, Clarendon Press, Oxford, 1913.

Charlesworth, James H (ed), 'The Testament of Solomon' (trans, Dennis C Duling), in *Old Testament Pseudepigrapha*, Doubleday, Garden City, NY, 1983.

Charpentier, Louis, *The Mysteries of Chartres Cathedral*, Research Into Lost Knowledge Organization and Thorsons, Wellingborough, 1992.

Clarke, Samuel, *The Lives of Thirty-Two English Divines*, William Birch, London, 1677.

Clayton, Peter A, *Chronicle of the Pharaohs*, Thames and Hudson, London, 1994.

Clébert, Jean-Paul, *The Gypsies* (trans. Charles Duff), Visita Books, London, 1963.

Collins, Andrew, *From the Ashes of Angels*, Michael Joseph, London, 1996.

Colonna, Francesco, *Hypnerotomachia Polyphili* (trans, Joscelin Godwin), Thames and Hudson, London, 2005.

Conway, Moncure Daniel, *Demonology and Devil Lore*, Chatto & Windus, London, 1879.

Cooper, Thomas, *Pleasant Treatise of Witches*, London, 1673.
Coulton, CG (ed), Life in the Middle Ages, Macmillan, New York, NY, 1910.

Cox, John D, *The Devil and the Sacred in English Drama, 1350–1642*, Cambridge University Press, Cambridge, 2006.

Crowley, Aleister, *Magick in Theory and Practice – Magick: Liber Aba*, Book 4, Castle Books, New York, NY, 1961.

— *Liber AL vel Legis: The Book of the Law*, Mandrake, Oxford, 1992.

Dalton, Michael, *Country Justice* (London, 1630), The Legal Classics Library, Gryphon Editions, New York, NY, 1996.

Deacon, Richard, *A History of the British Secret Service*, Grafton Books, London, 1982.

Defoe, Daniel, *A System of Magic or a History of the Black Art*, Oxford, 1840.

— *The Political History of the Devil*, AMS Press, New York, NY, 2003.

De Lancre, Pierre, *Tableau de l'inconstance des Mauvais Anges et Demons: ou il est Amplement Traite des Sorciers et de la Sorcellerie*, Paris, 1613.

Demos, John Putnam, *Entertaining Satan*, Oxford University Press, Oxford, 1982.

Dendle, Peter, *Satan Unbound: The Devil in Old English Narrative Literature*, University of Toronto Press, Toronto, 2001.

Douglas, Mary, *Witchcraft Confessions and Accusations*, Tavistock, London, 1970.

Drake, Samuel G, *Annals of Witchcraft in New England and Elsewhere in the United States*, Scholarly Publishing, University of Michigan, Michigan, MI, 2005.

BIBLIOGRAPHY

Duffy, Eamon, *The Stripping of the Altars: Traditional Belief in England, 1400–1580*, Yale University Press, New Haven, CT, 1992.

Dupont-Sommer, André, *The Essene Writings from Qumrân* (trans, Geza Vermes), Basil Blackwell, Oxford, 1961.

Earle, John, *Anglo-Saxon Literature*, Society for Promoting Christian Knowledge, London, 1884.

Emerson, Richard Kenneth, *Antichrist in the Middle Ages: A Study of Medieval Apocalypticism*, Manchester University Press, Manchester, 1981.

Eusebius of Caesarea, *The History of the Church from Christ to Constantine*, Penguin, London, 1989.

Ewen, C l'Estrange (ed), *Witchcraft and Demonianism*, Frederick Muller, London, 1970.

Farrar, Janet and Stewart, *A Witches' Bible*, Phoenix, Custer, WA, 1996.

Fiedler, Maureen, and Linda Rabben (eds), *Rome Has Spoken*, Crossroad Publishing, New York, NY, 1998.

Finamore, Frank J (ed), *Devilish Doings*, Gramercy Books, New York, NY, 1997.

Fiske, John, *New France and New England*, Houghton Mifflin, Boston, MD, 1902.

Flögel, Karl Friedrich, and Friedrich W Ebeling, *Geschichte des Grotesk-Komischen*, H Barsdorf, Leipzig, 1887.

Florescu, Radu, and Raymond McNally, *Dracula*, Robert Hale, London, 1973.

Frazer, Sir James George, *The Golden Bough*, Macmillan, London, 1907.

Freeman, David (ed), *Anchor Bible Dictionary*, Doubleday, Garden City, NY, 1992.

Frassetto, Michael, *The Year 1000: Religious and Social Response to the Turning of the First Millennium*, Palgrave Macmillan, London, 2003.

Gardner, Gerald B, *Witchcraft Today*, I-H-O Books, Thame, 1954.

Geis, Gilbert, and Ivan Bunn, *A Trial of Witches – A Seventeenth-century Witchcraft Prosecution*, Routledge, London, 1997.

Graf, Arturo, *The Story of the Devil* (trans, Edward N Stone), Macmillan, New York, NY, 1931.

Graves, Robert, *The White Goddess*, Faber & Faber, London, 1961.

Grimm, Jacob, *Teutonic Mythology*, Thoemmes Press, London, 1999.

Guazzo, Francesco Maria, *Compendium Maleficarum*, 1608 (ed, Montague Summers), Dover Publications, New York, NY, 1988.

Hall, Manly P, Masonic, *Hermetic, Qabbalistic and Rosicrucian Symbolical Philosophy – The Secret Teachings of All Ages*, Philosophical Research Society, Los Angeles, CA, 1989.

Hastings, James (ed), *Dictionary of the Bible*, T&T Clark, Edinburgh, 1909.

Hausrath, A, *Der Ketzermeister Konrad von Marburg*, Leipzig, 1883.

Henke, ELT, *Konrad von Marburg*, Marburg, 1861.

Herodotus, *The Histories* (trans, Robin Waterfield), Oxford University Press, Oxford, 1998.

Hill, Frances, *A Delusion of Satan: The Full Story of the Salem Witchcraft Trials*, Doubleday, Garden City, NY, 1995.

Hutchinson, Thomas, *The History of the Colony and Province of Massachusetts-Bay in New England*, Boston, MA, 1749–74.

Huxley, Aldous, *The Devils of Loudun*, Chatto & Windus, London, 1952.

Hyatte, Reginald, *Laughter for the Devil: The Trials of Gilles De Rais (1440)*, Fairleigh Dickinson University Press, Madison, NJ, 1984.

Jacobus de Voragine, Archbishop of Genoa, *The Golden Legend or Lives of the Saints* (1275), William Caxton, London, 1483; (ed, FS Ellis), Dent, London, 1900.

James VI, King of Scotland, I of England, *Daemonology*, Edinburgh 1597. Reprint: *James Stuart, King James's Daemonologie in the Form of a Dialogue, Divided into Three Books*, Godolphin House, Mandrake, Oxford, 1996.

James, Montague R (ed), *The Apocryphal New Testament*, Clarendon Press, Oxford, 1924.

Jewish Encyclopedia, Funk & Wagnalls, New York, NY, 1906.

Johnstone, Nathan, *The Devil and Demonism in Early Modern England*, Cambridge University Press, Cambridge, 2006.

Jones, William, *The History of the Christian Church from the Birth of Christ to the 18th Century*, W Myers, London, 1812.

Josephus, Flavius, *The Antiquities of the Jews*, (trans, William Whiston), Milner & Sowerby, London, 1870.

— *The Wars of the Jews* (trans, William Whiston), Milner & Sowerby, London, 1870.

Kaltner, B, *Konrad von Marburg and die Inquisition in Deutschland*, Prague, 1882.

Kelly, Henry Ansgar, *Satan, a Biography*, Cambridge University Press, New York, NY, 2006.

Kemp, Betty, *Sir Francis Dashwood*, Macmillan, London, 1967.

Kieckhefer, Richard, *European Witch Trials: Their Foundations in Popular and Learned Culture, 1300–1500*, Routledge & Kegan Paul, London, 1976.

Kirk, Robert, *The Secret Commonwealth of Elves, Fauns and Fairies*, NYRB Classics, New York, NY, 2006.

Klaits, Joseph, *Servants of Satan: The Age of the Witch Hunts*, Indiana University Press, Bloomington, IN, 1985.

Kleist, James A (trans), *The Didache, The Epistle of Barnabas, the Epistle and the Martyrdom of St.Polycarp, the Fragments of Papias, the Epistle to Diognetus*, Ancient Christian Writers, Paulist Press International, Mahwah, NJ, 1948.

Kors, Alan C, and Edward Peters (eds), *Witchcraft in Europe, 1100–1700: A Documentary History*, University of Pennsylvania Press, Philadelphia, PA, 1972.

Kraemer, Heinrich, and James Sprenger, *The Malleus Maleficarum* (trans, Montague Summers), Dover Publications, New York, NY, 1971.

Ladner, Gerhart, *The Idea of Reform: Its Impact on Christian Thought and Action in the Age of the Fathers*, Harvard University Press, Cambridge, MA, 1959.

Lamont, William, *Puritanism and Historical Controversy*, University College Press, London 1996.

Lancre, Pierre de, *Tableau de l'inconstance des Mauuaisanges et Demons*, Nicolas Buon, Paris, 1613.

Larner, Christina, *Enemies of God – The Witch Hunt in Scotland*, Chatto & Windus, London, 1981.

Lea, HC (trans), *A History of the Inquisition of the Middle Ages*, Harper & Brothers, New York, NY, 1887.

Le Franc, Martin, *Le Champion des Dames*, 1451 (ed, Robert Deschaux), Honore Champion, Paris, 1999.

Legué, Gabriel, *La Messe Noire*, Charpentier et Fasquelle, Paris, 1903.

Lewis, Matthew, *The Monk*, Oxford World's Classics, Oxford, 1998.

Lukken, GM, *Original Sin in the Roman Liturgy*, EJ Brill, Leiden, NL, 1973.

Malan, Rev SC (trans), *The Book of Adam and Eve* (from the Ethiopic text), Williams & Norgate, London, 1882.

Malinowski, Bronslaw, *Magic, Science and Religion*, Doubleday, Garden City, NY, 1954.

Map, Walter, *De Nugis Curialium* (trans, Christopher Brooke), Clarendon Press, Oxford, 1983.

Marie de France, *Lays* (trans, Eugene Mason), JM Dent, London, 1954.

Marten, Anthony, *An Exhortation to Stirre up the Mindes of all Her Maiesties Faithfulle Subjects to Defend their Countrey in this Dangerous Time, from the Invasion of Enemies*, John Windet, London, 1588.

Mather, Cotton, *Wonders of the Invisible World*, reprinted: John Russell Smith, London, 1862.

Melech, Aubrey, *Missa Niger: La Messe Noire*, Sut Anubis, Northampton, 1986.

Melton, J Gordon, *The Vampire Book*, Visible Ink Press, Farmington Hills, MI, 1999.

Menghi, Girolamo, and Gaetano Paxia, *The Devil's Scourge: Exorcism During the Renaissance*, Red Wheel/Weiser, San Francisco, 2003.

Michelet, Jules, *La Sorcière* (trans, LJ Trotter), Simpkin Marshall, London, 1863.

— *Satanism and Witchcraft*, Tandem, London, 1970.

Michell, John, *Dimensions of Paradise*, Thames and Hudson, London, 1988.

Migne, Jacques-Paul (ed), *Patrologiae Latinae Cursus Completus* (*Patrologia Latina*), Foucher, Paris, 1844–55.

Miller, Elizabeth, *Dracula: Sense and Nonsense*, Desert Island Books, Westcliff-on-Sea, 2000.

Milton, John, *Paradise Regained*, W Taylor, London, 1721.

— *Paradise Lost*, Jacob Tonson, London, 1730.

— *A Treatise Of Civil Power In Ecclesiastical Causes: That It Is Not Lawful For Any Power On Earth To Compel In Matters Of Religion*, Kessinger, Kila, MT, 2004.

Molitor, Ulrich, *De Lamiis et Pythonicis Mulieribus*, Johann Prüss, Reutlingen, 1489.

Moncreiffe, Sir Iain, *Royal Highness Ancestry of the Royal Child*, Hamish Hamilton, London, 1982.

More, Henry, *Antidote Against Atheism*, London, 1653.

Morgan, David T, *The Devious Doctor Franklin*, Colonial Agent, Mercer University Press, Macon, GA, 1999.

Muchembled, Robert, A *History of the Devil: From the Middle Ages to the Present*, Polity Press, Cambridge, 2003.

BIBLIOGRAPHY

Murray, Margaret Alice, *The God of the Witches*, Oxford University Press, Oxford, 1970.

— *The Witch Cult in Western Europe*, Oxford University Press, Oxford, 1971.

Nevins, Winfield S, *Witchcraft in Salem Village*, Northshore Publishing, Boston, 1892.

Nicolson, Adam, *Power and Glory*, HarperCollins, London, 2003.

Nider, Johannes, *Formicarius, Anton Sorg*, Augsburg, 1484.

O'Brien, Christian and Barbara Joy, *The Genius of the Few*, Dianthus, Cirencester, 1999.

Oberman, Heiko, *Luther: Man Between God and the Devil*, Yale University Press, New Haven, CT, 1989.

Oldridge, Darren, *The Devil in Early Modern England*, Sutton, Stroud, 2000.

Osborne, Eric F, *Ethical Patterns in Early Christian Thought*, Cambridge University Press, Cambridge, 1976.

Ovid, *Metamorphoses* (trans, AD Melville), Oxford University Press, Oxford, 1986.

Page, Sydney HT, *Powers of Evil: A Biblical Study of Satan and Demons*, Baker Academic, Grand Rapids, MI, 1995.

Pagels, Elaine, *The Gnostic Gospels*, Weidenfeld and Nicolson, London, 1980.

— *The Origin of Satan*, Random House, New York, NY, 1995.

Patai, Raphael, *The Hebrew Goddess*, Wayne State University Press, Detroit, IL, 1967.

Patrick, AJ, *The Making of a Nation: 1603–1789*, Penguin, London, 1981.

Perez, Joseph, F, *The Spanish Inquisition: A History* (trans, J Lloyd), Profile Books, London, 2004.

Perkins, James Breck, *France in the American Revolution*, Cornerhouse, Williamstown, MA, 1970.

Pernoud, Regine, and Marie-Veronique Clin, *Joan of Arc* (trans, Jeremy du Quesnay Adams), Weidenfeld & Nicolson, London, 2000.

Perrin, JP, *Histoire des Vaudois* (Geneva, 1619), English translation by R Baird and S Miller, Philadelphia, PA, 1847.

Philip, Robert, *The Life, Times and Characteristics of John Bunyan*, Wm Carlton Regand, New York, NY, 1888.

Petrie, Sir Charles, *The Stuarts*, Eyre and Spottiswoode, London, 1937.

Perkins, William, *A Discourse of the Damned Art of Witchcraft*, Cantrell Legge for the University of Cambridge, 1616.

Phillips, Russell, *Benjamin Franklin: The First Civilized American*, Brentano's, New York, NY, 1926.

Platt, Rutherford H (ed), *The Lost Books of the Bible and the Forgotten Books of Eden*, New American Library, New York, NY, 1974.

Pollington, Stephen, *Leechcraft: Early English Charms, Plantlore and Healing*, Anglo Saxon Books, Swaffham, 2000.

Potts, Thomas, *The Wonderful discoverie of witches in the countie of Lancaster: with the arraignment and triall of nineteene witches*, W Stansby for John Barnes, London, 1613; facsimile reprint: Carnegie Publishing, Lancaster, 2003.

Prudentius, Aurelius Clemens, *The Hymns of Prudentius* (trans R Martin Pope), JM Dent, London, 1905.

Prynne, William, *Historio-Mastix: The Player's Scourge, or Actors Tragedie*, London, 1633.

Radcliffe, Ann, *The Mysteries of Udolpho*, Oxford World's Classics, Oxford, 1998.

— *The Italian*, Oxford World's Classics, Oxford, 1998.

Rawlings, Helen, *The Spanish Inquisition*, Blackwell, Oxford, 2005.

Rhodes, HTF, *The Satanic Mass*, Rider, London, 1954.

Roberts, Rev Alexander, and James Donaldson (eds), *The Ante-Nicene Fathers – The Writings of the Fathers down to AD 325*, T&T Clark, Edinburgh, 1867.

— *The Apostolical Constitutions*, The Ante-Nicene Christian Library, T&T Clark, Edinburgh, 1870.

Robinson, James M (ed), *The Nag Hammadi Library*, Coptic Gnostic Project, Institute for Antiquity and Christianity, EJ Brill, Leiden, NL, 1977.

Rougemont, Denis de, *Love in the Western World* (trans, Montgomery Belgion), Princeton University Press, Princeton, NJ, 1983.

Rudwin, Maximillian, *The Devil in Legend and Literature*, Open Court, La Salle, IL, 1973.

Russell, Bertrand, *History of Western Philosophy*, Routledge, London, 2004.

Russell, Jeffrey Burton, *A History of Witchcraft*, Thames and Hudson, London, 1980.

— *Satan: The Early Christian Tradition*, Cornell University Press, Ithaca, NY, 1987.

— *The Devil: Perceptions of Evil from Antiquity to Primitive Christianity*, Cornell University Press, New York, NY, 1987.

Rymer, James Malcolm, *Varney the Vampire – The Feast of Blood*, E Lloyd, London, 1847.

Saccho, Reinerius, 'Of the Sects of Modern Heretics' – *Summa de Catharis et Pauperibus de Lugduno, 1254* (trans, SR Maitland), in *Facts and Documents Illustrative of the History of the Albigenses and Waldensians*, CJG and F Rivington, London, 1832.

Salomon, David A, *The Glossa Ordinaria: Medieval Hypertext*, University of Wales Press, Cardiff, 2006.

Schaff, Philip (ed), *The Principal Works of St Jerome*, Christian Literature Publishing, New York, NY, 1892.

—·*History of the Christian Church*, Charles Scribner's Sons, New York, NY, 1910.

— and Henry Wace (eds), *Nicene and Post-Nicene Fathers*, Eerdmans Publishing, Grand Rapids, MI, 1997.

Schodde, Rev George H (trans), *The Book of Jubilees*, Capital University, Columbus, OH, 1888; reprinted Artisan, CA, 1992.

Schonfield, Hugh J, *The Essene Odyssey*, Element Books, Shaftesbury, 1984.

— *The Original New Testament*, Waterstone, London, 1985.

Schreck, Nikolas, *The Satanic Screen: An Illustrated Guide to the Devil in Cinema*, Creation Books, New York, NY, 2001.

Scott, Reginald, *The Discoverie of Witchcraft* (1584), Dover Publications, New York, NY, 1989.

Scribner, RW, *Popular Culture and Popular Movements in Reformation Germany*, Hambledon Continuum, London, 1988.

Seabrook, William, *Witchcraft: Its Power in the World Today*, Harcourt Brace, New York, NY, 1940.

Sellwood, Arthur Victor, *Devil Worship in Britain*, Transworld, London, 1964.

Seth, Ronald, *In the Name of the Devil: Great Witchcraft Cases*, Arrow, London, 1970

Seward, Desmond, *The Monks of War*, Paladin/Granada, St Albans, 1974.

Sharpe, JA, *Crime in Seventeenth-Century England: A County Study*, Cambridge Universsity Press, Cambridge, 1983.

Siefker, Phyllis, *Santa Claus, Last of the Wild Men*, MacFarland, Jefferson, NC, 1997.

Sinker, Rev Robert (trans), 'Testaments of the Twelve Patriarchs III' in *Ante-Nicene Fathers* (ed, A Cleveland Coxe, 1886), Eerdmans, Grand Rapids, MI, 1988.

Sitchin, Zecharia, *The 12th Planet*, Avon Books, New York, NY, 1978.

Smith, Homer M, *Man and His Gods*, Little, Brown, Boston, MD, 1952.

Somerset, Anne, *The Affair of the Poisons: Murder, Infanticide, and Satanism at the Court of Louis XIV*, St. Martin's Press, New York, NY, 2003.

Spee von Langenfeld, Friedrich, *Cautio Criminalis, or a Book on Witch Trials*, 1631 (trans, Marcus Hellyer), University of Virginia Press, Charlottesville, VA, 2003.

Stanford, Peter, *The Devil: A Biography*, Mandarin, London, 1996.

Stevenson, Robert Louis, *The Strange Case of Dr Jekyll and Mr Hyde*, Oxford World's Classics, Oxford, 2006.

Stoker, Bram, *Dracula*, Archibald Constable, London, 1897.

Stoyanov, Yuri, *The Hidden Tradition in Europe*, Arkana/Penguin, London, 1995.

— *The Other God*, Yale University Press, New Haven, CT, 2000.

Summers, Montague, *The Vampire: His Kith and Kin*, K Paul Trench & Trubner, London, 1928.

— *The Confessions of Madeleine Bavent* (1652), Fortune Press, London, 1930.

— *The History of Witchcraft*, Castle Books, Edison, NJ, 1992.

— *Witchcraft and Black Magic*, Dover Publications, New York, NY, 2000.

Swanton, Michael (trans), *The Anglo-Saxon Chronicle*, JM Dent, London, 1997.

Terry, Milton S (trans), *The Sibylline Oracles*, Eaton & Mains, New York, NY, 1899.

Thatcher, Oliver J (ed), *The Library of Original Sources*, University Research Extension, Milwaukee, WI, 1901.

Thiering, Barbara, *Jesus the Man*, Doubleday, London, 1992.

— *Jesus of the Apocalypse,* Doubleday, London, 1996.

Titus Livius ('Livy' c.59 BC – AD 17), *Ab Urbe Condita* (*From the Founding of the City*) – vol I, Loeb Classical Library, Harvard University Press, Cambridge, MA, 1919; vol II, Bristol Classical Press, Bristol, 1998; vols III, IV, Loeb Classical Library, 1989.

BIBLIOGRAPHY

Translations and Reprints from the Original Sources of European History, University of Pennsylvania Department of History, University of Pennsylvania Press, Philadelphia, PA, 1897–1907.

Tudor-Craig, Sir Algernon, *Mélusine and the Lukin Family*, Century House, London, 1932.

Van Dale, Anton, *De Oraculis Ethnicorum*, Amsterdam, 1685.

— *Dissertationes de origine ac progressu Idolalriæ*, Amsterdam, 1696.

Vermes, Geza, *The Complete Dead Sea Scrolls in English*, Penguin, London, 1997.

Waite, Arthur Edward, *Devil Worship in France*, George Redway, London, 1896.

— *Transcendental Magic*, Samuel Weiser, York Beach, ME, 1896.

— *Devil Worship in France with Diana Vaughan and the Question of Modern Palladism*, Red Wheel Weiser, York Beach, ME, 2003.

Wakefield, Walter, and Austin P Evans, *Heresies of the High Middle Ages*, University of Columbia Press, New York, NY, 1969.

Walpole, Horace, *The Castle of Otranto*, Oxford World's Classics, Oxford, 1998.

Wheatley, Dennis, *The Devil and All His Works*, American Heritage Press, New York, NY, 1971.

Wijngaards, J, *No Women in Holy Orders*, Canterbury Press, Norwich, 2002.

Williams, Charles, *Witchcraft*, Faber & Faber, London, 1941.

Williams, Gryffith, *The True Church, shewd to all Men that desire to be Members of the Same*, London, 1629.

Williamson, John, *The Oak King, the Holly King and the Unicorn*, Harper & Row, New York, NY, 1986.

Wray, TJ, and Gregory Mobley, *The Birth of Satan – Turning the Devil's Biblical Roots*, Palgrave Macmillan, Basingstoke, 2005.

Wright, W, *News from Scotland, Declaring the Damnable Life and Death of Doctor Fian*, London, 1592.

Yates, Frances A, *The Occult Philosophy in the Elizabethan Age*, Routledge & Kegan Paul, London, 1983.

INDEX
Compiled by
Walter Schneider

INDEX

INDEX

INDEX

INDEX

INDEX

INDEX

Lightning Source UK Ltd.
Milton Keynes UK
UKOW042357210513

211036UK00002B/6/P